Jessup Whitehead

Hotel Meat Cooking

Jessup Whitehead

Hotel Meat Cooking

ISBN/EAN: 9783744788809

Printed in Europe, USA, Canada, Australia, Japan

Cover: Foto ©Lupo / pixelio.de

More available books at **www.hansebooks.com**

VOLUME 2 OF THE "OVEN AND RANGE" SERIES.

❖ HOTEL ❖

MEAT COOKING

SECOND EDITION

Comprising Hotel and Restaurant Fish and Oyster Cooking, How to Cut Meats, and Soups, Entrees and Bills of Fare.

BY

JESSUP WHITEHEAD.

CHICAGO:
1884.

Entered according to Act of Congress in the years 1880, 1882 and 1884,
BY JESSUP WHITEHEAD,
In the Office of the Librarian of Congress at Washington.

ALL RIGHTS RESERVED.

ADVERTISEMENT

THE present volume, as will be at once apparent to the reader who glances at the numbers of receipts, constitutes a part of an AMERICAN HOTEL COOK BOOK that is being published serially; the preceding parts bound together form the volume called the AMERICAN PASTRY COOK that was published a year ago, at two dollars. That volume has met with a very encouraging degree of success, so that a second edition has become necessary, and the sales have steadily increased as the merits of the work became better known.

In the meantime, the most numerous and frequent inquiries have been received for instructions how to cook oysters and how to cut meats, questions which this book answers in a most thorough manner. Instructions for meat cutting, as practiced by hotel cooks, have never before been put in print, it is no wonder, therefore, that the demand for them has been urgent; and almost the same thing might be said of oyster cooking and all the other matters so far as regards hotel and restaurant practice, for the present is the first endeavor ever put forth to describe the conditions that really exist in hotels and make the cooking directions conform to them and not to a set of strange conditions that exist somewhere a long way off.

The merit most particularly claimed for the entire series is the reliable character of the directions, which offer to any intelligent person a chance to learn a trade that is an exceedingly good one for those who have the capacity to become skillful in it.

SECOND EDITION.

Since the above was first printed another part has been supplied, the HOTEL BOOK OF SOUPS, ENTREES AND BILLS OF FARE, which adds considerably to the value of this volume. It is the intention, when the series is entirely complete, to bind the whole in one large book, to be called the AMERICAN COOK.

THE HOTEL FISH AND OYSTER COOK

Showing all the Best Methods of Cooking Oysters and Fish, for Restaurant and Hotel Service, together with the appropriate Sauces and Vegetables.

BEING A PART OF THE

"OVEN AND RANGE" SERIES

ORIGINALLY PUBLISHED IN THE CHICAGO DAILY NATIONAL HOTEL REPORTER.

BY

JESSUP WHITEHEAD.

CHICAGO, 1884.

HOTEL FISH AND OYSTER COOK

AND

HOW TO CUT MEATS.

ROAST, BOIL AND BROIL.

803. To Dress Terrapin.

When there is a question of quantity required for a given number of persons it may be counted about the same as of young chickens. As they ordinarily run a terrapin weighs from two to four pounds alive. There are larger and better, but rarely obtainable away from the source of supply. The amount of meat in a terrapin is not over half the live weight. It is most serviceable stewed or in soup.

Drop the terrapin alive into a pot of boiling water. At the end of 15 minutes take it out and take off the bottom shell by chipping through the thinnest part where it joins the back shell between the openings. This can be done with the heavy handle end of a stout knife. Cut close to the shell, not to bring any meat away with it. Pour away the water that will be found inside but save the blood that collects in the deep shell afterwards. The gall about the size of a cherry, will be seen near the center and must be taken out without breaking; also take out the single fish-bait entrail. Loosen the meat from the back shell and cut through the spine bone that attaches to the shell at a point above the tail. Empty it into a pan. When all are done go over them, take off the heads and put them with the shells for soup; separate the hind and fore feet (or fins, as some call them) making four pieces; trim off the claws and scrape off the thin outside cuticle. It is worth while to take off the the rich fat that will be found at the shoulder joints of the females, because it boils away while meat is cooking tender, and should be added later. It is of a very dark green color, almost black. Preserve along with it all the eggs both large and small. Keep all the pieces of meat, fat and eggs in cold water. Put on the heads, shells and remaining scraps in water enough to more than cover, boil slowly for two or three hours, skimming when it first boils, then strain the liquor or stock into a clean saucepan, put the pieces of terrapin in and boil them one hour. The pieces that were like india-rubber at first will begin to be tender by that time, but before being finished as stew or soup or otherwise should be taken up on dish to cool and the liquor strained into a bowl.

Most of the terrapin soup now made in hotels is of canned terrapin. The raw article prepared as above directed is now the same as the canned, except that the latter has the meat and jelly mixed together. Both can be finished for table in various ways.

804. Terrapin in Shell, Maryland Style.

Take a baking pan large enough to hold as many terrapines as are wanted, half fill it with dry gravel or sand and make it hot in the oven. Kill or stun the terrapins, wash off and bed them back downwards in the pan of gravel. Bake nearly an hour. Take hold with a towel and pry off the belly shell, remove the gall bag and the single fish bait entrail from the inside and loosen the meat from the shell without taking it out. Work a cupful of soft butter and half as much flour together with a large teaspoonful of black pepper, the same of salt and juice of lemon. Drop a spoonful into each terrapin and replace them in the oven for the seasonings to cook. Serve in the shell on a folded napkin.

805. Stowed Terrapin.

The meat of six terrapins—about four quarts.
The liquor or stock—about four quarts.
6 ounces of butter.
3 tablespoonfuls of flour.
Herb and spice seasonings.
A cupful of sherry or maderia.

The terrapin and the liquor it was boiled in being ready add a little water to the latter to allow for boiling away and set it on to boil with a tablespoonful of bruised peppercorns, a piece of parsley root, a small bunch of parsley and green thyme, eight cloves, a b'ade of mace and a tablespoonful of onion. Stir the butter and flour together over the fire until it is yellow or light brown, add it to the boiling stock and also a tablespoonful of salt. When boiled sufficiently with the thickening in it strain it into a clean saucepan. That is the sauce. Take the pieces of cooked terrapin and chop off all the projecting points of bones and otherwise trim the joints smooth and shapely, then put them into the sauce to simmer at the side of the range. Add the wine, and the fat pieces if any saved, also the eggs, and strew them over the surface of the stew when served.

806. Soft Shell Crabs, Boiled.

Every part of a soft shell crab is eatab'e, shell, claws and all, except the sand pouch on the under side, but the small claws should be taken off when the crabs are to be cooked by boiling.

Drop the crabs into boiling water already well salted, cook 10 or 15 minutes, drain, and serve with a sauce at the side.

Tomato kotchup, mayonaise sauce, hot cream sauce or butter or parsley sauce are suitable kinds.

807. Soft Shell Crabs, Fried.

Bread it in the usual manner by dipping in egg in which a small proportion of water has been beaten, then in cracker meal. Drop two or three at a time into a saucepan of hot oil or lard and fry light brown in about ten minutes. The claws should be crisp enough to break. Garnish with fried parsley and serve mayonaise at the side separately.

808. Oyster Stew for Fifty.

A quart of small oysters bulk, "solid meat," contains eight dozen.

A quart of selects bulk, "solid meat," contains four to four and a half dozen.

A can of selects contains three and a half dozen generally.

The ordinary conventional oyster stew such as people expect to receive when it is cooked to order is a pint bowl nearly full, consisting of one dozen oysters and one or one and a half cups of milk or milk and oyster liquor. To serve this according to the letter a pint of small oysters should be sufficient for four stews, or a can of selects for three and a half or four; but as the stews for a large number are dipped up and guessed there is always a discrepancy, and a pint can only be relied upon for three dishes. Proceeding upon these calculations, for a dinner, or oyster supper, or church festival or other such occasion provide for 50 stews

9 quarts of small oysters, or
12 or 13 quarts of selects, or
14 or 15 cans of selects, and
1½ gallons of milk,
½ gallon of oyster liquor or water,
1 pound of fresh butter,
2 tablespoonfuls of salt.

Set the milk on in good time that it may heat gradually and not burn, and put in the required amount of salt which also helps to prevent burning. Cook the oysters separately and add them to the milk afterwards. It is better to boil the oyster liquor or water by itself and then drop the oysters in, because if they are set over the fire cold in bulk the bottom will cook hard before the top is warm.

As raw oysters do not drain well some boiling water should be poured over them, the liquor will then run abundantly and can be boiled and skimmed, the oysters added and then the milk and butter.

809. To Fry Oysters Without Eggs.

Mix cracker meal and flour together about a cupful of each, but the cracker meal the larger measure. If no cracker meal to be had crush some oyster crackers and put them through a seive.

Have some milk in a shallow pan. Dip the oysters out of their own liquor into the mixed meal and flour, out of that into the milk, then into the meal again, giving them a double breading. It does no harm to let them lie in the breading a while. Handle carefully not to rub off the coating in places for the grease to get in.

Have enough lard very hot in a deep pan to quite cover the oysters. Drop in a few at a time, fry three or four minutes, take out with a skimmer when light brown and drain free from grease before sending them in.

The milk causes them to fry to the same fine brown color as if eggs were used. If they are quite immersed and fried quickly in lard that is hissing hot they come out crisp and dry, yet full of the juice of the oyster. If simmered in lard that is only half deep enough the breading peels off like so much greasy pudding.

810. Clam Frittors Without Eggs.

The same as the oysters preceding, using raw clams, but bread them four times over instead of twice and dip them in clam liquor until the last time when dip in milk for color. They are better done this way than with egg breading or batter.

811. A Half-Shell Roast.

Choose oysters in the shell of a good shape for the purpose. Open them and preserve the liquor with them in the deep shell. Squeeze a little lemon juice into them, add salt, cayenne and a small piece of butter and set them on the hot top of the range until they begin to boil over. Or, for a little better way, set them in a pan having salt in to hold the shells level and bake them five minutes in a hot oven. This is a good way for clams.

812. Truffled Oysters.

4 dozen of the largest oysters.
1 can of truffles ($1.50 size.)
6 ounces of breast of chicken, cooked.
3 ounces of fat salt pork, raw.
Red or pickled pepper.
5 eggs. Flour. Toast.

Mince and then pound to a paste the chicken and salt pork and add a quarter pod of red pepper minced very small and a pinch of salt. Cut the truffles to the size of peas and mix them in. Lay the oysters out on a napkin, insert a penknife at the edge and split each oyster up and down inside without making the opening very large, then push in a teaspoonful of the truffle forcemeat.

As the oysters are stuffed lay them in flour and coat well with it, then dip in beaten egg in a plate. Drop a few at a time into hot oil or lard and fry for three or four minutes. The lard should be deep enough to immerse them and hot enough to hiss sharply but not smoking. When the oysters are of a golden brown take them up and drain on blank paper in a hot place. Dust with fine salt.

Cut diamond shaped pieces of thin dry toast and serve four oysters laid diagonally on each slice.

813. Stuffed Oysters, Broiled.

Grate the yolks of hard-boiled eggs—four or five for every dozen of the largest oysters—mince half as much fat salt pork or bacon and mix in, also black pepper and chopped parsley. Add a raw yolk to make a paste of it.

Split the oysters inside by moving a penknife up and down without making a very large opening at the edge and stuff them. Dip them in fine bread crumbs that have been minced and sifted through a colander, then into butter melted on a plate, then into the bread crumbs again and broil them over a clear fire. (See No. 831.)

As a matter of economy it is well to remember that where hard-boiled eggs are needed it answers about as well to break the eggs raw, save the whites for other purposes and poach the yolks alone in a shallow pan of water.

814. Oysters with Macaroni Milanaise.

1 pound of macaroni.
3 cupfuls of oysters, or two cans.
¼ pound of butter—¼ cupful.
1 pint of milk.
2 eggs.
1 tablespoonful of flour.
Pepper and salt.

It is the same as making macaroni and cheese, with oysters in place of cheese. Italians make it with fish.

Boil the the macaroni broken in pieces by itself first, throwing it into salted water already boiling and allowing 20 or 25 minutes. Strain it in a colander, put a layer on the bottom of a buttered pan and spread half the oysters on it. Drop pieces of butter, pepper and salt, more macaroni, the rest of the oysters and macaroni on top.

Mix the flour smooth with milk, add the eggs and rest of the milk, pour it over the macaroni and bake until it is set in the middle.

815. Oysters, Box Stew. Restaurant Order.

In answer to several enquiries as to "what is a box stew?" it has to be remarked that there is not much sense in the term away from the famous Fulton market oyster houses. "Box stew" may be found on the regular printed bill of fare of a very few restaurants, price 60 cents, and when served it is a stew of a dozen of the very largest oysters just taken out of the shells, with only a spoonful of milk and quite as much of the best butter. The oysters are dished upon a small square of buttered toast in a bowl and the rich milk and butter poured around. It is uncommonly good eating, although there is no reason for the name except that the largest oysters that are called counts in Chicago are called box oysters in Fulton market.

816. Box Fry.

Read explanation above, and a box fry is a fry of the very largest oysters in a paper box for the buyer to carry home.

816. Soft Shell Clams

Not soft in the same sense that soft shell crabs are, but a large kind with brittle shell. After taking out cut off the leathery dark portion that projected out of the shell and remove with knife and fingers the beard and string from the inside and throw the clams as they are trimmed into a pan of cold water. Fry them in any of the ways directed for oysters; the method of frying without eggs above described for oysters and clam fritters is excellent provided there is a sufficiency of hot lard, for these on account of their open form take up a good deal of room.

Stew same as oysters. Roast by replacing the clams in the shells after trimming.

Now, at last, it is the cook's turn to talk back about that hotel oyster soup that they say has only one oyster, which, of course, is no such thing. Some of the guests get a whole plateful of oysters, particularly if the waiters are girls and allowed to help themselves at the tureen. Why, anyway, does the man who gets only one oyster come so late? But the discontent, in truth, is not with the soup but about something else. The only really national soup of this country is the oyster stew; it alone fills the measure of happiness full, and that which is soup truly and properly is unsatisfactory in just the degree that it differs from stewed oysters. But after all the badinage, as stews cannot very generally be served as mere preliminaries to a great dinner, it is found that oyster soup meets with a readier welcome than any other that can be named, and in the interior when the expensive raw oysters fail will at least run even in favor with the best of other kinds if only made of the cooked canned or cove oysters.

The oyster soups made by the European methods have no resemblance to our universal oysters-in milk; with them the oysters are but an addition to a soup already made rich and high flavored with fish stock, vegetables and anchovies, or else the soup is almost a brown oyster sauce.

In some of our largest restaurants the soup receives so little attention that it amounts to nothing more than a pint of boiling milk poured over six small oysters in a bowl. And still it sells, though it might be better.

The lowest price of an oyster stew, such as hotel-keepers give for soup when they can afford it, in respectable restaurants is 25 cents. It is a dozen medium oysters with a pint or less of milk and bit of butter, with crackers, butter and pickles on the table. To furnish such for soup at places away from the great oyster markets would require over one dozen well filled cans for every fifty persons. But hotel-keepers go the dearest way if they buy oysters in cans at all, they are cheapest in bulk by the gallon. The dealers and packers, however, discourage the sale in bulk all they are able. The can of oysters is supposed by most people to be equal to a quart, but instead it takes 5½ or 6 to fill a gallon. So much for comparison, but we are not going to do anything so mean as discourage the making of the favorite soup by making out a hard case of expense against it and will treat of it not as stew but as soup —just what the bill of fare promises and not something better.

According to the rules of etiquette 2 gallons of soup ought to be enough for 50, and a still smaller quantity might be, of any other kind. Having made that suggestion, we will now suppose this is the Sunday dinner, and go on and make enough to fill the plates.

819. Oyster Soup.

1 gallon of oysters—5 or 6 cans.
1 gallon of good clear soup stock.
1 gallon of milk.
1 pound of best fresh butter.
1 tablespoonful of salt.
1 heaping teaspoonful of white pepper.
1 cupful of crushed oyster crackers.

The stock is used on the principle that the liquor that meat has been boiled in is better than water. It should be chicken or veal broth slightly seasoned with celery and parsely and other vegetables, and should be taken from the top, clear without sediment.

The things to be guarded against are, not to get the milk curdled by boiling it with the oysters, and to avoid having the scum from the oyster liquor floating on top of the soup. To get out of the trouble shiftless cooks sometimes throw the liquor away and wash off the oysters; of course that makes the soup poor.

An hour before dinner time set the gallon of stock on the range in one saucepan and the milk in another. Pour the oysters into a large colander set in another saucepan on the table and when the soup stock boils pour a few ladlefuls into the oysters, stir them and let them drain. Then set the oyster liquor thus obtained over the fire, when it boils skim it, then strain it into the soup stock. Next throw in the oysters and when they begin to shrink, showing they are fairly hot through take the vessel from the fire. Stir in the cupful of rolled crackers, (not cracker meal, from the barrel,) the salt, pepper and butter, then at last add the boiling milk and pour the soup into the tureen. Sprinkle a little chopped parsley over the top.

It is very poor policy to let the oysters ever reach boiling heat. They begin to shrink and dwindle the moment they touch hot liquor and never stop till the largest saddle-rocks looks like small oysters, and the small oysters seem to disappear altogether. At least it is hard to find them after the soup has been kept hot for some time.

820. Oyster Soup, French Way.

(Restaurant Order for 25.)

2 quarts of oysters — or 3 cans.
5 quarts of seasoned fish stock.
1 quart of French white wine.
3 or 4 anchovies.
18 yolks of eggs.
1 pint of cream.
Salt, pepper, and white butter-and-flour thickening.

Make the fish stock by boiling a 5 pound fish, or some eels, in plain broth, with a head of celery, a handful or two of parsley, salt, white pepper, the wine and anchovies. While it is boiling pour a few ladlefuls into the oysters and then drain them in a colander and add the liquor to the stock. When the fish has boiled slowly about three quarters of an hour strain off the stock into another kettle, add a little thickening, (roux,) let it boil and skim it; put in the oysters and while they are nearing the boiling point again heat the yolks and the pint of cream together and stir them in. Draw the kettle to the side of the range and watch till the soup becomes smooth and creamy but take care not to let it boil. Taste for seasoning.

The cans of oysters mentioned in the preceding receipts are intended to mean the raw fresh oysters in cans. The cooked kind or cove oysters, however, make soups that are as good at least as meat soups. As this is a matter never mentioned in print before I will take occasion to express the opinion that the boarders in hotels are not so much annoyed at being served with canned "cove oyster" soup, which is good enough on its own merits, as they are by seeing it paraded as fresh oysters, which insults their understanding. Far inland where the raw canned article is costly and rare the point of this is understood.

821. Brown Oyster Soup.

(25 Plates.)

Take the preceding receipt for quantities. While the fish stock is in preparation fry a small carrot, turnip and a piece of onion, all chopped small, in a little butter till brown, then put them in the boiling stock and let them cook in it some time longer.

Make some brown butter thickening (roux) by stirring together a cupful of butter and the same of flour in a frying pan and letting it bake brown in the oven.

Strain off the fish stock into another kettle on the fire. Add the brown thickening, stirring lest it sink and burn on the bottom. Add the oyster liquor and draw the soup to the side of the range to slowly boil and clear itself by throwing up scum. Put in the juice of a lemon mixed with a little cold water and skim when the soup boils up again. A few minutes before dinner time put the oysters into the soup and take off as soon as it once more begins to boil. If no anchovies have been used in the fish stock to heighten the flavor a spoonful of essence of anchovies may be added to the finished soup.

Where the bottle of white wine for the fish stock cannot be afforded the half cup of vinegar usually added to boiling fish answers the same purpose.

For the sake of helping a general understanding of terms it may be worth while to notice that stewards and cooks who write bills of fare and think they must have a style attached to every article named mean the milk soup of the first receipt when they write it *a la creme*, and clam soups are designated the same. If we must give any opinion at all we say that it is sufficient in the hotel menu to write it simply oyster, or oyster soup.

822. Clam Soups.

Cut the clams in four pieces and make the soups by the receipts for oyster soups. The French soup, number 820, like a true fricassee thinned down, with its dash of acid and partial thickening of egg yolks is better made with clams than with oysters.

823. Clam Chowder Soup.

Not to be confounded with chowder proper any more than oyster soup is oyster stew. It is a popular kind, and that is the only criterion our articles' worth is ever measured by. It is essential, to make a good looking soup, that the clams be neatly cut after scalding, into pieces the size of beans, and not chopped into tatters.

4 dozen clams, or 3 cans.
4 quarts of clear soup stock.
1 quart of raw potatoes cut in dice.
1 pint of broken crackers.
3 slices of ham.
1 medium onion, or ½ cupful chopped.
Salt and pepper.
2 quarts of milk,
Parsley, or a green celery leaf.

The soup stock should have been already flavored with vegetables in the stock boiler. Strain the required amount and set it over the fire.

Fry the pieces of ham at the side of the range brown on both sides, put them into the stock, without the grease and let boil in it for flavor, also, add the onions. Scald the clams in their own liquor a minute or two; take them out, pour the liquor to the soup through a fine strainer, and cut the clams in small pieces. Thirty minutes before dinner throw in the potatoes and seasoning of salt and pepper and take out the ham slices (which are no more needed in the soup), and skim as it begins to boil again. Add the clams and boil a few minutes, and the cupful of crackers and chopped parsley and the milk which should be already boiling.

The care required is to have the potatoes done and not boiled away, and the crumbled crackers just dissolved in the soup without making it too thick.

Nothing promotes the enjoyment of a dinner so much as a happy knack of plain seasoning in the cook. Very common food can be made to excite the appetite and seem equal to the better description by a judicious use of pepper and salt only. It is very well to talk about leaving it to the people to do their own seasoning, but in fact there is a different taste and finer flavor to articles that have been cooked with pepper, especially black pepper, than when they are sprinkled with the raw. In combination with potatoes, with cooked crackers and with flour the difference is especially noticeable. And half the people forget or are too indifferent to season the things set before them at table; they do not stop to analyze the qualities of the viands but carry away a sense that one dinner suits them and another does not. The question often arises, particularly concerning oysters. Discretion is needed and to keep on the safe side, but skill in seasoning is a great point in cooking.

824. Oyster Stew. Milk Stew.

Cook the oysters and the milk in separate saucepans. Dip the oysters from the saucepan into the bowl, add a ladleful of milk and a small piece of fresh butter. Serve crackers, butter and shred cabbage separately with the stew.

Oysters do not always curdle the milk when boiled in it, but there is always a danger that they may, so the rule is not to run any risk. Besides, to cook the oysters in the milk although good for flavor always makes a dingy looking stew with a scum on top. To obtain the best quality and appearance boil some oyster liquor separately and keep it ready for orders. As it reaches boiling point the scum on top can be skimmed off and after that pour it through a fine strainer into a clean saucepan, and you have the oyster essence clear and ready for use without detriment to the appearances.

It is with cooking an oyster as with cooking an egg. It may be either soft boiled or hard boiled, only there is the difference that an oyster boiled hard is spoiled. To cook oysters for stews set some of the liquor that has been boiled on in a little saucepan and drop in the oysters with a fork. Add a pinch of salt and pepper, shake them back and forth while heating and as soon as the liquor fairly boils they are done. Time about 3 minutes for 1 stew.

825. Plain Stew.

The oysters cooked as above with the liquor only served with them, and no milk.

826. Dry Stew.

(Restaurant Order.)

The same as plain stew without the liquor, or with only a spoonful.

827. Boston Fancy Stew.

(Restaurant Order.)

The milk stew with a slice of buttered toast floating in it and the oysters on the toast. Use a large, shallow bowl, put the square of toast in it first, drain the liquor of the stew into it and place the oysters neatly.

828. Oysters Single Breaded and Fried in Butter

(Restaurant Order.)

Not necessary to use eggs. Drop the oysters into a plate of cracker meal and give them a good coating, careful not to rub it off as it will not stick a second time. Drop an ounce of butter in the frying pan, and when melted lay in the oysters close together. Cook over a brisk fire to get a brown on one side without hardening them. Lay a small plate upside down on the oysters, turn over the pan, then slide the cake of oysters from the plate into the pan again without letting them break apart and brown the other side. Serve on the plate set in another plate. Ornament with lemon and parsley. There are oval shaped pans for such *sautees* as this to be in shape for a platter.

829. Fried Oysters. Single Breaded.

Dry the oysters by pressing with a napkin. Drop them into beaten egg, in which is a little salt, and out of that into cracker meal. Give them a good coating by pressing, with care not to rub, or leave a bare place for the grease to get in. Drop them singly into a frying pan of hot lard. Fry brown in 2 or 3 minutes. Dish neatly in the middle of a hot platter with a piece of lemon and sprigs of parsley.

830. Fried Oysters. Double Breaded.

Out of their own liquor into cracker-meal, coat well, dip in beaten egg and then in cracker meal again. Fry 4 or 5 minutes. Oysters look twice as large as they really are, when double breaded.

Various fancies are made known by different people in regard to fried oysters, the commonest being a preference for corn meal to dip them in instead of cracker-meal. Fried oysters can never be made to look very well in that way and they are only served so when so ordered. One hotel-keeper, of considerable traveling experience, used to say the best he ever ate were breaded with white of egg and cracker-meal and patted down flat, then served set on edge with very small and thin pieces of buttered toast between, like so many lamb chops set up on a dish. Where large quantities are fried for hotel meals they are generally double breaded and all available hands called in to help with that somewhat tedious operation, a pile of cracker-meal being spread upon the table and the remainder of it sifted to be put away for the next occasion. A large and deep meat pan is set on the range and half filled with lard, the oysters shaken in out of a large pan or colander and when done—there can be only a few at a time fried satisfactorily—taken out with a skimmer and drained in another colander, or, better still, on seives. Six or eight to a dish are enough, and there should be a squeezable piece of lemon, or two, of them to each dish.

Fried oysters are expensive over the other methods of cooking because of the lard destroyed. At the end of a meal the cracker sediment will have made the lard used dark and unfit for further use, and if clarified of that there still remains a sort of mucilage from the oysters that makes the lard boil over like butter melting, and almost useless. Consequently the charge for fries is, and has to be, higher than for other styles.

831. Broiled Oysters, Bread-Crumbed

The original meaning of breading has nearly been forgotten, so much better for most purposes is the meal of crushed and sifted crackers than grated dry bread. But the smallness of the demand for breaded oysters broiled—way that over the water is considered most delicate—is proof that cracker-meal is not the thing for it.

Oysters breaded in cracker-meal, then broiled, unless they are deluged with butter, are more like discolored pieces of buckskin than anything eatable.

Grate a stale loaf of bread or else mince the thin slices extremely fine with a knife. Shake the oysters about in a little beaten egg, dip them in the bread crumbs and gently press a coating on both sides. It is better to let them lie in the crumbs awhile if there is time.

Brush the wire oyster broiler with a brush dipped in butter, place the oysters, shut down the other side and as soon as the egg is set with the heat of the bright coals baste the oysters on both sides with the same brush in butter. Get a toast-brown on both sides without cooking the oysters too much. Serve on a dish the same as fried oysters, with a piece of lemon.

832. Plain Broiled Oysters on Toast.

Take the largest oysters obtainable. Brush the wire oyster broiler with softened butter, lay in the oysters and broil over a hot fire 2 or 3 minutes, basting once on each side with the butter brush. Dish side by side on one long slice of buttered toast in a dish. Garnish with lemon and parsley.

Where silver-plated griddles and silver wire broilers are used it is practicable to dispense with the butter basting altogether, and prevent sticking by rubbing the bars with chalk. Some of the greatest restaurants of the two continents have had a sort of specialty in this line, and probably proved not only the desirableness but the real economy of the mode.

833. Oyster Omelet.

(Restaurant Order.)

6 oysters.
2 eggs.
1 large basting spoonful of milk.
Seasonings.

Cook the oysters rare done in a little saucepan separately, with a spoonful of milk, scrap of butter and thickening to make white sauce of the liquor. Break the 2 eggs in a bowl, put in a spoonful of milk and beat with the wire egg whisk. Add a pinch of salt.

Shake a tablespoonful of melted lard about in the omelet frying pan and before it gets very hot pour in the omelet and let it cook rather slowly.

Properly made omelets are not exactly rolled up, but there is a knack to be learned of shaping them in the pan by shaking while cooking into one side of it, the side farthest from you, while you keep the handle toward you raised higher. Loosen the edges with a knife when it is nearly cooked enough to shake.

When the omelet is nearly done to the center place the oysters with a spoon in the hollow middle and pull over the further edge to cover them in. Slide on to the dish, smooth side up. Garnish with parsley and lemon.

One reason of omelets and all fried eggs sticking to the frying pan is allowing the pan to get too hot. They seldom stick when poured into a pan that is only kept warm till wanted. The pans should be kept for no other purpose, and be rubbed smooth after using, if not bright.

Scalloped or escaloped oysters (either is right) should mean oysters cooked in their shell, but there are several ways commonly practiced of escaloping oysters of which we give four. The best way must be that which suits the particular case. The large pan is the quickest, for hotel dinners, but the same thing of individual dimensions is served in many restaurants. The half shell method is the most stylish, and the most tedious for large numbers.

834. Escaloped Oysters. Large Pan.

The thing to be guarded against is the getting it all bread and dry and hard and for that reason uneatable. These proportions make it right.

8 dozen oysters and their liquor.
12 ounces of butter.
2 pounds of fine bread and cracker crumbs mixed.
1 pint of milk. Pepper and salt.

Use a shallow 4-quart milk pan. Spread a little of the butter all over the bottom and cover that with a layer of the mixed bread crumbs.

Scald the oysters in their liquor just enough to make them shrink a little and place half of them close together on the layer of crumbs. Then more crumbs, butter dropped about in small pieces, pepper and salt; then the rest of the oysters and cover with the remaining bread crumbs and butter. Mix the milk with the oyster liquor, strain it into the pan, moistening the top all over. Bake from 20 to 30 minutes.

The same thing as the foregoing can be baked in a shallow baking pan only one layer deep, but needs very quick baking to be good.

835. Scalloped Oysters.

(Restaurant Party.)

Baked on a platter of a size according to number. Put a border of mashed potato forced like a thick cord through a paper cornet all around the inner rim of the platter to hold in the liquor. The inside scooped out of baked potatoes is often the available thing for this.

Cover the bottom of the dish with finely minced or grated bread crumbs. Scald the oysters slightly in a saucepan and then place them close together on the layer of crumbs. Continue till the dish is piled up in the middle and rounded, with the butter, salt and pepper as in the preceding receipt, then mix the oyster liquor with a little milk and strain over the top. Wipe the edges of the dish dry. Bake to get a quick brown on top, on the top shelf of the oven.

Silver dishes are the better for such uses. The above way and the next destroys white dishes after a few times, but not so rapidly if they are wiped perfectly dry and clean before baking.

836. Scalloped Oysters.

(Individual Orders).

In small deep dishes, same way as shirred eggs. A few bread crumbs in the dish, 6 to 12 oysters, bread crumbs spread thinly over them, butter on top and bake on the top shelf in a hot oven.

837. Scalloped Oysters on Half Shell.

Select oysters of good shape for this—Blue Points, Scotch coves, or Shrewsburys. Loosen them entirely from the shell or they will draw to one side. Dredge fine bread crumbs in the shell, replace the oyster, cover with bread crumbs and bake by the panful on the top shelf. When lightly browned pour a teaspoonful of melted fresh butter over each one, moistening the crumbs with it.

It hastens the browning to have the bread dry already. Serve 4 or 5 to an order with a quarter of a lemon in the center of the dish.

838. Scalloped Clams on Half Shell.

Take the clams out of the shells and scald them slightly in their own liquor. Replace them in the half shell, pepper and salt, and then cover with fine bread crumbs, and bake quickly. Make a little white sauce of the clam liquor mixed with cream and a little butter and spoonful of flour thickening, and pour a spoonful of it over the clam in the shell when it has become browned. Serve same as oysters, on a small fish plate, with a piece of lemon.

839. Oysters—Shell Roast.

A bright and glowing charcoal fire is requisite for this. The oyster ranges are nearly all broiler and the bars are near the coals. Wash the oysters with a brush in water. Lay them on the broiler, flat side down, and endeavor to get the shell so hot as to slightly color the oyster. When the shell begins to open turn it over. Dish up in the deep shell, the other removed entirely, and if too dry pour over each one a small spoonful of hot oyster liquor and butter mixed. Serve a dozen on a platter, a half on a fish plate, with lemon.

840. Oysters—Fancy Roast.

(Restaurant Order.)

Cut two slices of buttered toast to fit a medium sized platter, when placed end to end, or cut fancy shapes of toast that when placed together will form a star shape.

Roast the oysters in the shells. Take them out when done and place them on the toast and pour some hot oyster liquor mixed with cream over the toast and in the dish. Garnish with parsley.

841. Oysters—Pan Roast.

An imitation of the shell roast.

1. Put 12 or 13 oysters in a bright pie pan, with their liquor. Dredge with salt and pepper very sparingly. Drop in some small lumps of butter and bake on the top shelf of a hot oven from 3 to 5 minutes. Slide them right side up into a hot dish, and garnish with 1 or 2 quarters of lemon.

2. A very common way in restaurants is to merely stew the oysters in a bright tin pan holding only about a pint, slightly season, and serve them in the same pan set in a plate. And, further, in the same style neat lids are used that fit the pans, to be placed when the oysters are done and sent in so. There is no difference, except in the imagination, betwixt that and a dry stew.

842. Steamed Oysters. Shells.

Scrub the oysters clean in water. Place the deep shell side down in the steamer and steam them about 5 minutes. Take off the top shell and save as much of the liquor as possible with the oyster in the lower one. Serve on a platter without seasoning or any addition, except lemon in quarters.

843. Oyster Pie. Individual.

A very popular sort of oyster pie is made with a bottom and top crust of short paste in a pie pan, like a fruit pie, but in size no larger than a tea saucer if to hold but a dozen medium oysters for a single order. Bake a few ahead of orders and keep them warm. Serve on a plate with hot oyster stew liquor poured under.

844. Oyster Pie or Pot Pie. Cheapest.

Put 4 quarts of small oysters pretty well drained from their liquor into a 6 quart bright pan and cover them with a sheet of good biscuit dough, or with a pot-pie dough made of a quart of flour, 3 teaspoonfuls of baking powder, salt and water and no shortening, but mixed up and rolled out very soft.

Bake about twenty minutes and then introduce at one side a seasoning of salt and pepper, a small piece of butter, a cupful of milk and a large spoonful of flour thickening. Stir about, replace the piece of crust and bake a short time longer. Sells well in restaurants where regular dinner is served. The crust should be as light as a sponge and lightly browned.

845. Small Oyster Pie

(Hotel Entree.)

2 quarts of oysters.
3 cupfuls of milk.
2 ounces of butter.
2 ounces of flour.
Cayenne, salt, parsley.
Puff paste for the crusts.

Set the oysters over the fire to scald but take off before they boil. Boil the milk by itself. Mix the butter and flour together in a saucepan big enough to hold all the rest, and when it bubbles up on the range begin stirring in the milk, thus making a thick white sauce. Let it boil up, stirring constantly. Season with cayenne and salt. Take the oysters out of their liquor and put them in the white sauce, and then stir in a little chopped parsley.

For the crusts roll out a sheet of puff paste quite thin, cut out flats with an oval cutter or biscuit cutter bent to shape, and bake them on a baking sheet. When to be served split them. Dish a spoonful of oysters on the bottom half and place the other crust on top.

846. Oyster Patties or Bouchees.

For directions for making puff paste and vol-au-vents or patty cases, see Nos. 28 and 72.

Prepare the oysters as in the preceding article, but make a yellow sauce for them by thickening with 8 yolks of eggs in lieu of part of the flour. The sauce must not quite boil after the yolks are added. At the last squeeze in the juice of a lemon. Take the lids out of the patties, fill with oysters, replace the lid and garnish with a sprig of parsley.

It may be hardly necessary to mention that the two oyster patty fillings above are suitable in other forms of patties. As to the names the oysters in white sauce are a la bechamel because cream sauce is so named, and the patties filled with the yellow are usually dubbed a la princesse. The particular exercise of taste and judgment required is to get the sauces just thick enough to coat the oysters and not run out of the patties, and yet not like a paste. The yellow sauce is thickest about one minute after the yolks are added and gets thinner and poorer afterwards.

847. Oysters in Cases.

Either of the oyster patty mixtures may be used with the difference that the oysters must be cut in small pieces after the scalding and before they are put into the sauce. A little anchovy sauce may be added. Serve a spoonful in each little paper case and band around hot. Paper cases can be bought by the dozen. They should be brushed slightly with clear butter and allowed to stand in the oven a minute before the filling. These *huitres en caisse* are served at luncheons, and as appetisers, after the soup at dinner.

848. Oysters in a Loaf.

(*Restaurant Order.*)

Take a loaf that has been baked in a tin mold, such as the bakers sell; cut off the top crust and lay it aside, remove most of the inside crumb, then cut the edge into ornamental notches or saw tooth fashion all around. Spread a little soft butter inside with the back of a spoon and set the loaf in the oven to toast. The top generally gets browned enough by the time the buttered inside is hot. Make an oyster stew in the usual way but dredge in a few fine bread crumbs to partially thicken it. Pour into the hot crisped loaf on a dish, no cover.

849.

The loaf above becomes a *croustade* when it is fried in hot lard or clarified butter, and pan roasts with their liquor and butter are sometimes served in *croustades*, so are fried oysters.

For individual hotel entrees the method is to use plain round rolls with the inside scooped out and fill with either of the oyster patty preparations. Or else to cut slices of bread in fancy shapes, fry and place three or four as a border in the dish and the oyster preparation in the middle.

The next is a method not at all especial for oysters since any other savory filling may be used, but the croustade small belongs to the class of hors d'oeuvre like the cases and patties that are served between courses. These cannot be recommended for large dinners, for though they need not be really wasteful they certainly have the appearance of being so. This is one of the methods of what is called fine cookery.

850. Croustades of Oysters.

Make some balls of cold butter by working them in ice water in a bowl, and shape them like eggs, or round or flattened or canoe shaped. Roll them in very fine bread crumbs, then in beaten eggs with a little milk mixed in, then in cracker meal; then in egg and cracker meal again. In short, you double bread the balls of butter after first giving them a solid coat of bread crumbs.

After rolling up the outside smooth in plenty of cracker meal drop the balls in hot lard and fry like any other breaded article to a deep yellow color. Take them out, cut out a circular piece of the top, turn the croustade upside down and let all the butter run out, or if not all melted take it out with a teaspoon. Drain well from grease, keep the cases crisp and hot, and when to be served fill them with oyster patty preparation the same as for cases, with the oysters cut small, replace the lids and serve. Garnish with lemon and parsley. Take care in making the balls of butter to have them small, for the breading increases the size greatly. Large sizes can, however, be made for restaurant parties.

851. Oysters Broiled in Bacon.

Dredge some large oysters with pepper and squeeze the juice of a lemon over them.

Cut large slices of fat bacon as thin as possible. Roll up two oysters together in each slice, run a skewer through diagonally and put six such rolls on each skewer crowded together to allow for shrinkage. Bake in the top of the oven for a few minutes, the skewers resting on the edge of a pan with the oysters raised above the drippings. Finish on the broiler. Serve on the skewers on buttered toast in a dish, and if common skewers are used slip a ring of fringed paper on the end.

Oyster sauce is the bait that catches the most people, and where the cheapest sort does so well there is little encouragement to try the artistic.

852. White Oyster Sauce—Common.

Take a quart of your fish soup or the liquor the fish is boiling in and pour it hot to about 3 dozen oysters. Drain it then from the oysters through a colander and boil it. Skim, stir in a large spoonful or two of flour-and water thickening, a little salt and then the oysters. Take off as soon as it begins to boil again.

853. White Oyster Sauce—Good.

1 level cupful of fresh butter.
1 level cupful of flour.
4 dozen oysters and their liquor.
1 quart of fish stock or soup stock.
1 lemon, cayenne, salt.

Stir the butter and flour together in a sauce pan over the fire till the mixture is hot and bubbling. Pour the quart of stock (or water) over the oysters in a colander set in a pan, and when it has run through add it a little at a time to the butter and flour. Stir up smooth and let it boil. It should be thicker than sauce, and the oysters now to be added should thin it to the proper degree. As soon as it begins to boil again take from the fire. Stir in a small lump of cold butter, the juice of the lemon and pinch of cayenne, and do not let the oysters cook hard.

854. Brown Oyster Sauce.

When to be served with baked fish or with roast turkey the very best is made by first making a gravy in the pan from which the fish (or turkey) has just been removed, and after straining adding the oysters to it. If not convenient to do that bake the butter and flour of the preceding receipt together in a frying pan in the oven till brown through, and use it to thicken the quart of stock. Add a tablespoonful of caramel for color, and the same of anchovy sauce.

855. Oyster Stuffing for Turkeys and Fish.

3 or 4 dozen oysters.
1 quart of crushed oyster crackers.
1 quart of fine bread crumbs.
8 ounces of butter.
2 eggs. Pepper and salt.

To get the bread finely crumbled it is best to slice thin and then mince it. The mixture of bread and crackers is much better than bread alone. Stir the softened butter, the liquor from the oysters and the two eggs into the crumbs and season to taste. Then mix in the oysters whole. Stuff the fowl loosely, that the filling may absorb the gravy. Enough for one large turkey or two geese or large fowls.

856. Scalloped Oysters in Silver Shells.

And now, since writing the receipts a little way back for scalloped oysters, thinking it best not to mention the silver scallop shells which cost $48 per dozen, with the air of the king's cook setting people to wishing for things it is not good for them to have, I have discovered that there are upon the market very good imitations stamped from heavy tin that are entirely practicable and with care to keep the edges dry while baking, and careful polishing, may be kept bright and presentable a long time. They cost $3 per dozen; are in scallop shell shape and hold about as much as a small tea saucer, but have more depth. They are calculated for an individual dish of half a dozen oysters scalloped. So, to re-state it for convenience sake, take

6 or 7 dozen oysters.
1 pound of fine bread crumbs.
1 pound of crushed oyster crackers.
12 ounces of butter.
1 pint of milk.
Pepper and salt.

Soften the butter and brush a coating of it over the bottom of the shells and strew in a layer of the mixed bread and cracker crumbs.

Shake the oysters about in a pan over the fire to make them shrink a little without boiling, take out with a drainer and place 5 or 6 in each scallop. Cover with the crumbs. Mix the butter with the hot oyster liquor, add the milk, pepper and salt to taste, and divide it by spoonfuls into the 15 or 18 scallops, moistening the crumbs all over. Wipe the edges clean. Bake on the middle shelf of the range.

857. Oyster Kromeskies.

Little pieces of a sort of croquette mixture rolled in thin shaved slices of bacon and fried in batter.

1 quart of oysters and their liquor.
1 pint of minced chicken meat.
1 cupful of milk.
½ cupful of flour—2 ounces.
Butter size of an egg.
4 yolks of eggs.
Black pepper, salt, little cayenne.
Juice of half a lemon.
50 little wraps of parboiled fat bacon.
Frying batter.

Scald the oysters first in their own liquor, take out with a skimmer and cut them small. Mince the chicken as if for salad, in the smallest possible dice. Melt the butter and flour together as if for butter sauce, and when it bubbles stir in the oyster liquor and the milk. Add the minced chicken and season-ing and stir till boiling hot again, put in the four yolks and when they have further thickened the mixture add the cut up oysters and then spread it in a bright pan brushed with butter, and let it get quite cold on ice.

Cut in strips the thickness of fingers, divide in two-inch lengths, roll up in bacon very thin, dip in fine frying batter and fry like fritters. Serve in place of patties, hot, with fried parsley

For directions for making the finest frying batter for the above see No. 252. Am. Pastry Cook, com-mon, for oysters and clam fritters, No. 253.

858. Oyster Fritters.

Scald the oysters first, or they will shrink too much, but they need not actually boil. Drain, sprinkle with pepper and salt and drop them into a pan of frying batter. Take two or three together with the batter coating them, and push from the spoon into hot lard. Very large oysters to be fried in batter singly without previous scalding should be dried first between two towels and dipped in the finest frying batter. They are done whenever the outside has acquired a yellow color. Serve same as fried oysters.

859. Clam Fritters.

The same as oyster fritters preceding. They are better with a cream sauce poured over.

860. Scallops in Batter—Marseillaise.

Scallops, the shell fish, not being universally known are often in an explanatory way designated New York scallops in the hotel bill of fare. Scallops of a smaller sort are known on the other side of the Atlantic as cockles. Our scallops, not gener-ally eaten raw, come to market in bulk without the shells. They are the little cream co'ored lumps seen in tubs at the fish shops. They have the tenderness of the oyster but the taste of the quahog.

Take 4 dozen scallops drained from their liquor, dredge with pepper and salt and squeeze the juice of a large lemon over them, and let remain in the pickle an hour or two. Make the fine frying batter

(No. 252). Make ready some lard, hot enough to just begin to smoke. Drain the scallops on a seive, take up two at a time with a spoon, dip them in the batter and coat them well, and fry for 2 or 3 minutes. Drain them on paper and keep hot.

Mash 2 cans of French peas (or use any other peas that are green) through a gravy strainer and season the puree thus obtained with butter, pepper and salt. Spread a small spoonful in each small dish, place two of the scallop fritters on the puree and serve hot.

Scallops may also be cooked in most of the ways that oysters are done, stewed, fried or roasted.

The process for the following is the same as for the yellow oyster preparation for patties at No. 846. Familiarity with one makes the other easy.

And it is here in place to mention that while a large piece of bread cut into a hollow shape and fried is called a *croustade*, as was stated a little way back, small pieces cut in shapes, such as may be used to ornament with, or to serve instead of toast with clams, etc., are called *croutons*.

861. Fricasseed Clams on Toast.

4 dozen clams and their liquor.
6 yolks of eggs.
1 pint of milk.
2 ounces of butter.
1 ounce of flour.
1 lemon, cayenne, salt.

Boil the milk. Take the clams from their shells and scald in their own liquor, drain them from it and cut them in pieces. Strain the clam liquor into the milk, add a spoonful of thickening, the butter, and the yolks slightly beaten, and the salt and cayenne to taste. Squeeze in the juice of the lemon. Then put in the cut clams. Dish spoonfuls on toast cut in neat shapes, or on fried crusts.

Which of these two mollusks has the best of it after all, the oyster, for which the regard is great but wholly gustatory, or the clam, for which the regard is more than half sentimental? Sorry indeed we all are that it is so, for we care nothing for the oyster further than that it is good to eat, but a hundred barrels of oysters may be sold as soon as one barrel of clams, and yet one far inland, homesick for a taste of the salt sea, will find it in the just opened shell of a small quahog or a large little neck as nowhere else, and not in the oyster at all, for the latter thrives most and fattens fastest where there is a mixture of fresh water with salt. But as if to offset this inequality in its market value the clam has got itself somehow mixed up with all the New England history, tales and traditions to such an extent that it can never be left out or disregarded or forgotten, so that even if we cannot eat the clam it interests us, and we wish it well and grieve because it is not as good as the oyster, and never can be. To learn something more about it let us quote from Thoreau, exploring the clam grounds of Cape Cod, like a Layard on the site of another Nineveh:

"There were, here and there, heaps of shells in the fields where clams had been opened for bait; for Orleans is famous for its shell-fish, especially clams. The shores are more fertile than the dry land. The inhabitants measure their crops, not only by bushels of corns, but by barrels of clams. A thousand barrels of clam-bait are counted as equal in value to six or eight thousand bushels of Indian corn, and once they were procured witout more labor or expense, and the supply was thought to be inexhaustible. 'For,' runs the history, 'after a portion of the shore has been dug over, and almost all the clams taken up, at the end of two years, it is said they are as plenty there as ever. It is even affirmed by many persons, that it is as necessary to stir clam ground frequently, as it is to hoe a field of potatoes because, if this labor is omitted, the clams will be crowded too closely together, add will be prevented from increasing in size' But we were told that the small clam, *mya arenaria*, was not so plenty here as formerly. Probably the clam-ground has been stirred too frequently, after all. Nevertheless one man, who complained that they fed pigs with them and so made them scarce, told me that he dug and opened one hundred and twenty-six dollars worth in one winter, in Truro."

Again: "We found some large clams, of the species *mactra solidissima*, which the storm had torn up from the bottom, and cast ashore. I selected one of the largest, about six inches in length, and carried it along, thinking to try an experiment on it. We soon after met a wrecker with a grapple and a rope. * * He also told us that the clam which I had was the sea clam or hen, and was good to eat. We took our nooning under a sand-hill, covered with bench-grass, in a dreary little hollow, on the bank, while it alternately rained and shined. There, having reduced some damp drift-wood, which I had picked up on the shore, to shavings with my knife, I kindled a fire and cooked my clam on the embers for my dinner; for breakfast was commonly the only meal which I took in a house on this excursion. When the clam was done one valve held the meat and the other the liquor. Though it was very tough, I found it sweet and savory, and ate the whole with a relish. Indeed, with the addition of a cracker or two, it would have been a bountiful dinner. I noticed that the shells were such as I had seen in the sugar-kit at home. Tied to a stick, they formerly made the Indians hoe hereabouts"

"The old man said the great clams (long necks) were good to eat, but they always took out a certain part which was poisonous, before they cooked them. 'People said it would kill a cat.' I did not tell him I had eaten a large one entire that afternoon, but began to think that I was tougher than a cat. In the course of the evening I began to feel the potency of the clam which I had eaten, and I was obliged to confess to our host that I was no tougher than the cat he told of; but he answered, that he was a plainspoken man, and he could tell me that it was all imagination. At any rate it proved an emetic in my case, and I was made quite sick by it for a short time, while he laughed at my expense. I was pleased to read afterward, in Mourt's Relation of the landing of the Pilgrims in Provincetown Harbor, these words: 'We found great muscles (the old editor says that they were undoubtedly sea clams) and very fat and full of sea pearl; but we could not eat them, for they made us all sick that did eat, as well sailors as passengers. But they were soon well again.' It brought me nearer to the Pilgrims to be thus reminded by a similar experience that I was so like them "

Having thus paid the tribute of a small space to the New England clam, let us proceed with our own narrative. For the large clams or "long necks" mentioned above come to market already strung on twine like old-fashioned dried apples. They are principally used for making clam chowder. They are strung through the "neck" and that part should be cut off before they are cooked.

862. Clam Chowder.

About 1 quart of clams, or two cans.
1 pound of salt pork.
2 quarts of sliced raw potatoes.
1 small onion.
2 teaspoonfuls of salt.
1 teaspoonful of pepper.
1 quart of milk, and the clam liquor.
About a pint of broken crackers.

This will take a pan that holds 5 or 6 quarts, or two small ones. Cut the pork in dice, put it into the pan and bake it light brown. Take the pan out and strew some of the thin sliced potatoes all over the pork scraps and fat. Shave some slices of the onion over them, then half the clams, cut in small pieces, then more potatoes, onion, and the rest of the clams. Potatoes on top and the crushed crackers over all. Mix the quart of milk with the clam liquor, add the pepper and salt and pour it over the crackers. Brush a sheet of thick paper with a little meat fat, lay it on top of the chowder and bake in a moderate oven about 2 hours. It will be partly browned on top.

More liquid may be needed if the chowder boils away fast. It is done whenever the potatoes in the center are done. Dish out spoonfuls on flat dishes.

863. Fish Chowder.

Fresh codfish and haddock make the best chowder but any other kind that can be freed from bones will do. Proceed as for clam chowder with the difference that the potatoes should be boiled first, the fish not needing much time to cook. Butter may be used instead of pork.

We have heard that on the coast of France the fish houses serve a pot-pourri of the chowder description made of a mixture of all sorts of shell fish, scallops, muscles, periwinkles, oysters, whelks, etc., with ship pork and ship biscuit.

Also, that the jambalaya of Florida is a mixture of different sorts of fish with tomatoes, peppers and rice, of a soup-like consistency. We have heard, too, of bisques of shell fish—soups thickened with the pounded meat of one kind of fish and several other kinds thrown in like plums into a pudding. And we have heard of clam chowder being made with tomatoes mixed in, and various high-flavored herbs besides. These things have to be mentioned because, as hotel cooks, the whole boundless continent is ours to make chowder in any way that we please, but the old Wellfleet oysterman, once above mentioned, we feel certain would never have owned that to be real chowder, and he should know, for all his world—as clams and oysters.

864. Raw Oysters and Clams.

The dealers now say that most of the popular names that oysters are sold by are but popular delusions, the Saddle Rock bed, for instance, having been exhausted twenty years ago, and the same with —but why should we meddle? The Morris Rivers or the Scotch Coves, the Blue Points and Shrewsburys are all small and fat and of good shape to serve in the shell. And with all the devices of china, glass and ice to serve raw oysters in, they never have the same taste out of the shell that they have when first opened and sprinkled with the juice from half a lemon. Four, five or six of these small oysters make a plate to serve preliminary to the dinner; fashion, it is said, even interfering in this small matter and making the proper number at present four. See that the shells are clean before opening the oysters. Put the piece of lemon in the middle.

"Counts," or New York counts, are the largest oysters sold by count and not by the gallon. "Culls" are the largest "selects." "Selects" are the ordinarily large oysters, sold by gallon or can. "Straights" come next and are supposed to be of all sizes unsorted. "Standards" are small oysters, and there is a grade below that known as "small."

The "paper shell," or little neck clam and the quahog of small size are served raw in the half shell precisely the same as oysters, and are not prohibited in the summer months as oysters are.

While the alarm of a threatened scarcity of oysters is raised regularly every season it is reassuring to be told, in an article by Mr. Gaston Fay, "That the cultivation of the oyster is so well understood, it is probable the supply will never cease Its deterioration or scarcity is due merely to local causes, and a barren bed of to-day may so to speak, become a bonanza to-morrow." And that is written in the midst of a number of instances showing how rapidly such fishes as the striped bass, white perch and others are disappearing And to show for how long a time oysters have already been abundant we will quote once more from Thoreau's *Cape Cod*, and then drop the subject for something else.

"Also William Wood speaks, in his 'New England's Prospect,' published in 1634, of 'a great oyster bank' in Charles River, and of another in the Mistick, each of which obstructed the navigation of the river, 'The oysters,' says he, 'be great ones in form of a shoe-horn; some be a foot long; these breed on certain banks that are bare every spring tide. This fish without the shell is so big that it must admit of a division before you can well get it into your mouth.' Oysters are still found there."

Mussels, or muscles, (the dictionaries allow both ways of spelling) are to oysters on the British shores what clams are with us—the second rate shell fish. They hang in clusters on the rocks by a "beard," a moss-like filament that has to be pulled off when they are cooked. Mussels are roasted in the shells, and steamed or boiled.

The number of kinds of fish that are eaten being enormous it would be a most bewildering task to attempt a set of different ways of cooking each one, such as have been set forth as inventions of cooks aiming chiefly at ornamental effects. The inapplicability of most of the elaborate foreign directions o hotel work is shown when we come to look over a few hundreds of bills of fare, ranging from hotels of every class, and find that all the fishes are cooked in the half dozen common ways, varied by the changes of at the most, a dozen different sauces.

Some of the "a la" styles do appear occasionally, but generally where the probabilities are altogether against the genuineness of the dish. Take, for instance the one that oftenest is seen, "*a la Chambord*." Chambord is a department or county in France, having an extent of sea coast, but probably a Count de Chambord was honored in naming the style A fish in that style is boiled, skinned, spread all over with a paste made of pounded fish, etc., and ornamented

then put into a fish kettle and simmered in a bottle of champagne, and when dished, the *cuisine classique* shows it with six different compartments in the platter occupied with as many different accessions of truffles, mushrooms, crayfish, oysters and other trifles, all separately prepared. Such dishes may appear at club dinners and for parties to whom expense is no object and where baskets of champagne to cook fish in are as plenty as baskets of potatoes, but when such names appear in the menus of hotels wherein the fish is cut and served individually there is reasonable ground for doubting its authenticity.

This is prefatory to saying that we are going to take up the few ways of cooking fish and a few fishes for illustrations, and then will mention the others only to show their adaptability to either one method or the other.

865. Fried Brook Trout with Bacon.

Provide in an average way about one eight-ounce fish for each person, or each probable order, which will be about forty-nine out of fifty persons. Also a thin slice of bacon for each one. Open the fish and clean them, wash and wipe dry with a coarse towel. The small fishes do not need scaling. Fry the slices of bacon well done in a deep baking pan in the oven, take them out with a skimmer. Roll the trout well in flour and fry them in the bacon fat in the same pan. Perhaps a little lard will have to be added.

Trout take from 6 to 15 minutes to fry, according to size. Drain them thoroughly from grease in a pan tilted up at one end and set in the open oven. Serve a slice of bacon with each fish.

It is a pleasant peculiarity of the speckled trout that the entire side or fillet parts readily from the spine, in one piece, not a bone remaining in the meat. Taking advantage of this the knowing ones have their trout fried in this way.

866. Boned Trout Fried with Bacon.

(Restaurant Order.)

Take a trout that weighs about a pound, split it down the back, open and clean it, leaving the head and tail on but clipping off the fins, and take out the back bone. Score the skin in three places on each side. Pepper the fish slightly, place a thin slice of bacon inside, close up and tie the two sides together again with two or three turns of twine. Roll the fish in flour and fry in hot lard about 10 minutes. Drain on a hot pan in the oven, take off the twine, dredge fine salt over, and serve in a hot dish with fried parsley and quarters of lemon, and minced potatoes in a side dish.

867. Fried Parsley.

One of the most desirable adjuncts to fried fish served without a sauce. Heat some lard in the potato fryer, but not hot enough to smoke, for too much heat takes all the color out of parsley. Put the parsley in the wire basket and immerse it in the hot lard about 1 minute, when it should be crisp, but still green. Drain it on a sheet of paper, and set for a minute in the open oven.

868. Minced Potatoes.

Chop cold boiled potatoes quite fine and season with salt. Spread a spoonful of drippings or butter in an omelet pan or small frying pan and place the minced potatoes about an inch deep. Cook on top of the range like a cake, without stirring. Invert a plate that just fits the pan over the potatoes. Let them brown nicely and slowly, then turn over on to the plate. Push in the edge a little all around and serve on the same plate with the brown on top. There are oval-shaped pans that make these suitable for a platter, and even in the round frying pan it can be managed to give the cake the flatter shape.

The fried bacon accompaniment to trout, bass, shad or perch is, however, very repugnant to some people. It is derived from the customs of the angler's camp life, and we find it never mentioned in the French methods of cooking fish, where even for larding several other things than bacon are used, except perhaps in the case of a dressing of a pike. The famous English white bait are simply rolled in flour, fried in hot lard, for only 1 minute, and eaten hot and crisp with nothing but salt. Every kind of small fish may be fried in the same way.

Says Brillat-Savarin: "Don't forget, however, when you have any of those trout weighing scarcely more than a quarter of a pound, and fetched from streams that murmur far from the capital—don't forget, I say, to fry them in the very finest olive oil you have." This is the dish that he says properly served with slices of lemon is fit for a cardinal.

This admiration for fish so small, "weighing scarcely more than a quarter of a pound," must be of the same kind as for whitebait, to be eaten bones and all.

869. Plain Fried Trout with Saratoga Potatoes.

Open and cleanse the trout, wash and dry them between two clean towels. The fins retain their red color after frying; leave them on as well as the head and tail. Roll the fish in flour and let them lie awhile in a pan of flour to get a better coating Drop in hot lard and fry from 5 to 10 minutes according to size. Dish with a border of Saratoga potatoes around and a slice of lemon on top of the fish.

870. Saratoga Chip Potatoes.

The common broadly sliced and fried potatoes are not Saratogas. These are thinly shaved, almost as thin as paper. When cut in quantities before the meal, as they generally have to be, they must be kept covered with cold water to prevent turning black. It is hardly practicable to dry them on a cloth, as, it is said, the original Saratogas were, but they will drain dry enough in a seive or colander. Throw a few at a time into hot lard. When first thrown in they sink. When they rise and float they are done, if colored enough. They should be yellow and curled. Good and mealy potatoes are required to make good and crisp chips. Dredge a little salt or them after frying, not before.

871. Brook Trout Breaded and Fried.

Cleanse the trout, leave the heads and tails on, chop off the fins, wash and wipe them dry with a clean rough towel. Beat some eggs—it will probably require about 2 dozen for fried fish for 50—and add less than a fourth as much water, some salt and white pepper. Dip the fish in the egg, then in cracker meal, coat them well by pressing, and let them lie in a pan after breading, for a little while before you fry. Drop them in hot lard, or frying fat, or oil; cook from 5 to 10 or 15 minutes according to size. Serve on a hot dish with a garnish of parsley and slices of lemon.

872. Some General Remarks on Frying Fish.

The speckled trout being always an expensive kind, and generally the most thought of by the anglers who bring them to the hotel to be cooked, we take it for example, as it must often be a source of disappointment to see the expected feast of "speckled beauties" come to table looking anything but inviting. Most frequently the breading comes off in patches, and the fish instead of having a crisp coating, and a moist and full-flavored inside, looks black and greasy. The breading comes off trout because, not needing to be scaled, it does not get scraped free of the fishiness that coats the skin. A vigorous rubbing with a rough cloth overcomes the difficulty, but the cloth becomes wet and useless after a dozen or so have been wiped. Either scrape the fish or have dry cloths plenty. The difference often seen betwixt the outside skin of a fish that is cut up before frying, and which comes out bare of breading, and the cut sides which remain coated, shows the above to be true.

Rolling the fish in flour before dipping in egg insures a good coating, but we have not so directed for the reason that it takes more eggs that way and uses up twice as much time before the egg will stick to the flour. These things count for a large number. There is nothing gained by filling the pans with too many fish at once. They reduce the heat of the frying fat and fry badly. The fat should be hot enough to hiss sharply when a drop of water touches it, but not hot enough to smoke.

Not long since a remark appeared in a New York publication devoted to such subjects of a correspondent who said there is only one way to cook a speckled trout—meaning only one way that it ought to be cooked—and that was to roll it in egg and corn meal. That is a dashing, off hand way of stating a thing but the one way wouldn't fit everywhere.

There are people enough who like corn meal breading better than cracker dust, but neither cooks nor any one else will choose it where the appearance of the article fried is cared for. Pieces of bread dried in a warm place can be crushed into a sort of meal and used for breading, and it is economical to do so, but the color is bad even of that, and not like the golden brown of the cracker-meal breading.

It is an advantage, when the fish has been nicely fried, to have it ornamented a little with parsley, young celery leaves, cress, water cress or cut lemons—whatever be obtainable—for it looks as if somebody cared for the appearance of the table, not forgetting that quartered lemons to squeeze over trout are a luxury. But there is seldom any one to do the garnishing at a fishing resort unless the waiters are allowed while waiting for their orders. They are generally anxious enough to "fix up" their dishes if the materials are placed ready, and the city hotel rules relaxed sufficiently.

873. Plain Fried Potatoes.

A good garnish for fried fish. Slice the potatoes thicker than Saratoga chips, and fry till they float and are yellow. Place them in the fish dish as a border.

874. Fried Mackinaw Trout—Breakfast or Supper.

Scale and cleanse the fish, split down the back and take out the back bone. Cut the fish in pieces, dredge with salt and pepper, roll the pieces well in flour and fry in hot fat. Time 8 or 10 minutes. Fish is best when just cooked through to the center and not dried out, unless when the order is for small fish done to a crisp

875. Mackinaw Trout Fried in Eggs.

Skin the trout, beginning at the gills. It can be done with a little help of a sharp knife. To dip the fish in hot water makes it easier. Take out the back bone. Cut the fish, if for breakfast, in suitable pieces, and dry them on a cloth. Dredge with salt. About one egg for every pound of fish is needed. Beat up without adding any water. Dip the fish in the egg, roll in flour, then in egg again and fry in lard not very hot. If carefully fried without too much heat fish looks richer this way than any other. It is of a yellow brown color. This is one of the methods for frying in sweet oil. Garnish with parsley.

876. Fried Black Bass.

For ordinary restaurant orders the fish should be selected weighing about one pound each. Scale and cleanse them, roll well in flour and fry. For occasional orders it answers to fry them in a frying pan only half full of fat, care being taken that a black burnt section does not appear where the thick part of the fish touches the pan. Garnish with sliced lemon, and fried or plain parsley, and potatoes.

877. Broiled Trout with Bacon.

Split a small trout and take out the back bone and place a thin slice of bacon inside. Broil the trout in the wire broiler over a bed of clear coals. Garnish the dish with parsley, and send in a dish of saute potatoes.

878. Potatoes Sautes, or Dutch Fried.

Slice cold boiled potatoes, not very thin, and brown them in a large frying pan, slowly, at the side of the range, with only enough frying fat in the pan to keep the bottom moist. When brown at bottom shake them over. Dredge a little salt.

879. Broiled Trout, a la Colbert.

Scrape and cleanse the trout and take out the back bone. Brush over with a touch of butter to prevent sticking and broil it in natural shape over clear coals. When done open the fish and put in a slice of maitre d'hotel butter. Garnish with lemon and fried parsley. If not inclosed in a wire broiler, or if a large fish in any case score the skin on both sides to prevent curling.

Simple as the word Colbert is I have recently seen it misspelt in two or three bills of fare. It is the name of a French statesman who kept good cooks and gave dinners. Maitre d' hotel is a clumsy term for us to use, and some are translating it steward, which it literally means, so that cold maitre d' hotel sauce, or butter, becomes steward sauce. An authority on cooking says the principle of cooking a la maitre d' hotel is in the mixture of acid with green herbs, which, however, is not explaining much. There are two sauces of the name, and beside that there is a way of rolling a nicely boiled fish in chopped parsley and fennel, squeezing lemon juice all over it and then pouring a rich cream sauce around it, and it makes a very pretty dish when the fish is of a suitable sort, a shad, carp, or whitefish.

880. Maitre d' Hotel Butter or Cold Sauce.

8 ounces of butter.
2 lemons—juice only.
Small bunch of parsley.
Little cayenne.

Soften the butter, squeeze in the lemon juice a little at a time, stirring till the butter absorbs it, add the cayenne and the parsley chopped small. Keep in a cold place.

881. Broiled Whitefish.

Take small ones for choice, scale, trim, split them in halves, take out the back bone and divide each half in two. Wash in cold water and dry them. Lay on a plate and brush over with the butter brush. Broil in the hinged wire broiler over a clear fire, till brown on both sides. Brush over with butter again, dredge with fine salt, send to table hot, with potatoes.

882. Frizzed or Shoestring Potatoes.

Slice raw potatoes thin and cut them in shreds, in size from a shoestring to a pencil, but all alike, and the longer the better. Fry in hot lard. Drain and sprinkle with salt. Serve as a border with broiled fish.

883. Broiled Striped Bass.

Scale, cleanse, split in halves and take out the back bone. Fish done this way are said to be filleted, the two sides being called fillets. Fillets of bass rayée, a la maitre d' hotel, a favorite dish for fine dinners, are these sides buttered and broiled and served with maitre d' hotel butter.

884. To Broil a Shad Whole.

Scale the fish and pull out the gills, and draw it without ripping open. Wash and wipe it dry. Mix a little butter, pepper and salt together, put a small portion inside the fish, and spread the rest upon the outside, roll it in two turns of oiled or buttered paper and broil it high above the coals about 20 minutes. When done open out, lay on a hot dish, and mark it with a red hot iron wire.

Manilla paper should be used. Paper well greased will stand a good deal of heat without being destroyed. To prevent dripping the butter and gravy double in the ends of the paper and fasten with a pin. Throw coarse salt on the coals to put out a blaze. The fish may be served with a sauce or with a surrounding of green peas, potatoes, toast or fried crusts.

Roe shad bring about one-third more than the others in market, the roe sells in the restaurants for as much as the fish. It has a sweet mealy taste when fried.

885. Fried Shad Roe.

Take out the roe without breaking it out of shape and let lie in cold water till wanted. Wipe dry, roll it in flour and fry in a little lard in a pan the same as fish.

Shad roe can also be breaded whole; parboiled and then split and breaded and fried crisp; or scrambled with butter in a frying pan and an egg or two added; and it may be boiled and served with cream sauce. The plain fry is the best way.

Planked shad is an American dish that is eaten out of doors, by a camp fire, on the river bank, in the spring of the year. Daniel Webster was fond of planked shad and he knew an old uncle who could cook it better than anybody else. But they always prepared it out of doors. It does not belong to hotel cooking.

886. Broiled Spanish Mackerel—Royal Sauce.

Cut the fish, if over one pound in weight, in four pieces, first splitting it down the back and taking out the bone. Dry it on a cloth. Dredge with salt and pepper. For each fish mix together two raw yolks of eggs and an equal amount of olive oil, roll the pieces (fillets) of fish in the egg mixture and then in fine bread crumbs (not cracker-meal) and broil carefully on top of the wire broiler. Spanish mackerel can of course be broiled plain like any other fish as well. It is a scarcer and dearer fish than the common mackerel.

887. Royal Fish Sauce.

4 ounces of fresh butter.
3 raw yolks of eggs.
3 tablespoonfuls of tarragon vinegar.
2 tablespoonfuls of India soy.
1 green gherkin finely minced.
Little cayenne and salt.

Stir the eggs and butter together in a little sauce-pan over the fire till the yolks thicken slightly, taking care not to let them cook hard. Take it off and stir in the other ingredients gradually. Set in a cold place and serve sliced cold with fish

888. Broiled Fresh Mackerel

Split the fish down the back, take out the bone, cut in four pieces if for hotel service, wash, and dry on a cloth. Brush over each piece with the butter brush and broil in the hinged wire broiler. Brush over with a touch of fresh butter when done.

889. The Mystery of the Fillet.

Probably we can do nothing more useful here than explain a matter that has never been explained before in set phrase, and is a source of evident confusion, not only among some cooks, and others concerned in cooking, but among the frequenters of restaurant and hotel tables.

The word fillet is used in cookery in its broadest meaning of a band or strip, and is strict in sense only in one point, that it always means meat without any bone. It does not always mean the same piece of meat in every animal, and it does not follow that because the fillet of beef is the tenderloin that a fillet of fish can be called a tenderloin likewise. When our big cook books that mystify more than they teach tell us to bone a fillet of veal they do not mean the tenderloin of veal only but the whole of the loin, the tenderloin being called the under or small fillet. The same with mutton and other small meats. A fillet of rabbit is the saddle of rabbit with the bone out. A fillet of fowl is the breast of fowl, but as that has a natural division each fowl furnishes four fillets according to cooks' talk, the upper fillet or portion of the breast, and the minion fillet or division of the breast that is nearest the breast bone. So with fish: the fillet first is the whole side of a fish free from bone, but technically any boneless piece of fish of considerable size is spoken of as a fillet (strip) of fish. When a bill of fare announces fillets of fish in any style it simply means sides of fish cut off clear from the bone. And that is not quite the same as a slice or a steak.

890. Lake Herring.

Either fry or broil it in any way that is directed for trout and other kinds.

This is an excellent fish of the trout family, having the same fins and the same freedom from small bones. It is white, both scales and flesh.

891. Fresh Water Perch.

Good pan fish. Fry and serve with bacon. The bones are not troublesome but large in proportion to the meat. It takes two perch to make a dish where one of some other kinds would do.

892. Smelt's Sauteed in Brown Butter.
Or, Au Beurre Noir.

Pull out the gills and cleanse the fish, wash and wipe dry and roll them in flour. Fifty of these small fish will take over a pound of butter. A very short time before they are wanted melt a part of the butter in a large frying pan, lay in the fish in close order, and let the butter and fish brown together but not get black. Turn over when half done, cook only as they are wanted, a panful at a time, adding more butter with each relay. The butter froths over them while cooking and they should be sent to table before it subsides, with potato pancakes, or croquettes, or toast in the same dish.

The smelt is a sea fish, but is caught in fresh waters. It can be cooked in all the ways previously mentioned. The foregoing does for any kind of small fish as well.

893. Potato Pancakes to Serve with Fish, Etc.

1 pound of mashed potato.
3 ounces of butter.
1 cupful of milk.
8 yolks and 6 whites.
Salt.

Mash the potatoes through a colander, work the butter in while warm, and the milk and yolks. Whip the whites firm and stir in just before frying Cook in omelet pans like sweet pancakes; roll up, place in the dish diagonally with a fish on each side. A spoonful of flour is needed in the mixture when the potatoes are not of a mealy sort.

894. Grayling.

Cook it in all the ways directed for brook trout. It runs about the same size from eight ounces to three pounds.

The grayling like the trout and the mullet possesses an interest apart from its value as food, which it is pertinent here to mention because it has lately been discovered inhabiting the lakes and rivers of the northwest, whereas it had been regarded as peculiar to Europe before. Old Izaac Walton mentions it: "St Ambrose, the glorious bishop of Milan, who lived when the church kept fasting days, calls the grayling the flower fish; and some think that he feeds on the sweet water thyme." Another tells us the grayling is one of the few fishes of the glacial period still in existence. A home authority says: "He has only very recently been discovered to be a dweller in certain American waters as well. They are quite abundant in many of the streams of

Michigan, and, it is said, in a few tributaries of Lake Superior so well. However this may be, it is certain that the rivers of Michigan, particularly the northern ones, are the chief abiding places of the grayling, and here he was discovered and the event announced to a doubting public. Extensive and systematic efforts are now being made to introduce the new comer into many and remote waters and there is no doubt that he will thrive in any suitable trout stream."

These, and similar attractions, go to make up the business of summer resort hotels. Let us in passing snatch another "flower fish" simile from Thoreau The epithet applied to the grayling is for i's great curved fins and its brilliant hues. This refers to another kind:

Anon their cousins, the true trout, took their turn, and a'teronately the speckled trout, and the silvery ronches, swallowed the bait as fast as we cou'd throw in; and the finest specimens of both that I have ever seen, the largest one weighing three pounds, were heaved upon the shore. While yet alive, before their tints had faded, they glistened like the fairest flowers the product of primitive rivers; and he could hardly trust his senses, as he stood over them, that these jewels should have swam away in that Aboljackenagesic water for so many dark ages; these bright fluviati'c flowers, seen of Indians only, made beautiful, the Lord on'y knows why, to swim there. But there is the rough voice of Uncle George, who commands at the frying-pan to send over what you've got, and then you may stay till morning The pork sizzles and cries for fish."

895. Cisco.

Either fry or broil it in any way that is directed for trout or any small fish.

The cisco and lake herring are varieties of the same family of fishes, the cisco being the smaller and darker of the two.

The following we quote from "*Fish and Fishing*," as having relation to our summer resort business:

"The cisco found in the Wisconsin and Indiana lakes, particularly the former, inhabits deep water through almost the entire year, and is rarely met with except during a very brief season in June. Then he makes up for his former absence by appearing literally in countless numbers, rising to the surface in pursuit of a fly called the "cisco fly," which abounds during an equally brief season in June.

Immediately on the appearance of the cisco fly rapid preparations are made for the approaching sport. Old fishermen claim to prognosticate the abundance or reverse of the cisco by the number of flies, saying "Many flies, many fish," or the opposite.

At Geneva Lake, Wisconsin, perhaps the most noted cisco resort, the fish appear first in one portion of the lake, gradually working towards the opposite extremity. Hence, while fishing is at its height in one locality, there are only scattering fish at another point but a short distance removed. The next day the boat has passed from its haunts of yesterday, leaving only a few stragglers behind A few days later, their course being completed, they almost wholly disappear, returning to the deepest portions of the lakes, and thence onward until the arrival of the next cisco season, the sportsman may fish a month without seeing a single individual.

But while the season lasts the sport is fast and furious. The residents at the lake telegraph to friends and *habitues* far and near that the fish have appeared, and the telegram must be responded to promptly or not at all.

On arrival, the fisherman takes a boat, and, provided with a bamboo pole, a common linen line, and perch hooks, rows out to where the school is then lying. Baiting with the abundant cisco fly, he casts, and almost before the flies have reached the water they are seized upon by the eager fi-h. Then, until he is fairly satiated, he has only to throw out his line and haul in the beauties.

On the table, the cisco is delicious eating, its flesh being white and translucent. In the hotels and restaurants of Chicago they have become a favorite item in the bills of fare."

And the following we quote from a ladies' fashion paper. The way of cooking trout described in the second instance—"however odd"—is the well-known, primitive Indian barbecue; the potting method ought to be tried with our home cisco in the season of its abundance:

"One of the greatest charms of trout fishing is the satisfactory culinary result of the amusement; and we now intend to give a little information regarding trout as a table luxury, which of itself might tempt many a lady to take a rod and go a fishing. Every one who has been in England, and many people who have not been there, have heard of the famous delicacy, associated with the English lakes, called potted char. Now potted char is, as often as not, potted trout. The distinction between the fish is difficult to determine, and one fish is quite as delicate as the other The following simple recipe for its preparation was given us by the landlady of the famous Ferry Inn at Ambleside—one of the most noted makers of the delicacy living:

896. "Take one dozen char (or trout), dress, and wipe with a dry cloth; strew a little salt in and over them, and let them lie all night; then wipe again with a dry cloth, and season with one ounce of white pepper, one-quarter ounce of cayenne, one-half ounce of pounded cloves, and a pinch of mace. Clarify two pounds of butter; then put the fish, with

their backs down, in a pot lined with paper, pour the butter over them, and bake four hours in a slow oven."

And now that we are on the subject of eating trout, we will add a delicate and delicious way of dressing trout at the water edge, invariably adopted by the hungry anglers in the Cumberland dales—one, however odd, that only needs to be tried once in order to be adopted by acclamation. We will, of course, suppose that a little bread, butter, and salt have been taken in the creel, or basket. If there has been this forethought, then let your attendant collect a lot of small dry wood, and set it on fire. When a sufficient quantity of ashes has been obtained, take a sheet of paper—an old newspaper will do—wet it thoroughly, shake off the drops of water, fill the mouth of the fish with salt, wrap him up in the wet paper, and bury him in the ashes. In ten or fifteen minutes uncover him, and if he is sufficiently done, the skin will come off cutire with the paper, and the trout be ready for eating, as white or pink as rose.

If we have have said enough to induce some lady to buy a rod and become a disciple of the "gentle craft," we shall have added somewhat to the happiness of the world."

397. Broiled Salmon Steak with New Potatoes.

One of the greatest luxuries that can be provided for a fine breakfast or dinner, not only for its high price but because the salmon is called the king of fishes.

Slice the fish with a sharp knife and sever the bone in the center by striking the point of the knife with a hammer—not to break or tear the meat. Lay the steaks in a bright tin pan or dish, dredge with pepper and salt, brush them over with olive oil, if you can, or with clear melted butter and let them lie till wanted. Then broil in the hinged wire broiler same as beefsteaks, about 10 minutes. Dish up on a large platter hot. Have some new potatoes ready boiled, cut them in quarters lengthwise and place them as a border around the steak. Shake a teaspoonful of chopped parsley over the salmon steak, melt a piece of fresh butter in an omelet pan and pour it hot over it, squeeze the juice of half a lemon over that. Place three or four green tufts of parsley among the potatoes in the border and send it in.

The above is *a la maître d' hôtel* by a short order method, suitable for a dish for a party, of almost any kind of broiled fish. A restaurant order for one is commonly a salmon steak weighing from eight to twelve ounces. A party dish may take three or four such. It takes at least fifteen pounds gross of salmon for broiled steaks for breakfast for fifty, in hotel service. People generally cannot eat as much of this rich fish as of other kinds and the individual steaks need not be large when the fish is only one item in the meal.

898. Broiled Trout Steak—Hollandaise

The largest lake trout are used to slice and broil the same as salmon. Serve the steaks in the same way, or with hollandaise sauce poured around; or, if individual small portions, with the sauce at one end of the dish. It is not sensible to pour a sauce of decided flavor and pungency upon the fish for the many who would rather have it ithout.

Most, if not all, of the old established favorite sauces have come down to us in two forms, the original French and the modified English; the pungent and the mild; it might almost be said the costly and the cheap, but it is too plain that the cheaper form is generally liked the better without regard to any difference of cost. It may seem trite to say it but it is necessary: the cook should be equally prepared and equally willing to make them either way, and if he finds, as is generally the case, that the cheaper form suits best for the hotel table he can reserve the more expensive, or the more concentrated, pungent or vinous form for particular or private requirements.

899. Hollandaise Sauce—French Way.

1 teacupful of vinegar.
1 teaspoonful of black pepper-corns.
½ cupful of fresh butter.
8 yolks of eggs.
Small piece of broken nutmeg.
Salt, if not enough in the butter.

Bruise the pepper-corns so that the flavor can be drawn and boil them and the scrap of nutmeg in the vinegar a few minutes. Then strain it into another saucepan, throw in half the butter and boil it again. Beat the yolks a little, pour part of the boiling vinegar to them gradually, then turn all into the saucepan and stir it on the fire. There is nothing very particular about making this sauce, but the one point of knowing when to stop the cooking. About one minute after it is set on the fire with the yolks in it thickens to the consistency and appearance of good mayonaise or soft butter, immediately after that it becomes thinner, and although not then quite spoiled it is not perfect or fit for a fine dish. When the sauce is at that thickest point drop in half the remaining butter and keep beating with the wire egg whisk till it is dissolved—still on the side of the range—then take it off and beat in the butter remaining. Salt if needed.

900. Hollandaise Sauce—English Way.

Make good butter sauce, or drawn butter as it is called, color it yellow with yolks of eggs and let them cook in it enough to thicken but not boil, and beat in a little more butter. Squeeze in the juice of one or two lemons, and add a pinch of cayenne.

901. Original Dutch or Hollandaise Sauce.

1 or 2 yolks of eggs.
1 cupful of butter.
½ cupful of vinegar.
Pinch of cayenne.

Flavoring of any kind of table sauce, anchovy essence, soy, or flavored vinegar.

No cooking is required, but the sauce is made with a knowledge of the fact that butter will mix with a liquid at the right temperature. Soften the butter but not melt it. Have the vinegar nearly milk-warm. Stir a spoonful of vinegar into the butter, and when that is absorbed add another, and after that the yolk of an egg. Then more vinegar, the flavoring of table sauce and another yolk. May be used as soon as mixed, or kept cold till wanted.

902. Broiled Pompano—Tartar Sauce.

The pompano is a southern sea fish somewhat rare and high priced. It has a decided flavor of its own that suggests the taste of black walnuts when broiled It has the flattened shape of the sunfish and scales almost as fine as those of the mackerel.

Scrape the skin thoroughly. The smallest size, weighing about one pound, may be broiled whole in the wire broiler previously greased. Split the large ones down the back and through the head Broil the cut side first—8 or 10 minutes—brush over with fresh butter and dredge with salt and pepper, then broil the skin side till done. Serve on a hot dish Squeeze a little lemon juice over, and serve cold tartar sauce in a sauce boat separately, or, for individual orders, the hot tartar sauce in the same dish.

903. Tartar Sauce, Cold.

Is mayonaise sauce with finely minced onion or cives and green pickled gherkin or chopped tarragon mixed in, and a good pinch of cayenne pepper. (See Nos. 693 and 738.)

904. Tartar Sauce, Hot.

1 teacupful of vinegar.
1 bastingspoonful of olive oil.
1 ounce of butter.
1 tablespoonful of finely minced onion.
8 yolks of eggs.

Little minced pickled gherkin and cives.
Salt and cayenne.

Boil the onion in the vinegar a few minutes, throw in the butter and yolks and beat till it cooks thick—one minute. Take it from the fire and whip in the oil gradually, and the seasonings.

905. Halibut Steak—Sauce Robert.

Dip the slices of halibut in flour and saute them with a little drippings or butter in a frying pan, like the common frying of beefsteak, and serve with the sauce at the side in the same dish.

906. Catfish Steaks.

Catfish especially needs to be well done. It is more oily than halibut and somewhat slow to cook. It may be plainly sauteed, or floured and fried, or breaded; or broiled plain. A good sauce is an advantage to it.

Rabelais mentions the originator of the sauce Robert in such words as these: "And Robert, another cook, who gave us the sauce, that is good with fish and capon and grilled bones," etc. Another writer refers to him as "Robert, one of the Parisian gastronomic masters." Sauce Robert briefly and simply is brown meat gravy containing lightly fried onion and garlic, or one or the other, and mustard, vinegar and pepper.

907. Sauce Robert—French Way.

2 bastingspoonfuls of olive oil.
2 cloves of garlic
2 small onions.
1 bastingspoonful of vinegar.
½ teaspoonful of white pepper.
½ pint of espagnole sauce, or brown gravy.
1 tablespoonful of made mustard.

Stew the onions and garlic, cut small, in the oil till they are tender and begin to color. Pour off the oil; add to the onions a spoonful of broth or water and a spoonful of vinegar and the ground pepper. Simmer a little longer, then add the ladleful of brown sauce, boil and skim and at last mix in the mustard.

908. Sauce Robert—English Way.

Fry a minced onion in very little fresh butter a the side of the range, only till light yellow, and not in the least brown. Put in a ladleful of brown sauce slightly diluted with stock, and throw in a little pepper. Let simmer a while and add a spoonful of vinegar. The butter when it boils again will come to the top and can be skimmed off if desired, but used not be when the sauce is for a dry kind of fish. At last mix in a tablespoonful of mustard moistened with vinegar. The mustard should not cook in it,

909. Chutney Sauce.

Used to mix with fish sauces and gravies. It is an article of the same order as tomato ketchup, Tabasco sauce, chili sauce and the like. It is brought forward here because the time to make it is at hand, as it needs sour apples.

1 pound each of sour apples, figs, tomatoes, brown sugar and salt
1 ounce of cayenne pepper.
1 ounce of ground ginger.
2 ounces of garlic.
2 ounces of onions
1 quart of lemon juice.
3 quarts of vinegar.

Pound all the articles of the first part, and the garlic and onions together in a mortar, mix in the ground pepper and ginger, put the pulp in a jar, mix in the lemon juice and vinegar and set the jar in a place warm enough to raise bread. Keep it there for a month, stirring the mixture twice a day. Pour off the top liquor and keep it tightly corked in bottles for seasoning fish sauces; put the chutney—the thick bottom portion—in wide-mouthed bottles for table use.

Bordelaise is of Bordeaux. Bordelaise sauce is Bordeaux wine sauce, and that wine is claret. A few French terms have, through some chance associations, been taken up and are perpetually repeated, often with little similarity of meaning, by those who speak of cooking, while the articles they stand for are inconsequential, but the admirers of the claret sauce or the fish cooked partially in claret or sauterne are numerous and enthusiastic while the term for such is scarcely to be heard beyond a very limited circle. A special affection for the *vin de Bordeaux* must have possessed Sir Walter Scott, for he seems never to have let an opportunity pass of mentioning it in his novels—in the cargoes of the smugglers, in the cellars of the Scottish gentlemen, and on their hospitable tables—and his liking for Bordelaise sauce is as evidently shown in various places as the liking of Thackeray for *creme au marasquin*. "The ducks" —he says, in *Guy Mannering*—"were roasted to a single turn, and the sauce, of claret, lemon, and cayenne was beyond all praise." But did even he, or his friend Thackeray when they dined together at the London clubs, as they often did afterwards, recognize the "claret, lemon and cayenne," sauce in the Bordelaise they undoubtedly were served with, after the club cooks had thrown in their extra flavorings? Probably they did, if the cooks were discreet in their seasonings, not to destroy the main characteristic of the sauce. For there has to be a mixture, or the sauce would lack consistence. At Col. Mannering's table the claret, lemon, and cayenne were mixed with the savory gravy of the brace of wild ducks. It had long before been discovered that a little puree of pounded ham mixed with meat gravy makes a fine combination, when the gravy of duck is not at hand, and since that it has been tried on with the lean of the comparatively recent sugar-cured ham of America with such savory results that the Bordelaise is getting further beyond all praise than ever

910. Bordelaise Sauce for Fish and Broiled Meats.

2 ladlefuls of espagnole or brown sauce.
1 ladleful of claret.
1 clove of garlic.
½ a bay leaf. Cloves. Mace.
Lean ham.
1 lemon. Pepper-corns or cayenne.

Pick some lean meat from the knuckle bone of a boiled ham, taking care that it is sweet, freshly cut and free from smoked outside, pound it to shreds in the saucepan, and boil it with the wine and brown sauce. Throw in the piece of bay leaf, two cloves, pepper and half a blade of mace. When nearly a third has boiled away strain the sauce into another sauce pan, let simmer and skim it. Pour in a spoonful more of claret, mixed with the juice of the lemon, to brighten and clear the sauce, and skim when it boils up again. If for broiled fish add in the boiling a flavoring of one pounded anchovy, or some essence to the sauce at last.

911. About Crimping Fish.

This is an operation generally beyond the cook's province, but dependent upon the fisherman for its performance. There is reason to believe that very vague ideas of what is meant by crimped fish prevail among the generality of cooks and other writers of bills of fare. Trout and salmon should be cooked the same day they are caught. When first taken, if they are to be in the most perfect condition when cooked, the fish should be instantly killed by a blow on the head, incisions cut in the sides down to the bone and about two inches apart, and it should then be placed in very cold water for two hours. The result is the flesh becomes firm almost to crispness, through contraction of the fibres, and congulation. In the case of salmon it is recommended to cut it in steaks at once, as soon as killed, and let them lie in the cold spring water, or under a stream from a pump till they can be cooked. That is crimping fish. It makes it flaky when boiled and preserves a certain creaminess between the flakes and a richness of flavor that passes away from fish long kept. The colder the water that is used the better. Crimped fish needs a shorter time to cook than the plain, it should be put on in boiling water, and not allowed to remain in it a minute after it is done, which may be in six or eight minutes for a slice or steak and fifteen to thirty for a whole fish.

912. Boiled Red Snapper, Shrimp Sauce.

The firm-fleshed fishes, of which this is one, and the groupers from the same southern waters are others, are a little better to boil than to bake, and rather to be chosen for boiling than the softer lake trout. They also need a little more time to cook in, regard being had to the weight and thickness. Scale and clean the fish and let it lie in a pan of cold water till wanted. Half fill the fish kettle with hot water, or part stock. Throw in a spoonful of salt, a small bay leaf, a small onion with six cloves stuck in it, a bunch of parsley, and half a cup of vinegar and let it boil.

Three-quarters of an hour before dinner put in the fish and cook it at the side of the range about 35 minutes. Lift it out on the drainer of the kettle and take off the skin of the upper side.

Dish up small portions on plates, with a spoonful of shrimp sauce poured over and a small spoonful of mashed potato on the same plate.

It takes from 12 to 15 pounds gross for the orders of about 50 persons, where there is but one kind of fish.

913. Shrimp Sauce.

Butter sauce colored light yellow with egg yolk, with a little lemon juice in it, and shrimps.

1 quart of water or stock.
6 ounces of butter—about a cupful.
3 ounces of flour—small cupful.
1 teaspoonful of salt.
2 yolks of eggs.
Juice of half a lemon.
1 can of Barataria shrimps.

Put half the butter in a saucepan with all the flour and stir them over the fire till mixed and bubbling. Then add the boiling water gradually and stir while it cooks smooth and rather thick. Drop in the other half the butter, take it from the fire, put in the yolks and beat till the butter is melted. Add the lemon juice and shrimps.

914. Boiled Codfish or Haddock, Oyster Sauce.

Boil in plain salted water generally about half an hour, or till the meat of the fish will leave the back bone. Serve with the white oyster sauce, No. 853.

915. Boiled Pickerel, Butter Sauce.

Boil it slowly at the side of the range half an hour or more according to size. The stock it is boiled in should be seasoned with salt, vinegar and a piece of horseradish chopped in pieces. The skin of the fish can be pushed off when it is dished up, and a spoonful of good butter sauce poured over each portion of the white fish in the plates. The pickerel comes from one pound to ten, in weight, usually, but is often seen of much larger size. Though a fine fish, solid and meaty, for some reason it is not as generally saleable or taken for choice as a number of other large kinds are.

"He was a good man, an excellent man; he had the best melted butter I ever tasted in my life"—was the eulogy pronounced upon a deceased English Baron, by an eminent Queen's counsel and member of parliament.

This universally serviceable "melted butter," the one sauce of the English, and the beginning of a number of others is a source of much difficulty for the hotel cook, because of its cost, as it consists, if made according to rule, of about one-half butter, and that must be of very good quality.

916. Butter Sauce.

Drawn Butter, or Melted Butter.

1 quart of clear strained broth or water.
8 ounces of butter, or more.
4 ounces of flour.
Salt, if not enough in the butter.

Take a large basting spoonful of butter—about 4 ounces—and the same measure of sifted flour and stir them together in a saucepan over the fire. When well mingled and bubbling from the bottom begin and add the boiling water or broth a little at a time, stirring till all is in and the sauce has cooked thick and smooth. Take it from the fire and heat in the other half the butter a portion at a time and do not let it boil again. It looks glossy and smooth as soft butter; may need thinning down for some purposes, such as for parsley sauce, etc.

917. Butter Sauce Substitute.

1 quart of clear-strained soup stock.
Flour and water thickening.
Butter size of an egg.
Salt.

Thicken the stock to the right consistency and add salt. Take it from the fire and beat in the butter, which takes away the transparency and whitens it. If not slightly yellow from the butter add the yolk of an egg. It must not boil.

The pike and pickerel are often mentioned as the same; there are, however, several varieties of pike. It looks familiar to see the pike that used to drive all the other fishes away and spoil the sport when we all went fishing, named in connection with a French river: "The Fureus, a clear stream that falls into the Rhone above Peyrieux. The trout caught in it have pink-colored flesh, while that of the pike is as white as ivory." The flesh of the pike is high flavored rather than delicate. It is firm and inclined to fall apart in flakes. Pike roe is nearly as good as shad roe, but must be small to cook well by frying.

918. Boiled Pike, Parsley Sauce.

Scale, cleanse, remove the head; boil according to size, from twenty to thirty or forty minutes. Serve cuts with a fish spoon, with parsley sauce poured over it, and potatoes on the same plate.

919. Parsley Sauce.

Butter sauce (No 916) with a handful of chopped parsley boiled in a minute, before the second portion of butter is beaten in.

920. Boiled Mackinaw Trout—Maitre d' Hotel Potatoes.

Half fill the fish kettle with soup stock and add a small onion with four cloves stuck in it, half a bay leaf, salt, bruised pepper-corns and a pint of white wine. Place two trout on the drainer and let simmer nearly or quite half an hour. Push off the upper skin as it is dished up. Serve with maitre d' hotel potatoes in the same plate in lieu of other sauce.

The above *bouillon au vin blanc* is what good cooks always *try* to use for boiling a good fish in, but is not very generally available and of course not absolutely necessary even for fine cooking. The lake trout has a delicate flavor but contains more water in its composition than some others, the pike, for instance, and is apt to be insipid when boiled in plain salt and water. It should generally have seasoned stock, though vinegar may take the place of wine. The stock sometimes can be used afterwards for fish soups or chowders, or for stewing fish steaks in.

921. Maitre d' Hotel Potatoes.

The French term is pronounced mater-dotel and is abbreviated in common talk to mate-o-tel.

Potatoes done this way taste like new potatoes. If new ones can be had so much the better

1 quart of cooked potatoes.
1 pint ladleful of hot water or broth.
1 basting spoonful of vinegar.
Butter size of an egg.
1 basting spoonful of chopped parsley.
Same of flour thickening.
Salt.

Steam some potatoes and cut in pieces into a saucepan, add the other ingredients and shake about over the fire till it boils It is a thin, semi-transparent, buttery looking sauce with considerable green in it.

922. Boiled Salmon—Hollandaise Potatoes,

Boil the salmon in the same sort of stock as for trout (No. 920). Where there is no regular fish kettle the difficulty can be obviated by cutting the fish into two or three and cooking in a common saucepan. Time from half an hour to three quarters, with slow boiling. Dish up spoonfuls with hollandaise potatoes on the same plate.

923. Hollandaise Potatoes.

Cut raw potatoes in some particular shape, either round with a potato scoop or "spoon," or with an apple corer and cut the long cores across, or else cut them in dice. Boil in salted water, taking them from the fire when just done and before they break; pour off the water and cover them with hollandaise sauce (No. 900) made a little thinner for the purpose. These boiled fish dishes shine with their white and green, pink, yellow, red, and cream colors.

924. Boiled Fresh Mackerel—Fennel Sauce.

Mackerel deteriorates with keeping very rapidly. Its special excellence can only be known when it is cooked when fresh caught. The fennel accompaniment is an English fancy. The green feathery leaves are given with the fish. A portion is boiled in the water and another portion chopped, is mixed with butter sauce in the same way as parsley.

The best way generally to boil mackerel is to roll it in a piece of muslin, cook about twenty minutes in salted water, roll out on to the dish without breaking and serve sauce separately or at the side. Tartar sauce is suitable, or the next variety.

925. Hot Maitre d'Hotel Sauce.

Add chopped parsley and lemon juice to some butter sauce and make it a trifle thinner with hot water.

926. Boiled Shad.

Sever the back bone with the point of a knife inserted where the cuts are to be taken off, before cooking, then boil it whole. Dish up neat shapely pieces or it will seem to be a mixed up lot of fine bones. Serve a simple sauce like the preceding, or potatoes.

927. Boiled Muskallonge, Caper Sauce.

A fish like the pickerel, but attains a larger size. Boil in seasoned stock with vinegar or wine in it, as for lake trout, and serve with sauce and plain mashed potatoes.

928. Caper Sauce.

Butter sauce with capers and caper vinegar. Mix a small portion of the vinegar from the capers with the sauce and strew a teaspoonful of capers over that on the fish as it is placed on the plates.

That great favorite the bass, too, is well spoken of over the water, but it looks odd to see it spelled basse. This is the sea bass, however. "The basse is not very abundant in the London fish shops; in the Channel Islands it is often plentiful in its season, but never, I believe, very cheap; and it abounds along our South coast, in St. Georges's and the Bristol channel, and on different parts of the Irish coast."

We have beside the sea bass some three or four fresh water varieties. They usually run from one pound to four or five in weight.

929. Boiled Bass with Green Peas.

After scaling and cleaning the fish sever the bone, by inserting the knife point at the places where it is to be divided when served, as directed for shad; that is, when it is black bass or others weighing enough to be served in portions. Boil in plain salted water about fifteen minutes. Peel off the upper skin when done. Place on the dish, pour over it some good butter sauce and green peas around in the dish. If to be served individually from the carving table remove the head before cooking. Pour a spoonful of butter sauce over the portion of fish and a tablespoonful of green peas over that.

If the white fish of the lakes were a scarce variety it would doubtless be held in the highest esteem. It is one of the best of fishes, and from a culinary point of view the most desirable in many ways. Firm, boneless, a splendid broiler and fryer; delicately white when boiled; takes on the best color in the oven, and is never rejected at the table. And yet people do not habitually boast of it as of the pet fishes. A traveler has written this in its praise:

"I shall never forget my first white fish. I had set out from New York for Niagara by a night train, and having fallen into sound slumber at Albany in a comfortable sleeping car, I did not awake till we stopped for breakfast at Rochester, near Lake Ontario, at nine o'clock next morning. Rising hastily fresh as a daisy after my good night's rest, I found myself shortly in a handsome refreshment room, seated before a cup of steaming coffee, a plate of hot cakes, and a broiled fish, which had been swimming un suspectingly in the lake at four o'clock that morning. The feelings of a true epicure who lights upon a new delicacy of the first order are indescribable. Whitefish is a sort of idealised mackerel, with a tinge of etherial salmon flavor; rich without greasiness, full without strongness, and delicate without insipidity I ate it with unflagging appetite every morning that I remained along the whole great chain of lakes and rivers, from Chicago to Saguenay, and every morning I thought it rather better than the last. If I could only succeed in acclimatising it in our own Scottish lochs—where it still lingered within historical times, and lived freely during late geological epochs—I should feel (as prefaces always say) that my work was not quite in vain."

930. Boiled Whitefish—Cream Sauce.

Let the fish lie in very cold water, after scaling and cleaning, till near dinner time. Boil them in seasoned stock with parsley or parsley roots in it, slowly for twenty or thirty minutes, taking them up as soon as the flesh begins to leave the back bone. Serve cuts with a spoonful of cream sauce poured over and a teaspoonful of very green peas in butter scattered on top for ornament.

931. Cream Sauce—Plain

1 quart of good milk.
1 large basting spoonful of flour.
Twice its weight of fresh butter.
Salt.

Make same way as butter sauce, mixing ha the butter with all the flour in a saucepan on the fire, adding the boiling milk and afterwards the remaining butter and beating it in.

932. Cream Sauce—Bechamel.

1 pint of condensed soup stock.
2 ounces of flour—a spoonful.
4 ounces of butter.
1 pint of rich cream.
Salt.

Take a quart of stock from the boiler, that has already been seasoned with the stock vegetables and bay leaf, etc., and boil it down to a pint. Stir the flour with half the butter over the fire and when it bubbles strain the stock into it and stir up while it cooks, then add the cream and butter, beat up, and take it from the fire just before it boils again.

933. Boiled Sheepshead—Lobster Sauce.

The sheepshead is a southern sea fish, something like the groupers. It may be known by its rows of teeth exposed on the very front of the mouth.

Scrape well, boil it in seasoned stock same as red snapper, and serve with lobster sauce poured over in the plates, and duchesse or dauphine potatoes.

934. Lobster Sauce.

3 pints of butter sauce.
1 small lobster, or half a can.
1 raw yolk of an egg.
1 lemon.

Pick out the reddest lobster meat, if you have none of the spawn, and pound it smooth. Mix it with the butter sauce. Add the yolk for color, and the juice of the lemon. Rub this through a gravy strainer. Cut the rest of the lobster in pieces as near as possible of one size and mix it in the sauce.

935. Boiled Slices of Fish.

We had, a little way back, some examples of fish steaks or slices broiled with appropriate sauces; the same steaks or slices can be boiled as well, and in short order, in a frying pan or tin pan, and it is very useful to remember it as the fish for dinner often comes in late. The slices only need to boil slowly for from six to ten minutes, and may then be served with any of the boiled fish sauces, with potatoes in cream sauce, potatoes in butter sauce, and the like. But there should in most cases be seasonings in the water the slices are boiled in. An insipid, washed out slice of fish with an imitation sauce may satisfy hunger and serve a present purpose but does not tend to draw custom. Expensive sauces may be out of reach, but plain seasonings for the boiling fish itself are always available. A panful of stock with an onion, whole pepper, salt, parsley and little vinegar in it, and perhaps some green thyme and a scrap of bay leaf, makes a slice of salmon, trout, sturgeon, cod, or halibut, a different sort of dish from the same boiled in fresh water—as they often are.

In cold weather the stock left from the previous day's boiling of fish will be good for boiling steaks. This mode of cooking needs to be encouraged for breakfast as well as for dinner dishes, to lessen the frequency of the more expensive mode of frying.

936. Egg Sauce.

A good and always available sauce for fish steaks or any boiled fish.

Make butter sauce (No. 916), color it yellow with yolk of egg, and mix in about a fourth as much hard boiled eggs chopped not too fine.

987. Baked Red Grouper—Sauce Andalouse.

Take two of these fishes weighing six or eight pounds each. When cleaned and scaled put them in a baking pan with salt, a little water, some cut up vegetables, and fat from the stock boiler. Bake about ten minutes, then peel off the upper skin, which is coarse and rough, baste the fish with the liquor in the pan and let it bake brown. This fish needs a long time to cook—nearly or quite an hour. Serve with the sauce at the side.

938. Sauce Andalouse.

Andalusian sauce is in effect a mixture of espagnole with tomato sauce seasoned with red peppers or chutney. When the fish is done and taken up put into the pan it was baked in two pounds of tomatoes, a dozen cloves, a spoonful of finely minced onion, half a bay leaf and a chopped red pepper. Add a pint of brown sauce, if at hand, if not water and brown thickening, and let simmer inside the range a short time. Strain through a coarse gravy strainer into a saucepan. Set it over the fire, at the side, to continue gently boiling, and skim off the grease as it rises. Add salt if necessary.

939. Baked German Carp with Green Peas.

Scale and cleanse the fish—always remove the head, which otherwise will impart an unpleasant taste—and let lie in cold water a while. An hour before dinner put them in a baking pan with a little salt and black pepper and a slice of salt pork for seasoning laid on the bottom, and just enough soup stock to keep the pan from burning. Bake the fish about ten minutes, withdraw it from the oven and peel off the skin of the upper side. Dredge a little flour evenly all over—stirred through a sieve with the fingers if you have no dredger—smooth it with the blade of a knife, then bake half an hour and baste with butter while it is baking. The fish will be light brown and there will be a small quantity of thick and rich sauce. Having taken up the fish put in some stock, stir up, boil and strain it and mix in a pint of green peas, already cooked. Serve the sauce and peas on the fish in the plates.

940. Fried Green Peas.

Very young new peas may be made of a brilliant green color for garnishing the plates of fish, by carefully sauteing them in a frying pan with the clear oil of melted butter.

German carp were introduced into American waters by the United States Fish Commissioners some six years ago. Some of the fish taken in the Potomac, said to be the first German carp ever seen at an American hotel table, were served at Willard's Hotel, Washington, March 29, 1882.

"This fish"—says an English author—"is held in high estimation on the Continent especially those caught in the Rhine and Moselle. In England they are seldom found good; when cooked they taste muddy; this is chiefly owing to their being taken from stagnant ponds."

941. Baked German Carp—Espagnole.

Scale and clean the fish and take off the heads. Wash and wipe dry, and stuff them with the bread dressing of the next receipt. Sew up the belly with twine. It takes about fifteen pounds of fish for the orders of fifty persons.

Slice up into your baking pan a small carrot, onion, turnip, and stalk of celery, and throw in a few cloves, half a blade of mace and a bay leaf. Put in the fish with salt and pepper and some fat from the stock boiler and water enough to cover the bottom. Bake about half an hour basting the fish frequently. When done and placed on the carving stand add more water or stock to the contents of the pan, let simmer in the range a while, then thicken and strain off the sauce. Serve the fish with a spoonful of sauce and a spoonful of French fried potatoes in the same plate.

942. Bread Dressing for Fish.

2 pounds of bread.
1 heaping teaspoonful of powdered herbs—thyme and savory.
½ pint of warm water—a cupful.
½ pint or less of butter, lard, or sausage fat.
Pepper and salt.
4 yolks of eggs.

Cut the bread in dice, all free from dark crust, add the herbs to it and pepper liberally. Mix the other articles together and pour over the bread. Stir up, but not mash it. This will not be liable to burst out when baking.

943. Potatoes Francaise.

Cut raw potatoes in slices and then crosswise in lengths with a sabatier scollop knife, which gives them a ribbed appearance. Fry them a light color in lard. They are done when they rise and float. Drain in a colander and sprinkle with salt.

The American carp is known as the "buffalo" fish, and "sucker." It is good enough to form the staple commodity of many inland fish markets along the great rivers of the West where it abounds.

944. Carp Baked Plain.

Bake the fish in a pan with salt, pepper, slices of pickled pork or bacon and water enough to keep the pan from burning and to baste with. Bake according to size, from half an hour to an hour. Make thickened gravy in the pan and serve the pieces of pork with the fish, and plain steamed potatoes.

945. Baked Salmon Trout—Au Gratin or Chevaliere.

Split the fish down the back and take out the back bone. Lay it, skin side down, in a baking pan in which there is salt, and soup stock or water enough to wet the bottom. Bake the fish a few minutes, or until it gets fairly hot, then take out and brush over the top with beaten egg, and on that sift some cracker meal, or finely crushed and sifted dry bread crumbs. Set the fish in to bake again and baste while it is baking with butter melted, or good drippings. When richly browned take it up. Serve with fine herbs sauce, or tomato sauce and potato croquettes. To be *a la chevaliere* the above should have grated cheese in the breading, to be properly *au gratin* there should be a coating of fine herbs sauce under the crumbs. There is no need to use either term.

946. Potato Croquettes

2 pounds of steamed potatoes.
2 ounces of butter.
2 yolks, or one egg.
1 teaspoonful of salt.

Mash all together. Make up in long rolls about the length of a thumb, roll them in beaten egg-and-water, and then in cracker meal and fry in hot lard

947. Fillets of Whitefish—Dauphine Potatoes.

Choose large whitefish, scale, split, and take out the back bone. Make some fresh lard hot in a baking pan. Salt and pepper the sides of fish, dip them in beaten egg (without water), then in flour, then in egg again. Lay them in the hot lard and set the pan in the oven. Care is required not to let the lard get very hot, but to cook the fish of a delicate deep yellow color. In about twenty minutes take up and drain the fillets from grease. Serve with parsley sauce and potatoes.

948. Dauphine Potatoes.

Mash some potatoes through a seive—about a quart dipper full—with butter size of an egg, two yolks, salt, and half a cupful of milk. Drop spoonfuls like cakes, conical in shape, on a greased baking pan and bake them of a light color.

949. Baked Spanish Mackerel—Sauce Piquante.

Take fifteen or twenty mackerel; scrape the fine scales off, pull out the gills and draw them without cutting open. Wash thoroughly and dry inside and out. Stuff the mackerel with the fish forcemeat of the next receipt. Lay them in a pan with the bottom previously well spread with fresh butter, add salt and a ladleful of stock and the juice of one or two lemons, and bake them in a brisk oven about twenty or thirty minutes, basting with the liquor from a corner of the pan, which should be dry at last and the fish richly glazed and brown. Divide neatly with a sharp knife point and serve portions with the sauce at the side and small potato croquettes on the same plate.

950. Fish Forcemeat.

1 pound of whitefish, raw.
8 ounces of bread panada.
8 ounces of minced suet
2 eggs—(4 yolks better).
2 tablespoonfuls of chopped parsley.
Pepper, salt, little nutmeg and lemon juice.

Steep some bread in cold water and wring it dry by twisting in a clean kitchen napkin. Take the required quantity with all the other ingredients, and mash them to a paste, taking care that the fish be free from bones. Use this to stuff small fish and to make little balls (quenelles), to be rolled in flour and fried or poached, for garnishing and for ragouts.

951. Small Potato Croquettes.

Make the potato preparation, No. 946, and make it up in little balls not larger than walnuts with plenty of flour on the hands, insuring the croquettes a good coating. Put them in a wire basket and immerse them in hot lard. Take out as soon as they have a yellow color lest they burst in the fat. Serve them with fish, on the same plate, or as a border to a large dish.

Potato croquettes are made difficult to fry by too much milk or water being mixed in when the potatoes are mashed. They then turn soft in the hot lard, and become shapeless and greasy. The potatoes for croquettes should be mashed separately and kept dry.

952. Speckled Trout with Fine Herbs.

20 to 25 pounds of trout.
Forcemeat for stuffing.
8 ounces of butter.
4 slices of pork.
1 bastingspoonful of minced onion.
1 can of button mushrooms.
1 spoonful of minced parsley.
1 pint of sherry.
Pepper and salt.

Scrape the fish, pull out the gills, and draw them without cutting open. Wash and wipe dry inside. Fill with the stuffing (No 950). Spread the butter on the pan, put in the fish close together, and the mushroom liquor and pork slices and shake the remaining ingredients evenly upon them. Add a ladleful of stock. Bake about half an hour, basting from the corner of the pan. Dish up out of the pan without other sauce, but with **Parisian** potatoes in the same plate.

953. Potatoes Boulettes, or Parisienne or Mitrailleuse.

Scoop out balls from raw potatoes with a potato spoon about like large cherries in size, and enough of them to fill a quart. Stew (not fry) them in butter, or in mixed butter and lard till they are done, then drain and set them in a pan in the oven a few minutes to get a rich color. Sprinkle with parsley and salt. Good to serve with every kind of meat, but especially for small dishes of fish. They are fine and ornamental likewise as fried potatoes.

954. Baked Bluefish—Bordelaise.

After cleaning and trimming off the fins wash the fish and wipe it dry. Fill the inside with the veal forcemeat of the next receipt, and sew up with twine. Cut up into the baking pan a piece of carrot and turnip, and put in a small onion stuck with cloves, a bunch of parsley, a ladleful or two of stock and fat from the top of the stock boiler, a ladleful of claret or white wine, some pepper and salt. Put in the fish, bake in a hot oven. While it is baking fry a slice of ham in butter, add a bastingspoonful of flour and let it become brown in the pan for thickening. When the fish is taken up pour into the pan another ladleful of stock and another of wine, thicken with the brown flour, and when it has boiled up in the pan strain the sauce into a sauce pan, simmer at the side of the range and take off the grease as it rises. Add the juice of a lemon and some cayenne.

955. Wine Sauce for Fish.

The above described method of baking a fish in wine stock and making a thickened wine sauce for it in the same pan, whether the fish be stuffed or not, is a favorite one both with the cooks and with those they cook for, and is resorted to with nearly every kind of fish that comes to the hotel table the designation, a very proper one, usually being "with wine sauce," the cooking wine available usually being sherry. Another most popular way is that directed for speckled trout with fine herbs (No. 952), which is also applicable to every kind of fish and is in general practice, it being merely optional whether the fish, whatever the kind may be, shall be stuffed or not. The skill of the cook, and natural taste is shown in the appearance of both the fish and the sauces, in making the latter of good color, bright, and not pasty; things at once appreciated in practice, if not altogether to be made plain in words

956. Veal Stuffing for Fish.

1 pound of minced cooked veal.
8 ounces of fat salt pork, or part suet.
8 ounces of bread panada.
2 eggs.
1 teaspoonful of mixed salt and pepper.
Same of powdered thyme and savory.
A pinch of ground mace.
Juice of 1 lemon.

To prepare the bread, soak the pieces in cold

water and squeeze dry in a cloth. Pound all the ingredients together. This veal forcemeat can be used in many other ways besides for stuffing fish.

957. Duchess Potatoes.

Prepare the potatoes as at No. 948, by mashing through a sieve and seasoning with butter, salt, little milk and yolk of egg, and for the short way spread in a pan or pie plate, egg over the top, bake light brown and serve out portions to each plate of fish with a spoon. To be more elaborate cut the thinly spread potato out in shapes, egg over, place on a greased pan and bake till colored, or shape the mashed potato in greased patty pans, turn them out, egg over and bake.

958. Baked Codfish Stuffed with Oysters

Choose small cod or hake or haddock for baking whole. Fill them with the oyster stuffing, No. 855, sew up and bake plain, that is to say, with only some fat from the top of the stock boiler in the pan, and salt. Serve with a portion of the dressing and brown oyster sauce made as directed at No. 854. This makes the cheap and abundant codfish equal to the choicer kinds.

959. Potato Cake to go with Fish.

1 pound of steamed potatoes—a quart dipperful
6 ounces of butter—a cupful.
2 ounces of flour—a bastingspoonful.
1 cupful of milk.
3 eggs. Salt.

Mash the potatoes through a sieve. Mix the butter in while still warm, then the flour, the milk and the eggs beaten very light. Pour the mixture into a greased baking pan like Yorkshire pudding, bake the same way, of a nice light brown, and serve out in squares or spoonfuls with plates of fish.

960. Fillets of Fish with Quenelle Dressing.

We will not specify any particular kind of fish, for this is a tasteful and handsome way for any variety. Neither is it necessary to write it at length for the bill of fare. The simple designation baked whitefish, or trout, or muskallunge or whatever it may be is sufficient.

Split the fish in two down the back, take out the bone, wipe the two sides (fillets) dry, and dredge them with pepper and salt. Then, having them on a board before you with the skin side down, spread the upper side over with an even coating of the fish forcemeat of the following receipt. It is a soft yellow paste and can be smoothed over with a palette knife.

Then lay the fillets in a baking pan, with a little salt dredged under, put in a spoonful of drippings

and the same of butter, and about as much water to keep the corners of the pan from burning. Bake about half an hour, or longer if the sides are large and thick, and baste twice with the contents of the pan. The surface should be of a rich yellow-brown color, and may need a cover of greased paper should the oven be too hot.

Serve neat cuts on the fish plates with potatoes, and a very little gravy of some sort poured under.

A whole fish for a party table can be prepared in the same way, and with wine sauce in the dish.

961. Fish Forcemeat.

The quantity of this receipt is about enough for one large whitefish laid open. It should be doubled for fish for fifty.

12 ounces of whitefish, raw.
8 ounces of bread panada.
4 ounces of butter.
3 or 4 yolks of eggs, raw.
1 tablespoonful of chopped parsley.
Juice of half a lemon.
Salt, pepper, and a slight grating of nutmeg.

Any other kind of fish will do if whitefish is not at hand. See that it is free from bones and skin, cut it up and pound it in a bright saucepan; throw in all the other ingredients—the butter not melted—and pound them together till smooth.

This delicate paste is useful in a number of ways, and should be made often enough for the ingredients to be easily remembered.

962. Bread Panada.

Shave the crust from some stale rolls or slices of bread and soak them in cold water, then twist up in a coarse cloth to squeeze dry. Hot water to steep in will not make good panada.

963 A Southern Way.

In the restaurants and hotels of the South a considerable use is made of coloring pepper for baking fish. The receipt for making it will be found in the miscellanea at the end of this work. It can be purchased in bottles the same as curry powder or *file gumbo*. Though mild in flavor it gives the fish the appearance of being covered with a coating of cayenne. Split the fish down the back and take out the bone. Wash and wipe dry, and lay it in a baking pan, skin side downwards and with butter in the pan under it. Dredge over salt and a plentiful coating of coloring pepper. Pour a ladleful of broth in the pan and bake the fish according to kind and thickness, from fifteen to thirty minutes.

964. A Plain Bake.

The method above indicated without the pepper, and with only butter and lemon juice on the fish and salted broth in the pan, is one of the best and simplest that anyone can practice for any good fish that comes along on short order, and a way that is designated by a high sounding French term in some places. Baste once or twice while the fish is baking, with soft butter from your butter can, and that will give brown color enough.

In the columns that have preceded this the reader now has all the good, straight ways of cooking fish for breakfast, dinner and supper, nearly all the necessary sauces for both fish and meats, and nearly all the ways of cooking potatoes to go with them.

It is to be understood, of course, that the sauces, etc., do not specially belong to the several fishes, but are to be changed over to other kinds according to the general intimation of fitness conveyed.

When a new kind of fish comes along consider first whether you can broil it, either in thin sides or slices; the best way for many reasons, but the broiling arrangements are seldom good enough to accommodate hotel numbers. Then consider the simple rolling in flour and frying in real hot lard, and after that breading and frying. For dinner give first preference to boiling and think over what good-looking sauce you will make to go with it. It is when fish is very plentiful and people seem to tire of it that the ways like stuffing with oysters and baking come in, and a little novelty of method is always to be kept in reserve for uncommon occasions.

There are other dishes of fish to be mentioned at a future time, of the class of made dishes, which we are all glad to adopt because of the necessity of sometimes making a fish entree to fill out the bill of fare, especially on Fridays and in Lent; and because there are times when the fish on hand is not enough for anything else but a side dish.

965. Turbot.

This is a summer fish, in season from early spring to late autumn. It runs from four or five to twenty pounds in weight, the small ones are considered the best.

Cook a turbot either by cutting the meat, after removing the bone, in pieces of even size and egging, breading and frying, or boil it whole in a broad kettle and serve a sauce unusual, or bake it in any of the ways heretofore directed for other kinds.

A turbot purporting to be broiled whole is only broiled on the white side, partially, then turned over into a baking pan and finished by baking, with a buttered paper on top to preserve the appearance. It must be split down the back to keep the white side from breaking while cooking.

Taft's Point Shirley bills of fare proclaim turbot king of the sea. Some folks call him only king of flat fish—a sort of chief plaice or boss flounder or jolly old sole. He is an historical fish, however, the great fish story originator, famous at the banquets of the Greek and Romans, recipient of the best attentions of the most ingenious maitres d'hotel and the chiefest of cooks, who delighted in him for his accommodating shape for a dish, and broad expanse of smooth white surface to draw sunflowers in lobster coral on.

It was turbot that caused the death of Vatel, maitre d'hotel and chef-de-cuisine to the great general, the Prince de Conde. The king was coming and they were preparing a regular Southern Hotel dinner for him. Vatel sent both to Blackford's and to Booth's for a fine turbot to come at the appointed time by Wells, Fargo & Co.'s Express, without asking the price or caring much what it cost. For Vatel had a special way of fixing up a turbot and wanted the king to see it. His way was to cut the fish down the back and open it enough to get out all the bones, then fill the inside with fish forcemeat (No. 961) and bake it with the white side uppermost, with wine, mushrooms and oyster liquor and various other things in the pan, basting till the fluids were nearly dried up and yet to glaze all over the fish. When he dished it up he had some rich cream sauce (No. 932) which he colored light green by mixing in some ravigote butter (No.   ) and that be poured over the fish. Then he took smelts enough to encircle it, took out their bones and stuffed them, then formed in rings by sticking their tails in their mouths, floured and fried them and laid them around. Then he took some fillets of soles, nice and white, and with a fine larding needle worked patterns in them with shreds of black truffle and red meat of lobster, simmered them in butter and then laid them around, and wherever they would do the most good, and then sent it in hot. But on this great occasion his great specialty could not be produced, he telegraphed and telephoned and sent couriers till he was tired. The king arrived and no fish had come, and Vatel went out and committed suicide. Not in any cold, clammy, disgusting way, but respectably as a gentlemanly chief cook should, by running his sword through himself.

A high literary lady of France saw the true merits of the case, and when most people were laughing at Vatel for a fool she wrote pathetically about the affair and made it look more like a tragedy than a joke. The rest of the French cooks were not ungraceful but gallantly named a soup after her, and consequently we have *consomme Sevigne* to this day. If any one thinks that a comical way of commemorating a person we ask them to consider how much longer the name of the soup will endure than any headstone, and how few, comparatively, would ever read the name of Madame de Sevigne if it were not in the *menu*.

Equally scarce, costly and impossible to obtain was this fish when a certain Cardinal Fesch unexpectedly received two at once as a present from a devoted friend. Not a hotel or restaurant in the city had a turbot or could get one for love or money. The cardinal's guests were invited. Some of them had not been able to obtain even a broiled turbot steak at their restaurant for months. They amused themselves while anticipating the treat in preparation with all the royal turbot stories they could think of, and when at last the great fish was brought in at the door they were thoroughly prepared for its enjoyment. But, alas, it never reached the table; the waiters slipped and the precious dish was scattered upon the floor.

Such a joker was this maitre d'hotel. He wanted to see how disappointed they would look, and to show how rich in turbot his employer was when nobody else had a speck. He ordered the second turbot to be immediately brought in and set on the table, showing that in that house they could afford to throw away what others were dying to obtain, and still have plenty more left to make a feast.

966. Plaice and Flounders.

Nearly the same, but the plaice the larger. Cut in pieces and fry, or fry whole, or bake with bread crumbs or cracker meal on top, or dipped in flour and egg.

967. Soles.

Among the best flat fish. The favorite way is to cook the fillets, rolled up, fastened with small skewers, dipped in egg and cracker crumbs. Also, fry them whole, after skinning. The skin can be pulled off after starting with a knife point.

968. Sturgeon.

May be seen in the market of every size, from one or two pounds weight to two or three hundred. The skin studded with ridges of horny substance is tough and must be removed by means of a knife. Cook in steaks same as halibut. Take middle cuts, remove the bone, fill the cavity with stuffing, and braise or bake same as meat, allowing plenty of time. Also stew and fricassee the same as veal. Sturgeon is salted and smoked in large quantities. The roe is converted into caviar. In England the fish is a rarity and every one caught in the rivers belongs to the crown. Sturgeon's head being very gelatinous is said to be a good substitute for turtle.

It is extremely probable that the names bestowed upon French dishes all had some tradition or historical association attached in the first instances. Here is a hint from a magazine article of the meaning of trout a la Genevese:

"At the same time Charlemagne encouraged the production of fruit and flowers, as adding to the enjoyment of the people, and was pleased when any special delicacy was presented to him. The Genevese trout are honorably mentioned in the capitularies, and it will be remembered that one of these trout, supplied to Cambaceres by the municipality of Geneva was charged 300 francs in their accounts."

969. Trout a la Genevese.

12 to 15 pounds of trout.
1 pint of champagne.
1 pint of sherry.
1 onion stuck with cloves.
4 ounces of butter.
A bunch of parsley and thyme.
A ladleful of broth.
Salt, pepper, brown roux, toast and lemons.

Cleanse the trout, take off the heads, wipe dry, score through the skin on both sides where the individual portions are to be taken off, and also sever the bone by striking the point of a knife through. Then dredge a little salt and pepper in a baking pan, put in the butter, and lay the fish in just touching. Add half the champagne and sherry, and if there is much vacant space in the pan the ladleful of broth likewise, and the onion and herbs. Set in a hot oven and baste the fish while it is baking, almost constantly. The gelatinous gravy from the fish makes a glaze with the wine, which is to be coated over it; by this means till there is no more liquid left in the pan. Remove the fish carefully into another pan when done, pour the remaining half of the wine into the fish pan, boil up, thicken with browned flour, and strain the sauce. Serve the portions of fish with a slice of lemon on top and the sauce poured under.

A fish cooked in this manner served whole should be raised upon a shape of fried bread cut to fit the bottom of the dish.

970. Eels.

Cook either by frying, rolled in flour or breaded, or by stewing, and either cut in sections or split and boned and then cut in lengths. They can also be broiled—boned and laid out flat for the purpose—and baked in a pan with wine, the pieces laid side by side, as so many small fish would be. Vast quantities of eels are sold in the markets, but only a small proportion go to American hotels. The large sorts are salted and smoked and find sale in large quantities in that form. Eel-pouts, bull-pouts and small catfish, ready skinned and cleaned likewise, are handled by the market men near the lakes in car load lots, which shows that the prejudice existing against these kinds is not universal. Clear meat of this description is, however, generally very cheap—often by the barrel only three cents per pound, more generally about five cents, and retails at seven or eight cents. Whatever good cooking can do to make such cheap, solid, and intrinsically valuable food acceptable to a larger number than at present unquestionably ought to be done. Cooks, at least, ought to have no prejudices that should make them s'ight one article to elevate another. Their art is essentially one of equalization.

Such articles as eel and fish pies, crabs soft and hard, mock crabs, matelottes or fish stews, turtle and terrapin, will be found in place in our forthcoming HOTEL BOOK OF SOUPS AND ENTREES.

971. Salt Mackerel.

As much care, if not skill is needed to have salt mackerel as good as can be as for anything that is done in the kitchen. The particular point is to put it on in cold water and remove it from the fire the moment it begins to boil. It is then soft and tender, but becomes dry if allowed to boil hard.

To prepare the mackerel for cooking, wash off the salt and steep them twenty-four hours in plenty of water, in a vessel set in a cold place. Lay them in with the skin side up, that the salt which is heavier than water may escape to the bottom; and change the water once or twice.

Scrape out the black skin of the inside of the mackerel, cut off the heads, divide—if for boiling—by cutting in three crosswise, but if for broiling split them lengthwise. Hang broiling mackerel up to dry about twenty-four hours before they are to be cooked. When dished up pour a spoonful of clear melted butter over the piece of fish in the dish.

It should be remembered by buyers of hotel stores that there is the utmost difference in quality between the different grades of mackerel, from fat mess to the thin and rusty number fours, which, if of any use at all, certainly are not fit to broil.

972. Salt Whitefish.

The remarks relating to salt mackerel apply to these as well. Watchfulness is needed to keep the vessel they are soaked in sweet and in a cold place, or the fish will have constantly a half spoiled taste and be soft.

When nicely freshened cook them only a few minutes, and serve with a cream or butter sauce, and sometimes with mustard sauce, which answers for any sort of salt fish.

973. Mustard Sauce.

Make butter sauce (No. 917), half the usual quantity may do, and add a tablespoonful of made mustard and a pinch of cayenne.

974. Salt or Pickled Salmon.

Freshen it by steeping in water two days, changing the water occasionally, then cut in pieces and boil only a few minutes, and serve with a sauce that has no salt.

It makes a good dinner dish also, cut in small pieces with potatoes cut to the same size, boiled together, then the water poured away and cream sauce poured to them instead.

975. Canned Salmon.

This should not be turned out of the cans. The greatest drawback to the use of canned salmon as a substitute for fresh fish is its liability to break into crumbs. Open the cans and set them on the back of the range a short time before dinner, and dish out of the cans on the plates. All the sauces, etc., suitable for boiled fish can be used with this. The large cans are to be preferred to small for the reason above given. Canned salmon cold is a good and convenient dish for supper and lunch.

975. Kippered Salmon.

Is smoked salmon. It is sliced, for breakfast and supper, and served cold without cooking; is toasted and broiled and spread with butter, and also stewed with potatoes.

976. Finnan Haddies.

Smoked haddock. They are commonly, for restaurant orders, plainly broiled over a slow fire or toasted, peppered, and brushed over with butter. May be improved by steeping in warm water before broiling, and by steeping in olive oil for several hours and then frying in the same.

977. Smoked Herring.

Picked apart in shreds and eaten without cooking, for lunch. Toast fine ones before the fire or on the broiler raised high above the coals. Serve on a hot dish. When large enough split them open and broil them flat on the wire broiler. Pepper while cooking and spread butter over when done.

978. Yarmouth Bloaters.

Oftenest now ticketed in the shops "bloaters," only. They are the largest and fattest herrings, selected like "mess" mackerel from the common, and mild cured. Can be broiled and served most elegantly rolled in buttered paper.

979. Smoked Whitefish.

Cook the same as herring or haddock.

980. Codfish Balls.

1½ pounds of raw pared potatoes.
1 pound of boneless codfish.
2 basting spoonfuls of melted butter.
3 or 4 eggs.
1 small teaspoonful of pepper.

Soak the codfish over night, boil it half an hour, pick over and mash it small. Cook the potatoes specially for the purpose. Mash all together, ball up with floured hands and fry brown.

981. Codfish in Cream.

Steep and boil a pound of codfish, pick it apart when cool and mash it, but not very fine. Pour to it about the same quantity of cream sauce made without salt, or add milk and butter to the fish and thicken it slightly when it boils.

982. Stewed Codfish.

Pick the fish apart in flakes after boiling, and cover with cream sauce, or boil the flakes in milk, add butter and a few cooked potatoes cut up and some butter, and thicken slightly with flour-and-water thickening when it boils up again. These are good Friday dishes, and good to alternate with salt mackerel and whitefish.

983 Fried Smelts

Draw the fish through the gills without opening them and wipe them clean. Dip in beaten egg and cracker meal, with care not to rub off the breading as it will not adhere a second time and the grease gets under the coating. Fry a few at a time in a pan of hot lard. They should be done and of a handsome light brown color in four minutes. May also be plainly rolled in flour and fried like trout. See No. 869.

984. Sea Bass Baked.

Scale and clean the fish, take the head off unless it is to be served whole. Make a stuffing for it of
4 pressed cupfuls of fine bread crumbs,
1 cupful of butter,
Rind of ½ a lemon finely minced,
Parsley, green thyme and marjoram,
Pepper and salt,
2 eggs and a cup of warm water,

Stuff the fish and sew it up. Mark it in slices as it is to be carved on both sides by cutting down to the bone and put a very thin slice of salt pork in each incision. Bake in a long pan with suet or drippings, stock and salt and pepper in it about 40 minutes or according to size.

Put a little strained tomatoes and brown gravy into the fish pan and water if necessary, let boil up, skim, and strain for sauce.

Sardines.

(*Magazine.*)

"In regard to our food, as in other matters, there is no gainsaying the fact that things are not what they seem. The dainty little fishes that come to our tables elaborately packed in tiny tin cases, and smothered with olive oil, are supposed to have been captured where the waters of the Mediterranean lash Sardinian shores. In reality they are frequently the product of what are known as the English and American Sardine fisheries. Sardines are simply the young of the pilchard (*clupea pilchardus*). They get their name from having been formerly caught in great numbers off the island of Sardinia. The Sardine is, in fact, a member of the herring family, and it is only its extreme youth and the manner of packing it that separate it from its relatives.

The following very "fishy" bill of fare was used at the annual banquet of the Ichthyopagous Club of New York city, held at the Palisade Mountain House, on the Hudson, June 6:

Little Neck Clams
Bisque of Razor Clams
Consomme Lady Morgan
Whitebait, Greenwich Style
Souffle of fresh water Clams en coquille
Moonfish Hollandaise
Cucumbers   Potatoes Duchesse
Turban of Skate Toulouse
Horseshoe crabs, farcis
Small fillets of porpoise, saute Bordelaise
Croquetts of dogfish, fine herbes
Lamprey eels fried in crumbs
Tenderloin of beef financiere
Asparagus   Green Peas
Stuffed Tomatoes
Salmon, sauce Tartare
Alligator garfish, Ravigote sauce
Brook trout in jelly
Pate of eels
Shrimp salad   Lobster salad
Punch du Chaillu
Albany beef, larded au jus
Lettuce   Grouper a la Fuord
Assorted cakes   Neapolitan ice cream
Cheese   Coffee
Fruits

A Good Hotel Refrigerator.

A refrigerator of a convenient medium size that is perfectly satisfactory in filling all the requirements of an ice chest for all purposes, and an object of pride to both the proprietor and his New England steward, is in use at the American House, Denver, Colo. The diagram below shows the form and arrangement. It gives a front view as the interior appears when the doors are open. The height inside is six feet; depth, front to back, five and a half; the middle compartment for the ice is three feet wide; the cold rooms on each side three and a half. The drip from the ice is led away by a zinc drainer, and the space below is both dry and cold. The outside walls are, of course, double, and filled in with eight inches of dry sawdust. This refrigerator is built close by the outer door on one side of a cellar basement, the store room being directly opposite. It is elevated a step or two from the floor.

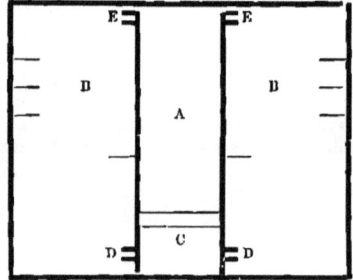

A Place for the blocks of ice, opening in front.

BB Cold rooms fitted with shelves. Front doors.

C Space under ice floor and zinc drainer where milk and butter may be kept. Front door.

DD Small doors open into the ice box letting the cold air in.

EE Small doors open into a ventilating pipe letting the warm air and vapor out.

—— Shelves.

HOW TO CUT MEATS

AND

 ROAST

BOIL AND BROIL.

The entire trade of the Hotel Meat-Cutter, Roaster and Broiler, including "Short Orders," Omelets, etc.

Being a part of the "Oven and Range" Series originally published in the Chicago Daily National Hotel Reporter.

BY

JESSUP WHITEHEAD.

CHICAGO
1883.

Entered according to Act of Congress, in the years 1877, 1879 and 1880, by JESSUP WHITEHEAD, in the office of the Librarian of Congress, at Washington.

RIGHT OF TRANSLATION RESERVED.

PUBLISHED BY THE AUTHOR
At the Office of the Daily National Hotel Reporter,
78 FIFTH AVENUE
CHICAGO, ILLS.

HOW TO CUT MEATS.

987. Hotel Beef and Beefsteaks.

One of those valuable citizens who live all their lives at a hotel or other similar public house, looked in where we were furnishing and getting ready to open a new restaurant and remarked with evident pleasure in the anticipation: "Ha! now we shall be able to get a good, *thick* steak, a steak that is a steak, and that is what I have been wanting a long time."

He meant that he would leave the first-class hotel where he was boarding and where the steaks cut in hotel style did not suit him, and would come where he could have a slice of beef an inch thick sawn through the bone and fat, upper loin, tenderloin and everything, just about where the figure 4 is seen in the diagram of a loin of beef below—that is if he meant to pay for a "porterhouse;" but if he would be content with a loin steak, only caring to have it thick and not beaten out, he would have it cut in a cheaper place, about where the figures 2 and 3 are found.

The remark and the satisfied tone of it might seem to cast a reflection somewhere, but as the same cook would be in charge at the restaurant who had been at the hotel, the reflection could not be upon the cook; and as nothing but good was spoken of the hotel table, it could not be upon the hotel in particular, but it was a reflection upon the hotel method to the extent that it did not suit this man's preferences. At the hotel table he took his meal in from three to five courses, and the portions of the viands were proportionately small, but this individual preferred a pound of beefsteak to all the variety and wanted little else. These are the reasons why restaurants and hotels both flourish side by side. Both have their ways and their admirers. If we cut the hotel beefsteak small it is because there is so much else offered that to cut it larger would be utterly useless and the price of board would rule higher for no other reason than to pay for the wanton waste. The restaurant steak cut in the first class shape supposed will weigh from a pound to a pound and a half, and will cost as much alone as the price of an entire meal at weekly board rates at many good hotels. Very few besides eat the whole of such a slice of meat; but as they pay a fixed price for it it is only individual loss. The hotel management culls and trims in a way to make the least waste, and the uneatable portions of bone and fat do not reach the table at all.

Most hotel cooks like cut up meat; the nicety of management, the methodical application of each portion to its particular purpose, the neatness and orderly arrangement of the trays of prepared meats when they are placed in the refrigerators ready for the next meal, or it may be the association of this part of the day's work with the quiet time between meals all go to make the cook look upon the meat-cutting as something not to be left to another without cogent reasons. It is difficult for the cook to "keep track" of his meats if he does not cut them himself, for an entree or some new use for the portion in hand will often suggest itself at the time that would not be thought of in an abstract way, and the make-up of the next bill of fare becomes so much the easier; and then when he has finished he knows to a pound how much he must order for the next day. So that in hotels where three, four, or five cooks are employed the head cook generally does his own meat-cutting; in larger hotels it becomes impracticable and another cook, the cutter and roaster, appears.

The hotel method of cutting up meat is different in some respects from the butchers'. It is a system apart, and understood to be different, though not written down—like certain oral laws or unwritten statutes that prevail for a certain class, while all the rest of the community are otherwise governed. The butcher sets apart for the hotel the "long loins" or "short loins," "short ribs" or "chuck ribs" of beef, and "racks" and sides of mutton, but he has different cuts with other names for other people. The butchers differ as well, there being London style, German style, and French style. Round or rump steaks it is said are unknown in France. The porterhouse cut is American and not known to London butchers except as it may have been adopted from this side. On the other hand the "aitch-bone," so common to London butchers and English cook books is unknown in American hotels, unless when the butcher to fill up the weight throws it in as a "butt"

988. The Porter-House Cut.

Said to be derived from a New York hotel called the Porter House, where a party of sp rtsmen one day found a roast like this prepared for cooking:

AMERICAN PORTER-HOUSE CUT.

But being unwilling to wait for the roasting they prevailed on the landlord to let them have it cut into steaks, and these pleasing them well they ordered more of the same cut for the next day, and afterwards brought hosts of other customers to eat the luscious Porter-House steaks.

This cut is called the sirloin in England, so, as we lost the sirloin when it became porter-house, we moved the name and call that sirloin which the English call aitch-bone, the heavy end of the loin, and the best and meattiest, beginning where the porter-house ends, in the point of the hip bone.

In our large diagram the porter-house cut is the section containing the figure 4; the sirloin is the section containing the figures 1 and 5; the thin end section with the numbers 2 and 3 is loin—a roasting or common steak piece.

The next cut shows the "aitch-bone," from which the well-known sirloin steaks are cut like the one below:

ENGLISH AITCH BONE CUT.

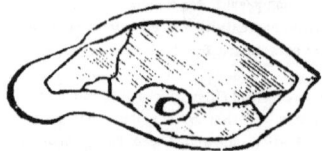

AMERICAN SIRLOIN STEAK.

The introduction of the new name, the porter-house cut, has, it is seen, caused a little confusion of terms. Restaurant keepers still find it convenient to retain the name of sirloin for the steaks of the upper part, when the lower or tenderloin has been taken away, and the "porter-house" is then no longer complete. A thick tenderloin steak alone sells generally at 50 cents, the porter-house at 75c. The number of porter-house steaks that can be cut from a loin is 10 or 12. The woodcuts show the first steak, cut nearest the rib end, and the last, cut at the line in the diagram near the figure 4.

FIRST PORTER-HOUSE STEAK.

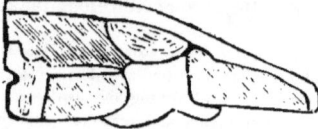

LAST PORTER-HOUSE, CUTTING INTO THE HIP-BONE.

The sirloin steak previously shown is cut at about the point marked by the figure 5 in the diagram, just where the bone is smallest and the tenderloin is the thickest. All three of the steaks represented contain a portion of the tenderloin—the small division of lean meat at the bottom.

So much for the restaurant cuts and their names. Though necessary to be known they have but little to do with the method of cutting up the loin for hotel use, in which the effort is made to equalize all parts and make good steak of the whole, and where this cannot be done to take off the roughness all in one piece so that it may be put to good use in other ways. The value of a cook's services depends greatly on his skill in this particular. One ignorant of the locality of the different grades of meat, or not knowing how to shape it neatly may easily hack and hew at a loin in such a way that there will hardly be a good and presentable pound of steak got out of a hundred. The cooks of small houses that depend upon the butchers to cut their meats are thereby spoiled for better positions. They may be good general cooks but if they cannot cut their own meats to advantage they may destroy more than they can earn, and an experienced hand may be cheaper at twice the wages. The writer has known well-meaning but untaught cooks to gouge out the fillet or tenderloin from a loin of beef to feed the cats on, or make beef tea, or gravy, under the supposition that it was the gravy meat or "roughness." Our instructions here are going to be very plain, and our cut is not that of a small and fancy loin, but of a large and long and rough one, that the lesson in cutting may be thorough.

989. Cutting Up the Loin of Beef.

The dotted lines in the diagram show the location of the tenderloin or fillet in the *under* part of the loin It is to be taken out whole, either to be cut into steaks afterwards, or roasted. The cutting out of the tenderloin is the first thing to be done. It will be found when the loin is turned over, covered over with the kidney fat, that must be taken off carefully so that the fillet will not be cut in doing it. Then begin where the figures 2 and 3 show the beginning and cut down along the backbone, raising up fat and all that comes, then raise the point of the fillet and cut under it close to the bone and then down from 3 to 4 and 5, raising up the fillet as you go. The thickest part is at figure 1. There the fillet dips down into the meat of the other side. It must be pulled over and cut along carefully with the point of the knife according to the apparent natural division. The fillet ends at the high bone in the buttock.

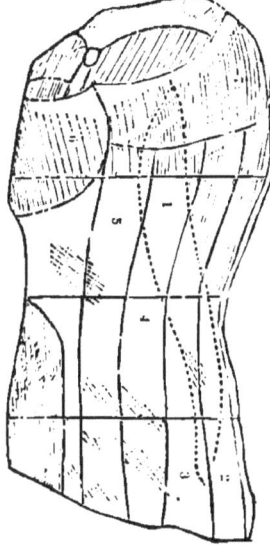

The tenderloin lying on the table with the side, that was next to the bone downwards, you proceed to shave off the surplus fat and skin that was brought away with it. On the upper side that is covered with this fat there is a smooth skin that covers the whole fillet. When the intention is to cut the fillet into steaks the fat should be cut level off to the top of it, and then a strip of the skin about as wide as a finger cut off the top of the meat the whole length. This prevents the steaks from curling up when they are broiled, and is neater looking for the steaks than cutting notches in the edge as they are sliced off. When the fillet is to be larded the whole of the skin covering has to be carefully removed and the surface left smooth.

The four or five long lines that mark the loin in our drawing show where the steak meat is to be cut into strips, the point of the knife going clear down to the bone. The strips are to be cut out as the tenderloin was, then cut off in two inch lengths and beaten out flat with the side of the cleaver on the block.

Now, the fortunate people who choose exactly where their meat shall be cut, and who can make it at the butcher's peril to send them anything but small and tender meat do not need to make as many cuts or strips as this, except when they have a loin of fat Christmas beef, which is pretty sure to be large.

A short loin, as it is called, is cut off at or about the straight line that is drawn across between the figures 5 and 6. A close-trimmed loin besides has the flank portion cut off at about the line that runs lengthwise, also between the figures 5 and 6, and the choice little loin remaining will be further shortened at the thin end down to about 2 and 3. After that the knife of the cutter is run down along the back bone, and again, only once along that middle long line that runs between 3 and 4, and all the meat taken off in two length pieces, then to be sliced into steaks. This, we repeat, is the way for small, tender, close-trimmed loins.

There are several reasons why hotel loins cannot be always of that choice sort. In many places the butchers will not take hotel trade at all, because hotel meat always has to be the choice portions, and they cannot sell what is left on their hands. And even if the best hotel does get the pick and choice *somebody* has to take the remainder, or the long untrimmed loin, or even the forequarter. So to commence in detail:

Your long loin of beef being before you on the block, and you having to do your own trimming, commence by cutting out that piece of lean meat marked 6. The knife will be guided by the bone at top, and by the adjoining fat and gristle of the inner part. Having trimmed off the roughness hang up the piece on a hook. It is good steak and only has to be cut in three lengths and then sliced across. Next, take off the flank in one piece, not only the section marked 8, but all the rest by the long line above. This is of but little use except for corning and mixing off with some that is too lean. The part marked 8 is streaked with lean and does to roll up and bruise tender, and does for spiced beef rolls, etc., and perhaps for rough steaks. The thin end of the loin has one rib in it, which the butchers cut with the hind quarter to keep it stretched in good shape; it is a question whether you want a roasting piece off the loin, and if so you will take off the the piece marked 2 and 3; if not, commence and take all the meat off in three or four strips, according to the size of the loin, as we mentioned in the beginning. Always cut these strips into pieces with the knife slanted, the edge cutting towards the tail, so as to cut across the grain.

Cooks are generally expected to have the magic power to make tough beef tender; for this reason we cut it into lumps instead of slices, and flatten it out with a blow. There is no method known, nor has any appliance yet been patented so effective for subduing obstinate beef as the disintegrating flat slap with the side of a heavy cleaver. It does not make bad meat good but makes it passable: While we must allow that it is better if the beef is of the tender sort that may be sliced to the proper thinness in the first instance, and only needs the customary tap with the cleaver to smooth it down to shape; the fact is that in nine cases out of ten the heavy-handled course of treatment is a benefit to the public. Nor is that a method for poor beef alone. The huge tenderloin steaks, large enough to fill a dish, that are served with the choicest garnishings of peas, asparagus, mushrooms and the like might sorely puzzle a person who had never beaten out a steak to know where they come from so large.

990. A Restaurant Tenderloin.

Cut off a section of a fillet of beef about 3 or 4 inches in length, or according to the thickness of the meat; remove a portion of the skin that encircles it and flatten it out to form a large steak 1 inch in thickness, on the block with the cleaver. Trim off the rough edges.

The poorest eating, unless the beef itself be fat, of what are called first-class steaks are cut from or close to the ribs—about figures 2 and 3; but these, cut thick and not beaten, form the staple "loin steaks" at many restaurants. Their neat shape is their recommendation, and stands there instead of a higher quality. The best steaks in any quality of beef are cut about and above figures 5 and 1. The meat here is better than the tenderloin, although that has the greater name on account of its comparative scarcity. Where the long lines end in the dark part of the diagram is a mountain of bone. A solid piece of meat of good size at figure 7 is good if cooked five hours, or more—braised or a la mode. If there be a portion of the solid lean meat of the round on the great bone of the long loin, slice it in any way that will cut across the grain and make 2 or 3-ounce steaks. To know whether you are cutting the steaks to the right size weigh some occasionally; they are large individual steaks when they weigh 3 ounces each or 5 to the pound—equal to half a pound each of beefsteak as the butcher sells it with the bone and roughness. The loin from which our drawing was made, years ago, weighed 108 pounds, and was all cut into steaks that weighed 7 to the pound, and they were the regular size and large enough. For your hotel people take for breakfast—fruit—mush—fish, either salt or fresh—beefsteak, mutton chops, bacon, breaded cutlets, and potatoes—ham and eggs, tripe, liver and pigs-feet—rolls and butter—toast, milk, batter-cakes and syrup—coffee, chocolate and tea, and a few extras. It is well to keep the few steaks that come larger than the rest, by accident, and not large enough to cut in two, for those who wish beefsteak only. Such are known among the cooks and waiters as "a *full order* of beefsteak," etc.

Always notch the edge of the steak through the fat, that it may not curl on the gridiron.

Contrary to what might be expected the proportion of bone to meat is as great in a short loin as a long one. the fleshy piece marked 6, ballancing in the long loin the preponderance of hip bone above. The short loin does not get quite all the tenderloin. If the long loin be cut so as to have five or six inches depth of the round attached, which is all solid meat and the best quality of that cut, it will furnish a larger proportion of small steaks than any other shape of loin.

991. Results of the Cutting.

The size of a hotel's business is often concisely stated among the employes by the number of loins of beef cut up for supper or breakfast, or per day. Two or three loins for supper represents a rush of trade, only it has to be taken into account whether they are long or short loins. As only one-third of the gross weight makes first-rate steaks, and the cutting is usually done in haste, it becomes a matter of some concern to know what to do with and what becomes of the rest.

The loin having been cut up as marked out in the last article we find it in seven different portions—(and what rules in this case is nearly the same in all meat cutting)—namely:

Sirloin steaks—first-class.
Tenderloin steaks—first-class.
Coarse steaks or corning pieces.
Roasting piece, rib and flank.
Scraps, shapeless odds and ends.
Tallow and kidney.
Bone.

Nothing can be easier than to ascertain that such grading is necessary. Let a man take up the piece of the thick rich-looking flank of fat beef, that will usually weigh ten pounds, and see the impossibility of getting steaks out of it that would do to send to a first-class or second class table. The loin roasting piece may be cut into steaks, but it is not over five pounds and the shallow and fat portion attached with the rib will weigh much more, and does not furnish a single steak that will pass for first-class.

A tally kept of ten successive loins of beef some years ago, at a summer hotel, where, while everything was bought of the best quality that money could procure, the meat supply was simply just what the town butcher was able to furnish with his limited facilities, and contracts for special cuts or strictly prime qualities were out of the question. Consequently the following exhibit may be supposed to represent a fair average for the great majority of hotels the country over.

	Weight, lbs.	Sirloin Steaks, 5 to lb.	Tenderloin, 7 to lb.	Coarse Steaks, lbs.	Flank, Meat.	Rump Roast.	Scraps	Tallow	Kidney.	Bone, lbs.
1st Loin—Medium size, lean...............	67	135	18	15	18	18	5	5	2	14
2nd Loin—Small beef, fat, short............	59	110	20	20	17	12	6	5	2	20
3rd Loin—Medium size, lean...............	74	145	36	22	19	15	6	5	2	19
4th Loin—Small, fat, with ½ the round.....	86	110	20	24	21	17	4	5	2	21
5th Loin—Medium, fat, no round...........	70	110	19	36	16	15	4	6	2	22
6th Loin—Medium, fat, with ½ the round..110		152	30	22	14	13	4	6	2	24
7th Loin—Large beef, middling fat, short..	74	132	39	18	13	11	5	6	2	19
8th Loin—Small, fat, with ½ the round.....	59	126	22	15	11	11	4	4	2	18
9th Loin—Middle size, lean, no round.....	51	115	28	18	15	10	3	4	2	13
10th Loin—Medium beef, no round.........	82	135	24	30	16	12	4	4	2	23
Totals 10 Loins,	**983**	**265**	**49**	**175**	**165**	**80**	**50**	**178**		

The averages of the above totals are bone, one-fifth, or 20 lbs. in every 100; tallow 6 lbs ; scraps, sinews, shapeless ends 7 lbs.; thin flank, rib and roasting piece 12 lbs ; tough, coarse meat that may be cut into steaks or used in better ways, one-fifth or 20 lbs. in every 100; tenderloin 5 lbs.; good culled steaks, all designated sirloin, three-tenths, or 30 lbs. in every 100.

992. What To Do With the Pieces.

Some beef that is furnished is so good and tender that an enjoyable steak may be cut off the brisket or at the back of the horns. Other beef comes along that is tough even to the upper portion of the porter-house. There are butchers who carry on a trade in nothing else but young and tender meat, and to have any that the cook would need to cull and sort could be for them only the result of accident. These must still, however, be regarded as the exceptional few.

It is common enough to make a practice of cutting up everything that will make a steak, in a mechanical sort of way, cooking and sending it in to the sufferers—for as the cook justifies himself by saying "he does not make the beef."

In Europe where they don't know how to keep hotel, they let the deck-hands get away with the thirty pounds of choice sirloin steaks and send the steaks cut from that we have designated as coarse meat in to the guests at table, who thereupon go away anathemising the hotel, though the deck-hands say the cook is a fine man. They manage these things differently in the United States.

Some cooks, and others, who "do not make the beef," but who do know that it can be sorted, avoid that as far as possible by mixing off the good and bad whenever there is a chance so to cut that one eatable mouthful will carry two uneatable with it. The uneatable will afterwards be found among the waste and refuse scraped from the dirty dishes. Some sort of system that would leave such uneatable portions intact on the cook's books in the meat house, to be made eatable and even delicious by proper cooking must be preferable to such an absence of any system whatever. The portions that are uneatable as steaks, except in very good fat beef, are all that marked 7 and below it in the diagram, and the upper or outside of the round, and another portion that is too fat. The other deduction called the flank roast in our table will be understood by a glance at the two drawings of porter-house steaks. It is the fat, narrow, and coarse textured meat of the right hand side. In the same list go the scraps and shapeless ends.

Hotel entrees are in the main only devices for using up these odds and ends of meat. All the science and skill there is to learned in cookery is needed in this direction, and all the tact and taste in the individual is called into play to make these generally supposed to be the worser portions appear the better, and make them more sought after than even the selected cuts.

As to the tenderloin—5 lbs. out of a hundred—the cook and the head-waiter together vote that away in steaks. As these steaks are generally cut larger than the rest, and twice as large as our table of weights and proportions says they ought to be, and as there are not enough for everybody they are generally bestowed as rewards of merit. Sometimes they are given to the best looking people. Sometimes to the people who do the most good. Where there is any danger that the waiter and the head waiter may differ in opinion of who these people are, the latter has checks printed—"good for one tenderloin steak"—which the waiter may obtain upon proper representations, and they will be duly honored by the cook as long as his bank remains solvent and there is a steak left in the pile; due watchfulness being exercised to see that the checks are not cleverly executed counterfeits of the waiter's own.

Another reference to our table of figures shows that the tenderloin varies greatly in size according to the make-up of the different beeves. The choicest loin in ten had only 3 pounds of tenderloin.

Sometimes the steward is incredulous and says: "What, no tenderloin left? Why, you cut up a loin this morning." Yes, but the weights vary from three to six pounds each.

The six pounds per hundred of beef suet can be put to very good use, saving that amount of butter or lard for pastry and puddings, and when rendered out in a baking pan in the range serving for frying fat. The kidney, if included, is worth its piece as meat. It weighs a pound, and is useful in the bill of fare.

The 20 pounds of bone in the 100 goes to make the soup, along with the bones of other meats, and the boiled fowls and legs of mutton. With this object in view, all the bones should be taken out of the meats that can be without detriment to their juiciness and good shape, and very little, if any, more than what the hotel meat house furnishes of this sort, with the few really surplus cuts—the shanks of veal, etc.—will be needed to make the best of stock.

993. Short Loin Average.

Short loins, close cut and trimmed, averaging 30 pounds, when cut up, will average as follows: Bone, 7½ lbs.; tenderloin, 4½ lbs; sirloin steaks, 13 lbs; coarse meat and fat, 5 lbs.; or, about 85 individual steaks of five to the pound, and 20 rough steaks or stewing meat—all more or less.

994. Cutting Up the Fore Quarter.

The choice rib roast of beef is the portion marked 11 in the diagram—it is generally known as the short ribs. The next best is the chuck ribs, marked 2. Where the hotel or restaurant buyer can take choice he takes all of those portions that are clear of the shoulder blade, which is marked by dotted lines. It is generally made compulsory, however, for the buyer to take the whole from B to B, and often a longer cut, including the lower part of the ribs. The butcher's own idea of the best roast for a hotel is to cut from A to A and send all—roast, ribs and brisket. In such a cut the roast weighs half of the gross amount, the ribs and brisket the rest.

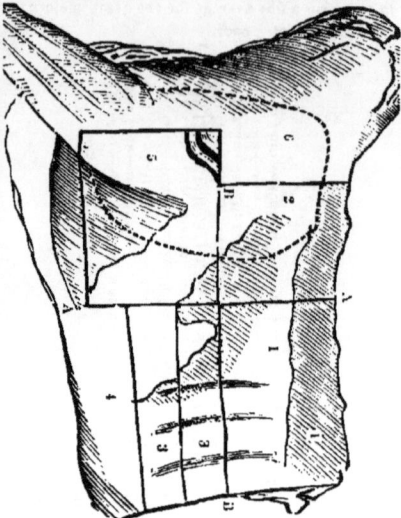

Supposing the house buys the entire fore quarter, and out of it you have to cut the roasting pieces and steaks, as well as the corning, boiling and stewing pieces, we will proceed as with the long and untrimmed loin.

First, with knife and saw, take out the roasting piece, from B to B, and upwards to the top of the shoulder. The choice roast cut, whether in hotel or restaurant, is a slice clear of bone off the end, above B, and the same cut with the same slant of the knife towards the tail, is to be continued clear to the other end at 2. Observe, therefore, that there is no use in cutting it any lower down than the proper length of a slice for the dish; it is better to let the surplus be a cut to itself, as marked 3, than to hang a useless string on the roasted slice. Where three or four of these whole rib roasts are used every day, the difference amounts to something. At figure 2 the piece of blade bone divides the roast in an inconvenient manner. The piece of meat on top of the blade is called "the cap." The butchers skewer it up tight after taking out the bone and sell both parts together, but for good hotel roasting it is better to take off the cap in one piece and make the lower part uniform in size of slices with the other end.

BUTCHER'S ROAST.

HOTEL ROAST.

The object of coiling up the roast is to get rid of the thin meat. The best end roast is made up so by cutting down both sides of each rib and taking it out, the thin fat meat marked 3 3 in the diagram being then coiled around No. 1. After roasting the thin meat is to be disposed of by slicing off the roast horizontally.

Whether or not that is the best way must be altogether determined by the circumstances governing each case.

Where there is a bill of fare and a variety of viands to choose from, and where the persons served with a slice of such coiled up beef would be likely to select from it only the choice inner portion, leave the rest on their plates and make a dinner from the entrees, it is better, as in the case of the loin management, to keep this thin, straggling and fat meat back and put it to good use in other ways. The best way to use the cuts marked 3 3 is as rib ends of beef, baked till tender, or boiled, and served with some good accompaniment.

The brisket marked 4 is a choice boiling and corning piece.

The square, 5, contains the best steak; a small portion of it is as tender and good as any part of the beef. The first of the steaks shown is cut across where the bone is smallest, at 5, the other is cut at 1 B, above. To get at these it is necessary to cut off the shoulder, raising it up and cutting under so as to bring away all the meat from the ribs beneath it to make the cuts the larger on the shoulder. These are the butcher's steaks; the method for individual steaks does not require the bone to be sawn through, but the meat is to be divided in lengths and then sliced crosswise of the grain, and beaten out with the cleaver.

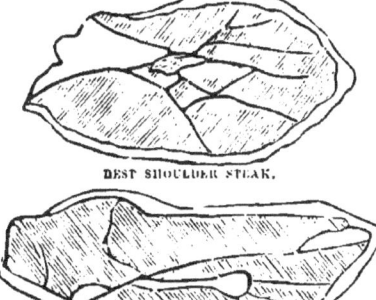

BEST SHOULDER STEAK.

CHUCK STEAK, FROM SHOULDER.

The shoulder having been removed the ribs beneath will be almost bare and fit only for the stock boiler, but the breast, or brisket—called "the plates" by the butcher—makes the best corned beef, and boiled beef, and the bones make the richest soup.

The meat at 6 makes a thin roast, of poor quality, unless the beef be fat, but, with all the rest of the neck, it is as good as the best to stew, or salt and boil, or to roll up and braize tender with vegetables and gravy.

The "cap," taken off at 2 and B, makes either steaks or a roasting or braizing piece. It is disfigured with a streak of grist that runs through it the flat way, but which dissolves with long cooking and makes the meat the better.

The shank, being broken up, is one of the principal reliances for the soup boiler.

In some of the large city butcher's shops great trays or baskets full of pieces of beef boneless and all of a size and of the same appearance, may be seen prepared evidently for some special purpose. These are roasts—as we will call them for convenience sake—taken off the necks of beef, the dark-shaded, throat part in our cut, perhaps unsaleable in the shops, but to be sent to the prisons and workhouses and other such institutions, there probably to be cooked by steaming or boiling in a way to make them as good for nutriment and health and strength as the best cuts in the beef.

The fore quarter of beef averages nearly one-third bone.

995. The Round of Beef.

The long loin untrimmed containing bone to the amount of one-fifth its weight, the short loin divested of the rough meat of the flank having one-fourth its weight, and the fore quarter entire about the same, it will be seen that the most profitable cut as regards the amount of meat for the buyer is the long loin with the larger half of the round attached, which is nearly all solid meat. In a good fat beef the round steak is the juiciest, and not inferior to any other cut, allowance always being made for the difference between the "silverside," as the English call it, and the tough portion opposite that is scarcely eatable as beefsteak, but needs different cooking.

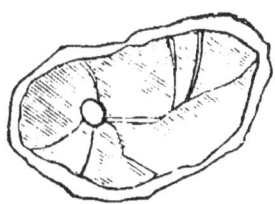

ROUND STEAK.

The tough side is only about one-third of it In cutting up the round for individual steaks selection should be made, the good side cut lengthwise into suitable pieces and these sliced across the grain and the tough side should be taken off entire, and where such meat will not answer for beefsteaks, but a better quality is required, it should be either cooked tender by boiling in the stock boiler and then quickly browned in a baking pan and served with gravy as well done roast, or else as boiled beef, or stewed, or salted, or à la mode.

996. Veal Tenderloins.

Where veal is used every day it will be found advisable to take out the tenderloins and reserve them to make entrees. "Milk veal" is not often eaten by Americans, but that of from three to six months old generally furnished yields tenderloins of good size, and they are apt to be overlooked and lost in the haste of carving if left on the roasts. Anything with the name of tenderloin has a passport to public favor already—beef tenderloin, pork tenderloin, veal tenderloin—and the latter makes some dainty dishes. It needs short and quick cooking to keep it moist and juicy, and a dash of lemon juice or vinegar in the preparation, the same as sweetbreads.

SIDE OF VEAL.

Number 1 is the loin best end, nearly all meat, and answering to the porterhouse cut in beef. No. 2 is nearly all bone. Many a buyer is deceived by it who takes it for a roast for dinner. A few cutlets may be got off it, the rest is for the soup pot. No. 3 is the fillet in veal, the same as the round of beef, nearly all meat except at the bulging knuckle.

It is sometimes, the bone being taken out, stuffed and roasted or braised, but is most serviceable in the form of cutlets, both plain and breaded, while the shoulder and ribs do better to roast. No. 6 is called the neck, as well as No. 7, and takes in all the ribs like the rib roasts of beef. When a large roast of veal is required, after taking off the shoulder saw through all the ribs at the place of the dotted line the entire length from the neck back to about figure 2, leaving the brisket 9 and 0, and the flank part of 1, all in one piece, to be used in various other ways.

To make the rib or "neck" roast of veal convenient for the carver take off all of the back bone and the strip of gristle along the edge before cooking, but leave the shortened ribs in it. If of proper size every alternate slice as it is carved will carry a bone with it, which can easily be detached with the carving knife.

When taking off the shoulder, which should be the first cut, run the knife upwards very close to the blade bone at the place marked by the figure 6, so as to leave all the meat on the ribs and none on the under side of the shoulder.

The shoulder can be roasted entire, or boned and rolled and roasted, or boned, larded and cooked as a fricandeau, etc.

The two shanks, 4 and 5, may be closely trimmed and the meat used for stews and pies, if they can be spared from the soup.

Veal, or the bones and trimmings, imparts the richest color to brown gravy, and makes the most excellent soups and broths.

In regard to the names, it is to be observed the "neck" roast is never seen in hotel bills of fare on this side the Atlantic; the word neck would not convey the idea of the choice rib portion that is intended. When it is not written plain "roast veal" it is either loin of veal or fillet.

The French cooks who had to introduce French cooking into England—Careme and his followers—were evidently impatient at having to call the round of veal a fillet, according to English usage, for after dismissing the fillet of veal shortly and curtly they ran to extremes in this way: Take—their directions say—a fine neck of veal and *fillet* it, lard the *fillet* closely with alternate *fillets* of red tongue and *fillets* of fat bacon; place the *fillet* thus prepared in a saute-pan, etc., etc.—thus running in a dozen repetitions of the fillet in a way to sadly confuse one who had just learned that the fillet of veal is the leg.

In the flush days of Leadville two cooks were one day talking over this matter over their beer. One of them was gray haired, traveled, learned and mysterious. Said he: "One thing I have learned, any way, and I want you to believe it and mind what I tell you: Every living thing in creation's got a fillet, but don't you never het you know where it is no more than you would on three card monte, 'cause it's never there."

997. The Side of Mutton.

There is a curious and most inconvenient disproportion between the number of orders for mutton chops and for mutton in any other form; making the hotel demand for "racks" alone of mutton as burdensome to the butchers as the demand for short loins of beef. In many places the prices are so arranged that the hotel buyer can get the racks if he will pay enough for them, but the remainder of the side of mutton is offered so cheap that it is like getting it for nothing in comparison, and the next thing the entire side, or entire sheep is found hanging in the hotel meat house.

In the accompanying cut No. 1 is the leg; 2 is the loin, and the two loins undivided make the saddle of mutton, to be cut out according to the dotted lines. But a choice loin of mutton roast takes in also six ribs, marked 3. That is to say, if the butcher sells you a loin of mutton it should consist of both 2 and 3, according to the butcher's names of cuts, and 4 and 5 together are called the neck, best end and scrag end. In the butchers' shops, also, the shoulder, No. 6, is generally sliced through with the ribs, to make chops, and those who buy must necessarily fry such large and bone-divided slices as they are. Our directions for trimming and shaping will not apply unless the cook cuts up the side or the quarter himself.

SIDE OF MUTTON.

998. Cutting Up the Side.

First take off the shoulder small, leaving all the meat under the blade on the rib chops at figure 4, which may be easily spoiled by too deep a cut. Next, saw off the brisket at the dotted straight line that runs between 3 and 7, beginning at the throat and taking off all the length back to the leg in one piece.

Then cut the side in two in the middle and you have the rack ready for trimming into chops.

Where several racks are to be cut up the workmanlike way is to cut a strip of the meat an inch wide from the ends of all the ribs at once, finishing the scraping of the ends after the division into chops; but for one rack at a time it is as quick to cut first and trim one by one after. The same with the back bone. It has to be taken off, and may either be sawn off the whole length of the rack at once, or taken off each chop piecemeal.

Cut the loin also into chops, each with the portion of bone belonging chopped through till the great hip bone beyond No. 2 is reached, when it is best to cut the steaks from the bone with the point of the knife, and all the way from the ribs keep the handle slanting towards the inside of the leg till the last steak is taken off parallel with the leg bone, and when the fleshy part of the other side of the leg at 1 is cut off in one piece the bone will be left clean trimmed.

Trim the outside skin to prevent curling up on the broiler, and flatten them with a tap of the cleaver.

A side of mutton cut from end to end yields about 30 chops and cutlets, (or steaks) without including the leg, but only 20 are first-class. There is the same inquiry for "a chop with a bone in it," or "a chop with a handle to it," that there is for tenderloin steaks. There are but 10 fine rib chops and 3 rough and tough ones. The loin chops at No. 2 are the best eating, and many people appreciating the fact are well content with them. Still, after that concession is made, the American indifference to roast shoulder and boiled leg of mutton makes the sheep seem a remarkably ill-proportioned animal, its racks so few, its legs and shoulders so numerous.

The shoulder of mutton, if fat, is best roasted as it is, with the bone in it. It is sweeter and juicier that way, and furnishes a few good cuts lengthwise. But it is more economical boned and rolled up with twine, and can be most readily disposed of if stuffed, nicely seasoned and cooked tender. The brisket and neck can easily be used to advantage in stews and pot pies.

The leg of mutton is supposed to be in demand to boil and serve with caper sauce. In point of fact the orders for it from a bill of fare will run about four out of fifty on an average, and of those four two will refuse it if cooked rare, English fashion, and the other two will refuse it if cooked well done. Better cut it up for breaded mutton cutlets for breakfast and plain boiled for supper.

999. The Side of Veal.

Every portion of the side of veal being tender and fit for the best uses there is but little selection to be made. When it is a question whether to buy the hind quarter or the fore quarter it can only be said the difference in quality does not justify any greater price being paid for the former. The knuckle and shank and hip bone are largely in proportion to meat in the hind quarter. The fore quarter yields the best roasts and rib cutlets and more useful side dish material than the other. But the whole side is better, for with that in the absence of poultry, brains, sweetbreads and the like small meats, the cook who has a bill of fare to make up is still pretty well provided.

1000. English Mutton Chops.

(RESTAURANT ORDER.)

Cut the chops of double thickness, two ribs in each one; then take out one rib and leave all the meat on the other. Flatten it very slightly to smooth it, but leave it thick. A rack of mutton only furnishes four, composed of the eight best ribs.

1001. The Side of Lamb.

The dainty dish of spring lamb may easily be spoiled, or at least made very unsatisfactory by careless cutting. If you take off the shoulder it will scarcely make two good orders when roasted, and the ribs underneath it will amount to nothing. Nearly all who choose their cuts ask for the ribs ("with some meat on 'em and well covered with fat") and the carver needs all that the cook can furnish. Instead of taking the shoulder off bona it where it is, beginning at the throat. Cut along on both sides of the blade bone and pull it out. There will not be much time for careful boning, nor is it necessary, five minutes or less will do. Saw the ribs across the middle, back through the back bone with the point of a sharp cleaver at two ribs apart and hack the brisket through ready for serving in the same manner. Then pull the meat of the shoulder well over the brisket and fasten it with a skewer or two. When carved, the ribs will carry a good, meaty slice of the shoulder with them, and with a little management the brisket ends of the ribs can be equally well portioned off.

The side thus prepared should be roasted in one piece, loin and flank included, but the leg requiring more time to cook, should be made a separate cut. The loin should likewise be carefully hacked through the back bone ready for carving into slices like loin chops.

The saddle of lamb is the same as of mutton, the two loins undivided. It is a roast for a family dinner or small party, the meat to be neatly carved in slices without hacking through, precisely as at the hotel carving table the thin white slices are carved from the leg and loin.

1002. Lamb Cutlets.

For cutlets proceed with the side of lamb the same as with mutton, taking off the shoulder, leg and brisket. Take off the back bone the whole length in one piece carefully without losing any of the meat (there should be a small, sharp saw for the purpose), then cut off the two ribs together, take out one bone and leave all the meat on the other. Scrape the end of the bone, flatten the cutlet, notch the edge, trim off rough ends and gristle. Cut the loin into chops (cutlets) the same thickness, and the leg, if needed. The shoulder, if used for chops, must be sawn across through the bone, making four slices.

When making up your breakfast bill of fare always write them lamb cutlets and not chops, for all the world and his wife will call for lamb chops, but if they are lamb cutlets there will be a great saving. Everybody knows what a chop is too well.

For breaded lamb cutlets the slices cut from the leg should be used, unless for an ornamental dish, when the prepared rib cutlets will be required.

The brisket or breast* of lamb is a choice portion for side dishes, broiled, fricasseed, curried, etc., etc.

1003. Rocky Mountain Sheep.

The meat is not easily distinguishable from venison except when it is very fat, then it has a decided flavor of mutton. Fat bucks will sometimes weigh as high as three hundred pounds each, but the ordinary weight is about a hundred and fifty pounds. The hair is like that of a deer. The yarns that every hunter tells to every "tenderfoot" as soon as this species of game is mentioned, of how the Rocky Mountain sheep can throw itself from the highest precipices and land on the rocks below on its ponderous curled horns unhurt, the hunters themselves do not believe.

The choice morsel is the rib chops cut of double thickness and broiled or fried rare done. The loin and leg can be cut into chops and steaks, and broiled, or can be roasted and served with currant jelly, and in all the ways that venison is served It is good meat, and every part can be made use of.

1004. Antelope.

Those who think the highest pitch of excellence in meat is excessive tenderness should be happy with antelope, which is tender even to softness.

However, the meat has a peculiar musky flavor and little or no fatness, and is but little called for after the first day or two of novelty. Only the hind quarters are used. Cut it into steaks to broil or fry, or roast and serve with jelly or game sauces.

1005. Elk.

Good for a brief novelty, but is intrinsically not so good as poor beef, which it closely resembles. It is cut into roasts and steaks in all respects the same as beef.

1006. Venison.

Doubtless the best of wild meats and best worth buying for hotel use. Every part is valuable, good soups being made from the neck and coarse pieces and stews and hunters' pies from the rough cuts. The choice morsel is the rib chops cut of double thickness and broiled. The shoulders may be roasted, care being taken not to dry them out. The hind quarter is the choice roasting portion.

The English term *haunch* of venison seems never to have become Americanized, but remains an unfamiliar word and unsuitable for the hotel bill of fare. Some seem to expect from it something peculiar and unusual like the hump of a buffalo. Saddle or leg of venison are common and well understood.

1007. Bear.

Who buys a bear buys a curiosity, something for the guests to talk about and be pleased with, but makes them a present to that extent, for nothing appreciable is saved in the meat bill by it. It is ordered very generally in addition to the usual meats, to be tasted and ventured upon carefully rather than to be actually eaten, while those to whom it is no novelty rarely order it at all, unless they know it to be young.

The meat of the black bear is the best. It is good in the fall when fat, and to be tender enough to eat must either be of a young animal or have been kept after killing long enough to be on the verge of spoiling. The meat has the sweet taste of pork, but is very dark colored, and, like pork, it is hard to cook done. Bear steak will generally bring forty or fifty cents per pound in market, owing to its rarity. A bear ham makes the best roast served with jelly or cranberry sauce. The flank and breast can be made into hunters' stews, ragouts, etc.

1008. The 'Possum and the 'Coon.

Though insignificant as articles of provision these two sleek animals, the one a marsupial with a prehensile tail and the other a fighting rodent, are blamable for much of the troubles of hotel keeping in the South and Southwest. For if the hotel help and especially the colored cook and his helpers, who have to work seven days in a week as it is, go raking through the woods all night, with axes on their shoulders and 'possum dogs" at their heels and fell ree after tree by the light of lanterns and help the dogs in the chase after the game when it jumps out of the falling 'simmon bush, it is not to be expected that the fire in the range will be made very early, nor the rolls light, nor the corn bread well done, nor the meats ready cut, nor the griddle hot, nor the biscuits anyway but burnt black on top through firing up the range with grease while the inside is still dough, to say nothing about the prospect of dinner where the cook is asleep in a chair at eleven o'clock in the morning.

Nevertheless the opossums will be fat and large—not at all like the poor runts to be seen exposed for sale in South Water street, taken in northern corn fields, but which no Arkansas 'possum hunter or 'possum dog would be seen in company with—and must be prepared for roasting with sweet potatoes in the pan. For it is more than likely that with the prospect of having one of these, the largest of course, for supper for himself and friends, the colonel who keeps the hotel will forget and forgive the troubles of the morning, whether his wife does or not.

The opossum if you hold him by the natural hold, the tail, will climb up on it and bite. He must be killed by a blow on the head. Then dip him in water that is hot enough to scald but not boiling, with a shovelful of wood ashes in it, and scrape him clean as you would a pig. The skin is very fat and easily scalded too much so that the hair cannot be removed, and a skinned 'possum is of no good at all. Draw it, wash, truss and bake it whole.

The coon, on the contrary, has to be skinned, the skin being worth something beside, and should then be split in halves lengthwise to bake.

1009. Buffalo.

Buffalo more nearly resembles beef than anything else, but is not so good. It is ordered by most people while still a novelty, but not sought after. Cut up the same as beef, into tenderloin, loin, round and rib roasts.

It will probably not be long before the buffalo will be extinct, the spanning of the great plains by railroads having made the destruction of the vast herds easy to the hunter for their "robes." There was a time when the first Pacific railroad was being constructed, that buffalo meat was plentiful enough in the markets to materially interfere with the sale of beef and lessen the price, and when it was a drug at the stalls at three cents a pound. It has already become a rarity only to be obtained in freezing weather from remote territories in the northwest.

1010. Cutting up a Porker.

As "times change and men change with them," fresh pork has gone out of fashion, being no longer the favorite kind of meat it was twenty years ago, unless it may be in a few remote localities.

The great wastefulness of pork as an article of hotel provision is consequently a matter of but little concern, though hotel buyers need still to observe critically the difference between a butcher's porker, which is not more wasteful than a fat sheep, and a fat bacon hog, which will hardly yield five pounds of meat for the plates out of twenty-five, even after the butcher has made a show of taking off the thickest of the lard from the outside. In a great many hotels this is the only kind of pork furnished the year round, nobody observing the difference, while all the figures in the meat bills are high numbers.

A PORKER.

Number 1 shows the extent of the shoulder blade, which may be sawed through and the little piece taken out of the shapely roast, number 4. Some good cutlets can be taken off at 2, if the shoulder is cut carefully, leaving the spareribs under it bare. The butchers call number 4 the fore loin and 5 the hind loin. The entire length can be cut into chops or roasted, the skin being first taken off. It is not customary to trim the ends of the bones of pork chops as mutton chops are trimmed, though it would be hard to advance a reason why there should be a difference. The leg, number 6, is equally good for roasting or to be cut into pork steaks. The belly, number 3, is somewhat hard to dispose of economically, being too much streaked with fat to roast or broil. It can sometimes be used in the form of brown stews, for which the meat is first fried and freed from fat; it does to fry in slices to go with chicken in the Maryland style, but best of all it may be put into pickle and used in the score of ways and dishes that require salt pork. The head may be prepared for the table in many ways, both cold and hot, as may be found fully described elsewhere,

1011. Cutting up a Bacon Hog.

Take off the head. Split the carcass in two halves down the back, not through the back bone as in cutting roasting meat, but sawing or chopping down both sides, taking the back bone out entire, and generally it is thought worth while to leave a good portion of lean meat on it, for the back bone makes several good dishes and the lean meat is of but little account in the bacon.

The chine of pork is the thick part of the back bone taken with considerable meat from between the shoulders. It is either to be stuffed and roasted, or cut in pieces and stewed.

Lay the sides on the bench and take off the leaf lard from the insides. Cut that into small pieces—the smaller the better—and put into the kettle, to be rendered out. Then take off the spareribs, cutting them bare or with a covering of meat, according to circumstances. If in a hotel the spareribs will be found very serviceable for the bill of fare.

Then make two straight cuts across, dividing the side into three, one portion being the ham, another the shoulder and the middle taking all the meat between.

All the roughness, loose ends and corners should be trimmed off, the lean to make sausage, the fat for lard; the feet are then to be taken off and the meat put in salt pickle. The head of a fat hog is either cut up for the lard kettle or salted and smoked, eventually to reappear as jowl with spinach.

1012. Good Country Pork Sausage.

12 pounds of lean pork.
6 pounds of fat pork.
3 ounces of salt.
1 ounce of good home ground black pepper.
1 ounce of powdered sage.
1 quart of water.

Or, twice as much lean as fat, and seasonings in the above proportions at the least for any smaller quantity of meat.

It does very well when you are seasoning sausage meat to pat out a cake of it and fry it on the range top and then ask everybody within reach to taste and tell you whether it is seasoned enough, but there are disadvantages about it; for if the tasters are hungry they will often prevaricate so as to obtain another section, and if they are not hungry their judgement is not worth a pinch of salt. On the whole it is better to trust the scales.

The butchers are always found willing to trim the fat from the pork they sell and from the pig's heads, because a mixture of such fat with minced beef makes the ordinary sausage meat of the shops in which such a large trade is carried on, that but few can keep up a constant supply. With proper conveniences for the work a better article and better seasoned can be made in any hotel when there is a surplus of similar material.

1013. To Cure Hams.

12 hams.
3 pounds of fine salt.
8 ounces of saltpetre pounded fine.
1 pint of molasses.

Mix these articles together and rub each ham with the mixture. Pack them skin side downwards in a barrel and let remain 4 or 5 days, according to the temperature. Turn them over, sprinkle plentifully with salt and let remain 5 days longer. Turn them skin side down again and add to the pickle in the barrel enough of brine made strong enough to bear an egg (about 5 pounds of salt to 3 gallons of water) to just cover them. In six weeks hang up the hams and after five days drying smoke them.

Home cured hams, jowls and shoulders are often ost by spoiling through being packed frozen in an exposed place The salt never penetrates the frozen meat, which remains fresh to spoil when the weather turns warm. The cellar and not the smokehouse is the place to do the pickling in. If necessary to keep hams in summer it is best to wrap them in paper and keep in a dark place.

1014. Cutting up a Ham.

We must dwell a little on the ham question, for a pile of hams being highly concentrated food, trimmed already, smoothed, shaved down, pickled, dried, smoked, packed and repacked, watched and labored with, also concentrates within itself a goodly pile of the hotel-keeper's money, and when the cook has to go at it with knife and saw, the man who pays the bills is very apt to begin a great thinking; and the indications are that every one such thinks, or has thought until he tried it, that there must be something wrong in the hotel cook's way of cutting a ham to pieces to slice it, and that it ought to be sawn across, slice by slice, from end to end.
In most restaurants that has to be done for the reason that the customers paying a stated price for their dish are apt to look more to its size, weight and thickness than to its fineness, and making a meal of one or two articles they expect a sufficiency. But a fine dish of ham has to be cut thinner than can be done with a saw, and smoother, neater and handsomer slices are required for the best hotel tables than any meat saw is capable of turning out. It takes a Sabatier knife with a keen edge to produce them and for once style and economy go together. If pretty fair progress is made at one time in sawing a ham, that is dry, cold and hard, it becomes next to an impossibility to proceed the same with a fat, bulky ham in warm weather, and altogether too wasteful.

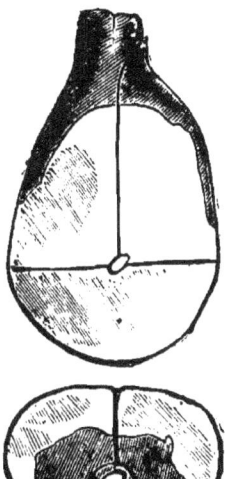

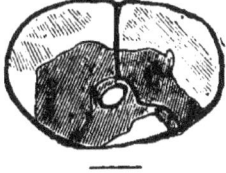

To cut up a ham, first saw off the butt end at the horizontal line in the cut. There is a center bone that is shown that stops the knife cutting down from the shank and there is another bone not shown that projects from the ham at a point on the right hand, in the line. That bone is the guide where to saw through, because hams are not all cut quite alike. The section of clear meat on the right that is taken out when both cuts are made is the principal portion of the ham from whence those thin, shapely slices are cut that make a first-class hotel dish of ham and eggs inimitable by any restaurant sawyer. The section on the left contains the leg bone and the slices are one-third shorter than the other side and can only be cut to about the extent of the dark shading in the drawing, the great knuckle bone filling out the rest. It is generally best to boil that left section and shank and not use it to slice for broiling at all.

The butt end shown in the lower figure is to be held on edge and, if of a large ham, cut by the black marks making two pieces cut clean from the irregular shaped bone. The rind having been taken off these two are to be cut in slices, and where too small cut them not quite through, two slices attached together, open and flatten them with the cleaver. When the ham is small the slices have to be taken the entire size without dividing at the middle line, and loosened from the bone below with the knife point.

Very generally it is found that the choice right hand sections of the hams are all that the house needs for broiled ham while the butt as well as shank are keeping up the supply of boiled ham for dinner and supper. In other words, don't boil the best portion if you can help it, as the ham is of less consequence at dinner than at breakfast.

Hams cut as above make about half their gross weight of broiling slices. One weighing 20 pounds may be cut into 100 presentable slices; a 14 pound ham has yielded 63, weighing 8 pounds—8 to the pound; an 18 pound ham 10 pounds of such broiling slices, 80 in number. Beside this there is a boiling portion of sufficient amount to bring the eatable part up to two-thirds of the gross weight.

On an average it is found that one-third of every ham is waste—bone, shank, rind, thin-shaved outside and superfluous fat; the ham bought at 14 cents per pound when placed upon the gridiron has cost 21 cents.

The hams that are too large and too fat for family use, at last, most frequently, find a home in the hotel storeroom. Every scrap of lean meat and even the knuckle bones can be put to some use, but all their surplus fat is unmitigated waste, good for nothing.

1015. Cutting up Fowls.

Nothing in this article should be so construed as to discourage the good carver from going on making six or more orders out of one chicken where such is required, but of really first-class cuts, shapely, complete and satisfactory, each fowl only yields four, no matter how large, and the best course where such good cuts are wanted is for the buyer to select small fowls and buy them by weight.

The four good cuts are, 1st, the leg, thigh, (second joint) and side bone of the roasted fowl, taken off with a horizontal cut all in one piece. The fowl having been trussed with the legs in the body before cooking this cut lies in compact shape, but the joint should be severed on the under side before it is placed on the dish by a quick cut with the handle end of the carving knife. When it is a large and coarse fowl, the drumstick may be kept back and the rest will make a large enough dish; 2nd, one side of the breast (a fillet), sliced off all in one, the knife cutting through under the wing joint and the wing going with the breast. This fills the dish handsomely with the clear white meat properly covered with the brown outside unbroken. The wings should be taken off before cooking, all but the meaty first joint. This taking one side of the fowl, the other side is carved in the same way and the breast bones nearly bare and the most of the back bone remain on the carving board. On each side of what may be called the small of the back of a fowl there is a little piece of meat known to epicures as the oyster; it belongs to the dark meat portion and shou'd be sent in with the side bone.

It is so nearly true it may almost be taken as a rule that wherever the fowls for dinner are carved as above the fragments remaining on the carcasses will be sufficient for an entree or salad or some other side dish for the same number of people the next day, making it as economical to send in first-class cuts as to chop up both back bones and necks to make dishes of, and the same consideration making it worth while to provide an extra fowl or two to allow of a surplus. Wherever it takes say 16 fowls roasted or boiled for dinner for 75 persons (some not taking chicken), 4 fowls or about 5 pounds of clear chicken meat without bones will make one of the favorite entrees for the same number of people, and half the number of pounds does for cut chicken meat to put in soup.

These chicken entrees made of 4 fowls are not, of course, a satisfactory substitute for the roast requiring 16, but the greater dish and the lesser, we wish to point out, can be had for about the same cost with good management.

It is much the same in cutting up raw fowls as in cooked. The writer once set a young fellow of considerable experience in cooking, who was on the night watch at a railroad house, the job of cutting up the fowls for the next day's chicken pie, and found next morning that he had the entire three dozen chopped into little bits of even size not larger than guinea eggs. That was entirely wrong and a bad blunder at that place, but it had been the right way in his former situation. He would perhaps have been dismissed for doing otherwise, for first-class houses, after all, are the few and not the many; but wherever fine cooking has been done and taught great attention has always been paid to the method of cutting up fowls, which for first-rate dishes—supremes, salmis, fricassees, blanquettes, pies—does not vary much from what has been shown in relation to the fowls after roasting.

To make first class dishes of chicken cut them raw into four choice portions, the two legs and second joints cut off large and rounded, and the two fillets with the wing joints attached, and the carcass left over. Then chop up the carcasses either for second-rate stew or pie, or cook them for soup or salad.

1016. To Truss Fowls to Serve Whole.

Make no opening at the crop but insert a long and narrow knife and cut the meat from the breast bone inside without cutting through, and when the ridge of the bone is reached cut into it a little so as to get away the skin without a rent. When all is cut over and the bone loosened twist it free from the wing sockets and pull it out. The object is by removing the high breast bone to give the fowl the smooth and plump appearance of a fat goose or duck, and make it suitable to be larded ornamentally with strips of fat bacon and filled out with stuffing.

1017. Cutting up a Turtle.

It is in every way easier to cut up a turtle if it is first well scalded before being touched with a knife, except to kill it by partly severing the head. If of large size lower it by a thin cord attached to the hind fins into a stock boiler of boiling water. It need not boil after the turtle is immersed as it is not to be cooked, but so large a body sufficiently reduces the temperature and the turtle may remain in it fifteen minutes or more. All the black cuticle can then be peeled off the fins, head and neck and much of the horny coating from the shells.

Then take off the bottom shell, not dividing the two shells at the edges as that cut into shreds some of the best of the meat, but by cutting into the bottom shell at an inch or two from the edge all around and then cutting under, bringing away with the shell as much of the "chicken meat" or calipee as may be without cutting into the entrails.

Take out the entrails, heart liver and lights, and with especial care not to break the gall. These inwards are cleaned and eaten by some people in some countries as are likewise pig's chitterlings, and the heads and feet of geese and the like, but are always thrown away in this country, unless an exception is to be made for the negroes of the Florida Keys However, it is necessary for the cook to know that these parts are by some considered delicacies and capable of being made into fine entrees.

Next, take off the four fins at the sockets. The thick joints afford some of the choicest meat, the thin ends also make some fine dishes besides the whole being used for the soup.

Then take out the dark meat from the back shell in as large and long pieces as possible—if wanted to make entrees gather up—when the turtle is large enough and good enough to possess any—all the green fat from about the fin sockets and around the edges of the shells and keep it by itself steeping in cold water.

Lastly, cut and saw the shells in pieces convenient to go in the stock boiler. You now have: The "chicken meat" or calipee from the bottom shell, easy to cook tender, for the soup, or for white fricassees or stewing in wine etc.:

The fins, requiring at least two hours to stew tender, for the soup or for entrees, stewed with wine and rich gravy and with various accessories of mushrooms and vegetables:

The "beef" or dark meat or calipash, from the back shell, capable of being cooked in the same ways in the same time as veal for the soup, or to be larded with fat bacon and braised as a fricandeau of turtle; the smaller pieces to make stews and ragouts: The green fat or "fish" most prized for turtle soup:

The shells and head, to be boiled in water till their glutinous parts are dissolved, making the turtle stock.

Says Fielding: "The turtle, as the alderman of Bristol, well learned in eating, knows by much experience, besides the delicious calipash and calipee, contains many different kinds of food."

But the dried turtle both from Australia and South America, and the canned turtle of our home packers now present in all the markets ready for almost instant use almost put out of mind and out of use the nice distinctions of the old time turtle tasters, though it is true the packers, some of them at least, do still advertise both calipash and calipee.

Turtle soup at the very best is but turtle added to rich mock turtle already made of veal and beef as a foundation, and the preserved article may easily enough answer for the fresh and generally does, for people who do not claim to be "well learned in eating." Dried turtle sells at about eighty cents to a dollar per pound. It should be steeped in water a few hours before cooking in the soup.

1018. General Management of Small Meats.

Some three or four years back a reporter of one of the New York papers—it may as well be stated that it was the *Graphic*—went out like Lord Bateman, "strange countries for to see," and visited the various hotel kitchens, we picked up the paper and of course perused the article with interest; and what does the reader of the "Oven and Range" suppose struck that reporter as the most noteworthy object encountered on that tour of observation in an unknown region? It was the orderly arrangement of the cut meats in the trays placed in the refrigerators of one of the prominent hotel kitchens—perhaps it was the Brevoort, perhaps the Hoffmann House—where, says the reporter, "the cook can go in the dark at any time of day or night and pick up any kind or cut of meat that is called for."

We call the attention of young and inexperienced cooks to this point in this manner in order to say to them that notwithstanding the too prevalent idea that a hotel kitchen is a place of disorder, dirt, grease and general disarrangement, it is in fact in every hotel where the business is properly understood and carried on a place of as perfect method and mechanical precision as any other description of workshop or factory whatsoever, and the man who cuts and takes care of the meats is as much of a skilled mechanic, and as little of a "roustabout" as the operative, in any other industrial occupation. In a case where the circumstances vary so widely as between such great hotels as the Tremont House and Grand Pacific of Chicago, that keep two men employed doing nothing but cutting meats, and the small houses where the one cook can cut all that is needed in the half hour before the meal it is of course impossible for all to follow the same rule as to times, nevertheless there ought to be as much order and precision in one place as in the other.

Whatever may be the convenient time of day, whether in the early morning, at four in the afternoon, or in the hour or two after supper let there be a strict rule of changing the cut meats into clean trays or pans—baking pans are always available and are generally used—and a replenishment of the stock laid ready in other pans to be commenced on when the older lot is gone.

The largest tray is for beef, for with all its faults they love it still. In an average way four-fifths of the people take meat for breakfast and two-thirds or three-fourths take meat for supper—varying with the seasons—and of the whole number one-half take beefsteak. In other words if you have one hundred persons it is safe and expedient to prepare fifty individual beefsteaks. The rest of the orders are divided among the other meats promiscuously, mutton being next in demand; veal being run upon occasionally, when the beef is whispered about as being poor for the time being; then ham, breakfast bacon, sausage, liver, salt mackerel, tripe, pork and kidneys. The one greater favorite than beef is chicken, and that and eggs at the first incoming in spring, or venison or brook trout or other such novelties and delicacies may materially change the amounts of other articles required. More curious than useful it is perhaps, but it is observable that certain leaders of the style in most hotels can set fashions of eating certain articles of diet cooked in certain ways that will be followed by a great proportion of the other guests for the time, but which when these leaders leave all the others will abandon. Occasionally some very simple article of diet is in this manner elevated to the place of highest importance and it becomes uncomfortable for the cook who happens to be deficient in that particular.

As nearly as possible, however, the cook tries to prepare just enough for the meal and no more. Whatever surp'us of raw cut meats there may be when the meal is over should be placed on ice till the next meal and then changed into clean, dry pans with the utmost care to prevent their acquiring a sour outside, one of the commonest and most damaging faults found by the fastidious in connection with hotel meats.

1019. Roast Beef Rare—Blood Gravy.

That is the way it is ordered, but in the bill of fare blood gravy is always softened into dish gravy, or in some cases into "au jus"—with natural juice or gravy. Certain restaurants make this dish a specialty to such an extent, and their patrons who esteem it have so separated themselves from those of contrary predilections that hardly two cuts of well-done beef are ordered out of fifty.

To cook beef just to the right point, and not only that but to cook it so that the blood gravy will flow in a stream as soon as the beef is cut is an effort of some skill and great care. It cannot be done if the beef is put into a cold range to heat up gradually, nor if it is put into a pan of water and scraps to simmer and become sodden, nor if crowded among other meats to be cooked rather by the steam than by dry heat; nor can it be done if the meat is stabbed and pricked with the fork continually, letting the gravy ooze out at every pore while it is cooking. For a large proportion of your people all the rest of the fine dinner will be as nothing at all if the roast beef is not medium rare and with plenty of gravy. Take the roast as shown at No. 994 and put it, if practicable, in a pan by itself, or if it must go in with the other meats, put it in when they are half done and all hot through and give it space not to crowd against any other. In a pan by itself put in with it a handful of salt, a ladleful of drippings or fat from the top of the stock boiler and set it in the range already fairly hot, only about 1½ hours before dinner, for trimmed roasts seldom need more than 1 hour or 1½ to roast, rare done; it is hard to keep them hot without too much cooking afterwards, and they are best and juiciest when just done.

Probably the most perfect roasts of this kind are those (already trimmed, ready and hanging in the meat house) which you throw hastily into the hot meat pan already in the range when a car-load of people arrive unexpectedly to dinner and another roast is needed. The sudden heat immediately sets the outside of the meat, which holds the juices within like a bladder. You roll it over and over in the hot fat and the salted glaze that is on the bottom of the pan in the effort to hasten the cooking. You calculate the weight—each rib weighs about three pounds—the length is nothing, only the thickness of the meat counts—3 pounds thickness will cook rare in three-quarters of an hour. Then you slice and send in the beef piping hot. Our entrees are all very well and we have hundreds of them, but this is the important part of the hotel dinner.

1020. The Blood Gravy.

Our carving tables are defective in their lack of appliances for keeping the gravy in the natural state and a little scheming is necessary. The juice from the beef flows into the usual steam-heated receptacle and becomes cooked and is no longer the thing that is called for. Where only one rare roast is used it is possible to get along with the carving with the roast on a large white platter set on the carving board which certainly looks clean and preserves the gravy, and can be set in a warm place occasionally between the rush of first and second table. Some set the roast on a small carving board on the carving table, set a dish under the edge to catch the gravy as it runs from the beef and set a board under that dish to prevent the heat of the carving table making it hot enough to cook.

1021. Roast Beef Well Done.

Well done beef can be juicy and the gravy will flow, although in smaller quantity, the same as rare if managed in the same way. Where the rare roast requires 1 hour let the well done remain in the range 2 hours. Or, put the thin end of the rib roast in for well done and the thick end with the shoulder cap left on, both in to roast at one time. The cap will preserve the inside portion rare while the other will be done through.

The spoon basting that was an important matter with the old-time spit roasting before open fires is not so necessary where the meat can be rolled over frequently in the baking pan, answering the same purpose. But always catch with the fork some bony or projecting end, not to puncture the meat and let the juice escape.

Apropos of natural gravy; Says Brillat Savarin: One day I was conducting two ladies to Melun, and on reaching Montgeron, after several hours traveling, we felt hungry enough to eat au ox. Alas! the inn we stopped at, though looking decent enough, had nothing but an empty larder. Three stage coaches and two post-chaises had been before us, and, like the Egyptian locusts, had devoured everything.

Looking into the kitchen, however, I saw turning on the spit a leg of mutton, the very thing wanted. The longing glances of the ladies were in vain, for it belonged to three Englishmen who had brought it, and were now patiently waiting, chatting over a bottle of champagne. "But, surely," said I, in a mixed tone of annoyance and entreaty, "you might fry us those eggs in the gravy of this roast; what with that and a cup of coffee with country cream to it we shall be resigned to our fate." "Certainly," answered the cook, "the gravy I have a right to dispose of, and in two minutes you'll have your dish."

Whilst he was breaking the eggs I went to the fireplace, and with my traveling knife made in the forbidden *gigot* a dozen deep wounds, letting every drop of the gravy run out. Then, watching the preparation of the eggs, lest any thing should spoil my plot, I took possession of the dish and carried it to our room. We of course made a capital meal, laughing loudly every time we thought of ourselves having the best part of the roast, and our friends, the English, chewing the remainder.

1022. Roast Rib Ends of Beef.

Take the ends of the ribs that are sawn off the rib roasts, the pieces marked 33 in the diagram at No. 994, and if needed the piece likewise marked 4, and put them in to cook early, while breakfast is still going on. Let there be in the baking pan, which should be a deep one, a handful of salt, 2 or 3 ladlefuls of sweet fresh drippings from the previous day's roasting, and about as much water or soup stock, and let simmer in the oven, never getting quite without water in the pan till very nearly time to serve dinner. If, as is almost sure to be the case, other meats have to be crowded into the same pan let these rib ends be at the bottom, they will be so much the richer and keep on cooking in the gravy till tender and glutinous. At last, the water being all evaporated out of the pan, roll these rib ends over and over in the natural glaze that remains on the bottom and take them out brown and shining before they likewise get dry. Serve cuts of 2 or 3 ribs with gravy.

There are certain popular restaurants where the above simple but delicious dish of meat sells side by side in equal amount with roast turkey at the same price per dish, and twenty to one more than any of the marinaded, spiced, larded and braised entrees of the French cuisine. In every hotel the rib ends are in demand fully equal to the supply of that cut, unless when pushed aside through the greater attraction of the rarer roast chicken or turkey or game. As the question of how to use up everything that comes from the butcher's is our most troublesome problem the proper way of roasting so as to make this meat always attractive deserves attention. To nicely glaze the meat when done is not always so easy as might be supposed, the pan gravy not being always boiled down in time, but the long and tender cooking is easy and of more consequence, for if a person orders that cut one day and finds it hard, tough and uneatable and a disappointment in his dinner, he will hardly call for it the next day though it may be never so unctuous and savory. The meat must have 3 hours slow baking. It is naturally too fat to eat at first but the long cooking expels the most of the fat and dissolves the gristle.

It is a common practice, but erroneous, to write the rib ends of beef in the bill of fare as short ribs. Such they are in one sense, but, properly, the short ribs of beef is the choicest roast, marked 11 in the diagram, and a person who knows that and expects perhaps a slice of rare beef from the best part is apt to be disappointed with a dish of the very well done rib ends. And those who have learned to call these short ribs at one hotel in the same contrary manner find themselves served with a slice of beef which they did not call for at the next. We need uniformity of practice in these particulars more than in any others.

1023. The Flank Roast.

See Nos. 991 and 992. Cook it in all respects as directed for the rib ends in the preceding article. It is not named in the bill of fare but makes a rich, unctuous cut and is acceptable to all who call for well-done beef. Slice it across the grain.

1024. Roast Mutton.

All the remarks concerning roast beef apply equally to mutton, which is sometimes called for rare done and is sure to be in a house where there are many English people. "Saddle of Southdown mutton," so frequently seen in bills of fare has relation to the fact that there are breeds of sheep raised for mutton, of which the Southdown is perhaps the favorite, (though there are also Cotswolds and Leicesters and others,) and others for wool. A carcass of the latter small kind, the staple supply of the markets in some parts of this country, will weigh only from 30 to 50 pounds, while a Southdown will weigh 150 and even 200. A leg of mutton of the small kind will weigh 4 or 5 pounds, but of the large and fat from 10 to 20 pounds. Consequently no rule as to the time of roasting can be given that will be so good as the cook's own experience marked by the kitchen clock.

1025. About Boning and Rolling Meats.

Many good cooks make a practice of boning and rolling up all their roast and boiled meats without exception, even the rare roast beef being so converted into a beef roll. We think this a decidedly objectionable practice, destroying the individuality of the meats, if we may so express it, making them look all alike and giving grounds for the complaint sometimes heard that hotel meats all taste alike. It is better only for the carver, who simply has to slice off the roll of meat from end to end. But such a roll being easily penetrated by the fat and liquor in the baking pan while cooking is not the same thing when done as a solid mass of meat that so far from mingling with the others holds its own juices ready to burst out at the first puncture.

The only meat that is better for being rolled is the shoulder of mutton of the poor sort previously mentioned; all the other rolls should be in the entrees with their appropriate seasonings, an exception being made perhaps for the standing hotel dish of veal with dressing.

1026. Roast Lamb—Mint Sauce.

It cooks in from 30 to 45 minutes. Should be fairly done through and no more. Needs to be in a pan by itself.

Having prepared the meat as directed at No. 1001, wash it in cold water, dredge both sides with salt and flour, by pressing both sides down into a pan of flour and shake off the surplus. Place it with the outside upwards in a baking pan already hot and containing a little salt, water and drippings. When the upper side has cooked so that the flour will not wash off begin to baste it and repeat frequently. If a quarter pound of quite fresh butter can be had melt it and baste the lamb with it at the finish. The butter froths upon the meat and gives it a fine color.

1027. Mint Sauce for Roast Lamb.

The proper sort of green mint not being an article in steady demand is very hard to obtain outside of the great cities and a number of execrable substitutes are employed "to fill out the bill of fare." There is in fact no proper substitute and the makeshifts are calculated to disgust people both with the sauce and the lamb. Peppermint, whether green or as essence, is not the thing, neither pennyroyal nor catnip nor wild mint. The gardeners know the proper article that makes the much be-praised English mint sause for roast lamb as orange mint. We often hear the order for lamb "with plenty of mint sauce," or with "more of the sauce in a dish,' showing that it is liked by many; still it is best when carving to pour the sauce under and not over the meat on account of the many who are unaccustomed to it. When there is no mint serve brown gravy instead.

Mint sauce is cold, a mixture of finely chopped green mint with sugar and vinegar. To a cupful of vinegar add 2 tablespoonfuls of white sugar and 4 of mint. With very strong vinegar a little water should be mixed in.

1028. Roast Veal.

When the veal is young and white proceed with it the same as directed for lamb. It must always be well done but taken out as soon as done and not dried out, as if overdone it will part into loose strings when carved. Serve the brown veal gravy made in the same baking pan after the veal is taken out. It is usually of a light reddish brown and a finer gravy than that from the beef.

1029. Roast Veal With Dressing.

The real purpose of dressing or stuffing is to impart a flavor of the seasonings to the meat while it at the same time absorbs the gravy. This is not accomplished when the dressing is baked in a pan separately.

Take a shoulder of veal, cut out the bone, split the thickest parts of the meat and cover the thin places. Spread over it thinly the bread dressing No. 942, or the sage dressing as made for roast chicken and turkey, roll up, fasten with skewers and roast about 1½ or 2 hours.

The dressing as put into the meat is rather dry. Whatever is left to be baked in a pan separately should be made quite soft with more water.

1030. Roast Pork—Apple Sauce.

Pork must always be well done, and is slow to cook; an ordinary roast will usually require 2 hours, a leg of pork about three hours. Serve a little of the brown sauce under the meat as well as the apple sauce at one side of the dish.

1031. Apple Sauce for Meats and Poultry.

Pare good, ripe apples and slice them into a bright saucepan. Add water enough to come up level with the apples and stew with a lid on till done—about 30 minutes. While they are stewing throw in a little butter. Mash at last with the back of a spoon. No sugar. Serve hot.

The above is the proper apple sauce for pork, duck and goose. When sour apples must be used of course a little sugar has to be added. But the apple sauce being for some unaccountable reason extremely liable to be forgotten till the carver calls for it nothing is more common than for the stewed apples of the supper sauce or the pie fruit from the pastry room with all the sugar and flavorings of lemon, cinnamon or nutmeg, to be pressed into service as sauce for the roast pork. The noteworthy thing about it is that this kind of apple sauce seems to give entire satisfaction and no objection is ever heard; which only proves that our people generally love apple sauce not so much as a sauce to certain kinds of meats but as apple sauce for itself alone. Moral: These considerations should make us tolerant of the seeming errors of others, which may be better in their effects than our own right doings.

1032. Roast Sucking Pig, Stuffed.

Cover the pig in the oven with a sheet of thick paper well greased. This being easily moved for basting and removed for the last crisping gives you command over the heat of the oven and shields the outside of the pig from becoming too brown before it is done through. When the pig is small and the skin still moist it can be scored with a sharp knife before going in the oven, care being taken to make the marks correspond with the slant of the ribs that it may be carved in clean cuts. Also sever the shoulder and leg joints inside. When the outside has become dried it is easier to put the pig in the baking pan first on its back and after 15 minutes take it out of the oven and score the skin which will then be soft. After having been stuffed with the following dressing the belly should be sewn up with a packing needle and twine. A whole sucking pig will require 2 hours careful roasting. Serve brown sauce made in the pan and some of the stuffing in the dishes and have apple sauce ready for those who call for it. Apple sauce and stuffing should not go together.

1033. Sage and Onion Stuffing.

2 quarts of finely minced bread crumbs.
2 tablespoonfuls of minced onion.
1 heaping tablespoonful of powdered sage.
Same of pepper and salt.
1 egg.
1 cupful of warm water.
1 cupful of fat from fried sausage or of lard.

Mix the ingredients all together in a pan, not trying to make the dressing too moist as it will absorb gravy while baking. The egg or eggs should be mixed with the warm water before it is poured over the bread crumbs.

1034. Roast Pig With Apple Sauce.

Pigs weighing from 30 to 40 pounds are more frequently furnished to hotels than the very small ones, and, as they are not sent to table whole are considered more satisfactory. They are too large to be cooked whole but are split in halves, carefully hacked through the bones inside the skin scored across and across in diamond squares, according to the directions for sucking pig, and basted and crisped light brown in the same manner. Serve with the apple sauce No. 1031. To insure its being done through the joints fully 2 hours slow baking will be required and perhaps a longer time.

1035. Roast Ham With Spinach.

A favorite and very saleable dish in the restaurants in the winter and spring months, and equally

1035. Roast Ham with Spinach.

A favorite and very saleable dish in the restaurants in the winter and spring months, and equally good for the hotel table, the difference being made in the size of the dish, which at a restaurant constitutes a dinner. Usual price per dish 35 cents—in first-class restaurants.

Scrape and carefully shave off the outside of a ham and saw off the rank end of the knuckle bone. It is an improvement to soak the ham in water 12 hours before cooking.

Boil it in the salt meat boiler from 2½ to 3½ hours, according to size. Take out, remove the rind, trim a little and bake it brown and shining—about ½ hour.

Serve like corned beef and cabbage with spinach in the dish and a slice of ham on top.

1036. To Cook Spinach.

It will probably take a bushel-basketful raw for 50 persons' orders. There is a winter spinach, hardened by slow growth that may need half an hour to cook. The tender spinach of spring growth will hardly bear to boil 10 or 15 minutes before it wastes away in the water. It shrinks in cooking more than any other vegetable.

Pick it over, cut off thick ends of stems, wash it well in abundance of water to free it from grit, put it into water that is already boiling and has in it a little salt and a little baking soda—say, from the size of a bean to half a teaspoonful. A little soda keeps the spinach green, too much is an injury.

When done pour all into a colander and let stand to drain itself. Season with salt and a spoonful of fat from the salt meat boiler.

1037. To Cook Radish Greens—a Substitute for Spinach.

Use the young leaves of radishes to serve with both roast ham and boiled jowl when spinach cannot be obtained. Proceed as for spinach. Boil half an hour, or till the stems are soft.

1038. About Roasting Hams.

Hams will absorb moisture if steeped before cooking, hence the practice where the highest possible excellence is aimed at of steeping them in wine with spices and herbs and then baking them enveloped in a covering of flour-and-water paste to retain the flavors. They will also absorb moisture in boiling if put on in cold water and heated slowly. For this reason, although a ham can, of course, be baked like any other meat in a pan of water and fat with a greased paper over it the common, almost universal practice of boiling first, then browning in the oven is doubtless the best as well as the least troublesome.

1039. Roast Ham, Wine Sauce.

Sometimes we see it in the bills of fare "au vin madere," or "sauce amontillado." These are the harmless little flourishes like those the good penman makes when he writes a card; that do no harm as long as they do not make the writing illegible or obscure the meaning.

For wine sauce see No. 955, or add wine to brown gravy in about equal quantities.

1040. Champagne Sauce for Roast Ham.

The pleasant sharp sauce so commonly served with roast ham and named champagne sauce, bears about the same relationship to real champagne that champagne cider, and champagne (or white wine) vinegar do. Possibly very skillful cooks could make the same thing with real champagne. This, however, seems to be generally esteemed as an accompaniment to roast ham, since it is nearly always consumed, which is more than can be said of some of the sauces of greater fame.

1 pint ladleful of good brown sauce or gravy.
½ cupful of vinegar.
½ cupful of sherry or native wine.
1 large tablespoonful of sugar.

Mix and serve hot. This it will be seen is of the same sour-sweet nature as mint sauce to roast lamb. The brown sauce, which is best for the purpose if taken from the roast veal pan, should be thick enough to bear the reduction of the added liquors.

If a ham were steeped (marinaded) in wine before cooking for some extra occasion the wine remaining would afterwards be strained and added to the brown sauce and boiled up in it.

1041. Roast Ham Bread-crumbed.

Boil and trim a ham as heretofore directed. Mix 3 cupfuls of the sifted crumbs of dried and crushed bread with 1 cupful of grated cheese. Brown the ham in the oven only very slightly, take it out and press upon it all the bread crumb mixture that can be made to stick. Put back in the pan and brown it in the oven carefully all over alike, basting the dry places with a little clear fat from the pan. The cheese mixed with the crumbs acts as a cement for the coating, gives a rich color and a good flavor. A ham done this way is good either for hot or cold.

1042. Leg of Venison Baked in Paste.

We have never seen the line above in any hotel bill of fare, but if there is really any merit in the very old-fashioned method of enveloping the venison in coat of dough there seems to be no good reason why it should not, and the people informed they are partaking of a dish of the old English and old Virginia style. The saddle of venison is most benefited by the covering because the thin parts are preserved from drying out. But this is the easier for a trial.

Trim a leg of venison, antelope or mountain sheep by sawing off the useless shank and shaving off the hard and black outside, or at least the worst parts, and wash the rest. Dry it and brush over with a little butter to keep the paste from sticking to the meat.

Mix 2 pounds of flour into a very soft paste with about 2 cupfuls of cold water and nothing else. Spread or roll it out, cover up the meat in it and close all holes

Put it in a baking pan that it will nearly fill and a little water to keep the corners from burning,

A joint that would take an hour and a quarter to roast just slightly rare done without the paste will take about half an hour longer with it. Keep the paste from burning in the range by moistening the outside with water occasionally.

When the meat is nearly done take it out of the paste and brown it quickly in another pan in a hot oven without allowing it to dry out. Serve with currant jelly and the natural gravy.

The objection in hotel work to the paste covering is not that it is any particular trouble or at all difficult, but the apparent waste of eatables.

The value of the two pounds of flour is at most 10 cents for each joint, but as the baked crust is thrown away it goes to swell the always enormous waste, and somebody is tolerably certain to put a veto on the method.

By the old spit roasting it was probably found that half an inch depth of the already dry venison became utterly dried like a crust before the inside was done, and the paste resorted to as a preventative.

1043. Roast Venison.

Trim and wash the meat, put it in to bake in a baking pan that contains a handful of salt, a little water or soup stock and as much drippings or fat from the top of the stock boiler. Never let the pan be quite devoid of water while the venison is in, and there will never be any dry crust. Roll the meat over or baste frequently, but take care never to stick a fork in it. A leg of ordinary size will be done in an hour to an hour and a half. It should be slightly rare around the bone when cut. A saddle or loin will cook in three-quarters of an hour.

Serve either with fruit jelly and natural gravy—which will, of course, be scarcely a teaspoonful to moisten each slice—or with game sauce made by mixing currant or other fruit jelly with brown sauce, or with brown sauce alone, according to circumstances. The expense of the currant jelly accompaniment to venison is in many places found more onerous than the expense of the meat itself.

Venison and all the similar wild meats must be roasted in pans apart from the butcher's meats. They impart strong flavors and also make the pan gravy very dark. The brown sauce or gravy made in the venison pan often is useful in small quantities to give color to the other from the beef and pork.

1044. Hotel Turkey and Chicken.

Hotel poultry is always bought in lots at advantageous times, with one eye open to the quality and another eye perhaps a little wider open to the price. We remember a time back in a Missouri town when it was an "Uncle Mose," who wore a Number 13 shoe, that did the buying for the City Hotel and always bought the chickens at $1, $1.25 or $1.50 per dozen, or did not buy at all, although the retail market price at the same time might be $3.

He circulated a little amongst the market wagons, posted himself as to their contents, and got himself known by sight, and then waited for the bell that closed the market.

"Got a heap o' stuff left over, aint yer?"

"Oh, no, not much," says the farmer, turning around briskly, and trying to appear cheerful, as if everything was lovely.

"No, it wouldn't be much to me 'cause I runs a big hotel, and what you got there wouldn't be no more than just nothing to us," says Mose, starting to go away, "but it's a right smart for a man like you that's come so far to get left on his hands. I'd like to help you out and let you go home, if we didn't have so many in our coop now. I'll tell you what I can do—I'll give you a dollar a dozen and clean out the whole lot."

Then when the farmer looked horrified at the very idea:

"Well I don't care for no two bits, if that makes a difference to you. I'll give a dollar and a quarter a dozen and take all the coops you got on both wagons."

And it generally ended with:

"Now you better let me have 'em. The market bell's done rung. You can't sell 'em anywheres in town, the merchants won't let you. You got to lay over till to-morrow, and there's your expenses; and some of the chickens will die, and there's a powerful sight of chickens coming in on the road every hour a'most, and maybe in the mornin' you can't sell a one. You better take it, and there's your money in gold right there in my hand—all right, drive right up to the back door in the alley—both wagons, you recollecks."

Then he would shout across the street:
"I wants you one-hoss hotel niggers so stay away from this man. Ole Uncle Mose done bought all dem chickens; you hear me!"

1045. Sorting Mixed Lots.

The old and mature turkeys may be known in a dressed lot by their larger size, by their general freedom from pin feathers and smooth skin, by their wattles, and by the unbending firmness of the end of the breast bone; also, generally, by their being fat, which immature turkeys never are.

The choice turkeys that the markets are culled for by dealers who supply high-priced family stores are the fat hen turkeys of about a year or a year and a half old. They are clean looking as to feathers, of desirable medium size, and will do to roast without previous boiling, as the old and very large ones will not. Young turkeys are the better the nearer they are to maturity. They are generally full of either pin feathers, or the marks of them, are thin and scrawny, with high bones and little meat. They have, however, the one great requisite of tenderness, and are bought exclusively by some restaurant keepers because, being light, a half of the breast with the bone in it, or a correspondingly large appearing cut of the dark meat can be served to each dish, which has a more liberal appearance than a slice and a single joint from a large turkey.

1046. Roast Turkey, Cranberry Sauce.

Take the the large turkeys such as are known to be old and not suitable for straight roasting—it will take 25 pounds raw weight for 50 persons, or 45 pounds for 100, varying according to the rarity of the dish and the method of carving—singe, wash, and truss with the legs in the body. Boil them in the stock boiler, in the soup stock which may have vegetables in it and a little salt, but no spice flavors nor bay leaf for about three hours, or till tender. They can be tried by lifting on a fork and pulling the wings, which will part from the body when done, or by raising the meat of the drumstick. Then take them out on a baking pan.

Your turkeys are now good eating, hardly to be improved by roasting, and all the harm that is done to them, the deterioration into dryness, stringiness and insipidity that brings hotel turkey into disrepute takes place afterwards by ruinous dry baking in the oven. They are already cooked, and you can let them wait till there is room and the range is hot. Dust them lightly with flour. Pour enough water or stock into the pan to keep it from burning, and some of the fat from the top of the stock boiler, and brown them off quickly. If fresh butter is cheap enough baste them with it and the turkeys will soon be of a rich deep brown, will cut moist, compact and tender without parting into only dry strings.

The common mistake in cooking old turkeys is in boiling them half done and thinking to finish the cooking in the oven. They dry out.

Serve with cranberry sauce on one side of the dish and a little brown sauce made with the residue of the butter in the turkey pan poured under.

Turkey stuffing and cranberry sauce ought not to go together. It makes too much of an incongruous mixture in one dish, and, as the dressing needs gravy as well, it takes too much time in the carving.

1047. Cranberry Sauce for Turkey.

2 quarts of cranberries.
12 ounces of sugar.
1 small cupful of water.

Wash and pick over the cranberries, put them into a bright kettle with the water, spread the sugar on top, shut in the steam and cook at the back of the range where they will not scorch at the bottom. When done, stir up to break the berries. Serve warm.

1048. Cranberry Jelly for Roast Turkey.

Cranberry jelly for wild turkey and game and cold dishes and pastry is easily obtained by draining off the syrup from well cooked cranberries before they are stirred or mashed and letting it get cold. The berries then stirred up with a little more sugar make equally good cranberry sauce.

1049. Roast Turkey, Stuffed.

Take fat hen turkeys or young but full grown gobblers, singe, and pick over and wash them. Stuff them with the bread dressing No. 942, or the same seasoned with sage, and twice the quantity, and roast for two hours, according to the general directions for roasting.

It is a good sign that a turkey is done when little jets of steam burst out of the breast and fleshy parts.

Young turkeys will cook in about an hour plain, or an hour and a half when stuffed.

1050. Roast Turkey, Brown Oyster Sauce.

Roast young turkeys not stuffed, about an hour, or till just done. Serve with the brown oyster sauce, No. 854.

1051. Roast Turkey, Stuffed with Oysters.

Read No. 855. Twice the quantity of oyster dressing will likely be required for turkey for 50. Serve the dressing with the turkey in the usual manner, and a little brown sauce made in the turkey pan.

1052. Roast Turkey, Stuffed with Chestnuts

There are two or more ways commonly practiced. One is to mix the whole chestnuts with enough of the common dressing to keep them together, and fill the turkey with the mixture; another is to mince the chestnuts very fine after boiling them tender, season well with butter or part suet, and salt and pepper, and stuff the turkey with the preparation, which results in a dish scarcely distinguishable from turkey stuffed with mashed sweet potatoes—a way that is really very good, but takes too many chestnuts.

For the first of the above ways make for two turkeys the veal stuffing No. 956, in twice the quantity, and boil about 80 or 100 of the *large foreign chestnuts* much as you would potatoes, in salted water, then peel and scrape them off the inner skin. Mix them with the veal forcemeat and use to stuff the turkeys.

Sausage meat can be used instead of the veal forcemeat. Also, turkeys are stuffed with sausage meat mixed with one-third as much fine bread crumbs added dry. There is a style called *a la chipolata* that means with little sausages, made by twisting link sausage into short lengths like chestnuts in size. These are used like whole chestnuts in stuffing, and also in the sauce or gravy.

1053. Chestnut Sauce for Turkey.

Boil chestnuts tender, peel, cut them in halves and mix them with the brown sauce made in the turkey pan.

1054. Puree of Chestnuts for Roast Turkey.

A puree is a pulp of meat, vegetables or fruits pressed through a sieve.

Boil 50 large chestnuts for half an hour, peel them, scrape off the furry inner skin, wash free from dark specks, then boil them in a little soup stock one-half hour longer. Mash them like potatoes, season with salt, thin down to the consistency of a thick sauce with hot milk and a little butter, and stir it through a gravy strainer. Best sauce for turkey or chicken stuffed with sausage.

1055. Wild Turkey with Cranberry Jelly.

We can dispense with the somewhat expensive covering of thin slices of fat salt pork or bacon for domestic turkeys, but not very well when a wild turkey is to be roasted. The most considerable part of it is the solid dark meat of the breast. Cover that part, at least, with very thin bands of fat salt pork, tied on, cover the whole upper part of the turkey with a moveable sheet of thick paper well greased, and roast the turkey in the oven for nearly or quite 2 hours. Wild turkeys sometimes weigh as high as 25 pounds each, and even more, and in such cases need long cooking in a moderate oven with very frequent basting. Let the water dry out of the pan at last, increase the heat, take off the paper and slices of pork and brown the outside quickly.

Wild turkeys should not be stuffed as long as they are a rarity in any place and there is a curiosity to taste the natural flavor unalloyed with herbs and seasonings.

Serve cranberry jelly No. 1048 cold, or currant jelly in the dish and a little brown sauce poured under the meat.

"The flesh of the wild turkey has more color and flavor than that of the domestic turkey. M. Bose tells me that he has shot some in Carolina much finer than those we have in Europe, and he advises all rearers of turkeys to give them as much liberty as possible, to take them out in the fields and even the woods, in order to heighten their flavor and bring them nearer the primitive species."—*Gastronomy*.

"There are three places in France rivals for the honor of furnishing the best poultry: Caux, Mans and Bresse. As to Capons, there is some doubt in deciding; and that which a man has his fork in must be the best. But as to chickens, the finest are those from Bresse, which are as round as an apple. It is a great pity they are so are in Paris where they only arrive when sent with a present of game."—*Ibid.*

1056. Roast Capon.

This, so often present by name in the hotel bill of fare, there is no reason to believe is seldom, if ever, outside of New York, present in reality.

A capon is a young male chicken gelded, by making an opening in its side and then sewing it up again, in order to make it fatten. So that although an immature turkey is never fat, an immature fowl, if caponized, may be made extremely fat if put through a course of cramming. These fat, young fowls are first choice as they can be roasted in the same time as a chicken and have twice the substance.

1057. Roast Spring Chickens.

Cook them only about half an hour in a hot oven with drippings and salt in the pan and very little water—barely enough to keep the pan from burning. They are better for being rather crowded together than in a pan too large. Tumble them over several times to get them light brown all over without drying out. A final basting with good butter is an improvement both to the chickens and the gravy that is to be made in the pan, but the most of the drippings should be ladled out first. Serve halves or quarters of the small chickens cut through the bones.

1058. Roast Fowl, Brown Celery Sauce.

All the remarks concerning the skillful cooking of old turkeys to make them as good as the young at No. 1046 apply equally to fowls. There is no difference in the time required for cooking. Some fowls will not be tender in less than 5 hours boiling, then they should be browned in the oven as quickly as possible.

1059. Brown Celery Sauce.

Take the outside stalks of celery, white, tender and good, but such as are left in the celery glasses when the people have picked out all the hearts, scrape off the back of each stalk, laid on the table, to remove coarse fibres and make it look smooth. Cut into bits about like the halves of chestnuts in chestnut sauce; boil them in salted water or stock till tender—20 or 30 minutes. Drain and put the pieces into the chicken or turkey gravy, and let simmer awhile that the whole may be mildly flavored.

1060. Bread Dressing for Chicken and Turkey.

"Chicken with plenty of dressing," and "some more of the dressing on the side," are some of the orders that come and make hotel cooks think the dressing or stuffing is something worth giving attention to, to make it good. It can be made so that it is actually better eating than the fowl itself, being savory and exciting the appetite. The sense of having dressing to fowls at all lies in the intention that the seasonings shall be imparted to the meat in cooking and the juices of the meat be at the same time absorbed by the stuffing. It should not, therefore, be made so wet that no more moisture can be absorbed, nor yet be crammed in solid.

The hasty way, when time is short, but not the best, is to shave off all dark crust from the rolls or slices of bread and throw them into a large tin pan. Turn on plenty of cold water, (hot water will not do as the bread can never be squeezed dry after) and after 5 minutes soaking turn into the large colander, let drain, and then press dry with a plate, and the colander tipped on one side. After that, season according to the proportions of the following receipt.

But this is not a difficult method, and if it takes a little longer cutting the bread, is better for everything except for baking separately in a pan.

4 pounds of bread (30 to 40 cold rolls).
2 heaping teaspoonfuls of powdered sage.
Same of mixed pepper and salt..

1½ pints of warm water—3 cupfuls.
1 pint of the fat from fried sausage, or lard, or butter.
2 eggs, or 4 yolks (not essential.)

Cut the bread in dice all free from dark crust, put in a large pan, add the sage and salt and good black pepper enough to season well. Mix the warm sausage fat, water and eggs (if afforded) together and pour over the bread. Stir up well but do not try to mash it to paste.

Finely chopped suet answers well in the above instead of other shortening, and often is the means of saving its weight of butter. More water will be needed when suet is used.

1061. Roast Chicken, Stuffed.

The best fowls for roasting are young, fat hens about a year old, as they can be roasted as they ought to be without previous boiling.

Singe, draw, wash thoroughly, and stuff with the bread dressing of the preceding receipt. Truss the legs in the bodies. Roast in the oven about 1½ hours.

1062. Bread Sauce, Brown.

This made in the pan the fowls are roasted in, savory, rich and liked by everybody, has no resemblance to the English bread sauce that is sometimes heard of but never wanted. English bread sauce is a white puree, made by boiling milk with a cut up onion in it and putting in white bread crumbs till it makes a sort of mush, seasoned with butter, salt and white pepper.

Brown bread sauce can only be made good in the chicken or turkey pan by great care to prevent the stuffing, that either has escaped from the roasting fowls or is mixed in the gravy for the purpose after they have been taken out, from burning on the bottom and getting a smoky taste like burnt espagnole while it is browning.

Set the pan (after the chickens or turkeys have been taken out) on the upper shelf of the range, should the bottom be too hot, until the bread crumbs (stuffing) in it have become brown, the water that was in the pan has all dried out, and the fat remaining is quite clear and can all be poured off almost to the last drop, the gravy and bread all sticking to the bottom.

The grease being got rid of pour a quart dipperful of hot water or stock into the pan and stir up the contents and let boil without scorching for a few minutes, then strain it into a saucepan by rubbing through a gravy strainer with the back of a spoon. If not thick enough it can be thickened in the saucepan while boiling at the side of the range. It is already seasoned with the salt that is invariably put into every pan that meat is roasted in, and the dressing.

1063 Spring Chicken, Maryland Style.

These can be done in a skillet or frying pan over the fire, as they doubtless generally are for a family party, yet we have always found in southern hotels that even "Old Aunty" herself was glad to slide the big pan containing three or four dozen into the range and be done with them all at once. And they seem just as good. The boarders at such hotels having chicken cooked this way for breakfast almost unfailingly during two-thirds of the year and for a period in the fall for supper likewise, learn a good many things about chickens that others in less favored localities never become poultrywise in. They learn the differences of quality in the different breeds of chickens, how, when all are cooked precisely alike, some kinds are white-fleshed, succulent, juicy and even fat, while others are little better eating than so much basswood—such differences as exist between Dorkings and Shanguis.

Singe and pick the chickens free from pin feathers. Instead of the usual posterior cut draw the chickens by splitting down the back bone and opening them. Cut off the neck and vent and then divide in halves through the breast bone. Wash them thoroughly, then lay out on board or table, dredge with salt and good home ground black pepper, then dip each piece into a pan of flour, flouring it on both sides.

Cover the bottom of the baking pan with slices of dry salt pork, not smoked, cut very thin that it may not take much in weight, and bake light colored to extract the fat.

Take out the slices and fill the pan with the chickens laid close together, the skin side down. Bake in a hot oven about ½ hour, basting with the fat from the corner of the pan (it almost always needs some fresh butter added) and when the upper side is light brown turn the pieces over and brown the other side—raised on to the shelf of the oven if necessary, as the pan should not be allowed to get brown.

Take out the chickens, pour a dipperful of milk into the pan and let boil up with the gravy and flour that is on the bottom and when done strain it. Serve a slice of the crisp pork on each piece of chicken and gravy in the dish.

1064 Domestic Goose and Duck.

One of Chicago's best known and most successful restaurateurs, Mr. Charles W. Baldwin, who is one of the oldest and best buyers in the market says, jestingly, about choosing geese: "Try whether you can push the end of your finger through the skin; pull the wing and see whether it will crack as if pulling off; try the legs, try the breast bone, then shut your eyes and guess at it and you will know no more about its age than you did before," which is equivalent to saying there is no way of knowing an old goose from a young one after it is dressed. An old goose is a very undesirable article of food, but young or "green" geese can often be obtained direct from the farms.

If stuffed with bread the proper kind is the same as for sucking pig, No. 1033.

Besides that all the stuffings used for turkeys are suitable, the oyster dressing, No. 856, being generally esteemed.

Not to go over the same ground again, those who, having a goose of doubtful age would make it good, should take the hint from the directions for roasting rib ends of beef at No. 1022.

1065. Roast Domestic Duck, Apple Sauce.

The same as domestic goose preceding. Apple sauce is served both with goose and duck. See No. 1031.

1066. Young Ducks, with Green Peas.

An early summer luxury. Roast young ducks like spring chickens, not over thirty minutes, without stuffing. Serve carved in halves with young green peas in gravy.

1067. Wild Geese and Brants.

The writer of these articles might have been inclined to ignore the process called braising—of which more will have to be said when we come to the entrees—as of little consequence in a system of cooking in which the meats are baked in gravy in a closed range had it not been for one bit of experience. Every one, almost, knows how wiry, tough, dark, dry, scraggy, bony, hard, and generally unsatisfactory wild geese and brants are, notwithstanding the pride the hunters feel in capturing such large game, at least after the ordinary method of roasting.

This was an old fashioned kitchen in the southwest in a region full of reedy lakes and swamps where wild fowl abounded and, whether or no, these wiry wild geese were continually piled in upon us to be made the best of. And there was nothing that gave us poor returns for the trouble or that one could take as little interest in carving; they were all carcass and no meat worth calling a good cut, the india rubber wings being condemned before hand and the legs barely tried, being mostly thrown away.

There was in the kitchen one large iron pot made of metal half an inch thick, that had a lid made to screw on. When closed it was almost as steam-tight as the screwed on lid of a modern glass fruit jar, and it had a safety valve like the cork of a bottle, that rose and let off steam when the inside pressure became too great.

I made this kettle and the intractable wild geese and brants acquainted with each other. The bottom was covered with slices of salt pork. One or two uions were thrown in, a dozen cloves and some bruised peppercorns, and salt. Then, as the wild geese were not stuffed or otherwise occupied, in order to economize the space, the meanest small wild ducks in the pile were sometimes crammed into the biggest geese, and the kettle was filled to its full capacity. A little water or soup stock and fat from the top was then added, the lid screwed on and the cooking began.

She would blow off steam sometimes like any other safety valve boiler—otherwise there would have been an explosion.

As most people know, water when once boiling never gets any hotter in an open vessel, but the added heat changes it to steam which goes off. But the steam if shut in can be made so hot that the pipes that confine it will brown a loaf of bread placed within a coil of them. Thus the wild geese with the steam shut in were subjected to a roasting degree of heat without the roasting dryness At the end of two hours they were as tender as young chickens, and fine and full flavored. The grease was then skimmed from the liquor remaining, and gravy made by adding water and thickening and straining it. Wild goose cooked this way soon became "all the rage." In keeping hot in the oven the outside would dry and glaze as if roasted, but in fact nobody cared whether roasted or braised, they merely called for more of that wild goose and the traveling man came again another day.

That particular pattern of iron kettle I have never met with nor been able to buy since, but imitate the method as closely as possible with the largest size of iron pots, with greased paper covers and tight fitting lids and weights on top.

1068. Roast Wild Goose, Giblet Sauce.

The method described in the foregoing article being essentially one of braising, we give here the details for the satisfactory roasting of wild geese.

It is well to remember that scalding does no good in removing the feathers, they have to be plucked dry, or partly plucked, then singed with lighted paper, and then picked over, singed again, and washed.

Take off the wings all but the first joints—the bony pinions have nothing on them. Draw the geese, and save the gizzards and hearts, but not the livers. Also keep the necks, cut off close to the body, to make the gravy. Cut off the lower part of the legs. Then wash the geese thoroughly.

Make the deepest baking pan in the kitchen hot beforehand, with salt, water and drippings in it. crowd in the geese so that they will lie close together, dredge pepper over, lay a dozen or more slices of fat salt pork over the top and slide the pan into a hot oven. Where salt pork cannot be afforded take the suet out of a loin of beef and beat it out to a sheet.

Let this cooking commence three hours before dinner, and when the pork slices are browned and shrunken cover the geese with a sheet of thick paper well greased. Baste frequently.

At the end of about two and a half hours the water should be all gone, only fat and glaze remaining, and the geese rolled over two or three times—without a fork ever being stuck into them, however—should be light brown and well glazed Then take them out before they become dry and hard.

1069. Giblet Sauce.

Boil the gizzards, hearts and necks of geese, ducks or fowls in a saucepan of soup stock or water for three hours. Add an onion and some peppercorns while they are cooking, but no salt. When tender, strain off the liquor into another vessel and cut up the gizzards, etc., into dice shaped pieces.

When the clear grease has been all poured off from the pan the geese are roasted in put in the giblet liquor instead and let it boil up and dissolve and mingle with the glaze on the pan. Strain off the gravy thus made and put into it the cut up giblets.

1070. Roast Wild Goose, Stuffed.

For stuffing, use the sage and onion dressing No. 1033. In other respects proceed as directed in the preceding article. If, as is most likely, the roasting pan should be so coated with the dressing from the geese as to be unsuitable to make sauce in, mix the cut giblets with the brown sauce of the other meats.

It takes about eight wild geese for dinner for fifty persons choosing from a bill of fare; or 12 mallard ducks or 18 small wild ducks, depending somewhat on the method of carving and on what other attractions in poultry and meats are offered.

1071. Wild Ducks.

Some South Water street game dealers who have felt interest enough in it to make note of the matter, say that about or nearly 100 different varieties of wild ducks come to their hands in the course of trade. One of them—a Mr. Maltman, I believe—has the proof of the statement to show in a stuffed specimen of each variety which he has preserved. Nine-tenths of these, however, are scarce and seldom met with, the remainder comprise the familiar varieties that are plentiful in the market and known to all. The Mallard, largest and most abundant, is fortunately one of the best as well, being a half domesticated frequenter of the cornfields and other such cultivated feeding places. The common price ranges from $2 to $3 per dozen.

The highest priced is the Canvas back, which bears a factitious value because of its reputation for a certain fine flavor said to be derived from feeding on water celery on the eastern coasts; but being found in all parts of the West, even to the Rocky mountains, is still always in demand for shipment to the eastern markets, the price being usually about $6 per dozen. The duck that is equal to the western Canvas back is the Red head. The Teals, fattest and tenderest and smallest, are in like manner very nearly equalled in quality by the Butter balls. Price, $1 to $2 per dozen.

The above mentioned are the kinds for the buyer to choose for good qualities. Then come a mixed company of Pin tails, Spoon bills, Divers, Fish ducks and others that are in the same category of hard cases with the brants and wild geese, but have the redeeming quality of being low priced.

1072. Roast Canvas back and Red Head.

These ducks are not to be stuffed; their excellence consists in their own natural flavor; but pepper and salt them inside and out. They are not to be washed, but being picked over, singed, and drawn carefully, are well wiped both inside and outside with a cloth.

Put them into a pan already hot in a hot oven— the pan only just large enough to hold the ducks, having the usual moistening of water and stock boiler fat or sweet lard in small amount, and a little salt. Roast them only from 20 to 30 minutes.

They are said to be unfit for the table if cooked five minutes too long.

They are the good carver's delight, each duck making only two dishes. With the carving fork holding the breast bone take off the meat of the entire side with both leg and wing, skillfully separating them from the carcass at the joints. No gravy required, but the natural gravy that flows from the ducks preserved and served with them the same as with roast beef.

They should be carved on a warm dish.

Serve fried potato cakes or croquettes or fried hominy cakes with canvas backs in Maryland style. For the French way, *"au cresson,"* place a bunch or border of water cress, fresh but quite free from water, in the dish.

1073. Roast Mallard Duck.

Being naturally tender, it will cook in 25 or 30 minutes, if not stuffed.

It is generally an improvement to stuff it the same as wild goose or turkey, and roast it an hour. A duck will make four dishes with dressing, cut in quarters through the bones

1074. Roast Teal and Butter ball.

These are commonly kept for broiling. Roast them in 20 minutes without stuffing. Serve halves cut down through the bones and good brown gravy poured under.

1075. Common Wild Ducks.

May be made good in the ways directed for wild geese, by slow baking. From 1 to 2 hours cooking is necessary. They can be used to good advantage in other ways besides roasting.

Articles such as small birds not found in this list of roasts will be found in place in the BOOK OF ENTREES.

1076. Boiled Ribs of Beef, with Horseradish.

Boil the same cuts as directed for roast rib ends of beef in the soup stock for 3 hours. Serve cuts 2 or 3 ribs long with a tablespoonful of grated horseradish in the dish. Less than half as many orders as of the roasted ribs are needed to be cooked this way.

1077. Boiled Salt Beef, with Vegetables.

The English and French make a more decided distinction between plain salted beef and corned beef than we do.

It would, perhaps, be difficult to gain any appreciation for the merits of plain salt beef at the American hotel table, and yet there are public eating houses, and many of them in London, where huge rounds of beef plainly salted and plainly boiled, with the gravy running out abundantly, are cut up every day. The popular accompaniment is boiled carrots; sometimes turnips, stewed peas, Brussels sprouts, (a species of small cabbage that grows in bunches on the stem) or dumplings.

Put the flank roasting piece, or the tough side of the round, in a jar with some salt and rub it with salt every day for a week. Then wash it and boil 3 or 4 hours.

The American equivalent and substitute for the foregoing is the universal corned beef and cabbage. The meats denominated *a l'ecarlate* in the English-Fresh cook books are corned meats—round of beef *a l'ecarlate*, scarlet or reddened beef. Tongue the same way. And chicken or other meats that are not corned when *a l'ecarlate* are ornamented, larded or mixed with corned meats, such as red tongue.

1078. Corned Beef and Cabbage.

This is a dish almost as permanent in the hotel bill of fare as the roast beef itself, and almost as necessary.

The whole subject of corned beef—making the brine or pickle, general management and cooking—has been fully treated of already at No. 792 and succeeding articles. Were any tender cuts of meat ever corned in the hotel economization of material two or three hours' boiling might be as good as the five hours' there recommended. But the first requisite to making any dish of meat popular is to have it sufficiently tender. The best brisket pieces for corning are the gristliet, and when it is a matter of choice betwixt starting the cooking of the corned beef before the busy time of breakfast begins or waiting till the opportunity arrives afterwards, which will probably be not till 10 o'clock, it is always advisable to take the early hour.

1079. To Boil Cabbage.

Cut one large head or two small ones, if to go with corned beef alone, or twice as much if to serve as a vegetable besides, into quarters, and cut away the thick stem. Let remain in a pan of cold water till wanted.

Two hours before dinner put it into a pot of water that is already boiling and has a little salt and a pinch of baking soda in it. Young summer cabbage will cook in from 30 minutes to 1 hour, solid winter cabbage from 1 to 2 hours.

It does not follow because a little soda in the water is good that more must be better. Use, say, half a teaspoonful. It keeps the leaves of summer cabbage green and softens winter cabbage so that it cooks in half the time required without soda.

When nearly done, drain off the cabbage in a colander, fill up with liquor from the corned beef boiler, or with part water, if that is too salt, and boil again. At last drain off again and chop it a little in the same vessel.

Dish a spoonful in a flat dish and a slice of corned beef on top.

1080. New England Boiled Dinner.

One of the first favorites in restaurants where each dish bears a stated price, being a complete dinner or two kinds of meat and a variety of vegetables, with bread at the side.

The price in the best Chicago restaurants is 25 cents, (the cuts and the dish it is served on being both of a liberal size.

The New England boiled dinner is generally disfavored by hotel keepers as a hotel dinner dish, because, however good and complete it is, through the unbreakable routine of the waiters and cooks who dish up the vegetables, the person ordering is pretty certain to get a duplicate set of vegetables placed before him along with the additional meat or entree that he will call for himself. The result is the waste of about the amount of one person's dinner.

The dish consists of:

1 or 2 slices of boiled corned beef.
1 smaller slice of boiled salt pork.
1 spoonful of boiled cabbage.
1 potato.
1 parsnip.
1 carrot.
1 turnip.
1 onion.
1 beet.

Or, pieces of the above vegetables equivalent in size to the spoonful of cabbage. Place the vegetables in the dish (a 7 or 8 inch flat platter) and the meat slices on top.

1081. Boiled Mutton, Caper Sauce.

The leg of mutton is the proper cut to boil. If there is sufficient demand for it there should be two at once, one cooked rare in about one hour, the other well done in one and one-half hours.

Drop the mutton into water or the soup stock that is already boiling, and be careful never to put a fork into it. The gravy should run from a leg of a mutton when cut the same as from roast beef.

When the boned scrag end of the neck, rolled up and tied with twine, or the rolled shoulder is cooked for boiled mutton the above rules do not apply, but these should be boiled three hours to make them tender.

For caper sauce, see Nos. 916 and 928, or the following.

1082. Pickle Sauce, for Mutton and Tongue.

1 pint of clear strained soup stock.
Flour and water thickening.
Butter size of an egg.
1 pickled cucumber.
Salt.

Set the stock or water on to boil, thicken it to the consistency of butter sauce. Beat in the butter a small piece at a time, and salt to taste. If not good yellow butter the yolk of an egg will improve the color. Chop the pickled cucumber and mix it in.

1083. Boiled Tongue.

An ox tongue needs to boil three hours to be tender. When done, take it up, dip in cold water, and peel off the skin. Serve sliced with caper sauce or sauce piquant.

1084. Piquant Sauce.

Is brown sauce made pleasantly sharp and relishing with vinegar, a piece of onion, some bruised peppercorns, and half a bayleaf boiled in it. Strain it and add a few capers or chopped pickle, making it in effect a brown caper sauce.

1085. Boiled Corned Tongue.

Boil the tongue three hours. Dip it in cold water and peel off the skin. Carve it slanting across to make long and thin slices and serve like boiled ham without sauce.
Directions for corning tongues at No. 792.

1086. Boiled Ham.

See directions at No. 1035. To glaze a ham to slice cold, No. 812.
The butt end of a ham and shank left over when the rest has been sliced for broiling will be sufficiently well done in one hours' boiling.

1087. Boiled Ox Heart, with Gravy

A fair proportion of this kind of meat which usually goes slowly or not at all can be disposed of by cooking it as follows:
Boil it not less than three hours in the salt meat boiler, or, if not there convenient, in the stock boiler. Carve it in broad slices and serve brown gravy with it. One such heart per day will generally be consumed if it is cooked tender. It is poor policy to warm any over and use it the second day, when a fresh one may be had for the asking. Wash the inside cavities free from blood before cooking.

1088. Boiled Turkey, Oyster Sauce.

Detailed directions for boiling a turkey may be found at No. 1046.
White oyster sauce at No. 852.
The same sauce is suitable with boiled chicken.

1089. Boiled Chicken, with Salt Pork.

Boiled fowls go a little further than roast, perhaps because no part of them is dried, but all can be carved and served advantageously.
Boil the fowls in the soup stock, salted, but without any spice flavorings, for a time, according to the kind. Chickens may be done in one-half hour, old fowls in 2 to 4 hours. They can be tried occasionally while boiling.
Parboil about 3 pounds of salt or pickled pork and afterwards finish cooking it in the same boiler with the chickens—it will need to cook about one and one-half hours. Serve a small slice of the pickled pork with each dish of chicken.

Chicken cooked as above in liquor slightly salted does not need a sauce, but if needed for better appearance use either butter or cream sauce, with perhaps, a little parsley minced and mixed in.

1090. Boiled Chicken, Egg Sauce.

Boil chickens and serve with egg sauce No. 936, Boiled turkey the same way.

1091. Boiled Chicken, Celery Sauce.

Boil chickens and serve with the white celery sauce of the next receipt. Boiled turkey the same way.

1092. White Celery Sauce.

Boil the outside stalks of celery, about 6 or 8—white, tender and good stalks, but such as are left in the celery glasses when the hearts have been picked out—for about 20 minutes. Cut them in small pieces.
Make cream sauce, No. 931, put the pieces of celery in and let simmer a short time to extract the flavor.

1093. Boiled Jowl and Spinach.

Steep two jowls in warm water and scrub off the rank, smoky outside with a brush. Boil for three hours in a vessel by themselves. Trim and shave along the lips and on the outside fat. Serve sliced on top of spinach in a dish. See hams and spinach, No. 1035.

1094. Boiled Pork and Sauer Kraut.

Rinse off the sauer kraut in cold water. Boil it from 2 to 3 hours. Drain, and keep it hot in a sink of the steam chest.
Boil a piece of pickled pork about one and a half or two hours, the latter part of the time in the sauer kraut. Serve slices on top of the kraut in the dish.

There are people of other nationalities who evidently think they know more about making sauer kraut than Americans do. But then even the doctors disagree.
A German has been heard to say of American sauer kraut: "It is too salt. Barrel should have two inches of salt laid on bottom, then filled with shred cabbage very hard pressed down. Stand a week or two, then put in a gallon of vinegar—that's better than all your salt."
And a Swede answers:
"We don't put any vinegar in. Let the cabbage stand till it makes its own sourness; always hard pressed down."

1095. Imitation Sauer Kraut—Made as Wanted.

Shred some white cabbage in the usual way of shaving up for sauer kraut over night, press it down in a jar and cover it with a mixture of vinegar and water and salt. When to be cooked next morning take it out of the pickle, wash it, and boil it in water with a cupful of vinegar in it, a little salt and piece of pickled pork. Cook two or three hours. The same pickle in the jar can be used again. It should be one-third vinegar.

1096. Keeping Meat to Make it Tender.

Our friends, the butchers, have always the answer ready to the complaint that the meat is tough, that we in hotels don't give it a chance to become tender for we don't keep it long enough. They say' with good reason too, that the best meat they kill is not tender the day after it is killed; that game, even the largest game, is tenderer than butcher's meat, partly because such a considerable interval elapses between the killing and the cooking of it; that their beef shipped by rail and vessel improves in the time and is just right for eating when it reaches its destination; that in the old countries where the study of good eating has been carried to the highest pitch the rich hang their meats till they are in danger of spoiling, both for tenderness and enhanced flavor.

While all this is true it is a matter generally beyond the control of the cook. It is easy to see that the large butchers who can keep a stock of meat on hand have an advantage over the small butchers who cannot though the latter may buy equally as good stock; and easy to see that if the butcher kills regularly every afternoon and the hotel buyer buys regularly at nine o'clock the next morning, and the cook has to put the meat to the fire immediately for dinner, that that hotel may go on the year round always having tough meat, although it may be cut from equally as good animals and bought at an equally high price with another hotel that always has good meat because it has a good place—cool, dry and dark—to keep it a few days in, and because it has a buyer who is aware that keeping does make a difference.

1097. The Vinegar Remedy.

It has been published before, notably in a book dated 1857, and has since been revived, the statement that to rub or steep tough meat in vinegar would make it tender. It is mentiond here for the purpose of saying with genuine sorrow that the remedy is no good. It is possible to keep cut beefsteaks that would spoil before night a considerable time longer by covering them with vinegar, but as they are then sour all through their last state is not much better than the first. However, our readers will try it for themselves.

1098. Hotel Broiling.

The propriety of having a hotel cook book for hotels especially is apparent in nothing so much as in the peculiar conditions of hotel broiling. It seems to have been the fashion ever since the art of printing was discovered and cook books began to be made for the cook to broil the meats as he pleased or rather as he was told by the instructors to do and for the people at table to receive what was given them gratefully, never questioning, but what the cooks in their superior wisdom sent them must be the best. But evidently now "the times are out of joint;" the tables are turned; it has got to be so that the people at the hotel table will not have it that smooth and easy way, but they have learned to do the ordering and the cooks have to do the obeying, and all our teachers' authoritative instructions have not now the weight of a feather. This makes the hotel broiler's a very difficult position. He is baffled about by every wind of opinion that blows about the dining room tables. He must be all mind, yet have no mind of his own; must understand and remember everything and feel nothing, either ludicrous or offensive. There are very few really good hotel broilers.

Of course it is not merely to broil for this one rare, that one medium and another one well done—these simple movements are varied like the movements in a grand dance, in a large and good hotel, and the broiling cook gets dizzy.

Let us both for direct instruction and for the exhibition of a matter that is very little understood suppose a case in a medium sized hotel having, say, two hundred guests attended at table by twenty waiters.

Breakfast is a little the most troublesome meal and there is always what is known to the hands as the first rush, when probably 15 out of the 20 waiters will come at once, each giving perhaps five person's orders for probably five different articles each. In preparation for this commencement there are a long range glowing with heat and two bright glowing charcoal broilers. At least, as we do not love pictures of misery, we will hope there are two charcoal burners for so many. We will hope, too, that the charcoal will glow; that it is not kept where it gets snowed upon or rained upon and that it is not half dust and dirt, and that the chimney has a good draft.

The pans of cut meats are brought out of the refrigerator at the minute of opening the doors. There are two, perhaps three of them, with beef, veal, mutton, lamb, fresh pork and chicken, ham, bacon, salt pork, liver, tripe, pig's feet, kidneys, venison and sliced dried beef; salmon steak, salt mackerel and whitefish, and they are set on the zinc table in front of the girdirons. There is a dish of various cold cooked meats somewhere near at hand. The short order cook has the middle of the table and the middle of the range for cooking eggs and omelets, frying breaded articles, and perhaps he has the potatoes and onions, fried mush and tripe in batter, and the like. There are, already prepared, a dish of grated or minced cheese for cheese omelets, minced ham and parsley for omelets of those descriptions, tomatoes and garlic, onion and minced peppers for Spanish omelets and beefsteaks, and a shallow pan half full of eggs ready broken stands ready with a ladle in it to dip them out for cooking, and another with ready made omelet mixture of eggs with a little milk and salt. Shallow saucepans are simmering on the range for poached eggs, and if there are no steam cooking apparatus, others, at least two, are ready for boiling eggs, while a tray of dishes ready buttered are there for eggs shirred. A row of omelet and frying pans rest on the bright bar along the front of the range ready for fried and scrambled. It would lead too far from the broiler to note the stews, the special sauces, the boiled mushes, two or three kinds; the hot breads and cakes, hot milk, coffee, teas and chocolate, and how, after all, some persons will send out for the special sort of cocoa or broma that is not there.

At first it runs along smooth and straight. Some three or four veal cutlets have been breaded and fried beforehand and perhaps two each of pork and mutton. Some more ready breaded are in the pans and will be cooked as ordered after the first rush is satisfied. On the left of the broiler's position there is a little side shelf or bracket used for nothing else, on which he has a plate, a small pan of melted butter and a tin bound flat brush. The ordinary orders come and he takes the steak or chop, lays it on the plate and draws the butter brush over it, oiling it just sufficiently to prevent sticking to the girdiron but never enough to drip. Then he once more polishes the girdiron by rubbing it as hard as possible with a coarse cloth, lays the meats on it and then dredges them all at once, so as to save time, with a mixture of two-thirds fine salt and one-third black pepper. These are beefsteaks or chops or cutlets either rare or well done as ordered without further comment—except that an order comes—"and be sure to season it well while it's cooking," which is immediately followed by an order for "plenty of butter gravy but no salt and pepper on it." These two orders of course must be kept in view separately among all the others on the girdiron, but that is nothing but routine. Presently, however, a waiter comes, and after crying off an order for four or five, or a family, taking an assortment of articles from here and there over the whole length and breadth of the kitchen winds up with—"and 3 steaks, 3 poached eggs and 2 boiled mackerels and 1 broiled for the Three Old Butter Maids."

As the orders, not of this waiter alone but of half a dozen before have been dropped the different cooks or assistants have picked up each the items that fell to their department, and the broiler, with his girdirons full of meats ordered to be of several different shades when done is supposed to have them all in his head in regular routine and still listening ready to store his mind with more, but the order of the three old butter maids proves to be a disturbing element.

The appellation given to the three distinguished guests has no suggestion of humor in it for these workers; it is not even disrespectful; it is merely an abbreviation or sign understood between the waiter and the broiling and frying cooks and by no one else, adopted through necessity where there is a difficulty in even getting heard in regular turn. Really it should have been "the three butter old maids," but the word butter was out of rythm and the waiter was conscious of it and placed it the other way. The parties alluded to are not even old maids at all, but a mother and her two young daughters, but the necessity of having a sign for them overrode all trifling facts like that. The simple explanation is that when they arrived they impressed it upon the waiter, who took a leisure minute to impress it in turn upon the cook, that butter was their particular abhorrence, that their physician had forbidden them to eat butter, that they could not touch any article that had been prepared with it, or had any in its composition, and they could not stay in any hotel twelve hours unless they were guaranteed perfect exemption from butter. Consequently the late order means that the steaks are not to be touched with the butter brush, nor yet the broiled mackerel, that the boiled mackerel must not have the usual tablespoonful poured over it in the dish, and although the poached eggs must be served upon toast the toast must be unbuttered, and all this and much more is conveyed in the four words. It adds to the disturbance of the routine when an instant after another waiter in loud and significant tones calls for "a full order of breakfast bacon for the Twice-turned-over-and-done-to-a-crisp Old Man," because the bacon creating flame and smoke will perhaps give a taste that the butter maids will swear (figuratively) is butter and raise a rumpus about it, and the trouble increases when the next wants "pork chops in crumbs and butter for the family-with-no-eggs," the latter meaning that these have as thorough an aversion to everything containing eggs as the others for butter, and their breaded and broiled cutlets must be specially prepared for them either with batter and crumbs, or crumbs pressed on plain and buttered on them while broiling. The family-with-no-egg will send out and ask whether there is eggs in the soup and the ice cream and the entrees before they order, and have special puddings and cakes made for them. But that is neither here nor there. Neither, perhaps, is the fish that ought to be when the order comes for "a broiled big trout for The General-split-down-the-back-and-bacon-inside," which, of course, is an unexpected order from a great man who pays extra, and the broiler must try to procure that trout even if he has his two gridirons full of meats at the time.

While, therefore, we wish the broiling cook well and hope he will survive where it is a case of the survival of the fittest, it is sad to have to say that very little help can be offered, seeing that no cast iron rules can ever be adapted to the circumstances.

It is wrong and very foolish for him to lose his temper and his patience and get to quarrelling with the waiters and losing track of things and mixing orders, even if the steak that he has sent in cut thin and dried like a shoe sole is sent back to him for "more fire," because the person has succeeded by hard pressure in forcing out one drop of gravy and declares it not done; or the steak barely warmed is returned as too well done by another, who sighs as he declares that he has searched half the country over for a hotel where he could get a steak cooked rare. The broiling cook should remain imperturbable. The people in the dining room are not fighting him but are having their own duels across the table. The well done party opposite has contrived to show intense disgust at this man's raw beefsteak, and he, perhaps, for pure deviltry, has sent out for one redder yet.

Seriously, the most of the difficulties that arise and lead to the frequent changes of cooks and the host of small inconveniences resulting, and get for the cooks the stigma of being "always on the wing," and worse things, begin over the meat broiler, but might be prevented, and in well governed hotels are prevented, by some quiet person in authority keeping watch for one hour and bringing up a little help when the skirmish grows serious—to mince the cheese for an omelet, that was forgotten, to replenish the meat pans, to prepare the unexpected trout order, possibly, in extreme cases, even to give the half roasted cook a spell long enough to wipe the perspiration from his face and get a drink—of water, of course.

1099. Broiling Beefsteas.

The exceptions and provisos being noted above it remains to be said that it is not quite optional whether in regular course the steaks and chops should be previously brushed over with butter or not, for when the meat is poor and lean that is the only way there is to prevent it from sticking to the bars and being torn in turning and causing delay. Most people like the butter seasoning, the meats go in looking the better for it, and most hotel keepers make it a point to provide good, sweet butter for that purpose. Where such is not the case the fat from fried breakfast bacon is the best substitute—to broil with, not to pour on the steaks when done—and failing that, fresh roast meat drippings can be used. Where it is desired to broil the meats absolutely plain rub the bars of the gridiron with a ham rind and be careful not to let the bars get too hot.

When broiling fat mutton and pork chops and the flames are troublesome and make the meat throw coarse salt on the charcoal, it will generally extinguish them, and another expedient is to raise the gridiron to the highest position, shut down the front and so create such a draft that the flames will be carried horizontally towards the chimney without the meat above being touched by them.

1100. Beefsteak with Natural Gravy.

Beefsteaks and other meats carefully broiled with the fork never thrust into them except in the fat edge or a loose corner yield a gravy of their own on the dish after a few minutes. In addition to this a few rough and coarse slices cut thick can be broiled half done and kept in a pan or dish, and if pierced with a fork several times will yield perhaps a cupful of gravy for special orders. Invalids often beg for this sort of sauce where it seems to be thought impossible to furnish it.

1101. "Old-Fashioned" Broiled Beefsteak and Gravy.

Probably the term is a misnomer for the same sort of steak must still be in fashion in some places, but that is the way we hear it spoken of. Orders and polite requests from people who have made themselves at home in the hotel sometimes reach the kitchen that are quite unintelligible. When it is for a fried steak with old fashioned gravy, and the brown sauce or stew gravy sent them does not fill the bill, we begin to think they mean this following; but it is not in the regular routine, and they will hardly succeed in obtaining it.

You take a whole sirloin steak, pretty nearly as long as your arm and proportionately broad, notch the rough edges to prevent curling, and make a show of beating it out a little on the kitchen table. Put a shovelful of charcoal in the ash-pan of the steamboat range, or the front of the country hotel stove, draw some hot coals on that, and when it is all aglow, put on your four-legged gridiron and the steak and pan inverted over it, and let it cook medium well done.

Put one-half pound of butter into a pan and about a tablespoonful of black pepper, and as much salt, and mix them together; take the steak up into the pan and press it into the butter, and press out all its juices, then pour in a cup of hot water, set the pan over the coals, and when it begins to simmer the meat gravy and pepper will have thickened the water, and there is your old-fashioned steak. The sequel is, somebody will carve it into pieces about the size of two fingers, and the people will pass up their plates and get their spoonful of the gravy.

The next thing to broiling for that kind of beefsteak is frying over the fire, but a little piece in a pan does not come out natural-looking, but burns around the edges—it must be a full pan or nothing.

1102. Broiled Porterhouse Steak.

An expedient adopted in some restaurants for getting a large and thick beefsteak done in a reasonable time, and to preserve its flat shape is to have two fire bricks, well polished, on the gridiron hot, and place one or both on the steak while broiling the first side. After turning over the brick must be set aside to allow the gravy to collect on the top of the steak.

Time for broiling six to ten minutes. Serve with some sort of potatoes around and quartered lemon on top.

1103. French Beefsteak.

A tenderloin or fillet steak broiled, and fried potato balls or other fancy cut potatoes around it in the dish with butter and quartered lemon.

1104. Beefsteak Maître d'Hôtel.

Broil a beefsteak and place it on a hot dish, chop up a lump of butter in a small frying pan over the fire, when it is melted throw in a teaspoonful of chopped parsley, then pour it over the steak. Cut a lemon in four. Squeeze the juice of two pieces over the steak, and place the other two quarters in the dish as a garnish.

1105. Beefsteak, Sauce Piquante.

Broil a beefsteak fairly well done and pour over it the following sauce:

Put into a small saucepan one-half cupful of brown sauce, a basting-spoon of stock to thin it down, one half a bay leaf, a level teaspoonful of bruised pepper-corns and a basting-spoon of good vinegar or caper vinegar. Let is boil rapidly while the steak is cooking, then strain it and throw in a teaspoonful of capers.

1106. Beefsteak with Champignons.

Broil a beefsteak and pour around and over it a quarter can or more of French mushrooms prepared as follows:

Put the mushrooms drained dry into a small frying pan with a little butter, shake about on the range until they begin to brown. Draw the mushrooms to one side, and work into the hot butter a small tablespoonful of flour. Pour in half mushroom liquor and half water, stir smooth, season with salt and pepper and a squeeze of lemon, boil up and dish.

1107. English Rump Steak with Mushrooms.

Broil a slice from the "silver side" or tender side of the round of beef, cut rather thick, and a little underdone, and serve it with broiled, baked, or fried fresh mushrooms, as follows:

1108. Fresh Mushrooms.

For an accompaniment to broiled meat the canned button mushrooms bear no comparison in richness with the large, wide-open, fresh mushrooms from the fields. At least fifty varieties of mushrooms are eaten in European countries, and there are kinds that are poisonous. We know but one kind and take no risks on the others. The true mushroom is of a delicate pink or flesh color on the under side when it first opens, and darkens to chocolate color and then black, according to the time it continues growing.

When such can be obtained cut off most of the stem, peel the top of the mushroom, shake about in cold water to free it [from grit or sand, and fry (saute) enough of them together in a little butter in a frying pan to touch and cover the bottom while cooking. They shrink very much, but give out a gravy of the richest description, which should not be allowed to dry up in the pan. Season with pepper and salt. When the mushrooms are done—in six or eight minutes—place them on top of the beefsteak and pour the gravy and butter over likewise.

Another way, most suitable when the mushrooms are to form a dish alone, is to place them top downwards in a baking pan, dredge with salt and pepper, put a small piece of butter in each, bake done and serve without turning over.

1109. Spanish Beefsteak.

Broil a beefsteak fairly well done, and serve it laid on top of the following sauce in a hot dish: Put into a frying-pan an ounce of butter, and while it is gradually melting cut up a clove of garlic and a small onion, and fry them slightly yellow; put in either four peeled tomatoes or two basting-spoonfuls from a can, and one-half pod of red pepper minced, and a little salt. Let stew down nearly dry, and place in the dish neatly with a spoon.

1110 Beefsteak with Tomatoes.

Mash a few peeled tomatoes—or use some from a can—in a saucepan over the fire. Season with butter, pepper and salt, and let stew down thick without burning. Dish around the steak.

1111. Devilled Beefsteak.

Broiled beefsteak with a sauce made of half brown sauce and half Worcestershire or Halford sauce mixed together and made hot.

1112. Beefsteak with Onions.

Shave two onions thin as possible into a frying-pan, put in a little lard and butter, turn a plate upside down upon them and fry them done in five minutes. Take off the plate and let them begin to brown. Drain from grease in one side of the pan, then dish them on top of the steak in a hot dish.

1113. Beefsteak Milanaise.

Boil four sticks of macaroni broken up in salted water for twenty minutes. Drain out, shake it up with a spoonful of butter and a spoonful of tomato sauce; turn it into a hot dish and place the broiled beefsteak on top.

1114. Beefsteak with Oysters.

Broil a beefsteak and serve it with brown oyster sauce (Nos. 853 and 854.)

1115 Hamburgh Steak.

Beef chopped into sausage meat—one-fourth fat or suet—and seasoned with onion and a little garlic, pepper and salt.

Chop the beef or put it through a sausage cutter. With a four ounce pat of it mix one-half clove of garlic and a teaspoonful of minced onion, both minced fine, and one half teaspoon of mixed pepper and salt. Flatten it out to a cake in a frying-pan, quite thin, fry on both sides, dish with its own gravy poured over and Lyonaise potatoes around.

Numbers of people who like Hamburgh steak either cannot or dare not eat the garlic and onions, in such cases those seasonings can be omitted, and only salt and pepper used. Hamburgh steak should be made of tender meat, but the ill-shaped and small pieces left when cutting the loin answer for it. The attempt to use really tough beef in this way defeats itself, for the steaks are not good, and are then no more called for.

1116. Lyonaise Potatoes.

Cold boiled potatoes sliced into a frying-pan with a little drippings, and browned more or less, as at No. 878, and called in the restaurants saute or Dutch fried potatoes, are also most frequently served in public places as Lyonaise, because of the very general objection that exists to eating fried onions. That is to say the onions are left out of Lyonaise for accommodation, just as they are out of Hamburgh steak when so ordered.

To make Lyonaise potatoes mince an onion—about a tablespoonful—into a frying-pan, put in as much drippings, and fry the onion a light color, then put in cooked potatoes cut thick, pepper and salt. Let them slowly brown on the bottom at the side of the range, then shake the pan so as to throw the brown side on top, and continue cooking until they are evenly colored.

See also minced potatoes, No. 868. Among the various contrary orders that reach the hotel and restaurant cook, some wish them that way. Minced onions can be cooked and mixed with the minced potatoes.

1117. Broiled Mutton Chops.

Single chops broil about four or five minutes, and serve with a small spoonful of melted fresh butter and sprigs of parsley in the dish. They are called for and served in all the same ways as beefsteak.

1118. A Dish of Mutton Chops.

Broil the required number, and cut as many pieces of thin buttered toast to the same shape. Set the chops on end leaning in the dish, and the pieces of toast placed alternately between them. Garnish with parsley and lemon.

1119. Mutton Chops with Tomato Sauce.

Broiled mutton chops and pour around them tomato sauce made as follows:

1120. Tomato Sauce.

Boil a few tomatoes, or part of a can, mash with the back of a spoon, and throw in three or four cloves, and a teaspoon of minced onion. Thicken with a teaspoonful of flour, and twice as much butter browned together in a frying-pan, then rub the sauce through a strainer, or if in haste, through a small colander. Season with salt and pepper.

1121. Lamb Chops with Green Peas.

Broil lamb chops three or four minutes, place two or three or more, leaning and overlapping, in a dish and pour green peas made hot, either in butter or in cream sauce, around them.

1122. Broiled Pork Chops with Milk Gravy.

Fry the chops first, then lay them on the gridiron, as they are hard to cook, while you pour half a cup of milk in the pan, pepper and salt, and thicken with browned flour-and-butter, or with plain thickening. Strain the sauce into the dish and lay the chop in it.

1123. Broiled Slices of Salt Pork.

Dip the slices in flour before broiling; they color better and do not drip so much fat.

1124. Broiled Ham and Eggs.

Broil broad thin slices of ham over clear coals, nicely colored on both sides in four minutes. Place the ham a little towards one end in a roomy dish and the fried eggs partly resting on the ham and partly in the dish.

1125. Broiled Liver and Bacon.

Calf's liver is the best. The liver should be sliced broad but thin. Brush over the slice with bacon fat, pepper and salt it and broil five minutes. Serve with a strip of bacon on top.

1126. Broiled Breakfast Bacon.

The endeavor should be made as far as possible to avoid broiling bacon whenever frying or baking will serve the purpose as well. It is not only exceedingly wasteful, as most affect it done to a crisp, a mere crackling, but it destroys the broiling fire, flares and smokes more than any other article. If fried carefully most of it will be saved in the form of fat, which is useful in sauteeing potatoes and otherwise.

1127. Broiled Liver, Plain.

Dip the slices of liver in flour and broil them. When about done spread a teaspoonful of soft butter on each side, let it continue broiling until the butter is in a froth, then serve it hot

1128. Broiled Honeycomb Tripe.

Cook precisely as directed above for liver, with care not to have any surplus flour filling the cavities. Serve the honeycomb side up and garnish with parsley and a cut of lemon.

1129. Broiled Kidneys.

Sheep's kidneys are the best, calf's are next best, Slice them for broiling through the suet, before taking them out, then trim off the surrounding fat, except a small rim all around. Put them in the hinged wire toaster, pepper, salt and butter them and broil a little longer time than beefsteaks, or until fairly cooked through. Serve with a little butter and whatever of their own gravy may have collected on top.

Kidneys are good at two periods in cooking: when they are barely done through, and again after they have been stewed two or three hours. In the intermediate time they are hard and undesirable.

1130. Economy of Broiled Meats.

Chops, steaks, etc., that are cooked through mistake of orders or are sent back as too well done and for other reasons, should be put into a small pan of well-seasoned gravy, like the "old-fashioned" beefsteak at No. 1101, and so kept fresh and savory. They will always be in demand for some persons.

1131. Easy Broiling of Fish.

Fresh fish now transported for long distances, often, after frost, comes out too soft to be easily broiled. Dip the pieces or sides of such in flour, and butter while broiling, the same as liver and tripe, and they will not adhere to the gridiron nor break up.

Salt mackerel that has not had time to get dry and would not brown otherwise can be well broiled in the same way.

1132. Broiled Chickens.

Split down the back to draw them, wash, and wipe dry. Flatten the chickens down with a blow of the cleaver. Brush over with butter and broil about ten minutes. If large, place the hot brick on top, mentioned at No. 1102.

Make some butter gravy as at 1101, in a pan, and press the chickens down in it as cooked until enough have been broiled for the hotel breakfast. Restaurant orders have various accessories such as peas and tomatoes to go with broiled chicken.

1133. Broiled Quail on Toast.

Everything, so to speak, is in the looks. It should not lie on the toast humped up and with the limbs pointing many different ways, but should lie flat, round and compact. This is accomplished by flattening the quail, after opening and cleaning it sufficiently, with a few pats of the cleaver to depress the breast bone and loosen the joints, not necessarily to mash the meat or make splinters in it. Split the quail down the back to open it, like a young chicken, rinse off in cold water and wipe it dry and brush over with butter. Broil it about eight minutes, perhaps with the hot brick on top if in haste. Have ready a little melted butter, pepper and salt in a pan, press the quail down into it, dish on toast and garnish if required.

To make a neat appearance, the toast should be cut to shape. Cut a square slice of toast diagonally across, making two triangles, and place the broad ends together in the dish.

1134. Broiled Snipe and Plover.

Not different from quail except in the time required for cooking, which is less than for quail, and the different sorts of potatoes, mushrooms, sauces, etc., that are required with restaurant orders.

1135. Broiled Young Rabbit.

Rabbits broiled are much neater in appearance and more evenly cooked if they can be had before they are dressed, and split down the back with a strong knife and so laid open. Wash and wipe dry, flatten them with the cleaver, brush over with bacon fat or butter, and broil about 15 minutes with the two hot fire bricks on top. Dip in butter gravy or pour a little over them. Broiled salt pork or bacon laid on top for restaurant orders and potatoes around in the dish.

1136. Broiled Squirrel.

The same as rabbit but taking less time to cook.

1137. Broiled Teal Duck.

Prepare for broiling like chicken and quail, cook with the inside downwards first and the hot brick on top, then turn them over, lay the brick aside and baste with a little butter. They take about 12 or 15 minutes to cook. Serve with butter gravy and lemon, or currant jelly, or orange sauce.

For hotel breakfasts they are best done in a pan on the top shelf in the range.

1138. Boiled Eggs.

The best furnished hotel kitchens have a kettle much like a long fish kettle in appearance, and a number of tin baskets, each with its handle, that fit in side by side. The kettle is full of boiling water, and the baskets with different orders of eggs can be withdrawn without disturbing the others. One hand is detailed to attend to the egg boiling, and he has sand glasses to time them by, or a clock or both. At ordinary levels two or three minutes for soft-boiled and four or five for hard-boiled is the rule, but at great altitudes in the Rocky Mountains as much as eight minutes is the least time for hard-boiled eggs. The low point at which water boils is the reason for the difference.

1139. Poached Eggs.

Also called dropped eggs.

It is no trouble to poach eggs handsomely if two or three rules are observed.

Have a roomy vessel with plenty of water, the frying-pan shape is good, but it is not deep enough. Have a little salt in the water. Never let the water boil furiously after the eggs are in, as that breaks them; keep it gently simmering at the sides.

The eggs break and are wasted because when first dropped they go heavily to the hot bottom and there stick, to prevent which set the water in motion by stirring it around with a spoon. The eggs dropped in are carried around a moment and the white cooks sufficiently to prevent adhesion.

Break the eggs carefully into little dishes and drop into the water one at a time. Take them out with a perforated ladle.

Serve either well drained in a small deep dish and a speck of butter on top or else laid neatly on a trimmed slice of buttered toast.

1140. Fried Eggs.

These are the most called-for of any form in which eggs are cooked and there is the widest possible difference between the work of a skillful and unskillful cook in this particular. The fried eggs that are a disgrace to any table are broken as to the yolks before they go in the pan, then they have black grease simmering up all around the edges and running over their surface, they are cooked nearly as hard as leather, they stick to the pan and cannot be turned over and finally when they are forcibly pushed into a dish the same smoky, black grease flows around them like gravy. That it should happen so sometimes is nothing to be remarked, but these lines are prompted by amazement that some will go on frying eggs that way always and habitually and do not seem to know that anything is wrong.

To fry eggs cleanly and handsomely, keep the small frying pans always rubbed clean, if not bright, and never set them empty upon the range but keep them warm on the bar along the front of it or on a hot shelf or a row of bricks at the back.

Put into the pan not more than a tablespoonful of clear melted lard. Break the eggs into small dishes if for a few people, two in a dish; for a large number break several dozens into a pail and take out by twos with a ladle. Put them into the warm pan and then set on the range and they will not stick or break in the pan. Shake them only after the yolks have begun to set.

Fried eggs are called for "straight up and soft"— which means only done on the under side; cooked hard, which sometimes requires the pan to be held inside the oven; half turned over, which is doubled in half upon itself; and turned over, which can be done with an egg-slice.

1141. Scrambled Eggs.

Not to be beaten up like an omelet but dropped into the frying-pan, sprinkled with pepper and salt and stirred around about a dozen times with a fork or spoon while cooking. Take out before they cook quite dry and hard; heap in the middle of a flat dish.

1142. Buttered Eggs.

Put two eggs, two tablespoonfuls of melted butter and a pinch of salt into a small saucepan or tin cup, set it in the boiling water on the range and rapidly beat it until cooked thick enough, either to serve on toast or like scrambled eggs in a dish.

1143. Shirred Eggs.

Some people keep little yellow-ware dishes for this purpose, or other dishes that cannot be damaged by baking. Spread with a teaspoon a slight coating of soft butter over the inside of the dish, drop in two eggs, not beaten, and set them inside the oven, or, perhaps, on the top of the range on one side. Try by shaking, and take them out when the whites are quite cooked. Send in in the same dish set in a flat one.

1144. Plain Omelet.

Two eggs and one tablespoonful of milk. Add a pinch of salt, beat in a bowl enough to thoroughly mix but not make it too light, as if the omelet rises like a souffle it will go down again, so much the worse. Pour it into a small frying pan, or omelet pan, in which is one tablespoonful of the clear part of melted butter, and fry like fried eggs. But when partly set run a knife point around to loosen it and begin and shake the omelet over to the further side of the pan until the thin further edge forced upward falls back into the omelet. When the under side has a good color, and the middle is nearly set, roll the brown side uppermost, with a knife to help, and slide the omelet on to a hot dish. Serve immediately while it is light and soft.

1145. Omelet with Parsley.

Mix a tablespoonful of minced parsley with the omelet mixture while beating it up. Make as directed in the preceding article.

1146. Omelet with Onions and Parsley

Mince two tablespoonfuls of onion and fry it in a little lard in a frying-pan with a plate inverted upon it. In five minutes take up the minced onion without grease and add it to the omelet mixture made ready with parsley in it; stir up and fry as directed for plain omelet.

1147. Omelet with Ham.

Have ready on the table some grated or minced lean ham in a dish. Pour a plain omelet of two eggs into the frying-pan and strew over the surface about a tablespoonful of the grated ham.

1148. Omelet with Cheese.

Make in the same manner as ham omelet, with grated cheese instead of ham.

1149. Omelet with Kidneys.

Have ready a spoonful of kidneys in sauce, the same as for patties or minced kidneys. When the omelet has been shaken to the further side of the pan and is nearly done place the spoonful of kidneys lengthwise in the hollow middle and roll the omelet over so as to inclose it.

1150. Omelet with Chicken Livers.

By the same method as with kidneys, using poultry livers that have been stewed, and cut up into a rich sauce.

1151. Oyster Omelet.

For omelet with oysters see No. 833. For another way cut the oysters in pieces in a brown butter sauce as follows:

Put a large half cupful of oysters into a frying-pan with their liquor, and salt and pepper, and keep them in motion by shaking over the fire until they are soft-cooked. Take up with a skimmer and cut them in pieces.

Stir a heaping teaspoonful of sifted flour and twice the measure of butter together in a very small saucepan over the fire until light brown, add half a cupful of milk and the cooked oyster liquor, if any, and when it has boiled up put in the cut oysters. Squeeze in the juice of a quarter of lemon. Make an omelet in the usual way and pour the oysters in sauce over it.

1152. Spanish Omelet.

Stew tomatoes down nearly dry with garlic, onions and minced pepper, as detailed for Spanish beefsteak, No. 1109, place the preparation in the hollow middle of the omelet and roll the edge over to inclose it.

1153. Omelet with Tomatoes.

Stew tomatoes down nearly dry, season with butter, pepper and salt. Inclose a spoonful in the middle of an omelet according to the preceding examples.

1154. Rum Omelet—For Three or Four.

6 eggs.
A third as much milk.
½ cupful of rum.
Powdered sugar.

Put the eggs and milk and a teaspoonful of powdered sugar in a bowl together, and beat enough to mix but not to make the omelet too light. Set the rum where it will get warm. Put a tablespoonful of the clear oil of melted butter in the large frying-pan, and pour in the omelet before the pan gets hot enough to make it stick on the bottom. An omelet should not be cooked through and the brown outside rolled in, but should be shaken and shaped in the further side of the pan, as soon as the edge is cooked enough to fall over from the edge into the middle shaken further over, so that the omelet is not a cake but a soft cooked mass with thick middle and pointed ends. A broad bladed knife is useful to help shape it.

Make an iron wire red hot in the fire.

When the omelet is done slip it on to a hot dish, dredge the top with powdered sugar, mark it with bars across with the hot wire laid a moment on the sugared top. Pour the rum around and set it on fire and send it in.

The sugaring and marking generally causes too much delay for individual omelets in large numbers, and has to be omitted in such cases.

1155. Sweet Omelet with Jelly.

For individual omelets break for each dish two eggs and put into the bowl with them about two tablespoonfuls of cream. Beat to mix, but not make it too light. Put a tablespoonful of the clear part of melted butter into the frying pan, pour in the omelet without waiting for the butter to get hot and discolored, let cook gradually, shaking it frequently to the further side of the pan until the thin edge, forced upward, falls over into the middle. When it is nicely browned and the upper side just set, put currant jelly, or other fruit jelly, in a long line in the middle that is made hollow for the purpose in the side of the pan. Roll over so as to shut in the jelly, slide it smooth side up on to a hot dish. Dredge powdered sugar on top and mark it with crossbars by touching the sugar with a hot wire.

1156. Omelet Souffiee.

It wants slow cooking like a meringue; not too much heat. After it has gone down it will be seen that the side that was cooked the most went down the flattest.

2 eggs.
1 small tablespoonful powdered sugar.
1 teaspoonful of water.
Extract vanilla, a few drops.

Put the yolks, sugar and flavor in one bowl, the whites in a larger one. Mix the yolks around, put in a few drops of water and beat till thick and foamy. Whip the whites firm enough to bear up an egg. Stir the yolks into them without more beating. Put a spoonful of clear melted butter into an omelet pan and when warm put the omelet in, smooth over the top and then if convenient cook it in the bottom of a slack oven. If on top of the range let it be at one side and hold a red hot shovel over the top. Sift powdered sugar over it before from the fire. Send it in on a dish almost as hot as the pan it leaves.

Omelet Frying Pans.

It is difficult if not impossible to fry eggs in a first-class manner, or to make individual omelets without the proper small frying pans, which are smallest size made, being no larger than a saucer in diameter, and scarcely any deeper. Frying pans that are too large for two eggs invariably blacken and burn the eggs at the edges.

ON THE ART OF CATERING.

First Principles.

It is the intention in these articles not to lay down any new laws upon so difficult a subject but to state the principal points made by the best authorities, the several questions of how many courses, how many dishes, how many wines and when to serve them admitting of endless discussion, for while there are certain established forms sanctioned by long usage and therefore safe for the inexperienced to adopt, some people grow restive under a set rule and inquire how far they may deviate without incurring dissentient criticism. Taking the wine question, the established custom, if the term may be used, is to begin the courses of a dinner with sherry or Madeira, or both, and end with champagne; the first, apparently, because the custom of taking Madeira after soup was introduced into France by Prince Talleyrand, and thus entered into the fashionable forms which have never been wholly controverted; the other only because a sweet wine has been conceded to be proper for the finish, and champagne has seemed the most available as well as the greatest favorite. But all champagne is not sweet. Under modern dinner customs another wine may be required before the Madeira, and possibly another draught after the champagne. One authority speaks of a banquet with thirty kinds of wine, "from Burgundy to Tokay," and imagines a dinner so prolonged by the pleasures of eating and of conversation that there would be no fixed data for finding what time might elapse between "the first glass of Madeira and the last tumbler of punch," and still speaks of an ideal bumble, but most enjoyable dinner with a half bottle of Madeira for two; another with some wine of the classical "Manlius vintage," and, again, a dinner with half-a-dozen friends regaled on a leg of mutton and a kidney washed down with "some Orleans and excellent Medoc;" the same as saying that it matters little what the kind of wine may be when there is but one or even two, further than that the light wine should be served first.

For artistic, even scientific, dining is achieved through the observance bf rules based on certain principles of which they who dine have not generally the first control, nor the direct opportunity of carrying out; they depend upon the executive officer who serves the meal. And the object in view is not the mere satisfaction of a keen appetite, although an appetite is the first requisite to enjoyment, but through that to gratify the finest sense of taste, to lead on from the commoner to the better, with small morsels of each dish, by courses, at each change to present new combinations of different viands and varied flavors; not to satiate with the first dish nor the first wine, but to lead on and prolong. That was the Roman idea of luxurious living and one of the most famous cooks of history is commemmorated as having become so skillful in serving courses that were each lighter, finer, more etherial than that which went before that the meals were never ended but a new appetite for substantials was experienced before the last flavored trifle was removed. Such have been the patterns for modern epicurism for those who seek the same exalted degree of gratification for the sense of taste as some do for the other senses. In the ancient models of conviviality all the senses were gratified at once, with music, with beautiful objects, with rare perfumes and divans of swan's down and velvet, but the sense of taste gave the occasion and was master of the ceremonies, for the banquet was the motive of all. In the endeavor to bring the art of catering for the appetite within the bounds of such exact rules as all cultivated arts are subject to, certain principles are laid down, such as, "In eating, the order is from the more substantial to the lighter. In drinking, the order is from the milder to that which is stronger and of finer flavor.

How To Drink Wine.

The following study shows how finely the sensations of taste have been analyzed in this pursuit.

"In drinking wine there is a pleasant but still imperfect sensation so long as it is in the mouth, it is only when swallowed that we can really taste and appreciate the special flavor and boquet of each variety, and a little time must elapse before the connoisseur can say, 'It is good,' 'middling,' or 'bad;' 'By Jove! 'tis genuine Chambertin,' or, 'Confound it! It is only Surene!'

"In conformity with these principles, and resulting from a well-understood experience, is that habit which all true connoisseurs have of sipping their wine, for each time they swallow they have the sum total of the sensation enjoyed had they taken the whole glass at one draught." And again: "A drunkard knows not how to drink, and he who eats too much, or too frequently, knows not how to eat."

The sipping and tasting, not rapid drinking, which constitutes the deferent duty of the guest in this reciprocal matter is minutely described by another student of the art of dining as follows:

The art of drinking wine is unknown except at Bordeaux, for with the Bordelais it is an art, and it is quite a sight to witness the operation. The butler, with a serious air, announces, on pouring it, "Chateau Giscourt," or "Lascombe," or "Margaux of 1849." The guest silently takes the glass between his thumb and forefinger, raises it to a level with his eye, and with a slight movement of the elbow gives the wine a rotary movement. This sets free the aroma. He sniffs the perfume circulating on the edge of the glass, looks at the ruby color scintilating in the glass, then drinks it off deliberately in small installments. Silence follows; the guests look at each other; the host has an anxious air, awaiting the verdict; then opinions are given in turn in a serious tone, and the wealth of adjectives at the command of a Bordelais is revived. If the judgment is unfavorable, the wine is declared as *rebelle, dur, sans ame, deplaisante, choquant, antipathique, imperatif.* If, on the contrary the judgment is favorable, eyes sparkle and the wine is styled *aimable, gracieux, seduisant, passionnant, elegant, riche, fier, grand, beau, doux, parfume, insinuant, coquet, ravissant, incomparable, plien d'amour.*

If this fine and critical judgment was not cultivated in some quarters the motive for maturing wine by years of keeping would be lost, for any sort of beverage would be acceptable to those who, like the sailor, on being told that the glass poured out for him was very old wine, would remark that it was very small of its age, and it is in consideration of this undiscriminating eagerness that is apt to be exhibited by anyone at the beginning of a meal that the commoner wines are served first and the best kept until last, and champagne may be the best in most cases; if of a choice and rare brand it may be that there is really nothing better, hence the custom of ending with champagne. It is the prerogative of the possessors of fine cellars to be able to end with something else. There are light champagnes that are more appropriate for the earlier courses of a dinner than for the close.

Wines in Courses.

"To maintain," says a high authority, "that a man must not change his wine is a heresy; the palate becomes cloyed, and, after three or four glasses, it is but a deadened sensation that even the best wine produces. The art of catering teaches how to put the wines on the table in such order as to produce for the guests an enjoyment constantly increasing up to the point where pleasure ends and abuse begins." Such being the object in view its attainment is a matter of more consequence than the observance of conventional usages in the order of the names of wines.

It was observed some years since that the viceroyalty of Canada was sanctioning a rule in the serving of wines somewhat different from the generally accepted mode and inquiry led to the ascertainment that the master of ceremonies based his procedure upon the following rule:

With fish or soup use sherry or Sauterne.
With roast meat use hock and claret.
With turtle use punch.
With whitebait use champagne.
With game use port or Burgundy.
Between the roast and confectionery use sparkling wines.
With sweets use Madeira.

With dessert use port, Tokay, Madeira, sherry, or claret.

Ice is never put in red wines even in summer. Burgundy should be slightly warmed. Claret-cup and champagne-cup should always be iced, and these are the only two wines in which ice is used. Every kind of wine has its different glass; champagne glasses for champagne only; goblets for claret and Burgundy; ordinary wine glasses for sherry and Madeira; green glasses for hock; large bell-shaped glasses for port. Port, sherry, and Madeira are decanted in the late style, but hock and champagne appear in their native bottles. Claret and Burgundy are always handed around in claret jugs.

That certainly seems to give latitude enough for the use of any sort of wine, and taking whitebait, a fish not known in this country, but comparable to small trout fried, for the admission, champagne may be used with fish.

In close connection with the above it is to be observed that new opinions are occasionally advanced and new deviations made on the other side of the Atlantic whose impressions are too quiet to at once strike the general observation. A certain master of ceremonies, once of the Paris Jockey Club, once of the Queen of England's household, put forth just such a set of rules as that above found not very long ago, but whether he learned from the palace or the palace from him, and whether the Paris Jockey Club should be considered as leading or following, are matters not to be determined. What he says is in these words, first quoting a learned French doctor's general remarks upon the use of wine in any case:

"For persons far advanced in years, old wine, in small quantities, is always to be preferred; taken in such a way it is a valuable tonic, but when taken in anything approaching excess, it loses all its beneficial effects.

"To those fortunate individuals in the prime of life who are gifted with a powerful constitution, I would recommend but a very sparing use of wine, and only of the lighter kinds.

"Where there is a chronic tendency to weakness, there will wine first manifest its injurious effects; thus in the same way as a weak sight suffers from too much light or wind, will it suffer from the use of alcoholic stimulants, and manifest the fact by inflamed and bloodshot eyes.

"My object is not to recommenced in all such cases the total abstinence from wine, but merely to advise its discreet use and judicious selection."

Thus far the physician, next the master of ceremonies:

In a general way, wine may be said to have the following influence on our frame. A light clear wine, with but little color and alcohol, gives a wholesome fillip to the circulation; a full-bodied and alcoholic wine, on the contrary, is rather calculated to make it sluggish.

A Parisian Authority.

"Having had many opportunities of testing the most pleasant mode of serving wine at dinner, and its most successful order of procedure I think it well to give a few hints on the subject.

"After the soup and fish, sherry, Madeira or Marsala are frequently served; but I would advise selecting lighter wines such as Sauterne, Graves, Chablis, Pouilly, Meursault or Montrachet; all these wines, as well as light champagnes, which can with advantage be served at this stage of a dinner, should be very cool.

"Such wines do not clog the appetite, as stronger wines would do, but, on the contrary, they give it a gentle fillip, and endow it with new vigor.

"Comparing a dinner to a brilliant orchestral composition, it strikes me very forcibly that, if, at the very first bars, I am deafened by the big drum, the double bass, and the trombone, I shall no longer be able to appreciate the sweet melodies which are about to follow. Similarly, if, at the beginning of a meal, my host is too persistent in helping me to full-bodied wines, he will deaden my palate, take off the edge of my appetite, and prevent my appreciating the delicacy of the cookery.

"At the beginning of a dinner, therefore, have only the lighter kinds of wine; with the roast serve those which have more body; they will prepare the palate for the more delicate wines which should follow, namely, such 'Burgundies as Corton, Clos-Vougeot, Romanee-Conti, and Pomard; or such as some of the undermentioned clarets: St. Julien, Chateau La Rose, Leoville, Lafitte, and Chateau-Margaux.'

"With dessert serve the following sweet wines: Malaga, Alicant, Rivesaltes, Malmsey, Lachryma-Christi, Constance, Tokay, and the higher brands of champagne, iced.

"My directions for serving wine will probably be criticised; but I would beg of those who differ from me to judge the question on its own merits: if the art of the cook is to provoke appetite without overtaxing the digestive organs, surely that of he who boasts of a good cellar is to induce his friends to drink without endangering their sobriety?

"I consider it bad taste to serve too many different kinds of wines; variety without profusion should be the aim; and quality should be the very first consideration, not only for the higher class wines, but principally for the more common descriptions of *vins ordinaires*, which, as they are most used during the meal, should be selected with proportionate care.

"Lastly, the following directions should be attended to before serving the different wines:

"*Vin ordinaire* should be served in claret jugs, and very cool; in winter it will be sufficient to bring it direct from the cellar, when wanted; in summer it should be very slightly iced, or put to cool in spring water.

"Claret of a choice vintage should be brought from the cellar a few hours before it is required; so that it may become of the same temperature as the dining room; it is a mistake to imagine that putting it before the fire improves it.

"Burgundy is best when cool, by which I do not mean *cold*; for, should the weather be very cold, it will be improved by being kept in the dining room some little time before it is served.

"Champagne, on the contrary, is never so good as when it is iced; icing brings out all its latent qualities; and your guests, when they drink it, will find therein the necessary eloquence to praise worthily the efforts made to please them."

Such are the amplifications and explanations of the concise set of rules before repeated, and they will be found to be in accordance although the sources of authority may appear to be so far removed; and, from first to last, from the prolonged feasts of the ancients to the most artistically devised banquets of the present, the scheme of catering has been for the utmost gratification of a refined sense without excess in anything.

An authority in American society says, ' If three wines are served, let them be a choice sherry with the soup, claret with the first course after the fish, and champagne with the roast. If a fourth is desired there is no better selection than a Chateau Yquem, to be served with an entree. If champagne alone is used serve it just after the fish. Many serve claret during the entire dinner, it matters not how many other varieties may be served; others do the same with champagne—for the benefit of the ladies, they say. I believe, however, champagne is considered with more disfavor every day."

Refreshments at Ball Suppers.

There are other occasions besides dinners, however, when the judicious method of serving beverages must be considered, as there are places where wine must not enter. A witty writer in a society paper made the sly remark the other day that in a new game of forfeits the young men who lose are compelled to bring a glass of water to the lady at the next hall, that being the hardest thing to obtain. No person can be said to be proficient in the art of catering who is not equal to this difficulty and is unable to furnish a sufficiency of that agreeable fluid, lighter than the lightest wine and less destructive to the appetite than the most delicate dish. The quicker perception of the needs of the occasion experienced by those accustomed to the course of the festivities by partaking of them frequently was shown in the preparations for a private party that has but just passed into the region of the bye-gones, when, for a refreshment to be handed around to the dancers an hour previous to the supper, a frozen marachino punch was determined upon, that which one of Thackeray's characters describes as having a flavor as seductive as the smiles of beauty, and it was intended to take the place of the proposed claret cup and lemonade, excluding everything but water. But the host observing, said that would never do; there should be frozen maraschino punch, of course, but there must be cool lemonade as well.

Pattern for a Dinner in Courses.

For an example of the safe pattern of a dinner served in courses the following is appended. It is the menu of an actual dinner served on a private occasion somewhere in New York. As a dinner menu it is good, excepting the affectation of a foreign language for an American party, and in size furnishes a convenient specimen. Whoever deviates from the regular track must consider whether any eyes are likely to be critical of the performance. It is something the same in planning a pretentious menu as in beginning a game of chess. There are certain well known safe openings which the timid player may follow, but the powerful masters of the game may indulge in brilliant eccentricities with equal safety:

Clams
Chateau Sauternes

POTAGE.
Printaniere Princesse
Amontillado

POISSON
Sea Bass a la Maitre d'Hotel
Concombres   Pommes Nouvelles

RELEVE.
Filet de Boeuf pique, aux Champignons
Choux-fleurs
Chateau Lamarque

ENTREE.
Ris de Veau aux Petits Pois
Asperges

Punch Romaine.

ROTI.
Grass Plovers on Toast au Cresson
Salade de Laitue
Veuve Cliquot, Yellow Label

DESSERT.
Creme Napolitaine.
Fraises   Fromage
Petits Fours   Desserts Assortis

The Explanation.

Clams—raw on the shell served with half a lemon, this being a May dinner, and Sauterne wine. Soup—Spring, or green vegetable (asparagus heads, peas, etc.), with a little rice in whole grains. Amontillado is the name of a brand of light sherry. Fish—sea bass, probably boiled, and maitre d'hotel sauce poured over in the dish, with cucumbers and new potatoes to complete the course. The releve or remove, as many menus have it, equivalent to the roasted or boiled joint of ordinary dinners, is tenderloin of beef larded, roasted and served with mushrooms in sauce, the vegetable to go with it is cauliflower. The wine, Chateau Lamarque, is one of the higher class of French wines, a claret. Entree —sweetbreads with green peas, probably larded and braised; the accompanying vegetable in this course is asparagus. Then comes Roman punch. Next comes the *roti*, meaning roast meat in general, but in a menu meaning game in particular, the English heading would be "game," for which the French word is *gibier*. That also sometimes appears instead of *roti*. The dish is roast grass plover, roasted over toast and the trail spread upon it, on which the birds are placed and water cress around, in the dish. Lettuce salad completes this course, and the wine between it and the dessert is champagne, and the last wine that is served. The last course consists of Neapolitan ice cream, strawberries, (*fraises*) cheese, (*fromage*) fancy small cakes, (*petits fours*) and *desserts assortis* includes such things as fruits, figs, raisins and nuts.

Where the clams are written in this early summer menu, oysters on the shell would be found in winter; only four, five or six are served to each plate, and they are supposed to increase the appetite for dinner instead of allaying it. The soup will be but a few spoonfuls, perhaps a third of a plate, the real dinner begins with the fish and the beef is the substantial part; the punch served in punch glasses gives an interval, and is supposed to renew the appetite for the acceptance of the dainty morsel under the head of *roti*, where vegetables would have no attraction, but a cool, refreshing salad takes the place as the accompaniment. The rest are but light sweets and pastimes.

American Plan, or Table d'Hote.

The best form of dinner is, however, the present American plan dinner, or, as the French call it, *table d'hote*. It is the only plan that is universally adaptable to either the smallest or largest numbers, either to the family dinner of four or five individuals or to the largest hotel with as many hundreds. The dinner served in single courses may be the dinner of wealth and culture, for occasions of ceremony and display, but none pretends that it is the meal of the greatest enjoyment. It requires a knowledge of gastronomy and epicurism on the part of the partakers that is not common in this country, and is not cultivated with any conspicuous degree of interest, a fact which it is common fashion to deplore, but without reason. Our people are too much interested in more active matters to resolve themselves into communities of professional eaters. They have the keenest enjoyment for good things to eat and drink, but prefer the enjoyment without the study. Let the stewards and cooks prepare the feast and the guests will do it justice if it is good and criticise or leave it if it is not, after a free fashion that is not admissable at a course dinner, where each person is expected to partake of every course, if not to eat it at least to pretend to do so and consume time while others do.

It is the American plan that needs to be cultivated, developed, improved by the grafting upon it of the peculiar excellences of the purely artistic dinner as well as the sociability of the family table. It already has such advantages in its favor as that it demands the highest degree of efficiency in the caterer and skill in the cook, and at the same time affords the means to pay sufficient compensation to secure them. Very few private parties can afford to pay what hotels and restaurants pay, consequently very few can enjoy the products of the best trained proficiency unless they go to one or the other of such establishments. Very few can afford to order at the highest class restaurants and give *carte blanche*, that is, leave it to the caterer to do his best without regard to the cost, and if they cannot they must stay within the bounds of ordering according to their own limited knowledge of dishes and combinations and their own ideas of the money value of the gratification desired. Those who dine at American plan tables do that in regard to pay, but they receive, according to what rate they pay, an amount, a variety, a style of cookery and service that could scarcely be obtained without a vast expenditure at a cafe, and in private houses is practically impossible.

Accordingly, those who have become accustomed to the best hotel tables are the most fastidious and critical diners in the world. They get the best, and soon learn to be exacting enough to be satisfied with nothing less. The viands that are prepared at some establishment at a distance and transported to the house of the private party would be criticised by the *habitues* of the highest class hotels as having been too long from the fire. They have their shell fish served direct from the refrigerators; their soups perfect, at a few minutes after the cook has bestowed the last touch of attention to their appearance; their meats, with the hot juices at the steaming point; their sauces, with the velvety appearance they have when fresh made; their souffles, light, distended, puffed up, but a minute from the oven; their pastry, absolutely fresh and new; their ices, when most perfect, without the mishaps and deteriorations of long waits.

The rolls served out by thousands of dozens by the bakers would be spurned by our exacting hotel guests as cold bread. They demand them fresh baked and hot. Fancy bread, muffins, waffles and all of those kinds are found in full variety and fresh made perfection only in American plan hotels. For these reasons those who regularly live at American plan hotels live better as regards good eating than any other people in the world, and know more in a practical way about dishes and cookery, and the flavors and qualities of the different edibles, but do not know and are not interested in the technicalities of cooking and catering. If any people fare badly at an American plan table they are the strangers to whom the method is new, but they are notoriously the most easily pleased at first and as they in turn learn to be critical they also learn how to avail themselves of all the advantages.

The Highest Praise of a Cook.

The highest praise of a cook ever printed appeared in the new French cook's journal very recently. It was but a sentence referring to the chief cook of one of the most celebrated catering establishments in this country, but it said that in over two thousand menus of his preparation that were under review there was not two alike. It was depressing to find another journal in the same line soon after repeating the commonplace part of the compliment that would fit any man and leaving out the essential point and pith. The ability to produce so large a number of bills of fare and never two exactly alike implies and includes all the knowledge of all the resources of the arts of catering and cooking that anybody can possess. If a cook builds up a fine ornamental center piece of figures moulded in tallow or wax it is pretty, but it is nothing because other artists can do better in plaster of Paris or metal. It does not make the eatable better; it does not advance the art of cookery; it does not help small hotels nor private houses; it is not practical art. But the art of producing variety and of making common things good and attractive is what the cooks are at present most deficient in and that most needs to be cultivated. There is an existing consciousness of the value of the power of constant variation but it has led to some very wrong notions and to some great absurdities in exhibition that are peculiar to American plan hotels, not being possible anywhere else, such as the crowding of unreasonable numbers of dishes on the bill of fare. The use of knowing how to cook everything in every manner is not to put it all into one dinner but to be able to make a dinner out of anything. To join much of the cheap with a little of the dear, not to make the dear article the worse by it but to help it and make both things the better by the combination. It is to know so many good ways and good combinations and so many ways of making people like it that when any particular thing is cheap and abundant that article can be used in large quantities, and when it becomes less obtainable the use of varied knowledge is to ta'.e up something else and provide equally as good meals without it. The opposite of all this is the helplessness that knows but a few dishes and can do nothing without a plentiful supply of certain articles that may be very difficult to obtain. The American plan cannot be the most money-making plan without the exercise of this faculty of change and adaptability on the part of the cooks, neither can it give the highest enjoyment to the lovers of good living, for a reasonable, intelligently regulated variation of the dishes is an essential matter. The peculiar demands of the American plan hotels are leading to their providers, caterers, stewards, cooks, pastry cooks and bakers being the best in the world and according to their grade they offer already the all-powerful inducement to the study of excellence, the highest pay for the most varied skill. The cook who can do but a few things, make but a dozen or two of dishes or articles, and is stopped and made useless by every little scarcity is not in much demand. The crowding of a great number of dishes in one bill of fare is not a evidence of varied knowledge. Most of the bills that contain ten or a dozen entrees at a time if examined day after day or Sunday after Sunday are found to contain the same few things everlastingly repeated.

The Restaurant Dinner.

There are hotel men who grow tired of trying to give so much in such good style under the American plan for so little pay and they say the restaurant plan after all is the only way to make profit. It restrains the hoggish wasteful eater wonderfully to see his check by the side of his plate growing to larger denominations at even pace with the distentension of his stomach. But it is difficult to keep up a place strictly on that plan, and there are few restaurants that do not find it necessary to adopt more or less of the plan of offering a regular meal for a certain sum total. This is the popular plan and the popular demand, for, as some one jocularly remarks: "O, the table d'hotes are a boon to men who are more certain of their own idea of desirable expenditure than they are of their companion's appetite. There is a charming definiteness about a meal for $1.25, claret included, that offsets an occasional disappointment in the viands. Dining rooms on this plan have multiplied in number and popularity within a year or two There used to be an Italian restaurant on Fourteenth street famous for the abundance of the dinner which it offered for $1 only."

But there is an epicurean class of customers to whom the question of expense is not a consideration and restaurants or cafes of the highest class thrive and high class cooking is done wherever there is enough of this class of patronage to warrant the outlay of the requisite means to serve the meals luxuriously. This field is very limited, for the particular class of customers soon form clubs, procure the best caterers and cooks and set up their own *menage* and the restaurateur seeks business among the wealthy dinner-givers at their own houses. The largest cities support only two or three completely equipped establishments of this sort, although every town with the least pretense to society has need of a public caterer, and because there are so few that really understand the business puts up with the assistance of the confectioner or baker or the village busybody who knows how to make ham sandwiches and pic-nic lemonade. In every town there are people like some city club members, who do not agree with the fashionable plan of a dinner in many courses with small portions of each, but if a delicacy be in store hold it best to attack it with the keenest appetite, enjoy it to the utmost, eat but little else at that meal and for the next seek something new. The establishment that caters to their requirements needs to adopt the same means for procuring the newest and rarest viands that a newspaper does for news. Leaving out the few exceptional establishments kept up by parties who do not need to count the cost, the general run of restaurants do not train their caterers and cooks to the perfection that hotels do, their business being so nearly like merchandising.

They call into exercise but a small part of the resources of the art of cookery for they make only such dishes as will sell and cannot set a table above the level of their customers' apprehension as American plan hotels can, and as good hotels constantly do. When a restaurant keeper can buy an article of cooked provision cheaper than he can get it made in his own house he does so, and when he says it is useless to make or prepare any kind of dish because he cannot sell it there is an end of effort in that direction. But people who eat constantly at a *table d'hote* where there is a new bill of fare each day become familiar in time with every kind of dish and insensibly become learned in the arts of catering and cooking.

French Terms.

None but a very few of the more exclusive sort of hotels can now afford to use French terms in their printed bills of fare, and it is of doubtful expediency even for them unless the menus are entirely French. That which was, perhaps, a good enough fashion once has become vulgarized like any past fashion in dress by every class of incompetent imitators trying it on and producing frightful effects. It is not well to be pragmatical in such a matter nor cultivate a sort of Franco-phobia, to cry out whenever a French word appears in a menu, for there are questions of taste involved and some know when and how to gain an advantage in that way. Such great novelists as Charlotte Bronte, Thackeray and Bulwer Lytton incurred lasting censure for indulging in the pedantic weakness of putting whole dialogues and whole pages of French in the middle of their books, that of course the vast majority of their readers could not understand and were much annoyed; and still, an occasional foreign word slipped in by the best writers seems to be thought rather rather ornamental than otherwise, besides being such an evident relief to the writers themselves who have more knowledge than they can possibly hold in. The plan and method used in introducing dishes more or less peculiar to other countries into England and America, with the principal thing named in English but the technical terms and the affixed style in French worked well when the cooks and stewards happened to be educated people. But, unfortunately, most of those who wrote the bills of fare did not read but only put down the words as they sounded when they heard them repeated, and the nonsense thus produced could not be set right by the printers, who always correct everybody's bad spelling except Josh Billings', when it is in English, but who are not expected to understand cooking terms.

As these cooks and stewards did not know the meaning of the terms which they could not even spell, they could not know much about the dishes that belonged to the terms, and traveling people and regular boarders alike soon learned that every dish that had a French name in the bill of fare was sure not to be fit to eat and that the whole hotel French entree list was a fraud and a farce. This has brought a good deal of undeserved odium upon French cookery among people who have gained their impressions of it in that way, and has done harm to the hotel business, so that even in the hotels where they are as near correct with their French terms and entrees as any one not really French ever gets to be, still the public feels the same suspicion and takes plain beef and turkey. Hotel keepers, therefore, very generally are doing away with the French ridiculousness and are stating what they have for dinner in plain language, and when they cannot find suitable English terms to tell how a thing is cooked they let it go without, and encourage their patrons to take the reputation of their table for the assurance that the dish is good anyway. Lest any reader may think he will be lacking in style if he write his bill of fare in English, here is what a high Washington authority wrote about it a few years ago:

"It is a pity that our own rich language is inadequate to the duties of a fashionable bill of fare. I would say that some tact might be displayed in choosing which language to employ. If you are entertaining a company of foreign embassadors, use unhesitating the French bills of fare (all French), but practical uncles and substantial persons of learning and wit, who, perhaps, do not appreciate the merits of languages which they do understand, might consider you demented to place one of these effusions b fore them— I would advise the English bills of fare on these occasions."

An American Plan Dinner.

SADDLE ROCK OYSTERS.

SOUP.
Cream of Asparagus   Consomme Royal

HORS D'ŒUVRES.
Sliced cucumbers   Small Patties   Sliced Tomatoes

FISH.
Fillet of Striped Bass, Italian Sauce
Potatoes Hollandaise

REMOVES.
Boiled Capon, Celery Sauce
Roast Spring Lamb, Mint Sauce
Roast Sirloin of Beef, Brown Gravy
Roast Saddle of Veal, with Dressing
Roast Ducklings, and Fresh Green Peas

Claret Punch.

SALADS.
Lettuce   Shrimp   Potato   Lobster

ENTREES.
Croquettes of Sweetbreads, and Mushrooms
Supreme of Chicken, with Truffles
Stewed Eggs, Alsascian Sauce
French Pancakes, with Jelly

VEGETABLES.
Fresh Asparagus   Fresh Green Peas
Stewed Tomatoes   String Beans
Boiled Potatoes   Mashed Potatoes

DESSERT
Steamed Fruit Pudding, Brandy Sauce
Apricot Pie   Cream Meringue Pie   Mixed Cake
Maraschino Jelly   Philadelphia Ice Cream
Fruits   Crackers   Cheese

FRENCH COFFEE.

GALT HOUSE, Louisville, Ky.,
March 25, 1883.

Service.

It seems like a species of irony to speak of the highest possibilities of excellence in furnishing a table with choice things to eat and drink in presence of a large number of hotels with whose proprietors the question of how to get what is due to them for board furnished at the lowest possible rate to their slow-paying customers is all the engrossing one, and the talk about high-priced rarities ordered from a distance, and high-priced cooks to prepare them skillfully, seems more like fancy sketches of free spreads furnished by private wealth than practical business matters. Perfection in any department is only reached in a few places, if ever, but there is always some degree of excellence that it pays to achieve in every situation. It is probably as essential in the hotel business as any other that the man should take an active interest in his occupation to make a success of it. As everybody must eat, whatever is true as regards one place must be true for any other according to grade, and the providing and cooking is not everything. The beef may be roasted perfectly in the smallest house, and coffee be made as good as in the largest, and bread and potatoes, which are by themselves such cheap articles of diet that the restaurant keepers find they can almost give them away if they but get pay for the meats, can be cooked as perfectly in the poorest house as in the richest. But it may be that in the poorest one there is no head waiter and none to perform the functions of the office. Perhaps the food looks, upon the dishes as if it had been dished up with a scoop shovel and hay fork. It may be brought in by tidy boys or round armed girls who are more amused with their own little affairs all over the room than interested in the commonplace business of placing knives and spoons, cream and sugar, a napkin or plate of bread within reach of the guest whom they have tantalized by setting a meal before him without the ordinary appliances to enable him to eat it, and sailing away into the distance never to return. Different sorts of people act differently under such circumstances; they hear the light hearted creatures singing or whistling in the kitchen and one will sit and sulk and mutter; another will boldly rise and walk to the other end of the table, or to the next table, to reach the mustard cruet, and then leave it alone because it is stale and dirty; another will lay aside the celery he had taken up because he cannot reach any salt, stirs up his coffee with his knife, and leaves the dining room as soon as possible; another hammers a plate with his knife, hates himself for it and is hated, but all of them regard it as a species of sarcasm in anybody to talk about the pleasures and luxuries of an American plan hotel—unless they have traveled further and seen better specimens. Under such a wretched sort of dining room service as that supposed, good cooking is thrown away. So with liberal providing. The writer has seen a house provided with early luxuries such as, for instance, strawberries, or California pears at nine dollars a box, of which never more than about a third were actually consumed by the guests. The proprietor had a steward to attend to those matters for him, and the steward was too good natured for anything, and too fearful of being thought stingy to lock up anything. The guests were always supplied, but what they ate cost somewhere near twenty-five dollars a box. The furnishing of occasional treats of things newly come in season is a borrowing of one of the principal attractions of the restaurant plan, and the experienced caterer does not expect it to pay the expense on the instant, but with a further temporary adoption of that plan of serving very little else beside the special article, and with a very proper degree of what is called stinginess, to see that it reaches those it is intended for, a great deal of this kind of attractiveness may be employed with profitable results.

The fear of being called stingy is one of the chief obstacles in the way of profitable hotel-keeping, and everybody except the very well bred is ready to hurl the epithet. There was a hotel keeper in a good sized town in the interior, a thriving county seat with but two hotels, whose method of table management brought upon him more than the usual amount of derogatory remarks and small witticisms, it being one of the chief points against him that the portions served on the dishes were so small that to order from his bill of fare was but a delusion, a man had to eat everything that was set before him, and call for it all in order to get enough; and another was that the newspapers were seldom without his advertisements for some description of help, leading to the inference that he was a hard task master. There is every reason for believing, notwithstanding the gossip, that he conducted his house upon the most correct principles and in the only way that a good hotel could be kept and make money in the place. The writer shared somewhat in the common prejudice and never saw him but once, at a distance—a white-haired old gentleman in broadcloth—but seeing from time to time how new parties took the only other hotel, with new spurts of energy and new promises to make it the only first class house, and seeing them all as surely fail, while the white-haired old gentleman kept on the even tenor of his way, paying everybody, owning his house, which bears his own name, and practically monopolizing the hotel business of his town, has led to the belief that all the gossip was but the malice of ignorance and the hotel keeper had his business upon a scientific basis.

To dish up small, and yet not absurdly small, is the hardest thing a man has to train his hands in. The *table d'hote* dinner is a failure, however, where the rule cannot be enforced. This style of dinner is based upon the same princip'es as the dinner of luxury and ceremony described in the first of these papers, in which there is a succession of viands in small portions, and the appetite is not to be appeased upon the first courses alone, but led on with enjoyment for the entire "square meal."

There is a mutual interest and should be a tacit understanding between host and boarder in this regard The boarder wants the lowest possible rate, and he would be horrified at the thought of having food presented to him that had already been served once or several times to others and returned; but if he and each one has two or three times as much set before him as he can eat, either he must pay for much more than he needs or the hotel keeper must fail in business. It is much more sensible for a person to have to order some dish that specially suits him two or three times replenished than to have before him half a dozen full dishes of articles that he does not want.

Conclusions.

The term caterer has been employed in making these observation as being more comprehensive than steward. There may be no steward in the house but still some one must be caterer or provider. Frequently the duty is shared by several, as the head cook and the proprietor, or his son, or some other attache of the house.

The caterer must know how to cook. Actual practice may not be necessary, but he should know all there is to be known about it short of that.

The public caterer or restaurateur must know all about cooking, buying, articles in season, and the next to be. He must be able to say what kind of a meal or banquet can be furnished for any stated sum, therefore he must know what every dish costs, in an average way, per one person or per one hundred. He knows how many hours or days it will take the coo s to prepare anything ordered; how much expense for fire and light; how much inevitable waste and shrinkage in provisions, and the proper charge to be made for use and wear and tear of silverware and china, teaming and attendance, and how many waiters are needed for a stated number.

The hotel caterer must know how good a meal can be furnished for a certain price, and to arrive at it must in like manner know the cost of provisions and the amount necessary for a given number of people, and make allowance for wear and tear, laundry expenses, service, and other matters belonging.

Following the highest tyle of dinner usages he serves small portions, and consequently must provide attentive waiters that the guests may have their dishes replenished if they wish it.

Following the same principles in the order of dishes, he should take care that the entrees are better than the plain meats, and most particularly should encourage excellence in making vegetable and farinaceous dishes and combinations, which his figuring shows him are the cheapest and best forms of food. Not regarding the pastry and dessert as a mere superfluity, to be given as an extra sort of bounty, but rather as an essential part of a complete meal, he shou d see that it is as good as the rest of the dinner; that those who eat may depend upon it for a new pleasure to compensate for any self denial they may exercise during the earlier courses. The perplexing questions of what to do with the waste; how to prevent waste; how to furnish a meal of several courses and a constant succession of good things in such a way that it shall cost no more than the pound or two of one thing bought at a restaurant; how to get the co-operative advantages that ought to accrue from the wholesale system of setting a table for a large number, and other such problems are only possible of solution through a thorough knowledge of the business called the art of catering.

Whitehead's Cook Books.

THE AMERICAN PASTRY COOK.

THE BOOK OF A TRADE.

Also contains the department of cold dishes, galantines and salads.

Volume 1 of the only Cook Book ever intended or adapted for Hotel use.

NEW EDITION.

Enlarged, filled out with the newest fashionable dots; improved in many ways.

PRICE, $2.00. By Mail Prepaid.

Address—

JESSUP WHITEHEAD,
Care JOHN ANDERSON & CO., 183–187 N. Peoria St.
CHICAGO.

"The receipts all work like a charm."
"I have seen the time I would gladly have given twenty-five dollars for the information I found in a few pages of it."—*What the Cooks say.*

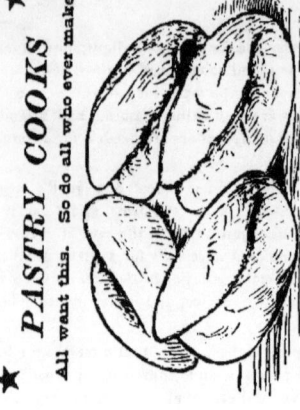

★ *PASTRY COOKS*
All want this. So do all who ever make

WHITEHEAD'S
Pat. French-Roll Cutter

A Labor-Saving Utensil that every Bread Maker ought to have.

Pastry Cooks and Bakers who are in practice at molding out the tedious split rolls by hand, will still find they can beat their own time about one-half with this new tool. Those who have never learned can make rolls quite as fast and as good looking after a few trials as the oldest hands. It is useful besides for various forms of fancy pastries. Directions accompany each one.

Sent by mail, post-paid, price 50 cts.

The pastry cook of a leading hotel, where several hundred split rolls are made at each meal, writes:

* * * "I should also wish for one of your Cutters, large size and one of small size. If you should not have any large size, if you could possibly get one made, for I am completely lost without one." * * *
N. B. N.

HOT ROLLS AND BISCUITS.
WHITEHEAD'S
PATENT ROLL CUTTER

Saves half the time and labor in making the popular split rolls known as *Cream Rolls*, *French Rolls*, or *Pocket Books*, made with biscuit dough. Price 50 cents. BY MAIL, POSTAGE PAID.

It is to your interest to make the finest rolls possible.

Three or four cents worth of flour produces 15 of the same delicious sort of rolls that made the Parker House famous.

Send for the cutter that makes them easy. Send for a book that gives a readable account of all sorts of fancy breads and buns and you will become interested in proving your skill.

THE

HOTEL BOOK

OF

Soups and Entrées.

COMPRISING SPECIMENS OF
FRENCH, ENGLISH AND AMERICAN MENUS,
WITH TRANSLATIONS AND COMMENTS.

Showing how to make up hotel Bills of Fare with all the different
varieties of soups and consommes in proper rotation,
and a new set of entrees or made
dishes for every day.

BEING A PART OF THE "OVEN AND RANGE" SERIES ORIGINALLY PUBLISHED
IN THE DAILY NATIONAL HOTEL REPORTER.

BY
JESSUP WHITEHEAD.

CHICAGO
1893.

Entered according to Act of Congress, in the year 1882, by JESSUP WHITEHEAD, in the
Office of the Librarian of Congress, at Washington.

ALL RIGHTS RESERVED.

PUBLISHED BY THE AUTHOR
At the Office of the Daily National Hotel Reporter,
78 FIFTH AVENUE
CHICAGO, ILLS.

ELECTROTYPED BY BLOMGREN BROS. & Co.
162 and 164 Clark Street,
CHICAGO.

PRINTED AND BOUND BY JOHN ANDERSON & Co.
185 187 N. Peoria Street,
CHICAGO.

SOUPS, ENTREES & BILLS OF FARE.

1161. The Failure of French Cookery.

If there be anything still in existence deserving the distinctive name of French cookery it has singularly failed of making itself understood among English speaking people, although it has had a hundred years of careful importation and nursing among them, with every possible advantage from the example of royalty and the fashionable world and the ceaseless iteration of the press of the superiority of the French in this department. It is a hundred years in the United States since French manners and methods were taken up sedulously with the intention of complimenting distinguished friends and visitors from that nation, while French communities have existed both on the north and south: still French cookery remains as much an unknown system as ever and has made no perceptible impression. It is mentioned as an example of progress and culture in a journal of recent date that whereas some ten years ago only fifteen wealthy New York families employed French cooks, now there are a hundred and fifty—a great rate of progress, truly, both numbers show after the culture of a hundred years, and even with that the employment of French speaking cooks does not necessarily imply the adoption of French cookery pure and simple.

Fashionable London and indeed all fashionable England employed French cooks because it was unfashionable to do otherwise from fifty to seventy-five years ago, but instead of the people being eager to adopt so excellent a system the results to the contrary were unconsciously stated a few weeks since in a London paper called the *Hotel World*, and the article was copied entire in the New York *Gastronomer* with evident approbation that the English cooks know really nothing about cooking and that the hotel keepers show their wish to set good viands before their guests have still to procure their cooks from France. And yet there is, as there has been since Queen Anne's time, an incorporated cook's company in London, and the truth of the newspaper article might be challenged, but that it suits our purpose to accept it as a statement of fact. But what has French cookery been doing all this time that it has not been universally adopted? The inference offered for our acceptance is that the people are too stupid to learn to cook. The same bewailment of American ignorance and stupidity is constantly to be met with when the subject of cooking comes up and the same invidious comparisons between us and the French in this regard. But what has French cookery been doing all this time that with all its immense advantages it has not reformed us all and made us French in our methods and tastes and skill through and through, from one end of the land to the other? These two peoples have not been too stupid to seize upon and improve every other good system and every useful idea of any other people, and even without the ability to acquire French cookery two great nations still eat and live and flourish. As between two parties perhaps the fault lies in the lack of worth in the system itself. Possibly there is nothing now left of what was once known as French cookery except a Babel of meaningless terms, and French speaking cooks are superior only because they are trained in countries where their calling is considered as respectable as any that can be named and are therefore good cooks without reference to their peculiar methods. But assuming that there is such a thing and that it is a system of great excellence we ought to know why it has failed to make itself generally understood.

It is an accepted axiom that all permanent reforms begin at the bottom, but the attempted reform of French cookery began at the top. Whether it was worth adopting or not it was necessary first to understand it, and to do that a certain degree of education has always been a requisite, and those who had the education did not do the cooking and have rarely been sufficiently interested in a matter of no pratical value to them to study the subject, while the real cooks always have been as they probably always will be among those having the least ornamental education such as a knowledge of foreign languages and the biographies of foreign celebrities.

Even when French cookery is understood it is found to be only partially applicable through the differences in taste between different nations of people. After all that has been said in favor of French cookery and the little mention of German, the fact is plain that the latter has the greater hold upon the people of this country through a similarity of inherited tastes for bread and all farinaceous articles and dairy products in preference to spiced meats and wine. So much having been written vaguely upon these subjects a little useful experience of our own may serve to point the meaning. The writer chanced to be employed at that receptive time of life when what we learn is never forgotten in a community where the cooking was strictly and thoroughly *a la Provencale*—for even in France itself the styles vary in different sections—where it was regarded as a serious misdemeanor to set anything on to cook in water; it must be weak and sour wine for many things, broth for others, their own juices or gravies only for others. Roast beef plain was never seen, but the nearest approach to it was the *entre-cote* or choice middle ribs of beef thrust full of strips of carrot, turnip, celery and bacon and stewed with wine and herbs until it was extremely well done. Butter was but little used, but the stewed okra seasoned with olive oil hung in ropes of slime from the spoon and black and blue beans and peas were similarly seasoned. A leg of mutton was stuck full of fine shreds of garlic and stuffed with minced ham, onions and herbs and cooked like the beef; a boiled fowl was filled with onions before cooking and a paste of onions highly seasoned was spread upon it when done. Beefsteak plain was never thought of, but it was always covered and even simmered in a sauce pungent with pepper or curry, garlic, onions, tomatoes and a dozen different herbs, and the brown sauce itself was as highly spiced as English plum pudding or American mincemeat. This was all skillful cookery and required training in the cooks to do it, yet the skill and training would be thrown away on such a dinner for an average American company. It is not a part of the business before us to deride the style described. Some people like all such dishes and therefore they are found among the hotel entrees, but they are exceptions, and a national system cannot be founded upon exceptions. The intelligent French, it is said, adopted plain roast beef underdone from the example of the English. The intelligent French cook in this country modifies his methods to suit the tastes of the people as he discovers them, but in just the same degree he leaves distinctive French cookery behind and furnishes a reason why it is not understood and appreciated by the native cooks.

Diverse Schools.

French cookery is incomprehensible because the French cooks themselves follow several different authorities, and our Francatelli is altogether out of date with them and one of the smallest authorities among them. It is very rare that any of Francatelli's terms are now met with in really French menus, and to see them in the bill of fare of any hotel is almost a sure sign that there is some other sort of a cook trying to be French. It is true that a few of the names of dishes are to be found the same in all books, such as *a la Richelieu*, *a la chasseur*, *a la Perigeux*, and so forth, but still there are so many that are to be found in one and not in the others that any one who is acquainted with them all can generally tell from a menu which authority the cook is most familiar with. The French speaking cooks of San Francisco, for instance, seem to show by their menus the greatest acquaintance with the terms of the *cuisine classique*, those of the Eastern summer resorts indicate Jules Gouffe.

It may be seen from the mere statement of these facts that if the use of a name for a dish is to convey a description of it the diversity of masters baffles the intention, for a cook may understand Careme and be well up in Francatelli and still be unable to describe the dishes of another who follows Bernard, or may compose his menus for years from the dishes of Urbain-Dubois, and still pick up a menu containing terms and dishes he knows nothing about from Jules and Alphonse Gouffe. Besides the cooks in the most prominent positions are continually setting out, what are by courtesy called new dishes. And supposing that these differences could be cleared up by means of the cooks meeting in conventions, as has been proposed, the utter uselessness of ever reaching an agreement would still be felt in the impossibility of making the general public for whom cooks exist—even the French public itself, understand any better than before.

Too Extravagant

The French cookery that we hotel cooks have been expected to know originated as the pastime of kings and princes at a period before the age of great inventions and when the rich idlers had nothing better to think about than to imitate the profligacy of the ancient Romans and vie with each other in the costliness of their banquets. It was a merit in a cook to make a dish expensive and the extravagant character of the whole system thus stamped upon it is still an integral part of it and unfits it for the adoption of a business-like people. The expedients resorted to to make the common food of humanity unnaturally costly by cooking it in rare wine and garnishing it with other articles costing more than their weight in gold were not so permanently injurious as a certain vagary of those days which led to a sort of worship of the reduced essence of meat as holding all that was worth having in the food, an elixir of life; a sort of hidden principle of nutrition that was to be extracted in some degree from vegetable substances as well, but when extracted whether from truffles or fish or birds or meats, all that remained was regarded as practicably worthless. It was a passing notion of the wise men of their generation—like the blue glass theory of a few years ago in this country, but less transient—that contained enough of truth to make a lasting impression. It made the cooks extremely important as the extractors of these precious elixirs. It led to extremes of extravagance. It led to the invention of numbers of new dishes which French cookery is still encumbered with, little better than a heap of rubbish now; dishes denominated *a l' essence*, the essential characteristics of which are that they are composed of the concentrated extracts of something or other, as likely as not of larks or ortolans, or it may be only wild boars head, but useless now because the fictitious value these essences once had has passed away. For the customer of a cafe to value such things at their former value—these dishes that made the cooks who composed them famous—it would be necessary for him to be imbued with the beliefs of the times of the dawn of modern chemistry, when it was thought to have been discovered that the principles of life lay in the gravy.

This exaggerated estimate was imbibed even by Brillat-Savarin, probably in his youth, and an example of it has been already quoted in this book in connection with the articles on roast beef and gravy. Our people esteem the natural gravy most highly but it is for its real value, as they value "the sweet taste of the wheat" in good bread, and not for any imaginary qualities. It is now known by those even of the least physiological education that man cannot live on condensed essences, but the stomach requires a certain bulk of food along with the nourishment.

An instance in illustration of what is above set forth is furnished by an admirer of that system of cookery as follows:

The Prince of Soubise, wishing one day to celebrate a fete, which was to finish off with a supper, gave orders that the bill of fare should be shown him beforehand. Next morning, at his levee, the steward made his appearance with the document handsomely ornamented, and the first item which caught the eye of the Prince was, "fifty hams."

"Hullo, Bertrand!" said he; 'you must be on, of your senses! Fifty hams! do you intend feasting all my soldiers?"

"No your highness; one only will appear on the table, but the others are equally necessary for my *espagnole*, my *blonds*, my 'trimmings,' my "

"Bertrand, you are robbing me, and I can't let this item pass."

"Ah, monseigueur," said the artist, scarcely able to restrain his anger, "you don't know our resources. Give the order, and those fifty hams which annoy you, I shall put them into a glass bottle no bigger than my thumb."

"What reply could be made to an assertion so pathetic? The Prince smiled, nodded assent, and so the item passed."

When "the artist" said he could put the fifty hams into a bottle no bigger than his thumb he meant that he could extract the essence of them and put it into such a bottle and as that would be all that was really of any value according to the craze of that time, the meat remaining might as well be considered as out of existence, it was all the same as nothing. And the Prince so greatly admired his skill, according to the craze of that time, that he smiled approvingly.

Impracticable.

The French cookery that we hotel cooks have been expected to know ; that we have gained higher pay for pretending to practice, is the same now that it was in the time of the Prince of Soubise. It is *founded upon "espagnole," "blonds"* and esse ces that take large quantities of meat to make. The French cook who is thoroughly imbued with the teachings of that system delights in the most costly dishes, and for every economical method he may be obliged to adopt he makes an apology to the genius of his art. It is in the impracticable nature of the system itself that it could not be adopted nor even understood by any set of people governed by business principles. Our familiar Francatelli, the book which most cooks possess, and which we borrow the big words from to terrify our hotel guests with and make them feel small and cheap because they don't understand French as we do—the book that cooks learn some things from, but which none can work by, is as irreconcilable with any practice that hotel-keepers can permit as the "artist" Bernard, of the anecdote, himself could have been.

In order to obtain this precious *espagnole, blond* and *veloute*, presumably for about twenty-five per-

sons—only the sauces for the dinner, it is to be observed, and not the dinner itself—Francatelli tells us we must use the following amount of material:
40 pounds of white veal, or 2 legs.
40 pounds of gravy beef.
40 pounds of leg of beef and knuckles of veal.
1 pound of fresh butter.
1 pound of lean ham.
3 wild rabbits.
2 hens.
1 pound of glaze (reduced essence of meat).
Some essence of mushrooms
Some chicken broth.
Some blond of veal.
Butter and flour thickening, vegetables and herbs.

When we have used up all that material—not to name that which has gone beside to make the pound of glaze, the chicken broth and the blond of veal and the essence of mushrooms—and gone through processes occupying two or three days, we shall have as a result some indefinite amount—supposably two or three quarts—of sauces and about an equal amount of precious soup stock ready to begin to make a soup with. Is there anything strange in the fact that French cookery has failed to take root among us?

Francatelli's book is practically the only medium there is for English speaking cooks to learn this French nonsense through, but although bearing the deceptive title of the "Modern Cook," it was really written about fifty years ago, and is out of date with those who can read French. So to make good our statement that the principle of French cookery is the same to-day that it was in the time of the Prince of Soubise and his maitre d'hotel Bertrand we will quote the directions for making the same fundamental sauces from Jules Gouffe, so late as 1871. We are first to have ready five gallons of good soup stock, that has consumed in the making already an incredible amount of meat and poultry, and then we are to take for the new beginning:
12 pounds of veal without bone.
4 pounds of gravy beef.
2 young hens.
2 pounds of fresh butter—the
5 gallons of stock.
Vegetables, herbs, flour, seasonings.

Gouffe is sufficiently definite in his statements of amounts. When we have have used up the above material and condensed the product we shall possess 3 quarts of brown sauce and 3 quarts of white sauce. Only this and nothing more. It may be left to the common sense of the cook to make use of the solid meat veal and the hens after this first use for making sauce, but there is no direction to do so, and no encouragement for it is expressly stated in these words:

"It is a mistake to think that by over-cooking the meat the consomme or sauces will be improved thereby; when thoroughly cooked, *all nutriment is extracted from the meat*

This, although dated so late as 1871, is the same old worship of the gravy. The meat is nothing; the sauce is everything. But the common sense of a people rises above the theories of the ancient alchemists and modern cranks. The workingman who finds it necessary to lay out so large a proportion of his earnings in butcher's meat would laugh such a theory to scorn; and for hotel men a system based upon such ideas is simply absurd and impracticable.

Every hotel cook repeats the current remarks, "Oh, you can't work by Francatelli," or, "It would break up any hotel in the world to follow Francatel i."

And yet they must read it; there is nothing else. If they could read further they would make the same remarks about all the French authorities. They read and then stumble along, doing as circumstances compel them, the best way they can.

But French cooks who have been trained have these impracticable notions drilled into them and are not always so accommodating as to lay them aside for money-making considerations.

Two little instances occur to mind that will serve to show how this irreconcilable system conflicts with hotel keeping interests. This one was a "French John," so called, who became second cook in a flourishing hotel, and on the second forenoon was required to make a tomato sauce. A small quantity only was wanted, a ten cents worth in cost, perhaps; a little sauce made in an omelet pan to go with an unimportant entree. There would not be more than a dozen orders called for. It did not require the expenditure of more than a few minutes' time when there were many larger matters needing attention. But John took the solid end of a good ham, a two quart can of tomatoes, a pound of butter, some onions, bay leaves and other seasonings and a saucepan of soup stock, which he set about boiling down to glaze, while the three pounds of ham was boiling in the tomatoes, likewise being condensed. For John was a conscientious disciple of the French culinary masters: the word sauce was one of immense meaning to him, and he thought the hour or two devoted to that one operation was worthily spent. The head cook, however, disapproved of the whole thing, and when at last a little of the precious sauce had been laboriously forced through a "tammy," and it proved to be scorched at the bottom and almost worthless, he sharply remonstrated, and poor John got upon his dignity. "What you want?" said he. "I cook French. I no make it you shlop, I make it you good things. If you want-it shlop for sauce get your pan-washer to make it; I'm a French cook." And so he folded up his jacket and left. All the sympathy goes with John in a case like this, because he will not make "shlop," and will not be cheap. We understand that very well, and he is welcome to it, for the system he works under is utterly impracticable just the same.

All French cooks are not so unreasonable, for they do not all live up to their books; we purposely mention two who did, to show how it works.

The other was a head cook, an ideal French chef, soft mannered, educated and polite, who could give a reason for what he did. He was extravagant in the use of material to a degree worthy almost of Urbain-Dubois, the Kaiser's cook himself. The hotel was doing a good business and could stand a good deal of expense, still there were some items that pinched with an uncommon pressure. One of these was butter. The proprietors were already educated up to the point of buying none but perfectly sweet butter, and it so happened that such an article at that time and place cost thirty-to forty cents per pound. A forty-pound tub of it was rolled into the kitchen every morning for the cook to use, and it seldom proved sufficient for the day. Another item was the wines and liquors, which this chef, working strictly up to rule, would not accept at all unless they were by the quart dipperful. Common wine for marinading and stewing and baking in, Maderia, Port and Sherry for soups and ragouts; rum and brandy for sauces. Sixteen dollars a day for cooking butter and about the same sum for liquors, in a hotel of no great size, made the proprietors murmur a long time, and at length they spoke to the chef about it. Couldn't he manage to run with less? The chef put on a dejected look, shrugged his shoulders and spread out the palms of his hands—"Yes, if you want to live common, but, if you want to be first-class—!" That was enough to quell the proprietors. Of course they wanted to be first-class. They did not stop to say it, but silently retreated. But a short time after they mustered up courage once again. Better not to be so thoroughly first-class than to be bankrupt, and the accomplished chef took his departure. He would have been a most valuable man in his position, if he had not been pursuing an impracticable system.

Where it once Flourished.

French cookery considered in its ornamental character also is a thing of the past. The sudden change to the fashion of serving dinner *a la Russe* killed it. The system which used to tyrannize over all who could not speak the language, had its head severed from its trunk by that swift stroke as neatly as in the story we read, where the blade was so keen the person decapitated did not know that it had passed through his neck until he began to move about and found his head was loose.

The allusions we often hear from "old-timers" to the splendor of the tables of the southern river steamboats of from thirty to fifty years ago are no part of the common peurile praise of "good old times," but relate to a time when everything ornamental in French cookery and French terms that now seem so nonsensical really was brought into full practice and exhibition. The peculiar conditions that made it practicable then and not now, on the river, resulted from there being then plenty of very wealthy travelers and no railway in that part of the country for them to travel on. They made their regular winter visits to New Orleans. The steamboats were the only means of conveyance. Whole families of the planters went at once and returned at once, and they were about a week, on an average, on board the boat each way. The swiftest steamers that set the finest tables secured the greatest numbers. There would be from two hundred to five hundred of the wealthiest, or at least the most extravagant class of people; there were bands of music on board, and grand balls were frequent, when perhaps the passengers from another steamboat of even speed going the same way would come on board as guests, to be returned to their own boat at some landing toward the morning. There was then nothing too good or too expensive for some of the captains to put on their tables. That was the time for display. It came to an end with the completion of the first northern railroad to New Orleans, and the steamboats changed in character from race-horses to mere beasts of burden.

Twenty-Four Entrees a Day.

The style of serving dinner then was to set one table the entire length of the cabin, and the dishes that composed the dinner were set upon the table in their entirety, in chafing dishes kept hot by alcohol lamps. To make a good show on such a table, as many as twenty-four entrees might be wanted, perhaps twelve different ones and two of each kind, or eight different and three of a kind, and dishes of vegetables to match. The people at table saw everything whether they chose to partake of it or not, and there was reason enough for building up, ornamenting and naming dishes then. The waiters took up each dish in turn, while the captain or steward was carving and serving the roasts, and offered them to each person, and helped those who accepted from the dish as they went along. The names of dishes meant something then to the cooks and stewards, for as every different named dish of fowl had a different division of the joints, a different way of building up in the dish and different color and ornamentation, one standing at the end of the table could tell whether a dish of fowl was a fricassee *a la St. Lambert*, or a fricassee *a la Romaine*, and whether another was a *turban* or a *chartreuse*, and whether a fish was *a la Chambord*, or *a la Chevaliere*. But i those dishes had been kept in the kitchen and served individually nobody could have seen where the name came in. That is what makes the French names so senseless now. You may take a certain number of breasts of chicken and build up a turban of fillets of fowl, and it *is* a turban—a definite something with a name. But if you serve it out of sight, in the carving room, you cannot persuade anybody that it is a piece of turban; common sense says it is a piece of chicken. To give the names of these dishes that are never seen is like winking at your girl in the dark; you may know what you are doing but nobody else does. At least half the French names of dishes were swept out of use when the individual style and small dishes and small tables came in vogue.

No More Sugar Toys.

So with centre pieces and ornamental gum paste temples. In ancient times it was the custom to set images of the favorite deities on the banqueting tables, to bring good luck. The French changed it for the *plateau*, a centre piece of almost any ornamental form, a vase or fountain or church set on a bed of moss, or something of the sort, not of eatable materials, and from that came the chateaux in sugar rock work and the Chinese pagodas in gum paste. But now the only centre pieces at the finest banquets are banks of flowers and the opportunities for displaying ornamental meat dishes and sugar work occur but seldom when there is a set supper for a party or a ball. This has swept away another feature of the old-time bills of fare, for except when the cooks get up banquets for themselves so that they may once and again have the joy of showing these things which they love so much but which nobody else wants, there are no more *grosses pieces* and *pieces montees*.

"The Tables Fairly Groaned."

Under that old method of setting the long table for dinner both in hotel and steamboat and summoning the people by bell or gong all to come and eat and see at once, there were strong reasons for doing many things in the way of producing variety that seem useless and silly now. There was the very extended table to be filled and after the meat dishes were removed, as many more of pastry and dessert were required to replace them, and if there was to be three stands of meringues, three of custard in cups, and three of charlotte russe, and so forth. if the pastry cook was skillful enough there was no reason why the charlottes should not be different in form and ornament, the custards all have a different topping and the meringues be white, rose-colored and chocolate instead of all alike, since they would be seen all down the table on account of their being on raised stands. In the hotels the finest dinner of the week was on Sunday, on steamboats it was the last dinner of the trip.

A boat would perhaps be three or four days from New Orleans to Memphis, or six or seven to St. Louis, or Louisville or Nashville or Huntsville or Tuscumbia; and the steward starting out with his ice chests full of provisions, had his Mobile Bay oysters, soldered in tin cans at New Orleans, packed down in ice that came from Maine in sailing vessels; his terrapins, turtle and best fishes, such as pompano and Spanish mackerel, all laid out and apportioned for each dinner that was to come. The first day out was common, the second day's dinner better, about the third dinner the extras began to show up, and in getting ready for the last two dinners of the trip the cooks and pastry cooks would work all night doing ornamental work, and when the boat was in port they had two or three days with nothing to do but a dozen officers to cook for, and the fine cakes and gum paste businesses on hand would do to start the return trip dinners with.

False Standards of Excellence.

The cooks who were eminent among their fellows for their skill in building up ornamental entrees and cold dishes to set up on high on these long tables for all to see; the cooks who had the largest assortment of ornamental silver skewers and who could cut the most marvelously fine roses and lilies out of beets and turnips; the pastry cook who could build the most architecturally correct churches of gum paste, with gelatine windows, and who had the most molds wherein to cast horses and things in either sugar or mutton tallow found their occupation gone under the new fashion of serving dinner at small tables and carving the meats in the pantry or kitchen, and each one had to throw away enough of that kind of knowledge to set up half a dozen cooks under the modern manner. Still the French cooks grieve over this state of things. There is nothing finer than a boar's head *a la St. Hubert*, for a cold dish, or a fillet of beef *a la Godard*, for a hot one, but the names relate solely to the manner of decorating and the ornamental stands they are served upon, and when either article is sliced up St. Hubert and M. Godard both vanish and the dishes are resolved into their original elements of pig's head and beef. But this is so difficult for cooks—and indeed a good many others—to realize, there is such a deceptive glamour about these play things that kings and nobles have patronized and former fashions have cherished that a false standard of culinary excellence is set up, that is unfair all around.

The hotel keeper of the present day says in effect, to his cook, when he opens his house; "Now, I can bring plenty of customers to my hotel, but I depend upon you to keep them." And if the cook does such good cooking that he does keep them and the house fills up and overflows, he does that which makes money for cooks and all concerned. But on account of the false standard set up by French cookery the mass of cooks never think that kind of success a merit, but they ask about another one, what has he ever done? and who has ever seen his work? They mean has he ever laid an ornamental cold fish in a dish on a bed of moss made by coloring butter green and pressing it like vermicelli through a seive, or has he ever made a castle out of pressed head cheese. These were paying accomplishments forty years ago, but they are only play business now. They are so much more of the French system swept away by the ruthless hand of time.

There is an association of French-speaking cooks called the Universal Society of Culinary Art, that seems to be a sort of international trades union with missionary, or perhaps propagandist tendencies, that has its headquarters in this country in New York and branches in all the principal cities. It ought to do good in teaching cookery, and perhaps it will. The prospect would be better if there were but one such union, but there is another association of French cooks in New York beside, and, it seems that the two are not in harmony. The leading motive of both is, however, the same. Like the children in the promised land, they have spied out the United States and found it a goodly land for cooks and they are going forth to possess it and its milk and honey.

Before they can succeed in this laudable enterprise, however, they must learn to speak United States when they 'talk of cooking or eating, for the people of this country positively will not go to the trouble of learning French words as a preliminary to getting their dinners, when they can have as good as they want without. They must not tell the domestic cooks who may be their pupils to *vanner* a sauce when they mean to skim until it is bright, nor say *bardez-le* when they mean cover it with bands of bacon, because these cooks have not generally made much progress in their French lessons at college. In the early editions of Francatelli the directions to *dauhe* a piece of meat were very frequent, but none of the English wanted their meat daubed, it was a "nasty" word to them, and accordingly in the later editions the word almost entirely disappeared, and *larded* has taken its place.

The domestic cook books of this country that have had the largest sales, reaching to the hundred thousand copies, and which have done good, have not required a French education for their understanding, for there is no more mention of a French name or dish or sauce in them than if such a nation was not in existence, and, which must seem most incomprehensible to French cooks who regard them as the very foundation for everything, they do not tell how to make *espagnole* and *veloute*, nor even mention them! And still we claim to be a civilized people.

One of the officers of this Universal society, a very good friend of the writers, was talking one day about this association and its objects. He himself is a regularly trained cook. When, a boy, he was called upon to choose what trade he would follow, he chose to be a cook, as much as a matter of course, as he would have chosen to be a printer or a carpenter or a builder or a bookkeeper, for that was in Europe. He said they had about four hundred members in New York. We replied that four hundred cooks were not many to cook for a million and a half of people. He said they they had forty members in Chicago.

We thought that forty were not many in a city of six hundred thousand.

"But," he said, "we are going to train cooks enough for all those small hotels and for all the private families who can afford to employ them—we shall train them from the beginning—we shal teach them to make *espagnole* and *veloute*."

One does not naturally continue a subject with a friend, on which there can be no possible agreement, and the conversation was dropped.

Espagnole and *veloute* will never be taught to any considerable extent in this country, because they will never be adopted nor wanted nor understood. Ever since the time of Ude, the cook or maitre d'hotel of Louis XV, and Bechamel somewhat later, and Careme, who cooked for King George, III, the French cooks have been trying to teach these two sauces to the Anglo-Saxons, and probably not one in a hundred thousand persons knows what they are to-day. They are, as we have already shown, a brown stock sauce and a white one, made by consuming about ten pounds of meat to produce a pint. Employers will not have them. They are not wanted. There is extravagance enough in dress and furniture and building, but in this country extravagance does not extend to the culinary operations.

What remains? Well, all the essential part of cookery remains under the rubbish. There is an excellent hotel system already in existence, but it has never been put in a book. There is good cooking going on in thousands of places, but in an individual go-as-you-please sort of way. One cook knows a half dozen soups and a dozen entrees and another knows the same number that are all different, and we propose to bring them together. These cooks who could not follow out French directions because they were inpracticable have nevertheless found something in them. Some dishes have been adopted from the Italians, some from the Germans, some from the Mexicans and Spaniards, some from the French Creoles, and a great number from "home cooking." A writer in a leading magazine just recently extolled the true Maryland cookery as being unsupassed in the world, although simplicity itself, and the remark might be applied to more than one state or section. They will be disappointed who are looking for a book of entrees that will furnish them with a bran new set of French names longer and harder than any other cook ever had, but, whenever in the following pages we happen to know what the foreign name of any dish used to be we will tell you. There is to be no pulling down of the cook's occupation, but a building up. But there are many deep rooted wrong ideas to be encountered.

A Frightful Example

Here is a cook who has sent us three of his best Sunday bills of fare. He is such a cook as hotel keepers are willing to pay fifty or sixty dollars a month to. He is perfectly satisfied with himself and his bills of fare, and thinks his hard to beat, and the only thing in the world he would be willing to learn would be some more French terms, because each of his bills has twelve entrees and only half of them are outfitted with French *a la's*, and then the stock gave out and the other five or six had to come out in common English. The entrees are in the same number that used to be required to set along those extended tables we have referred to, and this man does realize that he is behind the times, and two or three would be better now. Of his twelve entrees four are of the pudding order, being "Spanish cake with lemon sauce, macaroni and cheese, Welsh rarebits, and charlotte of peaches," forgetting that nobody wants them and the pastry part of the dinner too. Then, in all three of the bills the entrees are nearly the same over again. He has what was evidently *noix* of veal *a la* something—one of the stock dishes from Francatelli—changed into "knuckle of veal," and it is in all his bills. Perhaps, when he used to write it *noix* the printers boy used to run over out of breath asking what that word was, and the waiters did not know how to call it—such is the preposterousness of the whole business—and has construed it noix—nux—knucks—knuckles, and probably thinks that is what it is. If he is wrong in any of these particulars there is no book and no person to tell him and the like of him any better, and for this reason we have taken up our task.

1162. Common Sense About Entrees.

Entrees seem more intelligible if one has graduated from a cooks' college—when called by their other name, *made dishes*, in contra distinction from the plain roasted and boi'ed meats. About all the pleasure there is in meat cooking is to be found in making the entrees and soups, as they call for taste and skill, and there is a certain sort of delight, such as every good workman finds in his occupation, in the perfect fit of every article of provision to the place where it is wanted, either large or small, either prominent or unimportant, to keep up an even average in the bill of fare. Thus, when you have good meats or fowls or turkeys in the roasts the entrees are but of little consequence, any trifles that do not cost much will do, but when the plain meats are unattractive put in the best your skill can furnish of made dishes.

Entrees were so called because they were the first to enter the dining room, according to French usage. Then, as now, at small dinners of more or less ceremony the entrees took the place that the plain roast meats occupy in the hotel dinners. Though not with us the leading dishes they are very necessary as a means of making use of many pieces of meat and other articles that could not be used in other ways. One of the first thoughts, apparently, that a hotel keeper has in regard to cutting down the expenses of the table is that he will cut off the entrees, but perhaps that is what he can least afford to do. It depends, however, upon whether they are made an item of expense or a means of saving by the cook, and whether they are really valuable dishes or only things crowded in to make a huge bill of fare.

1163. Knowledge of Cookery Requisite.

These made dishes render life a burden to cooks who have not learned to consider them in a true light, they know no reason for them; there is a certain lot of padding to be done to fill the bill and it seems that the markets are never big enough and never well enough furnished to supply materials to make entrees; but, on the other hand it seems mere pastime when you get the business down to the proper focus. Then you find the made dishes are the means of saving you trouble with the goods you already have on hand. American hotels are the only perfect schools of cookery for that reason. There are ladies lecturing in the cities about how to choose meat, and telling that the worse parts of the animal are the better, but they can never give point or meaning to such statements until they observe how admirably skillful cookery converts the unpromising odds and ends of raw material into finished dishes in really good hotels. We may even make some things that we know will not be called for, merely to keep up the usual number when everybody is feasting on some specialty of the day. At the same time it is found that among the many guests of a hotel there will be a few who will choose viands that the majority would look upon with aversion.

1164. Different Tastes to Suit.

While most people will choose the plain roasts we ave known some German merchants and their families who never ate any but stewed meats. It mattered but little in which of twenty different forms the stewed meat appeared so that it *was* stewed. If there was no such entree in the list these good customers were deprived of their dinner. The roast meats are the dearest and stewed meats and pot-pies are the cheapest, consequently it is a merit to make them good. It is a source of pride to a cook because it is a proof of skill, when the plain meats are left alone and the entrees are all consumed. We knew an Italian cook once who made macaroni in some form almost every day and had succeeded in bringing it in great request, and the boys, and the steward too, quizzed him about serving so much macaroni *because* he was Italian. But he went to figuring and showed that his delicious specialty cost the house less than two cents a dish, and then we all looked upon his proceeding in a different light, for almost all in the house were eating it.

1165. Variety

The real difference between dishes of the same character cannot always be great and it is not necessary they should be. There is something monotonous about writing out a bill of fare every morning and a feeling that we are repeating the same words week after week never giving the people anything new. There is no need to account for it, it simply is so as every cook knows who has to tell the steward what dishes he is going to make for dinner. This is what causes the anxiety to acquire more French terms. The real remedy is to learn more dishes. Hotel-keepers themselves who do not go deeply into the daily routine sometimes question the necessity of so many changes, but the stewards who write the menus—in some hotels where there is luncheon, dinner, and five o'clock dinner served, three menus in one day—know that there are never dishes enough to select from.

People in private houses who have a salad perhaps but once a week or never except at a party, cannot see the use of our having five or six different styles of putting, say a shrimp salad on a dish. But if they had to serve salads at three meals each day, and two or more kinds at each meal they would discover in a few weeks that it would be difficult to show up anything to a banquet or party supper that had not already become an old story. It is the same in cultivating many kinds of fruits and flowers. We have peaches, grapes, strawberries, and they are good enough, and still growers go on producing new varieties; and no matter how good and sufficient one person's residence may be a thousand others will build theirs all some different way. "Variety is the spice of life."

But the solid comfort to a cook of knowing all the ways can be better illustrated in this manner: When the breakfast meats have been cut and laid ready, with the pork chops to be breaded, you have two briskets of pork left over and as they will not do for roast pork you plan the dinner bill with these pieces for the leading entree, stuffed and rolled. When that question is settled and the other made dishes are decided upon and the bill of fare as good as finished, here begins a game of "ten little Injuns" with your meat. It loses one slice and another slice until your dinner bill is all broke up again. The breakfast cutlets give out and a cut or two comes off the pork roll until there is not enough left to serve in that style, and you conclude to slice it and fry in flour and serve with tomato sauce. Another portion goes and you have only enough left for a meat pie; the remainder of that brisket is called for and the half of what you originally had will answer only for a brown stew eked out with potatoes. Another call and another and at last there is barely enough left to serve as seasoning for another dish and the bill of fare must be made all over again.

1166. Knowing How Much to Prepare.

It must seem like an assumption in any case to say in advance how much of any article to be offered will be ordered and consumed by a given number of people at a hotel table, but still every cook learns by experience to make a very close guess. There are scores of contingencies, of course, that throw the calculations out and require "gumption" in the cook to make allowance for them. There is nothing more provocative of disgust with the whole catering business than to have to begin before the meal is half over answering the demands with "it is all out," except the other extreme of having all the pans and saucepans left at the end of a meal full of fixed up messes that nobody wants or ever will want.

A cook can never learn how to avoid both difficulties without seeing for himself at the end of every meal just what has been eaten out clean and what has been passed by unnoticed.

Generally speaking all dishes containing chicken in any form, turkey, oysters and eggs will be ordored by the hundred dishes when curries and other highly flavored articles are only called for by the tens.

A very much disappointed cook we once knew had made a hundred lobster cutlets as one of his entrees for two hundred persons. He was from the seashore where he had been used to seeing such dishes held in great estimation, for people often go there with the intention of feasting on sea products who never care for them at home. The cook had destroyed a good many lobsters to make his flattened croquettes with the lobster claw in each one like the bone of a lamb chop and he dished them very handsomely with sauce and trimmings. But at the end of the dinner there had been no more than twelve or fifteen orders for his cutlets that had cost him four hours of labor, and he looked at them as a model maker might gaze on a machine that won't work, and shrugging his shoulders he said, "Well, I suppose I may eat my cutlets myself." He never made any more.

1167. How People Order Dinner.

There is no natural division in an American plan dinner where Roman punch or an equivalent for it can be introduced, although any sort of form may be instituted by mutual consent; and there is no propriety in placing the game in the bill of fare anywhere but in the list of roasts at the top.

The home coterie at the tables at one end of the dining-room, can order their dinners in courses from the ordinary hotel bill of fare, if they choose to do so, and in as many courses as they please without regard to the arrangement of the dishes in the menu. It is a matter between themselves, the inside steward and head waiter and does not concern the carver or the cook, because the dinner lasts long enough in any case and when a waiter comes for a set of late orders of game it is all the same whether it is a party taking game as a subsequent course or a new party taking game instead of roast beef for their entire dinner. It is not like the whole company setting down at once, all reaching the Roman punch course at once, and all taking game and salad simultaneously

The hotel is still an inn.

There is a natural way that people left entirely unconstrained order their dinner, which perhaps is not to be accounted for, but is instinctive, and the vast majority feel the more comfortable in a hotel the more easy it is made for them to fall into the natural course. Their ways and manners are formed elsewhere; the hotel is not to form them anew, but to accommodate them in their own predilections. If we set out the glass of frozen punch in the middle of the dinner for the average transient guest, when ice cream is afterwards offered at the finish, there is a great probability that he will remark he has already had ice cream. There may be a laughing in the sleeve somewhere, but no certainty that the hotel is getting the best of it; there are so many more people than there are hotels, and they have so much more time to prolong the laughter.

In the natural course people want no "waits" between the soup and fish. Where there is a bill of fare, they inevitably order these together. Where there is no bill and the dinner is "called off" by the waiters, the "call" should be arranged accordingly.

Then they look over the whole bill, and it makes no difference where you may have placed the game and salads, even at the very bottom, they order then whatever they want in the way of meats, game, entrees, salads and vegetables all at one time.

As a rule, a person does not call for more than one kind of plain meat, and if he takes a slice of venison or other game, he will not order beef or mutton likewise, as if he should take meat now and more meat in another course afterwards, but having his one cut he will choose with it one or two of the made dishes and one or two or perhaps three vegetables. The exceptions are when one kind serves as a relish for another, as when boiled ham or pork is ordered to eat with chicken; and where, again, no roast meat at all is ordered but the dinner made of some favorite entree, like a bird pie.

Then there comes a natural pause in the dinner and the "wait" between that and the third and last division is not annoying to any but business men, who have but a few minutes to devote to the troublesome necessity of dining.

1168. The Use of Sweet Entrees.

And that shows the use of having a sweet entree, and accounts for the common practice. It seems natural to end the dinner with a sweet, yet one half the customers of some hotels think they can not wait long enough to take the third course, and every one has inbred home manners enough not to order pudding and pie with his meats, when it is that some trifle of a rice cake with jelly or a fruit fritter goes right to the spot and answers every requirement. It is ordered with the meats and other entrees, despatched in the last two minutes and the merchant is free to hurry back to the store and let his clerk go to dinner, while those who live to eat take their new set-out of cakes, ice creams and fruits at their leisure.

We have already remarked that there is a good American system already in existence. It only wants pruning and shaping. The "sweet entree" is a part of it, and by diligent search a fair reason why has been found. But one is enough, and no conceivable reason can be adduced for having more than one at once, and there is no reason even for that one when it is a dinner of leisure and every person will remain to partake of the abundant third course, of pastry and pudding, and creams and fruits, cheese and coffee.

1169. Vegetable Entrees.

It is stretching the meaning of the word considerably to speak of entrees of vegetables, yet such is the practice, and it must be considered in the sense of *made dishes* of vegetables Then it is perfectly intelligible.

For vegetables appear in two ways, either plain, like ordinary stewed tomatoes, or as garnishes or made dishes, like tomatoes stuffed and baked. These vegetable garnishes gave names to a number of dishes under the old style, or would have given names if there had been sufficient common sense in them for ordinary people to grasp. Thus, a piece of beef or rather meat in a dish with greens around it, was beef *a la Flamande*—that is in Flemish or Dutch style; with maccaroni around it, it was *a la Milanaise*—or in the style of the people of Milan in Italy; if it had sourkraut it was *a l' Allemande*—or German style; if with dumplings in the dish it was *a l' Anglaise* or in English style; if with beets, it was *a la Polonaise*—in the style of Poland; with stuffed and baked tomatoes around, it was *a la Provencale*—in the style of the south of France; with a general variety of vegetables in the same dish, like the New England boiled dinner, it was *a la Jardiniere*—the gardener's style; with the same vegetables cut small and mixed together, it was *a la Macedoine*—with a mixed garnish; and from these simples the plan ran on to all sorts of mixed sauces and ragouts. They are all out of fashion now. These names only hold good when the dish was set on the table whole. When a man orders beef on one dish and greens on another and puts them together he knows he is eating beef and greens, and all who sit around the table may know it at a glance, but there is no possible way of making them see the sense of calling it beef *a la Flamande*, especially as they do not know how *Flamande* should be pronounced.

The use of having these made dishes of vegetables among our entrees is precisely this: Two persons will order roast goose from the carving stand. One likes onions with it and orders baked onions— which he finds on the same among the entrees; the other does not and eats his portion with spinach or peas.

Surely there is something comical in the fact that all the common cooks and all the domestic cooks and housekeepers are setting dishes *a la Flamande*, *a l' Allemande*, *a la Provencale* and the rest of it on their tables every day, and have not the remotest suspicion of the fact, while the cooks of the hotels who handle the big words without knowing their meaning, don't come within a mile of what they think they are doing.

It is to be distinctly understood, then, that vegetable entrees are proper to be made at certain times. Besides those mentioned they are such dishes as spinach with poached eggs, stewed mushrooms on toast, asparagus points in crusts, stuffed onions, fried cabbage and many more, which help in making an intelligible bill of fare and a sensibly arranged dinner.

1170. The Rule of Entrees.

Highest number needed daily in any hotel, 5. Necessary for the smallest hotel, 2.

1st. A Leading Entree—something to be carved —highly seasoned meats—braised and stuffed rolls —fowls stuffed with onions—or birds too dear to be served in large portions, as roasts.

2nd. A Stewed Meat Entree—including fricassoes with borders, and all sorts of meat pies.

3rd. A Vegetable Entree—including macaroni and spaghetti, cheese polenta and beans.

4th. A Minced Entree—such as minced ham, minced veal, brains, croquettes—trifles of various sorts to suit peculiar tastes—fish entrees for Friday.

5th. A Sweet Entree.

Every practical steward and cook well knows that no very strict rule can be closely followed, because of the first necessity of using to good advantage the articles of provision that may be on hand, yet those who find their daily perplexity in composing the dinner bill of fare find it an immense assistance to bear such a rule in mind.

The smallest hotels need two or three entrees, not only to make a more excellent dinner, but in order that small quantities of good things, like chicken and sweetbreads, may be served in patties and croquettes, when they will not make a large dish.

1171. Osmazome.

Another name for it is beef tea; another is blood gravy. To come as near as possible to describing a half-imaginary substance by showing the real we should say that osmazome is the meaty part of beef tea divided from the clear or watery portion. This is the essence of meat that we incidentally referred to some pages back as having had so much to do with the construction of that world's puzzle called French cookery. Osmazome is defined in one of the old books as a product of the muscular fibre of meat, which gives the characteristic flavor of soup and broth, and was formerly supposed to be a definite substance. The time referred to was when one of the old French kings had to be nourished on beef tea and the royal doctors gave it a Greek name and proclaimed it as a new scientific discovery for fear the common people would begin to suspect that the king was like themselves. The news from the palace was not then conveyed to every house by cheap newspapers, and the cooks and attendants were very proud to have it to say that His Majesty and a few of the most favored courtiers were nourished with the supreme essence and strength and concentrated nutriment of the most expensive meats, in short, with osmazome, which was by far too costly for the common people, and a thing which, indeed, was not intended for their concern. It is to the aged weakness of Louis XIV., that we owe the cordials of spirit and sugar delicately flavored, noyeau, orgeat, curacoa, vermouth and many more. "For, feeling sometimes the difficulty of living, which often appears after sixty, they made him a cordial by mixing brandy with sugar and scents—the germ of the art of the modern liquorist." In such manner doubtless commenced the excessive refinement of sauces and food essences. New beauties and new properties were discovered in a gravy. There was a peculiar fascination in the idea that the entire strength of an ox was in the osmazome contained in its carcass, and that it could all be served up in one bowl of soup. There was the exultation of unapproachable superiority in the reflection that the commonalty in order to obtain a small modicum of the precious substance would have to go through the laborious process of eating the ox itself, piece by piece. We read that a Canon Chevier used to keep a padlock on the stock boiler, and, that many cooks used to be dismissed for abstracting the first soup—the beef tea—and filling up with water again, so valuable was it considered. "For," says our authority, "it is osmazome which constitutes the real merit of good soups. It is osmazome which, passing into a state resembling caramel, gives meat its reddish tinge, which forms the crisp brown on roasts and which yields a flavor to venison and game. It is derived principally from full-grown animals, with reddish or dark flesh; and it is scarcely ever found in veal, sucking pigs, pullets, or even the best fed capons. This explains, by the way, why your real connoisseur has always in poultry, preferred the dark meat."

Now, the reader who goes along with us will probably learn more of the motives and real merits of French cookery than were ever presented to him to see before, for the world never lets any real excellence be forgotten. Covered up out of sight by the royal press and courtly euphemisms we shall find the first rudiments of good cooking. The cordials and liqueurs have a certain excellence of their own, they are nice for old people and sugar-and-water drinkers, yet if all the fine writers should advise all the people to drink them if they wished to show that they were cultured and not too stupid to learn French excellences, the people would go on taking no notice whatever and drinking something else precisely as they act in regard to the special exaltations and refinements of cookery. We have to separate the real from the fanciful. The commonest cook in the commonest hotel, who does the bad cooking that everybody knows is bad; that even common and stupid people understand is bad—the cook who crowds a lot of all kinds of meat into one baking pan and slings it into a warm oven long before it is needed and lets it warm up gradually, sees this valuable osmazome trickling out of the meat in red drops all over the surface for perhaps an hour or more before it becomes hot enough to cook the outside and stop it; and who lets these drops of essence run into the pan and bake there, and adds to them by constantly thrusting a fork into the meat and drawing fresh streams, is indeed doing a very French way of drawing out this supreme essence, but the grand difference is that while the French system allows that meat so treated is spoiled and is willing it should be in order to obtain the osmazome, which will be espagnole when it is flavored and finished, this unlearned and unskilled cook that we are supposing will throw the gravy away and serve up the meat; will have spoiled the meat for nothing, and will not know that it is spoiled. As we do not value osmazome with the exaggerated estimate of the French system and only need a small amount for the gravy for our robust people instead of drawing out all he can in that careless way he should strive to keep it all in the meat, and after he has done his best to prevent its oozing out it will be found that enough has escaped to make a little commonplace espagnole or pan gravy in spite of all he could do.

1172. Espagnole—Brown Sauce.

We took occasion to remark, some way back, the extraordinary esteem in which some dishes were held by customers of cafes who brought their imaginations to bear to give an exalted character to a rather commonplace spread. Here, now, is a story gravely told as showing the superlative excellence of a great man's cookery as if it were an art not to be compassed by ordinary mortals.

Many a cook, at the present moment, who sends in tenderloin steaks with plenty of natural gravy by the hundred a day and receives no special notice for it will fail to see why this young fellow should be so choked with wonder at the sight that he could hardly speak at all. This is the anecdote:

"The *Vicomte de Vaudreuil*, when appointed *chargé d' affaires* of France to the Court of St. James's, brought over with him a young cook, an *eleve* of the highest schools of the *cuisines* of Paris.

This young culinary aspirant to fame, shortly after his arrival in London, obtained permission of his master to go and witness the artistic operations of that established *cordon bleu*, Monsieur Mingay, the cook to Prince Esterhazy, who had been brought up under the Prince Talleyrand's famous *chef*, Louis, and previously under that most *bleu* of all *cordons*, the great Careme. On the *eleve's* return, the Vicomte, hearing that his cook was in a state of astonishment from something he had witnessed in Prince Esterhazy's kitchen, summoned him to his presence, and said, 'What is this culinary miracle, which I have heard astonishes you, and casts into the shade all other triumphs of the art?' Vatel's follower replied, 'Oh, Monsieur le Vicomte, when I entered the *cuisine* at Chandos House it was near the time of the prince's luncheon, for which his excellency had ordered something which should be very simple and easily digestible, as he was suffering from languor. The *chef*, Mingay, accordingly cut from under a well-hung rump of beef three slices of fillet, and rapidly broiling them, he placed the choicest-looking in the middle of a hot dish, and afterward pressing the juice completely out of the remaining two, he poured it on the first! Oh, monsieur, how great the prince! how great the cook!'"

To couch so simple an affair, in such marvelous language, seems extremely silly unless we remember that those were the days of what we have ventured to term the worship of the gravy. However, we commend anew this old anecdote to those *chefs* who discourage the broiler by calling him "only a broil and fry cook." We have at hand a letter just written by a traveler in the southern states in which he says dolefully that a good beefsteak can not be had south of Mason and Dixon's line. Probably he should have excepted a few of the hotels, but if it be all true the false notions about what constitutes good cooking are to blame for it. The French cooks do not think it their mission to teach how to cook the beefsteaks that the whole nation wants, but to teach *espagnole* and *veloute* and dishes *a la moonshine.*

The *filet a la Chateaubriand* is very much like the Prince's beefsteak, above described, it being either a thick steak for one or two, or a whole tenderloin for a party, cooked inside of the two other steaks, the gravy from which is pressed and poured over the fillet. There are seasonings and other additions, but that brings us to espagnole. It was the meat gravy that made such a dish valuable and does so yet. It was the imaginary excellence of the gravy that made it a wonder and the wonder has passed away.

It makes but little difference how the gravy or meat essence may be obtained. If you broil a few small but thick beefsteaks rare done and pile them on a warm dish the blood gravy will run in the dish, perhaps a cupful. But, considering that rather insipid you manage to add to it a flavor of soup vegetables by adding them and some water and boiling until the water has all evaporated and you strain off the espagnole. That is the original pure article as Littre, the great French lexicographer, defines it, but the cooks have gone a little further and improved the flavor with the savor of roast meat. The same gravy as that from your dish of steak is obtained as beef tea in a bottle. You cut or chop some lean beef, put it in a bottle without any liquid added, set the bottle in a saucepan of cold water over the fire and let it heat up gradually. In an hour you can pour out the cupful of beef tea, the juice of the meat; rich but insipid and needs vegetables and seasonings to make a sauce of it.

These are illustrations of the result to be arrived at, but the real way, on a large scale, as directed by Groffe, Francatelli and the others is to put the vegetables and other seasonings in with the meat in a saucepan with butter spread on the bottom and the kinds of meat selected for their fitness, drawing the gravy by slow heat—much as we have described as very bad roasting of our home cooks—allowing the gravy so drawn to become light brown on the bottom, then pouring off the butter and fat from the meat and putting in broth instead, and when the gravy (or glaze as it has then become) has dissolved thickening it with flour baked brown in butter, straining, simmering and skimming it until bright and velvety in appearance. That is the espagnole of the books. Put a dozen ladlefuls in a dozen different saucepans and add different articles to each and you have a dozen different sauces and ragouts.

This has all been done in a saucepan on top of the fire because in past times there were no such ranges as we use at present and the baking pans with their nicely roasted meats were not there to work with. But the evident richness of the gravy that is found on the bottom of the pan in which a lot of turkeys or chickens have been roasted to perfection has forced that kind of sauce into use through the mere operation of common sense and we wish to say in the plainest language possible, for the benefit of those who need to be benefited by the assurance that this pan gravy is to all intents and purposes and in all essential respects the same thing as *espagnole*. We mean not only from the pans of poultry, but of all roast meats, although beef well roasted will furnish the least. The differences of the ways of proceeding arise from the old ways being intended for saucepan cooking and open roasting fires, and the new way being for closed ranges. It is observable that all the cooks now who put their directions in print, acknowledge this pan gravy as brown sauce, and we know for a fact that *espagnole*, as it used to be, is made in but very few places. There can be a most detestable article made and used as brown sauce and so also there is often a most execrable *espagnole*, scorched and vile; it is a matter of intelligence and skill in both cases. Some kinds of meat make a light reddish and pleasant looking brown sauce, other kinds are dark and dull. In order to insure a rich sauce put in some shanks of veal and other trimmings to cook slowly in the pan before it is time for the roasts to go in, and after the roasts come out use soup stock that has vegetable seasonings in it to make the gravy or brown sauce with, instead of putting in water. The full and particular directions have been already given in the different articles on "How to Roast Meats." Read Nos. 1022, 1062 and 1063.

1173. Blond—Veloute—White Sauce.

It is not necessary to add much to what is already written to make this plain to any comprehension. We have instanced beef tea or gravy for brown sauce and other meats are added to give color and richness, such as veal and wild rabbits. But it was noticed that fowls and veal yielded a natural gravy that had no color and their extract flavored in the boiling was thickened with a mixture of flour and butter not browned and that was and is *veloute*. In common practice take the broth in which chickens have been boiled, add to it a shank of veal and celery and other soup vegetables and boil down until it is condensed and rich, thicken, not too much; strain, simmer and skim it and that is white sauce. Boil down thicker yet, then add boiling cream to bring it to its former consistency again and a little butter, and that is Bechamel—named for a noted cook. These have also been given plain directions in former articles.

1174. Soup Making.

The operation of hotel soup making has a good deal of similarity to that pleasing trick of parlor magic in which a dozen empty glasses are placed ready, and out of the same bottle the operator pours into one of them red wine, into another white, another brandy or ale, another milk and so forth; the changes of color being caused by the different chemicals the glasses have been rinsed with previously, and other chemicals contained in the bottle. In making the daily soups the stock boiler is our bottle, and the soup pots with their different contents the glasses.

1175. Clear Soups.

There are two divisions in which soups are classed, the thick soups or potages and the thin clear soups or consommes. In some hotels one of each class appears at every dinner. You can make as many clear soups as you can full soups and of the same material. There can be a turtle soup almost like gravy and again a clear turtle which you can see the bottom of the tureen through, it is so transparent, although rich, and every square-cut piece of meat and turtle egg shows clean and distinct. You can make a green pea soup thick as cream, and also again make a clear consomme with green peas in it whole, that neither settle to the bottom nor float on top, because the consomme, although clear as oil, is rich and dense. So you can have these clear soups with rice in whole grains, or tapioca, barley, vermicelli, macaroni, alphabet pastes, vegetables cut in shapes, asparagus points, cauliflower in little flowrets, and custards both white and yellow, also small quenelles or meatballs, always in small proportions, and it is not much out of the way to compare them in appearance to gold fish in a globe of fresh water, because in these consommes there must be no crumbs and specks, each article being cooked separately and washed free from flour and scraps before being put into the clear finished consomme. These clear soups may also be of different colors, such as green colored with spinach juice, brown or amber with the color from roasted fowls, or clear white, or beet juice pink. However the amber or brandy color is the best.

1176. Full Soups.

It helps, when the daily question comes up, "What kind of soup shall we have?" to have a list of the different varieties in mind like this:

1. Gravy soups—brown meat soups, such as beef, ox-tail, mock turtle, mulligatawney, etc.

2. Cream soups, such as French cream, cream of barley, etc.

3. Puree soups—many different sorts made by thickening with a paste of something pounded through a strainer, from puree of partridge or chicken to puree of potatoes or beans.

4. Fish soups for Fridays.

5. Vegetable soups—variations of all the others, like chicken with cauliflower, and Scotch broth with mutton in dice and barley, etc.

All these varieties of soup are made out of the same stock, generally, but in the best fixed establishments there will be two boilers of stock, one with the meats rich in osmazome—the beef tea kinds—the other with the white meats. The impracticables tell us to purchase several different kinds of meat suitable for the different varieties of soup, as might be proper if there were but one dinner to be prepared, but as in every place where cooking goes on constantly there must always be a large amount of soup material on hand, instead of choosing the kinds of meat we choose which are the most suitable soups to make at the moment When the stock is mostly of beef make the gravy soups. When veal predominates make veal soups, fish soups and mock turtle. Sometimes, once a week perhaps, there will be an excess of lamb and mutton; then keep out all the fat possible and make barley, turnip, tomato and vegetable soups and Scotch broth, for all of these are best made with a portion of mutton in the stock.

And when there is but little soup material of any sort on hand and the stock is not rich is the day to make a cream soup or one of oysters or clams that takes milk instead of stock.

1178. The Stock Boiler.

It is an object to have plenty of stock and plenty of room in the stock boilers to make it, and also to be careful with it, not to make more soup than is needed, because instead of throwing away the large quantity it should be condensed to greater richness, and whatever stock can be saved from the soup is wanted to be boiled down to put into the gravy pan instead of water to make the rich espagnole that French cookery sets so much value upon—the beef stock for that, the chicken and veal stock for the white sauce. You may not have use for more than a quart of sauce of those kinds, yet it will take three or four quarts of stock to boil down to make it of the best quality.

It is against all the science of cookery to let the stock boiler be in too hot a place and boil hard. That is the objection brought against the steam stock boilers in some places; the cooks say they can not regulate them and the stock goes on at a gallop. French authorities say the stock should only "smile"—meaning to simmer gently. Some of the largest public establishments have two regular stock boilers, steam-heated, that hold from 80 to 100 gallons each and another one or two of about 60 gallons for boiling chickens and turkeys, hams, corned beef, and tongues. Commonly the rule is that there must be thirty gallons of room in the stock boiler for every fifty persons a house entertains. Room for the soup material and the water; room for the false bottom that holds the meat up from burning, and room to prevent boiling over. Thirty gallons is about the size of a flour barrel; forty-five gallons is the capacity of a whisky barrel. In a house that entertains 200 people the moveable stock boiler that has to be set on top of the range becomes a rather troublesome affair. It is seldom large enough for true economy. If made of galvanized iron, double bound, it lasts but a few months. The only durable kind is made of thick copper and they take two men to handle them. Generally there has to be two and it requires considerable good management to keep them from monopolizing the top of the range at the wrong times.

1179. Management.

Setting on the stock boiler comes immediately after the meat cutting and the pieces and soup bones should not have to lie over till the next day to lose their best flavor through exposure and drying. Drop them fresh cut into the clean boiler and fill up with cold water, remembering always that cold water draws out the juices of meat to enrich soups and stews and hot water seals up the meat and shuts them in. Read directions about the soup material at No. 992—page 262. Set the boiler on the range to heat up gradually. If a large one and full it will be slow enough to reach a boil no matter on what part of the range it is placed. Skim it as soon as the boiling begins.

The best flavored soup is that for which the stock simmers only six hours. There may be a pleasant tasted bouillon or beef broth taken off when it has cooked only one hour, but not much of the nutriment is then obtained, and again a sort of meat porridge after twelve hours' boiling when everything is dissolved but the bones, but this is only a cheap and nutritious food and has no delicacy of taste left. Six hours' slow boiling, as above remarked, is a good rule to go by. Then there is a difficulty to be met. If you set the boiler on in the afternoon, it simmers along until after supper and the fire is allowed to go out, the boiler remains there warm possibly for ten hours or eight or at any rate six, before the fire again raises it to a heat that prevents spoiling. In that lukewarm condition it is very likely to acquire a bad taste that even the French name that you will give the soup next day will not quite cure.

Beside that, the meaty particles settle to the bottom when the boiling ceases and by the time the fire is made in the morning there is a compact coating that is extremely liable to burn sooner than the stock will boil.

These things can be prevented, but it is the care and watchfulness required that makes really good cooks so scarce. Still, certain times and rules may be established in the kitchen by observing which even the most heedless helper may do all that is required.

Where there is night cooking going on or a night watch, it is a simple matter to take the boiler off the range when it has boiled long enough, or, what is better, to draw off the stock at the faucet, having first taken off the two quarts or two gallons—as the case may be—of clear fat from the top, and letting it cool and settle in the new vessel.

But where there is no such night attendance the way is to set the boiler on late enough so that it will not much more than boil before the fire is done with; then, instead of letting the fire out keep a slow one with coal dust to maintain the simmering heat for several hours.

In the morning before the fire is started, if you draw off the clear stock at the faucet near the bottom of the boiler, you will see what is meant by clear *consomme;* it will be almost clear enough for ordinary clear soups as it is, and will be more or less like melted jelly in appearance according to the degree of richness. When half of it has been drawn off and the gravy portion begins to show take another pan or boiler to hold it for making the strong soup and brown sauce—but make both lots hot as soon as possible, if you can not make them ice cold instead, for fear of souring.

It is a rule, then, that whoever builds the fire in the range in the morning must first draw off the stock and take down the boiler.

As another precaution against spoiled stock avoid putting into the boiler any essence of meat or chicken broth or anything else that has salt in it, because salt starts fermentation as soon as the temperature is right.

It is one of the hard conditions of living in this mean world that there can be no real excellence without labor either of hands or head or both. When you read of a great cook who gets three thousand dollars a year and apparently (according to the favorite way of telling it) does nothing but wear a gold watch and draw his salary, you may be sure that in reality he is going around establishing rules for preventing things going wrong and seeing to it that the rules are observed, and the same sort of capable man in a lesser position avoids the mishaps by attending to the precautions himself.

A cook receives half his salary for making every article good and the other half for preventing anything from ever going to the table bad; some can not or don't want to be efficient in both directions, consequently they never get above half pay

1180. Good Soups.

A few months ago the writer stopped at a hotel one day for dinner, and at the same table there was a little party of three who had been in the house probably a week or two.

One of the ladies was immensely amused at something. In a half aside she said to her neighbor: "Why, it's only hash!"

"Oh," expostulated the elder lady, "you should'nt order those things, they always turn out that wa ."

"How strange,"—said the other; "the bill of fare gives it such a grand name—see, *a la Montmorenci.* I thought it was something good."

"There is one thing to be said for this house,"— the other replied—"you can always depend upon the soups. I had never imagined that they could be made so enjoyable."

The reputation of the table was saved in that instance by the soup when *a la Montmorenci* had nearly ruined it.

Everybody takes soup. The exceptions are so few as not to be worth counting. The motive for having two soups at once is to suit all tastes, for some can not indulge in the rich gravy soups with impunity, and they take the light consomme; others object to cream soups and purees that they take away the appetite for dinner, and others again dislike tomato soups or other special kinds and they take the alternative of the consomme with peas or rice.

To follow up the refinements of soup-making, however, takes up lots of time. A cook who knows what he is trying to do can stand an hour over the soup-boiler, clarifying, skimming and improving it, and one soup is all that can be attended to in most of the busy kitchens. It is found that if that one soup is made good invariably not only do most of the special aversions gradually fade away, but many people pay it the silent compliment of making a dinner of soup and only one more course, it may be fish, or an entree, or pastry, but soup always.

Although in favor of two soups each day where it can be compassed we give but one at a time in the following examples, the different kinds alternating so as to be suitable to put two days together.

The wonderful increase in the common affection for the tomato flavor has to be recognized in the fullest degree. It seems singular that a vegetable which was, in the memory of some still living regarded as poisonous and grown only for an ornament, should have become of the first importance, although still an object of dislike to many. Cooks should take care to treat it only as a flavoring as they would some herbs, and not use it in more than one dish each meal and it need not then be offensive to any, while they may be pleased who like it in sauces, in clam chowder, and even in turtle oup.

First Day.
Green Turtle Soup.

Larded Fillet of Beef.
Potted Breast of Chicken in Form.
Stewed Mushrooms in Croustades.
Blanquette of Sweetbreads and Oysters.
Cream Fritters, glazed.

1181. Green Turtle Soup.

Any tolerably good cook now can make a meat soup of beef and veal and add canned turtle to it, with wine and lemon and he makes a turtle soup that is good in a general way without being quite the proper thing. It is doubtful, however, whether any one ever made the genuine old aldermanic green turtle soup by directions alone without example.

It is called so because made of the green sea turtle, but it has also a green tinge imparted by the "puree of turtle herbs" and the use of these and the different cooking of different parts of the turtle, the preparation of flour thickening and the quenelle making all take up six or eight different saucepans and make the matter hopelessly obscure without a plentiful sprinkling of the reasons why.

The green tinge can not be insisted on, and indeed is rarely seen because, of the herbs, sweet basil is practically unknown in this country and thyme, marjoram and savory are to be obtained by the many only in their dry state. However, a large proportion of parsley can be used, a small amount of green chives and green onions and very young celery leaves just raised from the seed.

Every cook should know that when these are but just dipped in boiling water they turn to a deep green, but if long cooked they lose their green color. That is the sense of some of the complex instructions. Ude was so particular he picked all the little leaves off the herbs to be scalded and pounded for coloring at last and boiled the stalks alone in the soup for flavor. Sweet basil has the flavor of cloves and that spice is the substitute for it.

There are four kinds of meat in a turtle, and the fins furnish another, and, beside the desire to give to each plate a sample of each kind, they cook in different lengths of time—the fat in half an hour—the soft white meat in an hour; the coarse meat and fins in two or three hours, the shells and bones in six hours, and the skillful preparation of the soup requires that none of the parts that go in the plates be "boiled to rags," but all neat and trim. Hence the cooking different parts in different vessels, each with some seasonings, and bringing all the parts, liquors and all into the one soup at last. A cook who is crowded for time and range room if he knows the object of certain proceedings can often take a short-cut to reach the same result with half the trouble, precisely as in cooking a mixed lot of fowls you put the hardest to cook at the bottom and the chickens at top where they can be taken out as soon as done and kept on a dish until the others are finished.

Turtle soup is expected to be a plate full and as thick with meat and quenelles (or turtle eggs) as an oyster stew is with oysters. Some of the noted turtle soup makers persist in calling the soup itself the sauce, regarding the pieces of meat as the principal part.

Probably a good many cooks have met with the remark that "it is no longer the fashion to put quenelles or egg balls in turtle soup," but they should not take any notice of it. A noted cook wrote that along with his directions a hundred years ago and a thousand "made-up" cook books have copied both the directions and the remark since then; but meantime the fashions have been changing back and forth and egg balls are very much in fashion now if the cook has only the time and the skill to make them.

For soup for fifty persons you require:
A 50-pound turtle.
5 gallons of soup-stock—about 2 pails.
4 onions—½ pound.
1 teaspoonful whole cloves.
Same of allspice.
2 blades of mace.
2 bay leaves.
Herbs, either green or dry.
1 pound of slices of raw ham.
1 pound of fresh butter—2 cups.
12 ounces of flour—3 cups.
Salt, pepper and cayenne.
2 lemons.
1 pint of Madeira.

It is expected to make three gallons of soup after reduction by boiling.

The turtle will have been cut up the night before, (see No. 1017) the meat laid on dishes, the fat in ice water in the refrigerator, and the shells in pieces. Peel off the horny covering that has been loosened by the previous scalding.

The stock will have been prepared also in the usual way over night with care that it contains only beef, veal and fowl for the ingredients.

Very early in the morning draw off the stock from the faucet clear—the fat will not come, but remains higher up in the boiler. Put the turtle shells at the bottom of a clean boiler, cover with the clear stock, boil, skim off all that rises, and then lay in the pieces of turtle meat. Let simmer a good while at the side of the range with the lid on. Take out the glutinous parts first and the others as they become tender. If in haste, you will have to put them in ice water in order to get the meat separated from the bone—but perhaps you can let them cool on dishes in the refrigerator. Cut all the cooked turtle meat you have obtained into neat squares and keep it ready for the finish, but put the bones and head back in the boiler to make the soup richer, and at the same time put in the seasonings, that is, one of the onions, all the spices, the peel of half a lemon, a little black pepper, and if you have no green herbs but parsley you can put in a small teaspoonful each of powdered thyme and savory and keep the parsley for greening at last.

Along in the middle of the morning or two hours before dinner, prepare the flavored thickening in this way: Cover the bottom of a large saucepan with the slices of raw ham, put in a pound of butter and then three or four onions cut in slices, and let them stew in the butter with the lid on. In a short time they cease stewing and begin to fry which must be immediately stopped—put the flour in, stir all up and either set the saucepan a short time in the oven with the door open or let cook on the top with care not to let the flour get more than a very pale color. When that is done dip some soup into it, stirring it smooth, until the saucepan is full when the whole mixture of ham, onions, butter, baked flour and soup may all be turned back into the boiler to save room and the use of so many vessels, there to continue boiling gently for half an hour. Then strain the soup through a fine strainer into the regular soup pot, let it simmer and the butter will rise and can be skimmed off. Put in the juice of a lemon with a spoonful of cold water and scum will rise and can be skimmed off, making the soup bright. Add the salt, little cayenne and then the turtle meat and green fat (if any when a larger sized turtle is used) already cut in inch squares. Scald and pound the green herbs already mentioned through a seive and add them for greening, but if it can not be green make the soup a rich brown instead. Add the juice of another lemon and the wine in the tureen.

The turtle eggs, if any, should be stewed separately in a little soup and added last. Egg balls for a substitute can be made either with hard-boiled yolks pounded with a raw yolk to bind them, or with any kind of white meat pounded and mixed with yolks, and can have parsley mixed with them enough to make them green—all matters of individual fancy. So also are the additions to the soup of a pinch of curry powder, a spoonful of anchovy sauce or minced lemon peel or mushroom liquor. They are not essential and had better be left out.

Live turtles range in price from 8 to 20 or 25 cents per pound. The clear meat in them is but a small proportion of the gross weight.

1182. Larded Fillet of Beef.

Having taking out the fillet as shown at No. 989, shave down the suet so that there will be a covering of it about as thick as a steak left on the meat. Then raise the edge of the fat, separate it from the fillet and lay it over without detaching the other edge, so that it will be ready to cover the fillet with again after the larding is done. The skin of the upper surface should be raised along with the fat and should be scored across to prevent drawing up in the oven.

Prepare half a pound of strips of fat bacon or pork. The pork is better because milder it a piece firm enough to bear inserting can be found. Cut in slices, then in strips, about half a finger's length, a little thinner than a common pencil, all alike in thickness and with one end slightly tapered to enter the larding needle easily. Roll them in white pepper and salt. Commence at the thick end with the larding. Insert a strip of bacon in the end of the larding needle, using another needle to assist, and draw it through the top part of the meat pinched up for the purpose. One end of each strip so inserted will be left leaning backward and the other forward on the surface. Insert six or more in an even row across. One inch forward insert another row, so alternating that the ends will fall between those of the first row. Keep on till near the end. Cut off the thinnest part of the fillet.

Cover the larded fillet with the sheet of fat. Make a long and narrow baking pan hot in the oven with a tablespoonful of salt and ladleful of drippings and water enough to keep the pan from burning. Put in also a slice of turnip, carrot and onion and stalk of celery and the meat scraps trimmed from the fillet. Have the oven hot, put in the fillet and roast with the fat covering it half an hour. Then take of the fat, baste the fillet with the contents of the pan and allow about fifteen minutes more for the larding to brown handsomely while you baste it several times, causing a glossy surface to dry upon it. A gravy will flow from the fillet quite copiously when it is cut, which should be mixed with the made sauce at the time of serving.

To make the sauce let all the remaining moisture dry out of the pan, so that the clear grease can be poured off without the gravy, which will be found sticking to the pan. Add a ladleful of stock and liquor from a can of mushrooms. Boil up, thicken slightly, strain into a saucepan, boil and skim, and then add a little wine and cayenne.

Carve in small slices laid well up to one end of the individual dish with a spoonful of sauce at the other; or, for a large dish send it in entire, with a border of the finest button mushrooms obtainable, made hot in the sauce.

1183. Potted Breast of Chicken in Form.

Avail yourself of the fancy shapes of stamped tin patty pans for individual entrees of a delicate sort. The oval or long diamond form with scalloped sides are the best, but any sort from a plain muffin ring up will do, if small.

Provide 24 of these small molds.
4 large chickens.
1½ cupfuls of bread panada.
½ cupful of butter.
½ cupful minced salt pork.
2 whites of eggs.
1 tablespoonful of minced parsley.
White pepper or cayenne, salt, nutmeg.
1 pint of cream sauce.
½ cupful finest green peas.

Tender chickens only can be used this way. Take off the breasts raw with a small knife. Divide each side into three, the small fillet that lies next the breast bone makes one, the larger part of the breast split lengthwise makes two more. Each chicken furnishes, therefore, six of these bands of white meat. When they are trimmed along the edges and free from skin and sinew butter the small molds and lay a fillet smooth side down in each and keep them cold until the forcemeat is ready.

Boil the remaining parts of the chickens about an

hour, pick off all the meat free from skin and except any that may be very dark, mince it fine and then pound it to a paste. Add the panada (No. 962), the seasoning of minced pork and half the butter and the parsley, and white of eggs whisked light, and salt and pepper. Pound all together.

Then fill the prepared molds with the forcemeat, placing a little on each side of the breast of chicken at first carefully, not to let the meat be pushed from the center, press in well and level off. Steam in the vegetable steamers or bake, set in a pan of water about half an hour. Turn them out as they are ordered, fresh and with the juice that will have formed upon them. Pour a spoonful of smooth cream sauce around and sprinkle a dozen green peas with a fork, for ornament.

1184. Stewed Mushrooms in Croustades.

Empty a can of small button mushrooms without the liquor into a bright saucepan with an ounce of butter and let them become hot. Throw in a teaspoonful of minced parsley and add a few spoonfuls of the sauce from the fillet of beef. Cut ten slices of bread with a scollop cutter in oval shape to fit the small dishes, and half an inch thick, and mark the shape of a lid around with a knife point, not cutting through. Fry light colored and drain. Lift out the lid piece and as they are called for serve a spoonful of the mushrooms and sauce in each croustade. The piece removed need not be replaced. Let there be sauce enough for a spoonful in the dish to moisten the crust.

1185. Blanquette of Sweetbreads and Oysters.

4 calves' sweetbreads.
2 dozen oysters.
1 pint cream sauce.
Lemon juice, cayenne, salt.
Mashed potato borders.

Boil the sweetbreads until tender, in water, seasoned with salt, pepper and vinegar. Take them up, trim and cut in neat squares like large dice. Put the oysters in a deep strainer and dip them in the sweetbread liquor one minute to shrink them, turn on to a plate and cut them in halves. Mix sweetbreads and oysters together by shaking in a small saucepan with a squeeze of lemon and dust of cayenne and cover with boiling cream sauce just before wanted. Form rings of mashed potato on the dishes with a cornet and serve the white fricassee piled in the center. The sauce should salt the whole. You can form a thin potato border handsomely with the cheese scoop that they gouge out a pineapple cheese with. Blanquette is from blanc, white, like blanch and blank, and means a white dish.

1186. Cream Fritters.

Called *beignets de bouillie* by the French, and *bouillie* (not *bouilli*) means pap or baby food. We can not help it, however, if the grown people cry for them, glazed with transparent wine sauce. The English have a better name, which is palm tree pudding, in allusion perhaps to the appearance of a number of the spike shaped pieces arranged in order in a dish when all is served at once.

It is a sort of sliced custard breaded and fried, made of

1 quart of milk.
6 ounces of sugar.
6 ounces of mixed corn starch and flour.
7 yolks of eggs.
2 ounces of butter.
Flavoring. Salt.

Boil the milk with the butter and salt in it. Mix the sugar in the starch and flour dry and dredge and beat them into the boiling milk. Let it cook slowly at the side of the range about ten minutes. Stir in the yolks of eggs and take it off. Flavor with lemon, cinnamon, nutmeg or vanilla and let it get cold in a buttered pan. Roll the slices in egg, then in cracker meal, fry in lard, serve warm with the sauce No. 490, made thick enough not to run off, and simmered until it has become quite transparent.

Study of Notable Menus.

Banquet given in London complimentary to a popular tragedian, July, 1883. Covers laid for 520 guests. The words in quotation marks are but allusions to certain plays.

MENU.

POTAGES.
Tortue Claire a la "Rialto."
Bisque a la "Prince de Danemark,"

POISSONS.
Saumon d' Ecosse.
Filets de Soles, sauce "Matthias."

ENTRÉES.
Mazarine de Volaille a la "Courier de Lyon."
Chaudfroid de Cailles a la "Richelieu."

RELEVES
Quartier d'Agneau.
Aloyau de Bœuf.   Selle de Mouton.

REMOVES.
Poulardes Bardees.   Caneton aux Cressons.
Salade a la "Doricourt,"

ENTREMETS.
Mayonnaise de Homard.
Tartelettes de Peches.
Creme a la "Bon Voyage."
Gelee a la "Benedick." Gateaux "Freres de Corse."
Pouding Glace.

DESSERT.

TRANSLATION.

SOUPS.—Clear turtle (No. 1187)—Bisques are soups thick with a paste of fish or birds and choice morsels of the meat.

FISHES.—Scotch salmon, as in this country we say Kennebec or California salmon—Fillets of soles with a sauce (No. 967).

ENTREES.—Mazarine of fowl—same sort of article as No. 1183, probably large form—Chaudfroid of quails. No. 1191 is a chaudfroid, but we have no such word; styles of putting up various.

RELEVES.—Quarter of lamb—Sirloin of beef—Saddle of mutton.

REMOVES.—Chickens roasted in bands of bacon like No 1055—young ducks with cress (No. 1072) —Salad.

ENTREMETS.—Lobster in mayonnaise (No. 746)— Peach tartlets (No. 72)—Cream (No. 180)—Jelly (No. 208)—Cakes, Iced pudding (No. 127).

The banquet was served by a catering firm. The floral decorations were elaborate and the affair was a pronounced success.

Second Day.

Clear Turtle Soup.

Lamb cutlets with vegetables.
Potted pigeons with jelly.
Stuffed tomatoes.
Minced quail in border.

1187. Clear Turtle Soup.

A 40-pound turtle—or selected meat kept over from a larger one of a previous day.
4 gallons of soup stock.
2 onions.
1 can of mushrooms.
A bunch of chives and parsley—good handful.
1 teaspoonful of whole cloves.
1 bay leaf, a blade of mace.
1 pound raw ham.
1 pound of raw beef.
Salt and cayenne.
8 whites of eggs.
2 lemons.
1 cupful Madeira.

It is expected to make 2 gallons of soup after reduction by boiling and clearing.

Have a good rich stock ready prepared, draw it off clear and without grease.

Lay the slices of ham on the bottom of a clean boiler, place the turtle shells on that and cover them with the stock. Boil and skim off, then put in the turtle meat and let simmer gently about two hours, looking at it frequently and taking out the meat as it appears to be done and putting it away to become cold, after which take the bones out and return them to the boiler, along with the onions, spices and herbs and the rind of half a small lemon and the mushrooms or liquor from a can.

Two hours before dinner strain off the soup into a deep jar or pail, let stand one-half hour and skim off the top. Pour it without sediment through a fine strainer into a large saucepan and proceed to clarify it. Squeeze in the juice of a lemon, then add the whites of eggs mixed with a cup of cold water and the piece of raw beef chopped like sausage meat. Set it on the fire and when the egg is well cooked in it pour it through a napkin, laid inside a strainer, twice. Put in such pieces of turtle as will not float and eggs or egg-balls previously cooked and free from fragments. If any green fat simmer the pieces in soup separately and add a piece in each plate. Wine and thin quarter slices of lemon to be added just before serving. Let the soup be amber colored. It is troublesome to have this soup ready too long before dinner as a skin forms on top that may necessitate another straining if the clear appearance is to be preserved.

It will be a great inconvenience should the clear soup be so excessively rich that it will not run through the napkin or jelly strainer after boiling with the beef and white of egg, especially if the trouble happen when time is short till dinner. Read the remarks concerning aspic jelly at No. 735, and avoid the extreme of glutinous richness if clear soup is to be made.

1188. Lamb Cutlets with Vegetables.

12 lamb chops.
1 peck of spinach—or other greens.
24 small new potatoes.
1 small cauliflower.
4 ounces of butter.
Little white sauce.

Prepare the chops as for broiling; pepper and salt them, dip both sides in a little butter on a plate and lay them in a baking pan that they will just fill.

Boil the spinach *green;* take it up before it is quite done, drain on a seive and press the water away from it, then rub it through a strainer with a little sauce mixed in to help it through. Mix the green pulp with an equal amount of butter sauce. Have the new potatoes ready steamed and the cauliflower picked apart in branches. Cook the chops on the top shelf in a hot range about six or eight minutes, serve one to a dish with the gravy that collects upon them, the green sauce under them and the vegetables as ornaments at either side.

1189. Potted Pigeons with Jelly.

12 pigeons.
1 pound of sausage meat.
½ pound of butter.
1 pint of broth.
2 tablespoonfuls vinegar.
Pepper, salt, spice.
½ cupful currant jelly.
Flour and water paste.

Clean the pigeons, split in halves down the back and breast, wipe dry, dredge with pepper and salt and ground allspice. Place a spoonful of sausage meat inside and press the two halves together again. Spread a cup of butter on the bottom of a small earthen jar, lay the pigeons close pressed down in the jar, put in a cup of broth and little vinegar. Cover the top with a lid of plain flour and water paste. (See No. 1042). Set in the oven in a pan of water early in the morning and let bake three or four hours. Dish up out of the jar without disarranging the stuffing and sauce with the jelly mixed with gravy. They should be very tender. Half a bird to an order is sufficient at a plentiful dinner.

1190. Stuffed Tomatoes

20 tomatoes—large and smooth.
6 cupfuls of fine bread crumbs—not pressed.
2 tablespoonfuls finely minced onions.
Same of minced fat bacon.
1 teaspoonful of salt.
Same of pepper.
Same of sugar.
1 egg.

In case bacon is not at hand use an ounce of butter.

The intention is that all the inside except enough to make a case to bake in shall be taken out, seasoned and put back to bake, the tomato, therefore, should not be peeled. Cut a slice off the top, scoop out with a spoon into a strainer that will let the surplus juice run off. Chop the pulp with the edge of a spoon, mix the other articles with it and press into the tomatoes and round over the tops. Place close together in a buttered baking pan, dredge cracker meal on top and moisten with the back of a spoon dipped in butter. Bake about one-half hour.

1191. Minced Quail in Border.

For twenty-four dishes provide:
1 dozen quail.
1 cupful raw rice.
3 quarts of broth.
Soup vegetables.
6 ounces of butter—small cup.
6 tablespoonfuls of flour—large cup.
Seasonings.

Cook the rice as for a vegetable at dinner—that is, wash well and put it on in three cups of water and the lid shut down to keep the steam in. When done stir it up with salt and milk and smooth over the top.

Take the breasts off the quails raw with a boning knife, split them into flat, broad slices, season with salt and simmer them laid close together in a pan with one ounce of butter or poultry fat. When done on both sides without browning put a plate on top to press, and set them away to get cold.

Break up the bones and legs, boil them in the broth with vegetables and parsley. When all the richness is extracted strain the liquor off and thicken it with flour stirred up with butter in the usual way. Make it rather thick, add cayenne, strain it, take off any butter that may rise. Cut the cold cooked breasts of quails in dice, size of peas—they are made cold first in order that they may keep the shape—and mix them in the hot sauce just before dishing up. Make fancy borders on the individual dishes, quickly and easily, by cutting out small egg shapes from the rice with a teaspoon dipped first in butter. Place four or more on each side and dish the mince in the centre. A green leaf of parsley will relieve the whiteness of all.

Supper and "fete of the season" under royal patronage at the Fisheries Exhibition, London, July 1883: "The Princess Christian and 'a dream of fair women' were engaged in supplying refreshments at the modest charge of half-a-crown a glass. The Lady Mayoress presided over the American bar, where were dispensed such fancy drinks as 'Bosom Caressers,' a '*Pousse l' Amour*,' a 'Flash of Lightning,' manipulated by the skilled attendants of the caterers." After midnight a supper was served at cosy little tables, in the Prince's Pavilion, with the following

MENU.

Saumon a la Norvegienne.
Salade de Homard. Buissons de Crevettes.
Filets de Soles a la Regence.
Roulade d'Anguilles en Aspic.

Cotelettes d'Agneau a la Printaniere.
Croustade de Cailles a la Gelee.

Galantine de Volaille aux Pistaches.
Poularde pique.
Jambon d'Yorck.
Pate de Pigeons.
Filet de Bœuf braisee.
Langue a l'Ecarlate.
Salade a la Russe.
Salade a la Francaise.

Suedoise aux Abricots.
Gelee Macedoine.
Meringues Chantilly.
Mazarines glace.
Dames d'Honneur.

TRANSLATION.

FISH —Salmon, Norwegian style, probably ornamented, this being a fish exhibition. Soyer says the Norwegian way is to boil the salmon in sea or salt water and eat it with spiced vinegar—Lobster salad (No. 746)—Buissons of prawns (No. 749)—Fillets of soles with regency sauce—that is the liquor from stewed eels and vegetables, mixed with claret and brown sauce, with balls of fish forcemeat and mushrooms in the dishes for ornament.

Roulade of eels in aspic—cold—large eels split open, boned, rolled up, cooked in that shape and put in ornamental jelly like Nos. 798 and 786.

HOT ENTREES.—Lamb chops with new vegetables, like No. 1188—a la Printaniere means Spring-time style—Crcustade of quails — a "chaudfroid," or mince, like No. 1191 in ornamental cups of fried bread, and currant jelly in the dish.

COLD.—Boned fowl, studded with pistachio nuts instead of truffles (No. 785)—pistachios are a kind of almond, green in color and costly, sometimes two dollars a pound—Poulard or young fowl larded with bacon—York ham—because Yorkshire hams are reputed the best (No. 811)—Pigeon pie, cold, the pigeons boned and laid in a case of paste raised in a mold and lined first with forcemeat and bacon—Fillet of beef, well cooked with seasonings in a covered pot—Corned tongue (No. 1077, see note)—Russian salad (No. 745)—French salad, anything, perhaps No. 740.

SWEETS AND PASTRY.—Swedish bombe or shell of apricot ice with ice-cream inside, formed in a mold (see combinations at 73 and succeeding numbers). Macedoine jelly, different kinds minced and mixed (No. 208)—Meringues or egg kisses, with whipped cream inside (No. 139) — Mazarines glazed — the Mazarine of meat of a former menu is a case of forcemeat filled, these are pastry patties a la Mazarin, round, the fruit jam inside, pearl glaze (No. 2) on top, the same as No. 242. Maids of Honor, the old Virginia and probably old English name for cheesecakes (Nos. 247, 290, 292) made with fine puff paste in the patty pans instead of common short paste.

The foregoing supper was served by a London catering firm.

The *pousse l' amour* referred to is made by filling a tall and slender wine glass half way up with maraschino, dropping in the yolk of an egg, half filling the remaining space with vanilla cordial and filling up with brandy without mixing the different parts.

Third Day.

Ox Tail Soup.
Chicken pie—American style.
Lambs' fries, sauteed in butter.
Geese livers in cases.
Peaches with rice.

1192. Ox Tail Soup.

The ox-tails must be cut up raw and stewed for two or three hours to make the meat quite tender. This is a gravy soup, and while it may be bright, rich and free from grease, it should not be too fine strained. Ox tail clear will be found further on. Take

3 gallons of beef soup stock.
6 ox-tails.
1 head of celery.
2 carrots.
2 turnips.
6 cloves stuck in an onion.
A bunch of herbs with a bay leaf tied up in it.
3 cups of sifted flour for thickening.
Pepper and salt.

Cut the ox-tails in thin round slices by sawing, if you have a sharp little saw and plenty of time; if not, with a sharp chopper; wash, and then set them on to stew early in a saucepan of stock with salt and pepper in it. Cut the carrots and turnips in thin slices, stamp out all the shapes they will make with a round cutter to match the pieces of oxtail, and put them in water. Set on the stock with a fresh loin bone in it, the scraps of vegetables, the thin ends of the ox-tails that would not make slices, the celery, onions and herbs, and let boil.

An hour before dinner time strain off into the soup pot through a coarse strainer, getting all the gravy particles; throw in the vegetable slices, let them cook in it, and strain in the liquor from the stewed ox-tails. Mix up the flour with water and use it to thicken slightly. Add the ox-tail last. Before turning it into the tureen let the soup stop boiling and skim off the fat until no more rises.

There should be two pieces of meat and two or three of vegetables served in each plate.

1193. Chicken Pie—American Style.

Read remarks about cutting up fowls for chicken pie at No. 1015. About eight large ones will be required for fifty persons. These weigh twenty-five pounds as they come to market unopened, or seventeen or eighteen pounds net. The thirty-two choice cuts should be cooked in one saucepan and the necks, backs and hips in another. The supposition is that some will be left over and it had better be the rough portions than the best breast pieces. Some will not take chicken. When fowls of a larger size are used they will be fewer in number and the cuts must be divided accordingly.

Many wayside inns have gained a reputation for their excellence in this popular dish and stop-over tickets have been in request on that account.

It does not make much difference whether the fowls are young or old, but those at the mature age of twelve months are the best, the essential point being to cook them until tender, and the next necessity being a knack of plain seasonings to a degree that makes the pie savory. When you have good chicken pie the guests generally are indifferent about the quality of the beef and mutton for that day at least. Take

8 two-and-a-quarter-pound chickens.
6 ounces of fat salt pork.
8 ounces of butter (optional).
1 onion—2 ounces.
1 tablespoonful good black pepper.
Same of salt.
2 cups of sifted flour for thickening.
2 tablespoonfuls chopped parsley.
And for the crust:
3 pounds of flour
2 pounds of beef suet.
Little salt.

Set the cut chickens on in a boiler with hot water to a little more than cover, cook with the lid on from one to three hours, according to kind. When there is a large quantity take care lest those pressed on the bottom stick and burn there and spoil the whole.

Throw in the pork cut in squares, the minced onion, salt and half the pepper, and when the chicken is tender thicken the liquor moderately with the flour stirred up with a little milk.

Make the paste by mincing the suet extremely fine, having it soft, then rubbing it into the flour, wet with water and roll it out same way as puff paste four or five times, to give it a flaky texture.

Line the sides of a deep baking pan with paste, (but not the bottom) dip the pieces of chicken in with a skimmer, dredge the remainder of the pepper over the top, sift a dust of flour over that, put in the butter and parsley, then all the chicken liquor it will hold without boiling over, roll out the remaining pie paste and cover it. Bake in a moderate oven three quarters of an hour.

Better not brush over with egg wash, for a hotel dinner. There should not be enough gravy in the pie while baking to boil over the crust and make it heavy, but it can be kept ready in the boiler and poured in afterwards.

1194. Lambs' Fries Sauteed in Butter.

Lamb's fries can be purchased of the market men who furnish sweetbreads and brains. Wash and then blanch them in boiling water containing salt and a dash of vinegar. Let them get cold. Split in two, pepper and salt and then flour them on both sides. When nearly time to serve put some butter in a large frying pan on the range and when it is melted and froths up lay in the lamb's fries and cook them brown on both sides. Serve hot with tomato sauce around in the dish and the butter still frothing upon them.

1195. Geese Livers in Cases.

This is a delicate entree made by lining the bottoms of small paper cases with liver paste (like No. 805, without the cut meats) on that lay a slice of raw goose liver, and on that a covering of the liver paste again, smooth over, brush with melted butter and bake in the cases in a slack oven about fifteen or twenty minutes or until the slice of liver inside is cooked through. Then pour a spoonful of sauce in each one and keep in the oven until served. For 24 you require:

24 fancy paper cases, procured from the cook's supply stores, or made like shallow boxes at home.
12 goose livers to slice—the scraps and
½ pound of poultry livers for the paste.
½ pound of fat bacon.
½ pound of bread panada.
2 eggs.
Seasonings.

See Nos. 804 and 805 for particulars.

It is not necessary to be exact in the kinds of seasonings used, but herbs may be used instead of wine when there is wine in the sauce; and the panada will give a mild flavor to the paste without the use of chicken.

Before using the paper cases brush them inside with clear butter and make them hot in the oven.

1196. Peaches with Rice.

30 halves of largest peaches in syrup.
3 pints of cooked rice.
1 cupful of red fruit jelly.

Fine large peaches, already put up in syrup, can be used; or, if fresh, they may be simmered in the oven in a pan containing a little syrup and butter. Baste them with the syrup and keep an oiled paper over until they are done.

Cook rice as if for a vegetable, use but little salt but a spoonful of sugar instead.

Mix the red jelly in the peach syrup for sauce.

Put a spoonful of rice in the small dish, dip a spoon in butter or syrup so that the rice will not adhere, and make a neat shape of it, place the peach on top, pour a spoonful of sauce over all.

Dishes a la Joinville are doubtless so named in compliment to a person, but whether a noted statesman of an earlier period or a recent Prince de Joinville it may be impossible now to determine. Crayfish and truffles are indicated by the name and the chief merit of both articles consists in their comparative scarcity and costliness.

There is nothing definite in the term *bouchees a la Reine* (literally mouthfuls or morsels) or *boudins* or patties in the Queen's style, because so many variations both of form and filling bear the same designation and it can not be known which is t' e original or whether there ever was one. The dish is said to have been originated by Marie, the wife of Louis XV., who was fond of good living. But that queen was a Polish princess, and Poland was famous before that time as a land of good living, good cookery and profuse hospitality and the *bouchees*, as likely as not, were but introduced from that country's *cuisine*. And Bechamel, whose name is almost as frequently attached to patties or pastry *bouchees* of chicken flourished in the service of the king preceding this one. The term is, therefore, but little more than a verbal ornament and you are to take the Queen's name for it that it is good, anyway.

Study of Notable Menus.

Dinner at Hotel Kaaterskill, Catskill Mountains, August 12, 1883, Edward A. Gillett, manager. One of the largest of American hotels. Heighth of the season. Probably 800 guests.

MENU.

Blue Point Oysters, en Coquille.

Green Turtle   Consomme, Printaniere.

Bouchees de Volaille, a la Reine.

Boiled Salmon. a la Joinville,
Broiled Spanish Mackerel, a la Maitre d'Hotel,
Parisienne Potatoes,   Cucumber Salad.

Tenderloin of Beef, Larded, with Mushrooms.

Baked Chicken Pie, a l'Americaine,
Geese Liver, en Caisse, Italienne Sauce,
Lamb Fries, Tomato Sauce,
Peches, a la Conde.

Sorbet Moscovite.

Boiled Leg of Mutton, Caper Sauce,
Boiled Chicken, Egg Sauce,
Corned Beef and Cabbage.

Roast Ribs of Beef, a l'Anglaise,
Roast Lamb, Mint Sauce,
Roast Duck, Stuffed, Apple Sauce.

Mashed Potatoes,   Boiled Potatoes,   Green Corn,
String Beans,   Fried Egg Plant,   Rice.

Boned Capon, with Truffles,   Beef Tongues,
Cold Lamb, Ham and Chicken.

Tomatoes and Lettuce, Plain or Mayonnaise,
Chicken Salad.

Apple Meringue Pie,   Custard Pie,
English Plum Pudding, Brandy Sauce.
Assorted Cake.
Champagne Jelly,   Vanilla Ice Cream,
Punch Cardinal,   Boiled Custard.
Fruit—Nuts and Raisins.
English Dairy, Edam and Roquefort Cheese.
Coffee.

COMMENTS.

OYSTERS—On shell (No. 864)—it is said that raw oysters are served at this table all through the summer, seven to a plate. Prices high, business vast, all on a lavish scale.

SOUPS—Green turtle (No. 1181) — Consomme printaniere or spring soup or with green vegetables (No. 1197).

BOUCHEES—or patties to serve in this place are always small and generally made of two flats of fine puff paste with a teaspoonful of minced chicken, very highly seasoned, inclosed between them like No. 242, but the edges, wetted, are only pressed lightly together and not pinched. There are various other forms of patties and cases used.

FISH—Boiled salmon (Nos. 920 and 922) and garnished with truffles and crayfish or prawns in the sauce—Parisian potatoes (No. 953)—Spanish mackerel (Nos. 883, 886, and sauce 880) — cucumber salad (No. 772)—the cucumbers are usually sliced, allowed to lie sprinkled with salt to draw the water, drained and shaken up with oil and vinegar.

ENTREES—Tenderloin or fillet (No. 1182) with small but on mushrooms in sauce poured over the slices when served—chicken pie (No. 1193)—lambs' fries (No. 1194)—geese livers in cases (No. 1195)--peaches with rice (No. 1196).

SORBET—Moscovite or Russian—Sorbets is the French word for frozen punches, or ices that contain wines and liqueurs.

MEATS AND VEGETABLES—See index.

COLD DISHES— Boned capon with truffles—galantine as at No. 785 with the white meat inlaid with strips of black truffle and the trimmings of truffles mixed in the forcemeat. Truffles come in cans of various graded sizes, beginning at a dollar for about two ounces. Other cold meats and salads, see index.

PASTRY—Apple cream pie as at No. 50, or 52, or 53, with meringue on top (No. 42)—custard pie (No. 58)—plum pudding (No. 331)—champagne jelly (Nos. 202 and 203)—Vanilla ice cream (No. 84) Cardinal punch, red frozen punch made with port wine poured over a roasted orange, and sugar and water—for a red punch, see No. 135—boiled custard (Nos. 499 and 77) probably served in cups, very cold for those who are afraid to eat ices.

Fourth Day.

Clear Spring Soup.

Stuffed loin of mutton.
Small fillets of beef in glaze.
Egg plant fried plain.
Curried tripe—Italian.
Apple fritters with sauce.

1197. Clear Spring Soup.

The distinguishing feature is the addition of asparagus heads and green peas to a proportion of any other commoner kinds of vegetables in a clear consomme.

We have no English word for *consomme* but broth and that does not express the same meaning. Broth is the liquor in which meat has been boiled, consomme is the same liquor strained clear, perhaps clarified like jelly. It is pronounced in *three* syllables, though some old English books of cookery speak of "consumes" of meat and fowl in a very vague and misty manner.

Consomme printaniere is one of the favorite varieties because of the handsome appearance of the vegetables when skilfully cooked green (No. 741). But these clear soups are not called for at table as much as the stronger kinds. Two gallons of clear soup is plenty where three of the others would be consumed. Take

2 gallons of consomme.
1 cupful of very green peas.
1 heaping cupful of asparagus heads.
Same of little trimmed flowrets of cauliflower.
Same of carrots, turnips and onions scooped out in shapes with a potato scoop, or else cut in neat dice shapes.

The stock (which is but a grand broth of several kinds of meat) will have been seasoned in the boiler already with soup herbs and vegetables. When it is drawn off clear in the morning and strained through a silk sieve, it will be clear enough for this purpose. An hour before dinner bring it to a boil and skim it from the side. Season with salt and little cayenne, add a tablespoonful of burnt sugar both for color and mild flavor.

Cook the vegetables separately, drain them out of the water into the tureen and pour the consomme to them.

1198. Stuffed Loin of Mutton.

This is loin of mutton or lamb sliced down to the bone, a highly seasoned mince (*salpicon*) pressed in between the slices, tied to keep shape and baked tender. For the meat you need four of those pieces that lie between figures 1 and 2 in the side of mutton at No. 997, and a boiled neck of mutton beside. For the stuffing take

1 cupful of cooked meat finely minced.
1 cupful of raw meat same way.
1 slice of ham, or meat from a cooked knuckle
—also minced.
1 tablespoonful minced onion, a clove of garlic and a bayleaf, both minced, a teaspoonful of black pepper and same of salt.

After thoroughly mixing these, taking care to have a small proportion of fat meat included, spread a little between the cuts, draw a twine around from end to end, crowd the pieces close together in one pan, cover with oiled paper and bake not less than two hours with frequent basting. Make gravy in the pan as at No. 1062.

To serve, take the slices from the bone, each with its portion of stuffing, and the strained gravy pour over.

The pieces of mutton named above always accumulate in the hotel meat house because they will not make the shapely chops that are so much coveted and there is not sufficient demand for plain roast mutton. And yet the meat of this cut is of the best. If cooked with any of the savory stuffings that make chickens and turkeys good and roasted long enough to make them tender without drying them out they are soon brought into use. Half cooked meat mixed with half raw will set and hold the herbs and seasonings and be good, but if all cooked meat must be used an egg and little bread crumbs must be added to bind it together.

1199. Small Fillets of Beef in Glaze.

This simplest of dishes and prime favorite with the lovers of stewed meat we find among the dishes of Queen Victoria's dinners as "*Les petits filets de boeuf dans leur glace*." Sometimes it turns up in a menu as "*Escalopes de boeuf en demi glace*," because the natural gravy of the pieces of beef is boiled down to the condition known as half glaze. Fillet in this case does not mean tenderloin, but only a strip or band of meat, or, it is called a scollop if cut like very small steaks. Take

3 pounds of lean scraps of beef.
2 quarts of water.
1 teaspoonful of black pepper.
2 teaspoonfuls of salt.
Cauliflower in branches, or small new potatoes for a border.

The meat is the small lot of choice loin pieces that are not large or shapely enough for steaks (No. 992). Cut them into strips like fingers. Put them on three hours before dinner with cold water enough to cover them and the salt and pepper in i and let stew slowly. Skim off the fat

There is nothing to add, nothing to do, but let the liquor boil down to rich gravy, so rich that it stays on the pieces of meat and makes them shine, and dish them up that way with potatoes scooped in ball shapes or something else to border the dishes.

The cook who makes the entrees ought to be the one to dish them up, or else his second must be fully intelligent of the purpose and method. One-half the merit of the cooking done by a master of it, over the common, lies in the manner of placing the viands on the dishes. If you tumble a pile of meat on a dish in a disorderly way the little niceties of shaping, glazing, coloring, garnishing, and straining and smoothing sauces into a velvety (*veloute*) appearance count for nothing; but if it is only three pieces of beef scraps stewed tender and savory with their own natural gravy they should placed be in order, perhaps diagonally, in the dish, with the little garnishing accompaniment of whatever it may be, either string beans cut in diamonds, or green peas or the like p'aced in two straight lines, also diagonally, across the ends. It is impossible to explain the whys and wherefores of these trifles. But each dish becomes an ornament to its place and the entire course is an invitation in itself. There must be a natural aptitude in the cook to understand this feature of the dinner making and then through all the necessary baste of the operations of serving dinner somehow that effort at tasteful display makes a distinct impression.

1200. Egg Plant Fried Plain

Slice the egg-plant without paring into quarter-inch thicknesses, throwing away only the end parings. Boil the slices a few minutes in salted water to extract the strong taste, drain them and while still moist dust with pepper, dip both sides in flour and fry (*saute*) them in frying pans on the top of the range in a little clear drippings and send them in fresh done and brown.

1201. Curried Tripe—Italian.

1 pound of tripe—already cooked.
1 cupful of gravy.
1 small onion.
1 teaspoonful of curry powder.
6 hard-boiled eggs.
10 slices of bread.
Black pepper and cayenne.

Cut the onion across and across and shave it in little bits into a saucepan with a bastingspoonful of the clear tasteless fat from the top of the stock boiler and fry until it begins to brown. Sprinkle a rounded teaspoonful of curry powder over the onion, cut the tripe in shred's size of macaroni and two inches long and put it in and shake up over the fire until it is yellow-coated with curry. Add a little black pepper and cayenne and hot meat gravy enough to make it like a thick stew. Cut ten thin slices of bread to the shape of a long leaf, dip one side in the fat in the meat pan and toast lightly on the top shelf of the range. When you dish up put one of these pieces on the edge partly projecting outwards, the spoonful of tripe heaped in the dish and two-quarters of boiled egg cut lengthwise, at the other end.

1202. Apple Fritters with Sauce.

There is the widest difference in quality between apple fritters made in the usual rough and ready way and some others of the best possible sort, still while thirty or forty persons out of every fifty are found to take these with apparent satisfaction we will not be the first to complain, but will only suggest that they cook through in half the time without burning the batter almost black if care is taken to ascertain that the apples are of an easy cooking kind; for there are kinds that will never be done through. Take.

8 or 10 apples.
2 cupfuls of flour—½ pound.
1 cupful of milk or water.
2 eggs. Pinch of salt.
1 tablespoonful melted lard.
Same of syrup.
1 teaspoonful baking powder.

It is well worth while to always mix the batter by measure as it wastes time and is unsatisfactory to have to doctor it over again.

Wash the apples and dry them, cut in slices without paring and throw away only the end pieces. If good apples the slices should not be very thin.

Put the flour and all the rest into a pan and stir rapidly together and beat the batter thus made until it is smooth. Drop in the apple slices, take them up coated with batter and drop from a spoon into a saucepan of hot lard. Fry about 8 minutes. Break off the rough fragments as you dish them and pour over a large spoonful of pudding sauce or No. 477.

They are more elegant with the apples pared and cored and then sliced into thick rings.

Study of Notable Menus.

Says a newspaper: "Very simple was the menu of the dinner at Dantzic, when the emperors of Germany and Russia met. It was this:

Potage tortue, a l'Anglaise.
Turbot et saumon garnis.
Filet de boeuf, braise.
Legumes.
Filets de poulets, aux truffes.
Chaudfroid de cailles.
Salade.
Glaces.   Compote.
Dessert.

A glass or two of champagne, and the meal was over. To the dread of bombs their imperial highnesses do not mean to add the horrors of dyspepsia."

TRANSLATION.

The simplicity is rather apparent than real, the fewest possible words being used to indicate the dishes served which are: English turtle soup, two kinds of fish, turbot and salmon, both garnished or decorated perhaps very elaborately, and of course differently cooked, a braised tenderloin of beef with some sort of accompaniment not mentioned. Vegetables are bunched together in one word, "*legumes*." Fillets of fowls with truffles, in some shape, but whether as truffle sauce or otherwise not indicated. The favorite "chaudfroid" of quails occurs here again. *Salade* has but one word, Ices, which may have been various, the same. *Compote* may have been a work of art in the shape of a combination of fruits in syrup with cream in a border mould or with cake. Dessert, is but the title head for an unknown quantity contributed by 'terers, confectioners, cheesemakers and others.

Fifth Day.

Cream of fowl soup.

Ribs of beef with Yorkshire pudding.
Larded sweetbreads with green peas.
Celery and cheese—Italian.
Peach fritters.

1203. Cream of Fowl Soup.

This following is the generally received *Potage a la Reine*, but it should be known that there are several variations. A case has been known of a fashionable city *restaurateur* who sent for a noted cook from a leading eastern hotel that he might have the advantage of the best skill obtainable in his business, only to find that they differed on such points as whether *potage a la Reine* should be made with almonds or not, to a degree of positiveness that soon put an end to the engagement. There have been almond cream soups always, Spanish, Italian, and French, sweet, *gras* and *maigre*—native to countries where almonds were plenty, the latter mixed with oatmeal instead of chicken, but the Queen soup or *potage a la Reine* in present use seems to have originated with Ude, since he gave out what he termed his improved receipt for making it, setting aside his first way, and does not use almonds. Still there were others who thought they improved it, and Bishop, a Windsor Castle cook, gives us an especial "potage a la Queen Victoria" that does contain the paste of pounded almonds, as well as that of chicken and hard boiled yolks of eggs. Another calls that "puree of fowl a la Celestine," after a stage celebrity of that time, while he adopts Ude's *potage a la Reine* and calls it "puree of fowl, a la Reine." These points are of interest to stewards and cooks, and may remind them of how two knights, in the fable, fought over the question of what the shield was made of that they found set up by the highway and one of them had seen only

the side that was made of gold and the other the opposite side that was made of silver.

To make the soup take
3 gallons of chicken or veal broth,
Meat of 4 fowls, or 3 quarts when cut up,
1 quart boiled rice,
1 small onion,
2 heads of celery,
2 blades of mace,
1 quart of cream—or milk and some butter,
Salt and cayenne.

It is frequently the case that there is an abundance of chicken broth on hand when fowls have been boiled for dinner the previous day. Set it on to boil with the bones of the fowls and if necessary a veal shank to make it richer, the onion, celery and mace and no other vegetables or seasonings. Mince the chicken meat fine, then pound it and the rice together in a mortar, thin it down with hot broth and force it through a sieve. Boil the cream separately. At time to dish up strain the chicken broth into the puree, stirring all the while. Season with salt and cayenne and add the boiling cream. The soup should not be allowed to boil after the different parts are mixed together. Any kind of rich soup or stew liquor will curdle cream or milk if they are boiled together. This and similar cream soups will generally curdle slightly while keeping hot in the tureen, but not to a degree that makes much difference provided it is not allowed to boil and then settle.

1204. Ribs of Beef with Yorkshire Pudding.

It would be a very popular dish if better understood. According to the original usage it should be beef roasted on a spit with the pudding in a tin reflecting oven underneath catching the gravy and baking at the same time, and the next way to that is to set the meat on a trivet or frame standing in the dish of pudding and both baked together, the pudding being of course saturated with the gravy and drippings. But this requires the steady and moderate heat of a brick oven. Either way, it must be seen, a dish is made that is very different from what some restaurants offer with the same name, which is a square of tough pudding as dry as a piece of bread, made long before the meal, and thrust into the side of a dish of meat as if for a superfluous sort of ornament only.

It can be served almost in the original style with almost its original softness and richness by cooking the rib ends of beef carefully as directed at No 1022, and the Yorkshire pudding at No. 408, and put the latter in to bake only fifteen minutes before time to serve, and only half an inch deep in the pan. Then serve a square or oblong cut in the dish that cut of beef rib without bone, and the wisch gravy obtainable from the roast beef poured over them. Yorkshire pudding made from the receipt above referred to is rich enough for anything, even for pudding with sweet sauce.

1205. Larded Sweetbreads with Peas.

For 24 dishes take
12 selected calves' sweetbreads.
1 pound of salt pork or bacon.
2 quarts of chicken or veal broth.
2 ounces of butter.
Seasonings; mashed potatoes.
2 cans of French peas.

Take sweetbreads large enough to be split in two. Wash them and steep in cold water. Boil about 15 minutes in soup stock with a dash of vinegar in it—which helps to keep them white—then take them out and press them between two pans until cold. At the same time set the chicken stock on the fire to boil down to half the quantity.

Cut the pork into thin strips. Split the sweetbreads and lard them with it in regular order, drawing the strips through. Trim the edges to an even shape.

Butter the bottom of a shallow saucepan and lay in the sweetbreads with the remaining trimmings of salt pork and piece of onion, turnips and celery, bruised pepper corns, and enough of the reduced broth to fill the spaces without floating the sweetbreads. Let simmer with the lid on about half an hour.

Then take them up into another vessel; add the remaining broth to the gravy, strain it into another saucepan and not thicken it but skim and then boil it down to clear glaze and pour it over the sweetbreads just before dishing them up.

Part of these preparations can be gone through the previous evening when the dish is for dinner.

When to be served spread mashed potatoes thinly in a large dish and cut out flats, place one in each dish with an egg-slice or knife, setting it with a diagonal slant across the dish, a sweetbread on top, and green peas in a similar slanting line at each end of the dish.

1206. Baked Celery and Cheese—Italian.

A two-quart panful of celery cut small.
2 cupfuls of grated cheese.
½ cupful of butter or roast meat fat.
2 cupfuls of brown sauce.
Pepper and perhaps salt.
1 cupful of cracker meal.

Cut the celery in pieces an inch and a half long and split to about twice the size of macaroni and boil 15 minutes in salted water. Drain, put in a buttered small baking pan, sprinkle in the cheese, and pepper liberally; pour over good well-flavored brown sauce, or the gravy without fat from the roast meat pan, sift cracker meal over the top and bake it long enough for the cheese to be melted in it and the flavors well mingled. This can be made a very excellent dish and one in great request with a good quality of cheese and gravy not too salt. Serve in flat dishes with or without a fried crust or toast. The baking is not essential, but when the oven is crowded it will be almost as good gently simmered on top.

1207. Peach Fritters.

Take ripe freestone peaches raw, peel and cut them in halves. Mix up a batter the same as for apple fritters at No. 1202, and use the peaches the same way. Serve with wine or any other pudding sauce.

Study of Notable Menus.

Banquet at the Grand Pacific Hotel, Chicago, John B. Drake, proprietor, September 1883. Given by the citizens in honor of a visiting Lord Chief Justice. Covers laid for 400.

"The entire apartment was decorated in as profusely rich a manner. It seemed as if the gardens of the West had been despoiled to furnish floral trophies for the occasion. The chandeliers were draped with smilax, the entrance was gorgeously festooned. The brilliance of electric lights flooded the apartment, and the strains of music, now gay and now patriotic, crept through the perfume-laden air and added melody to splendor."

MENU.

Blue Points.

Green Turtle Soup.

Boiled Kennebec Salmon.
Sliced Tomatoes.

Fillet of Beef, with Mushrooms.
Lima Beans.

Young Turkey, with Jelly.
Baked Stuffed Tomatoes. Sweet Potatoes.

Sweetbreads Larded. Green Peas.
Peach Fritters, Claret Sauce.
Pate of Chicken.

Champagne Sherbet.

Roast Prairie Chicken. Broiled Snipe.
Dressed Celery. Chicken Salad.
Brandy Jelly. Biscuit Glace.
Cake. Tutti Frutti.
Fruit. Coffee. Roquefort.

The Steward of the Grand Pacific Hotel is James F. Atkinson; Chief Cook, Constance Wolff; Pastry Cook and Confectioner, Pierre Caluori.

COMMENTS'

The Chicago *Times* said: "The dinner was elegantly served in courses; it was an English dinner given to an Englishman. The bill of fare was the acme of good taste; it was printed in good Anglo-Saxon so that everybody could read it without hiring an interpreter."

Sixth Day.

Coney Island clam chowder.
Fricandeau of minced veal.
Pork tenderloin with cabbage.
Celery in cream.
Poached eggs—Andalusian.
Farina cake with jelly.

1208. Clam Chowder — Coney Island Style.

The clam chowder so popular in the restaurants as a lunch dish is more of a stew than a soup, being thick with clams and potatoes; a large plate of it makes a hearty meal for a person. It is consequently unsuitable to serve as soup at hotel dinners unless modified by the addition of more liquid. The following makes an available soup without materially changing its character:

2 quarts of clams and their liquor—or three large cans.
6 quarts of soup stock.
2 quarts of raw potatoes cut in pieces.
Butter size of an egg.
2 cupfuls of sliced onions.
2 large slices of raw ham.
1 quart of tomatoes chopped small.
2 teaspoonfuls mixed thyme and savory.
12 cloves, 1 bayleaf, parsley.
1 tablespoonful each of black pepper and salt.

The different articles should be made ready separately and placed conveniently for use. Have the clams scalded and then cut in pieces and the liquor saved. Cut the potatoes in large squares and slice the onions.

An hour before dinner put the butter and ham in a saucepan together and the onions on top and set over the fire. Stick the cloves in a small onion additional and tie that up with the bayleaf and parsley and throw in and also the powdered or minced herbs, and put on the lid and let stew slowly.

In about 15 or 20 minutes, or before the contents begin to brown, put into the same saucepan the soup stock, clam liquor, tomatoes, potatoes, pepper and salt, and let cook until the potatoes are done. Then take out the soup bunch and ham, put in the clams and let boil up once before it goes into the tureen.

It is expected that the potatoes will sufficiently thicken this chowder, but they should not be allowed to boil so much as to disappear altogether.

1209. Fricandeau of Minced Veal.

A *fricandeau* is defined as meaning something pleasant to the taste, also as stewed veal, also, a person fond of dainties. The dish following has become known to some extent under the name. The more elaborate larded, stuffed and braised fricandeau will be found further on. Take.

1 pound or quart of raw veal, minced.
1 pound or three pints of cooked veal same.
1 small onion.
2 bay leaves, savory.
1 cupful minced ham.
4 thin slices of bacon.
1 teaspoonful each of salt and pepper.

Let one-fourth of the meat of both kinds be fat. Shave all dark outside from the cooked meat before mincing it. Fry the onion cut up small in a spoonful of drippings and when it begins to brown mix it with the meat and all the other ingredients except bay leaves and bacon. Press the meat—which is like sausage—into a 3-quart pan of a deep and narrow shape, smooth over, lay the bay leaves and bacon slices on top and bake in a slow oven about an hour. Turn it out, cut carefully in slices like roast meat, and serve with a brown meat gravy poured under.

1210. Pork Tenderloin with Cabbage.

Select 4 large tenderloins—they weigh nearly a pound each—boil them in stock well salted for about an hour; take up and let them cool. At the same time cut a head of summer cabbage in quarters, take out the hard stem and boil the cabbage about 45 minutes or until tender. Drain it then, season and chop it.

Cut the tenderloins into round slices (scollops). When you have taken up one kind of your roast dinner meat let the pan dry down on top of the range until it begins to fry and the gravy sticks to the bottom and then put in the sliced tenderloin and let the pieces get a bright glaze and slight touch of brown on both sides.

Dish up cabbage in the dish with two or three slices of tenderloin pressed down edgewise, as in a border, and a spoonful of light-colored brown sauce.

1211. Celery in Cream.

Cut celery in lengths a little shorter than asparagus, split the broad stalks to make them all of one size, tie in bunches, boil in salted water about half an hour, then drain and lay in a bright baking pan, removing the twine at the same time. Make a cupful of cream sauce (No. 931) and pour it over the celery and keep hot on the top shelf in the oven where it will get a yellow bake on top without cooking and drying. Serve on flat dishes, the celery placed as it lay on the pan.

1212. Poached Eggs—Andalusian.

One form of *œufs a la religieuse* or religious people's eggs for Friday dinners.

Stew down some strained tomatoes with finely minced onion in it to a thick puree, and brown sauce likewise in equal quantity and mix them together and add pepper sauce to make it pungent. Have ready some beets in vinegar and capers.

Poach eggs as they are called for, in good shape as shown at No. 1139; put a spoonful of the thick sauce or puree in a flat dish and a poached egg in the middle and ornament with shapes stamped out of pickled beets, and capers.

1213. Farina Cake with Jelly.

3 pints of milk or water.
10 ounces of farina—2 cups small.
1 cup of sugar.
Butter size of an egg.
3 eggs.
Pinch of salt.

Boil the milk (or water) with half the sugar in it, sprinkle in the farina like making mush. Let it cook slowly at the back of the range half an hour or more, Mix in the butter and eggs. Pour it into a pan that will not soil the bottom—a bright tin pan will do—about an inch deep. Bake 10 minutes, then take it out of the oven and dredge the remaining sugar over the top. Bake it again and the sugar will melt into a crisp glaze. Dish up squares or oblongs with a teaspoonful of bright jelly in the dish.

Study of Notable Menus.

The following was printed in the *Daily National Hotel Reporter* at the time. It is valuable as an example of the most advanced methods of setting out a banquet:

On December 3d the publishers of the *Atlantic Monthly* gave a breakfast at the Hotel Brunswick, Boston, in h nor of the seventieth birthday of Oliver Wendell Holmes, the famous author and poet. The banquet hall of the Brunswick was a flower garden. Six long tables occupied the centre of the flo r. Four of these were arranged lengthwise with the room, while the other two were placed at right angles to them, one at each end of the room. The space between the tables and the windows looking out upon the street was filled with palm trees of huge size, placed in tubs of earth, which were in turn placed upon blocks or pedesta's. The decorations, exclusively floral, were very elaborate. The four large mirrors on the side walls of the hall were tastefully hung with festoons of smilax intermingled with flowers of various kinds. The mantels were also profusely filled with rare flowers and plants, while the tables themselves were so covered with roses, carnations, camellias and other flowers that it seemed doubtful at first how the courses could be served. Two large baskets of flowers were set at the end of each table, and at the corner of each were strewn, in apparently loose piles, a lot of flowers. It looked as if a careless elbow might disarrange and upset these fragrant heaps, but a closer inspection showed that their stems were neatly tied together. This is said to be the latest Boston wrinkle in the arrangement of flowers. In the centre of the top and bottom tables were immense oblong baskets of flowers, from which delicate trails of smilax, with here and there a bright colored flower, ran gracefully in and out among the silver dishes.

The guests enjoyed the following

MENU.

Fillet of sole, tartar sauce.

Stuffed Saddle-Rock oysters, roasted.

Omelette, with chicken livers.
Cutlets of chicken, French peas.

Fillet of beef larded, with mushrooms.
Potato croquettes, tomatoes.

Broiled woodcock, on toast.
Roast quail, stuffed with truffles.
Dressed celery.

Creams and ices, Cakes. Fruits.
Coffee.

COMMENTS.

The sole, we believe, is not found in American waters, although other flat fishes of a similar sort, such as plaice and flounders, are; and it is frequently written in a menu as English sole; the circumstance of their having to be imported enhancing the flavor of the viands for an exceptional occasion. They are filleted, whenever, after skinning, the bone is taken out and then may be cooked either by breading and frying, rolled up in coils—as would very likely be the way where a large number were to be served—or by broiling. Tartar sauce is, or used to be, only another name for mayonaise, with certain seasonings added as stated at No. 903; but in this country a hot tartar sauce has c me into use which is but slightly different from Hollandaise—being a rich yellow, like softened butter, the method of making it is at No. 904. Stuffed oysters (Nos. 812 and 813) for a large party might be finished as a pan roast (No.841) after stuffing. Omelette wi h chicken livers as at No. 1150. Chicken cutlets are sometimes flattened croquettes with a bone inserted to make the imitation of the shape of a lamb chop breaded, but it is more than likely these were a different and better article, the cuts of chicken wi h the trimmed joints, either broiled or fried as at No. 1217. Concerning the fillet of beef an American writer on dinner-giving remarks: "One sees a fillet of beef at almost every dinner party. 'That same fillet with mushrooms,' a frequent diner-out will say. I hope to see it continued, for among the substantials there is nothing more satisfactory." Potato coquettes as at No. 951 would be the elegant style for this course. The tomatoes were most likely plain stewed, but stewed down rich. Broiled woodcock on toast the same as quail on toast, (No. 1133.)

Perhaps the highest effort at luxury among the dishes served was that which required an acquaintance with the literature of gastronomy, such as the literary company present on this occasion might be expected to possess for a full appreciation of its merits, the dish of quail stuffed with truffles. Says Brillat Savario: Of all kinds of game, properly so-called, the quail is perhaps the chief favorite, giving pleasure not only by taste but by its form and color. Only ignorance can excuse those who serve it up otherwise than roasted or *en papilottes* (in paper; broiled, twisted up in a sheet of writing paper cut to fit, or boned, and roasted in a paper case), because its flavor is so easily lost, that if the animal is plunged in any liquid it evaporates and disappears. The woodcock is also a bird well deserving notice, but few know its good points. It should be roasted under the eye of a sportsman, especially the sportsman who killed it." It is the stuffing of truffles that makes this a dish out of the ordinary way, for it does not matter that the truffle in itself is not a thing that the generality of people would go wild over, least of all the truffle that has been canned, kept and transported across the ocean, it is its association in innumerable anecdotes of great and famous people, their feasts and presents, their dissipation of fortunes in the purchase of a luxury of which the superlative attraction lay in the exorbitant price it commanded, putting it out of the reach at some periods of any but the wealthiest individuals. Says the author above quoted: "Whoever says 'truffle,'" utters a word associated with many enjoyments. The origin of the truffle is unknown; it is found, but how it is produced, or its mode of growth, nobody knows Men of the greatest skill have studied the question; and some felt certain they had discovered the seeds and thus could multiply the truffle at will. Vain efforts and deceitful promises! Their planting produced no crop; and it is, perhaps, no great misfortune, for since truffles are often sold at fancy prices, they would probably be less thought of if people could get plenty of them and at a cheap rate. The glory of the truffle may now (in 1825) be said to have reached is culmination. Who can dare mention being at a dinner unless it had its *piece truffée* ? However good an *entree* may be, it requires truffles to set it off to advantage. In a word, the truffle is the very gem of gastronomic materials." The same author in another place outlining his conceptions of what might be regarded as third-class, second-class and first-class dishes, names in the ascending order, respectively, turkey stuffed with chestnuts; turkey "done" (stuffed) with truffles, and truffled quails with marrow.

A hotel keeper correspondent of the *National Hotel Reporter* a few years ago gave his experience in this wise: He said he had read and been interested in the stories about the truffle and the fondness of many noted people for it; had read how the once famous Haytien emperor Soulouque had beggared himself in their purchase: had read of the rich aroma of the truffle that had plunged royal gourmands in ecstasies, particularly by the method of filling a quail with one large truffle, closing it and roasting, and serving with no other accompaniment but that which not only permeated the bird, but filled the apartment with perfume, and he purchased some in cans—enough of them for a Christmas feast for many people—and he was disappointed. The truffle as he found it was not that kind of a tuber at all, but tame, flat, almost tasteless. Perhaps another remark of Brillat Savario's may help to explain the grounds of the difference between romance and reality in this case, without even considering the effect of the canning process, he says : "The best truffles in France come from Perigord and High Provence, and it is about January they are in full flavor. Those of Burgundy and Dauphine are inferior, being hard and wanting in flavor. Thus, there are truffles and truffles as there are 'faggots' and faggots.'"

The point we wish to make for those who get up banquets is, that a truffled dish, particularly a dish of quail stuffed with truffles, may be a far more interesting affair to persons who, like the hotel-keeper correspondent, have read and had their imaginations stirred by truffle stories than to those who may have never heard of the existence of such an edible, and therein lies the use or uselessness of truffles at an American feast. In regard to the breakfast in question at the Hotel Brunswick, it has to be remarked that fresh truffles, and very good ones, are imported in jars. without difficulty, at the time of the principal truffle harvest, which is in December.

1214. Braising—What it Means.

Braising is that way of cooking meat in a covered skillet or "spider"—or whatever the local name for the covered pot may be—by which the old Virginia and Maryland colored cooks, "to the manor born," make their favorite dishes so surprisingly appetizing both by the odor while the cooking is in progress and by the juicy tenderness of the fowl, pig, turkey or coon, or whatever else it may be when done. It is the way of cooking in front of an open wood fire over coals drawn out upon the hearth with live coals by the shovelful piled upon the rimmed lid of the oven or skillet, while the odorous steam shoots out in jets from beneath, all around. If it were thoroughly and popularly understood that that is the meaning of "braised" meats in the hotel bill of fare, it is obvious such dishes would possess an interest for a great many people that they do not now, and, besides, there would be a sort of standard of comparison to try the success of the hotel in imitating home cooking. The trouble evidently is that the word "braise" conveys no meaning whatever connected with edibles to American ears, and still there is no other, and this happens to be a proper term for the process. The native cooks call it 'smothering," if they give it a name at all, but they also call it smothering to bake a panful of meat in gravy in the oven. In fact there is no name for braise but "cook-it-in-the-skillet," and that designation is a little unhandy for the purposes of a bill of fare. *Brazier* is the English, and *braisiere* the French proper name for the camp oven or skillet above mentioned, a vessel made to hold burning charcoal upon the lid while set upon a bed of live coals. Braised meats are those cooked in a *braisiere.* The French *braise*, with an accent over the last letter, is the same as our braised. Formerly it was always spelled with a z, and is still so met with sometimes and occasional disputes. The reason for the confusion of methods may be found in attempted spelling reforms and certain lexicographical transmogrifications.

The good of the braising process is that it cooks the article in super-heated steam and softens the fibres in a way that baking and roasting cannot effect, and when, at length, the water is all expelled in steam imparts a surface brown without drying the meat. The hotel cook can either carry out the process in proper form or imitate it with a covered vessel set in the oven.

Seventh Day.

Chicken broth.

Braised fillet of beef.
Chicken cutlets with vegetables.
Spaghetti and tomatoes—Palermotane.
Terrapin in cases, Maryland style.
Rice croquettes, sabayon sauce.

1215. Chicken Broth.

2 gallons of chicken stock.
4 cupfuls of vegetables cut small.
2 cupfuls of chicken meat in dice.
½ cupful minced parsley.
Salt and white pepper.

Strain off the liquor in which chickens have been boiled, or chickens and and turkeys together, into the soup pot. It will be better flavored if there has been a small piece of salt port boiled with them, not enough for decided taste but only a seasoning Skim off all the fat; cut several sorts of vegetables. in very small dice and set them to boiling in the broth an hour before the meal. Cut the chicken in pieces twice as large and add it later, and the parsley last. The broth is intended to be thin and simple, but a bastingspoon of mixed starch thickening may be added to give a little substance. Avoid chopping soup vegetables if possible. Chicken meat, at any rate, should always be carefully cut to an even size. White pepper is commom black pepper that has had the outside hull rasped off before grinding.

1216. Braised Fillet of Beef.

Cut a pound of fat bacon or firm salt pork into long strips about the size of a common pencil and lard a fillet of beef with them, drawing them through the meat from one side to the other with a large lance larding needle, and in such a slanting direction that the slices of fillet when cut will show the spots of fat all through. Clip off the projecting ends to a uniform length. Put the scraps of bacon into a deep saucepan, the fillet on them, an onion stuck with cloves, a piece of turnip, celery, carrot, a bay leaf, and parsley, and a pint of soup stock. Cover with a sheet of oiled paper and the lid and simmer at the side of the range about two hours, adding more stock as it is needed but not enough for the meat to float in it. Then take the fillet up on a baking pan and brown it in the oven. Strain the liquor it was braised in, skim off the fat, then boil it down to half-glaze and pour it over the slices of fillet as they are dished up.

Beef thus permeated with the flavor of bacon and vegetables is no longer like plain beef but is suitable to be served in the middle of a dish of cabbage or macaroni, or with dumplings or potatoes in the same dish.

The objection against the use of the fillet or tenderloin of beef for hotel dinners is that it is a scarce cut and is needed in every hotel much more for cutting into steaks for breakfast than for a dinner entree. There may be no such an objection with a few city hotels that have well-supplied markets at hand, but there are other places, particularly pleasure resorts, in large numbers, where it is impossible to purchase a fillet even for a party dinner without buying a whole quarter of beef with it. In such an exigency it may answer every purpose to take a rib roast of beef and cut out the choice portion the whole length, like a tenderloin in shape, lard it and braise it tender. The appearance is the same as the real fillet. The remainder of the rib roast can be used in other ways so that there will not be much loss.

1217. Chicken Cutlets with Vegetables.

These are the four principal cuts of a chicken— the two legs with all the meat that can be taken off with them, and the two first wing joints with a side of the breast to each. Take them off raw. Chop off the knob ends of the bones, then scrape them up like a lamb cutlet. Simmer the cuts in broth for about ten minutes, then place them in press between two pans with a weight on top.

When cold remove the skin and trim them to look like a lamb chop. They will not retain any shape unless partially cooked as stated, and then made cold. Season them, dip in egg and cracker meal and fry in the wire-basket in a pan of hot lard. Only young and tender chickens can be used in this way.

To border the dishes cut different sorts of vegetables in shreds as if for Julien soup, cook them in water and then drain them dry and mix in some cream sauce. Place the cutlet in the middle.

1218. Spaghetti and Tomatoes—Palermetane.

The name of the style has reference to the city of Palermo in Italy.

Spaghetti is macaroni in another form; a solid cord instead of a tube.

This is a favorite way with the Italians. The dish need not be baked. They simply boil the macaroni and then make it rich, not to say greasy, with the other articles and gravy from the meat dishes.

1 pound of spaghetti.
1 cupful of minced cheese.
2 cupfuls of thick stewed tomatoes.
2 cupfuls of brown meat gravy.

Break the spaghetti into three-inch lengths, throw it into boiling water and let cook twenty minutes. Drain it, put it into a baking pan, mix in the cheese, tomatoes, gravy, and if necessary a lump of butter. Mix up and let simmer together about half an hour, either in a slack oven or on the stove hearth. It will be all eaten if not made too strong flavored with tomatoes or too salt—the common mistakes. The gravy and stewed-down tomatoes being already seasoned no more salt should be added to the dish.

1219. Terrapin in Cases, Maryland Style.

For 50 cases, 8 to 12 terrapins will be required, depending on the size. They reach to 7 or 8 pounds each in weight, ocassionally, but yield only a fourth of the live weight of clear meat free from bone, for serving in cases. Having prepared the terrapin and stock as directed at No. 803 cut the meat into pieces size of cranberries. Keep the black fat and eggs separate on another dish. Boil down the liquor the terrapin was stewed in, thicken it, strain and reduce as detailed at No. 805 and add half a pint of Madeira.

Take large paper cases, brush them inside very slightly with clear melted butter. Mince the crumb of a stale loaf very fine, partially moisten with spoonfuls of melted butter poured over and stirred about; then line the bottom of the cases with the crumbs and bake them about three minutes Take them out, neatly fill the cases with terrapin meat, place the terrapin eggs and bits of fat around the edge and pour in the thick reduced sauce. Fifteen minutes before time to serve set the cases in the oven on a baking sheet, and send to table hot. There should be little cakes of fried hominy served on separate dishes to complete the style.

1220. Rice Croquettes, Sabayon Sauce.

1 cupful of raw rice—½ pound.
3 cupfuls of water and milk.
Butter size of an egg.
Sugar same amount—2 ounces.
3 yolks of eggs
Little salt, and flavoring of nutmeg.

Wash the rice and boil it with two cups of water with the steam shut in. Add a cup of milk when it is half cooked and let it simmer soft and dry at the back of the range. Mash it a little with the spoon; mix in the other ingredients. When cool make up in long rolls with flour on the hands. Fry in the wire basket in a deep saucepan of hot lard till light brown. Serve with a spoonful of sabayon sauce thick and smooth, No. 493, or 495, which is simpler and good enough with rum added.

One quart of cooked rice is equal to the quantity named in the above receipt, but it must be dry and not enriched with butter. The common annoyance in making croquettes is their tendency to melt and fall to pieces in the fat, or at least come out soft and greasy. It is owing to too much moisture in the mixture; but even the least experienced assistant need not fail if the ingredients are measured.

Study of Notable Menus.

Dinner at the Leland Hotel, Warren F. Leland, proprietor, Chicago, September, 1883. Given by an eminent lawyer to a visiting Lord Chief Justice.

"The ladies' ordinary of the hotel had been transformed for the occasion into a bower of beauty. Covers were laid for seventy-five persons. The tables were arranged in horse-shoe form. The Southern window of the apartment had a curtain literally composed of smilax, and on the surface was the motto of the house of Coleridge worked in immortelles on a white carnation background, "*Qualis Vita Finis Ita*"—as the life is so the end. A wreath composed of white rosebuds was suspended from the curtain by a white satin ribbon, and on the window drapery overhead was the motto, "*Dulce est Desipere in Loco*"—Sweet it is to play the fool at the right time. Around the entire room streamers in gold letters on a blue background were neatly arranged, bearing the names prominent in English and American jurisprudence.

The menu cards and accompanying invitations were of the most elaborate kind and elegant specimens of typographical art."

MENU.

Huitres sur Coquille.
Purce de Volaille a la Reine.

Boudins a la Richelieu.
Caviar.   Foies Gras.

Filets de Pompano, Normande.
Concombres, Pommes Duchesse.

Roast Beef a l'Anglai e, Yorkshire pudding.
Selle de Chevreuill.

Terrapin en caisse a la Maryland.
Supreme de ris de Veau aux Truffes.
Beccasines a la Joinville.

Sorbet a la Marquise.

Canvasback Duck au cresson.
Celery.
Glaces.   Gateaux.
Cafe.

The steward of the Leland Hotel is Daniel Lace; Chief Cook, Xavier Grosjean; Pastry Cook and Confectioner, Henri Born.

TRANSLATION.

OYSTERS—On shell.

SOUP—Purce or cream of fowl, or *potage a la Reine*, (No. 1203.)

SIDE DISHES OR HORS D'OEUVRE—Caviar—probably spread on shapes of toast (No. 727)—*foies gras*—fat livers, goose livers, roasted in a pan with seasonings, trimmed and sliced cold and ornamented in the dish with aspic jelly. Richelieu puddings; hot side dish to serve in place of patties or *bouchees* at same time with the soup—*boudin* is the French word for pudding of the class known as black pudding, liver pudding and the like—the wiley Cardinal Richelieu seems to have been fond of fried onions since all the dishes and ragouts bearing that designation taste of them—this is a little pat of forcemeat like No. 961, but made with pounded chicken instead of fish, a spoonful of a mixture of light fried minced onions, mushrooms, and truffles inside, egged over the top; ornamented, and cooked by steaming a short time.

FISH—Pompano (No. 902) split and doubtless broiled, with Normandy sauce, a yellow hot sauce like soft butter, sharp with lemon juice, made like Hollandaise with parsley added—cucumbers—duchess potatoes (No. 957).

REMOVES—Beef and Yorkshire pudding (No.1204)—saddle of *chevreuil*, which is roebuck in particular and stands for venison in general.

ENTREES—Terrapin in cases (No. 1219)—supreme of veal sweetbreads with truffles, same as No. 1226 in the main, subject to the cook's own style of dishing—s ipe with truffle sauce.

VEGETABLES.

PUNCH—a la Marquise—receipt furnished by Mr. Grosjean: 2 qts ripe peaches chopped; 1½ lbs sugar; 3 qts water; 1 qt maraschino; 1 pt kirsch.

ROTI—canvas-back duck with cress (No. 1072)—the South Kensington authority states the case about cress with roast fowls or game birds this way: "The fashion of serving bread sauce with roasted turkey or game is unknown on the continent, and the French are especially intolerant of our '*panade*, as they term bread sauce. *En revanche*, the English will not accept water-cress as the best accompaniment to roast chicken, quails, or partridges. Nevertheless it is a delicious and appropriate accompaniment, and one we shall do well to adopt, at least by way of a change."

SALAD—celery.

Cakes, ices, coffee, brandy.

1221. Supremes—What they Are.

A *supreme* of fowl takes that name from the *sauce supreme* that is poured over the meat. The pieces naturally enough are built up in s me regular form when it is one large dish served for a party, but it is still supreme of fowl when it is but one fillet trimmed to a pear shape laid on the individual dish, masked over with the rich sauce and ornamented with whatever goes with it at that time—green peas, asparagus heads or black truffles.

This is worthy of more than a passing notice because the *supreme de volaille* is such a favorite, evidently, with great people of the Old World; among those who esteem stewed meats above the roast, and who follow the German-French styles of Bernard and Dubois. The reader of this book will find the *supreme* occurring frequently in the specimen menus in our book of salads. At a dinner for the two emperors in Potsdam it appears as "*filets de poulets aux points d'asperges, sauce supreme;*" for the royal family of Italy it is "*poulards aux points d'asperges;*" for the imperial family of France it is "*supreme de volaille aux points d'asperges;*" at a dinner of President Buchanan's at Washington it is "*supreme de volaille aux truffes;*" and it appears thus frequently in every collection of fine bills of fare.

As above remarked, these dishes of chicken, or whatever else, take the name of supreme from the sauce of that name, and it is simply the richest white sauce that can be made. It is cream-colored, made by boiling down clear chicken broth to a jelly, boiling down mushrooms in broth to an equal stre gth, adding white butter-and-flour thickening (roux), boiling, straining, and then some rich cream. The chicken must be first cooked, then made cold so that it can be trimmed to a symmetrical shape, then made hot shortly before it is wanted in seasoned broth. The sauce is bright and glossy and just thick enough to remain on a piece of meat and coat it without being quite a paste, then the asparagus heads or cut truffles are placed upon or around it in the way to produce the most ornamental effect.

Eighth Day.

Cream of asparagus soup.

Calf's head in omelet.
Small chicken pies, French style.
Macaroni and cheese—Bechamel.
Supreme of sweetbreads, with truffles.
Pineapple fritters, curacoa sauce.

1222. Cream of Asparagus Soup.

This soup can be made at any time of the year, with either canned asparagus or fresh, while the puree of asparagus can only be made properly when the fresh vegetable can be obtained and cooked green for the purpose. This is a nearly white cream soup with asparagus heads and Conde crusts
6 quarts of soup stock.
3 quarts of asparagus, raw, cut in pieces, or 2 cans.
A small knuckle bone of ham.
1 tablespoonful of sugar.
½ cupful of minced onion.
1 blade of mace.
3 quarts rich milk.
½ pound of butter—a cupful.
½ pound of flour—2 cupfuls.
White pepper and salt.

Draw off the soup stock already lightly seasoned with vegetables; set on to boil with the knuckle bone or a slice of ham or dry salt pork, onion, mace and some white pepper. Cut off the asparagus pens, or green ends of the heads, and keep them separate, and boil the rest in the stock about an hour.

Meantime take the milk, butter and flour and make cream sauce of them (No. 931). Then strain the soup into the regular soup pot, rub the asparagus pulp through a strainer into it, put in the cream sauce, salt and the asparagus heads, which, if canned, will be all ready, if not cook them in the soup about 15 minutes.

Have brown crusts ready the same as for bean soup and place a few in each plate.

1223. Calf's Head in Omelet.

Split the head carefully, dividing the joints with the cleaver but sawing through the rest to preserve the tongue and brains, which take out and, after washing, cook the brains and keep them ready.

Steep the head in water, wash well, then cook in the stock boiler, allowing from one to two hours, according to size. When tender take it up into a pan of cold water and remove the bones. Having drained it from the water dredge with salt and pepper, sprinkle with the juice of a lemon, and lay each half, skin downwards, in a frying pan slightly buttered.

For each half of the head make an omelet of 5 eggs, mix in a fourth their bulk of soup stock, add salt and pepper, beat up and then add the brains, cut small and pour into the frying pan around the calf's head.

Bake on the bottom of the oven about fifteen minutes, or until the omelet is set and light brown.

Turn it upside down and out of the pan on to a dish and serve by cutting slices of the meat and omelet together. Pour a little veal gravy on the meat.

1224. Small Chicken Pies—French Style.

The meat of four fowls.
1 quart of brown butter sauce.
1 quart of potato balls (Parisienne).
2 tablespoonfuls of minced parsley.
Seasonings.
35 oval flats of puff paste.

Cut four pounds of cooked chicken meat into slices an inch long and all of one thickness. Make a quart of sauce by lightly browning ¼ cup of butter and rather more of flour together in the oven, and thickening a quart of chicken broth with it; strain it, add a grating of nutmeg, salt, pepper, parsley, the shred chicken, mix all, and keep hot.

Cut thin flats of puff paste about three inches long; brush the tops with egg and water, bake a nice color and when done split them into top and bottom. Cook the potato balls as at No. 953.

When time to serve place a bottom crust of pastry in the individual dish, and a good spoonful of chicken in sauce upon it and the top crust on that and a spoonful of potato balls around.

1225. Macaroni and Cheese.—Bechamel.

1 pound of macaroni.
1 cupful of minced cheese.
½ cupful of butter.
5 cupfuls of water.
1 bastingspoon of flour thickening.
4 eggs.
3 cupfuls of cream sauce.

Salt. Parsley.

This is yellow macaroni and cheese baked, with a white parsley sauce for a top layer.

Boil the macaroni by itself first, throwing it into water that is already boiling and salted. Let it cook only 20 minutes. Then drain it dry and put it into a pan or baking dish holding three quarts.

Chop the cheese, not very fine, and mix it with the macaroni, likewise the butter. Beat the eggs, water and spoonful of thickening together, pour them over the macaroni and set the pan in the oven to bake.

While it is getting hot boil a pint of milk and thicken it like cream sauce and add chopped parsley. Pour it over the macaroni without mixing and bake a little color on top.

This makes a very attractive dish; the yellow cheese and custard showing up in spots among the white parsley sauce.

1226. Supreme of Sweetbreads with Truffles.

Parboil calves sweetbreads that are large enough to split the flat way and press them between two dishes until cold. Draw fine strips of fat bacon through with a small larding needle. Split in halves, trim to shape, simmer in butter and a few spoonfuls of broth, with a little lemon juice and bunch of parsley, until done, or about 20 minutes.

Place a little foundation of boiled rice (spread on another dish and cut out with a cutter) in each individual dish, a sweetbread with it and the sauce (No. 1221) poured over.

Have ready some black truffles cut in slices and stamped to some shape with a fancy vegetable cutter. Shake them up in the clear part of melted butter in a pan over the fire, and place the shapes as an ornamental border carefully upon the white sauce.

1227. Pineapple Fritters with Curacoa.

To make the old style frying batter with ale take:
4 cupfuls of flour.
1 cupful of ale.
2 eggs.
1 tablespoonful of sugar dissolved in the ale.
3 tablespoonfuls of melted lard.

Put all in a pan at once and stir up thoroughly. Let stand an hour before using and the ale will make the batter light.

Drain slices of canned pineapple from their juice, dip in batter and fry in hot lard. Drain, and break off the rough edges.

When curacoa is added to a starch syrup (No. 490) it changes the color to a beautiful rose pink.

Study of Notable Menus.

Dinner at the Galt House, Louisvil'e, Ky., A. R. Cooper, manager. Tendered by the Bar Associat on to a visiting Lord Chief Justice, October, 1883

MENU.

Shell Oysters.   HAUT BARSAC
Celery.

Consomme Imperial.   QUEEN SHERRY.

Broiled Pompano, Venitienne.   HAUT SAUTERNE.
Hollandaise Potatoes.
Soft Shell Crabs, Chancellor Sauce

Supreme of Chicken with Truffles.   PAPE CLEMENT.
French Peas.

Roast Fillet of Beef, Sauce Bernaise.
Cauliflower.   GIESLER SPECIAL SEC.

CHAMPAGNE PUNCH.

Roast Saddle of Kentucky Mutton.   "
Puree of Turnips and Mashed Potatoes.
Roast Grouse, Game Sauce   "

Pastry.   Cheese.
Vanilla Ice Cream.

Fruits in Season.
Cafe.   COGNAC VIERGE.

COMMENTS.

Consomme imperial is a sort of diplomatic broth, apparently, for it was named imperial when France was under the empire, and consomme royal when emperors went out and kings came in—in other words, consomme imperial and consomme royal are the same thing; a brandy-colored clear soup with little egg cus ards floating in the plates. Fish *a la l'enitienne* is the Dubois style of *a la Maitre d' hotel*, the refined form of butter, lemon juice and parsley in combination to form a sauce. These menus are in plain language, however, but something else needs to be named.

It is often a matter of regret in presenting these specimen bills of fare that they have to be so entirely divested of the attractiveness that the engravers and printers have bestowed upon the original card. Our own purpose is fully subserved when it is shown what dishes to choose for any particular occasion and how they are to be prepared, but beyond that there is a vast amount of ingenuity and taste to be exercised in making a handsome menu.

Thus, the bill of the Grand Pacific banquet, a few pages back, was printed with large script for the principal dishes, and small script for the vegetables and accompaniments, on two fine white cards joined by white satin clasps. That of the Leland was a costly souvenir of the occasion which the guests retained. The Brunswick of Boston regularly prints the names of dishes in lines of small capitals and adds the sty'e or accompaniment in small print. The Galt House is preeminent for the variety, as well as beauty of its menus, everything that is brought out in the way of fine cards and specialties invented for particular occasions being called into requisition for its luncheons, dinners and special parties. These things, of course, constitute another department of the business of preparing a banquet which we can only mention but not do justice to.

Regular dinner bill of the Galt House:
TABLE D'HOTE.
6 to 8 p. m.

SUNDAY, NOVEMBER 14TH, 1883
RAW OYSTERS.
Celery.
SOUP.
Cream of Celery
FISH.
Broiled Whitefish, Maitre d'Hotel Sauce.
BOILED.
Young Capon with Egg Sauce.
ROAST.
Young Pig, Apple Sauce,   Loin of Beef, au jus,
Young Turkey, Cranberry Sauce,
Saddle of Veal with Dressing.
(GALT HOUSE PUNCH.)
SALADS.
Potato   Lobster.   Italian.
ENTREES.
Cutlets of Lamb with French Peas,
Macaroni and Cheese. Sauce Tomato,
Banana Fritters, Sherry Wine Sauce.
VEGETABLES.
Boiled Onions,   Boiled Rice.   Stewed Tomatoes,
Sugar Corn,   Boiled and Mashed Potatoes.
PASTRY.
Steamed Raisin Pudding, Hard Sauce.
Apple Custard Pie.   Peach Pie.   Assorted Cake.
CHEESE.
Roquefort,   Edam   American.
DESSERT.
Charlotte Russe,   Taffy Candy,
Strawberry Ice Cream,   Fruit in Season.
Coffee.
GALT HOUSE, Louisville; Ky.

The Steward of the Galt House is Charles Astor Howard; Chief Cook, **Frank Rhul**; Pastry Cook and Confectioner; John Theobald.

Ninth Day.

Old plantation vegetable soup.

Smothered rabbit, country style.
Backbone stew, egg dumplings.
Baked corn custard.
Pumpkin bread.

1228. Old Plantation Vegetable Soup.

This plain soup lacks the element of mystery which makes the *bouilabaisse* and *garbure* of Provence, the *olla podrida* and *gaspacho* of Spain, the *pilaff* of Turkey and the *ouka* of Russia,—not to include the Mexican stew of green chilies, tomatoes and corn—strike such an impression in print, but as long as a soup is considered in the light of something which people like to eat this one will continue to "take the cake."

Not necessary to have any stock but, early in the morning, put into a large boiler.

All the marrow out of a leg bone of beef:

4 gallons of cold water.

1 large fowl, a beef tongue, a chine of fresh pork, three or four pigs feet, a piece of pickled pork—one or two or all of them according to what may be on hand at the time, but never put in any mutton.

All the soup beef besides that the water will cover.

Some more marrow out of the broken bones.

Let it stew four hours.

Then take out the meat and cut up portions of any kind that is not fat; about a quart; and put it in the soup, also,

Onions, turnips, cauliflower, celery, or any vegetables except carrots and beets—about a cupful of each.

1 pint of tomatoes cut in pieces.
pint of corn.
pods of red pepper chopped.
A small bunch of garden herbs—thyme, marjoram and parsley.

Let boil until the vegetables are done, then add a pint of flour and water thickening and salt to taste.

There is a good deal of needless anxiety in some places to remove every particle of grease from the top of the soup, some going so far as to use blotting paper and, perhaps, a microscope, to find the most minute particles. They would fail if they were to try to find such a horror of the fat that shines in spots on the surface of a good plate of soup among the people who consume it. Most people like fat beef, fat fowls, fat butter, and seem to be quite tolerant of a little fat—marrow-fat—on their soup that they sup with bread and crackers. However, it is a matter of taste, perhaps of training, and in any case we do not want fat by the spoonful in our tureen.

1229. Smothered Rabbits, Country Style.

Take eight rabbits and chop off the heads, feet and thin ribs, and divide them each into six cuts; the two legs, two shoulders, and two pieces of back. Keep back the pieces of young rabbit, if they can be known by their smaller size. Boil the large ones in a pot of seasoned stock about two hours, then put in the young ones and let stew half an hour longer. To ke up the pieces into a baking pan, put in half a cup of butter and a cup of milk, dredge with salt and pepper and flour and set in a hot oven. It is an object to get a brown outside on the pieces of rabbit as quickly as possible, which is the purpose of the milk and butter, for they both cause a quick brown. If not so managed the meat is dry and stringy and nobody cares for it. When slightly colored on all sides pour in the remainder of the liquor the rabbits were stewed in and serve it as gravy with each dish.

1230. Backbone Stew, Egg Dumplings.

2 pork backbones.
4 leaves of sage.
1 onion.
1 teaspoonful of minced red pepper.
2 cups of milk.
Flour thickening.
2 eggs and 2 cups of flour for dumplings.

Chop the backbones in pieces and wash in cold water to get rid of the splinters of bone.

Boil about 2 hours in water, just enough to cover, with the seasonings in it, and when boiled down low put in the milk and thicken to the consistency of cream.

To make the ribbon dumplings, mix two raw eggs with an equal amount of cold water, add a little salt and stir in flour enough to make dough. Knead on the table, roll out as thin as the back of a knife and cut in narrow ribbons with a rolling paste-jagger; divide in suitable lengths, drop into a saucepan of boiling water and cook about 10 minutes.

Dish up the stew in deep dishes and place the dumplings on top with a fork. They are yellower, and easier to place if cooked separately this way than if mixed in the stew.

1231. Baked Corn Custard.

2 cans of corn—dry, solid packed.
½ cup of butter.
1 rounded teaspoonful of salt.
¼ teaspoonful of white pepper.
6 eggs.
1 quart of milk.

Empty the corn into a pan and mash it a little; melt the butter and stir it in; mix eggs and milk together, stir them into the corn, put in a 4-quart pan and bake until just fairly set in the middle. Too long baking makes it watery.

1232. Pumpkin Bread.

Bake a pumpkin in large pieces in order to get pulp very dry. Mix with the mashed pulp all the corn meal it will take up, adding a little salt and a little lard, or some small broken cracklings from the rendering kettle, if in the season. Take up large spoonfuls and place them shaped like goose eggs in a greased pan and bake about an hour.

Tenth Day.

Consomme with vegetables.

Beef a la mode.
Mutton chops breaded, tomato sauce.
Hot spiced pigs feet.
Hulled corn and milk.

1233. Consomme with Vegetables.

This is a clear soup with plenty of vegetables in it and they should be of as many different colors and kinds as may be convenient, leaving out tomatoes, which make all soups alike, but including red carrots, yellow ruta-bagas, white turnips, green string beans, celery, peas, cauliflower, salsify, cabbage, lettuce, leeks, onions, and either green or salted cucumbers. Only a small quantity of each kind is wanted; about half a carrot, half cupful of peas, and so forth; the idea being that a vegetable soup can be made at any season with whatever kinds may be within reach. Take, for proportions,

2 gallons of clear soup stock.
1 quart of hard vegetables cut up.
1 quart of green vegetables.
8 tablespoonfuls of corn starch.
Salt and pepper.

Draw off the stock clear from the stock boiler through a fine strainer and set it on the back of the range.

Cut, first, some string beans into little diamond shapes and then cut all the other vegetables as near like them as possible (you can't get an assistant to do that any more than you can to cut julien vegetables fine, or soup nudles).

Boil those that take longest to cook first, in a saucepan alone, drain away the water and the strong taste and put the vegetables in the soup along with the cauliflower and peas, cabbage or lettuce and let boil until done.

If the clear soup seems not very rich stir up a little starch with a pint of cold stock and add at last. It gives apparent substance without destroying its clearness.

We give the following more space than it is really worth in deference to the curious interest in the name we have found among hotel cooks.

Beef a la mode appears to be a dish of English origin. The French would have called it *a la mode Anglaise*—"in the English fashion"—and then shortened it to *a l'Anglaise* or, *a la mode* something else, and not have stopped at *mode*. The English always were good at cooking rounds of beef plain, and perhaps this was the first attempt they made to do it up in a French style. It seems to have first come into repute in Prince Bladud's city of Bath. It proved to be pretty good, all things considered, but there are several spurious dishes passing under the same name; one we find is contemptuously alluded to by an English cook as "the hashed meat of the eating houses." Another, or possibly the same thing, is a brown stew of small pieces of beef; another is beef stuffed with veal and oysters, and so it goes. But the following is unquestionably the real beef a la mode.

1234. Beef a la Mode.

A way of making a tough piece of lean beef tender and well flavored:

Take a solid lean piece of beef that is not tender enough to cut into first-class steaks; and about as large as a common leg of mutton.

1 pound of fat bacon or dry salt pork cut in thick strips.

Some mixed spices in a plate to roll the strips of bacon in.

1 cupful of chopped onions.
4 cloves of garlic.
3 bay leaves.
1 pint of ale.
½ pint of common red wine.
1 teaspoonful black pepper.
Same of salt, and a pinch of cayenne.
Soup stock or water to cover the meat.

There should be in the kitchen a glass jar of prepared spices and herbs as directed at No. 789, if there is not mix some cloves, mace, allspice and herbs in a plate, roll the strips of salt bacon in the mixture, then insert them in the beef by means of a large lance larding needle. Put the scraps remaining in a deep saucepan with the other articles named, except the stock, and the beef on top, cover with the lid and let simmer until it is nearly dry, then put in water or stock to come level with the top of the meat, cover down, and keep it gently boiling at the back of the range 5 or 6 hours. Turn it over once or twice. When the beef is thoroughly tender take it up and strain the liquor that remains, skim off all the fat, and reduce it by boiling to the richness of melted jelly. Slice the meat crosswise of the larding and pour a little of the sauce over each slice. If you use no cooking wine add a spoonful of vinegar.

Beef a la mode is in better demand for a cold dish at lunch than hot for dinner.

The way unskilled cooks spoil it, generally, is by letting it boil dry and begin to brown at the bottom, when the onions and spices make an unpleasant taste, and, again, by serving it with common brown sauce instead of its own glaze. Another error is the addition of carrots and celery in excess of what may be in the stock. There may be people somewhere in the world as excessively fond of carrots as some French cooking directions would lead us to believe, still it is a perpetual wonder why they never come to American hotels. There is no surer way of getting a dish left unconsumed than to crowd into it the peck of carrots, turnips and celery that some of the teachers advise.

A way of procuring more of the glaze or gravy for a dish like the foregoing, or the scollops of beef at No. 1199, is to stew some soup beef in a separate saucepan and boil down the liquor nearly dry, then add it to the other.

1235. Mutton Chops Breaded, Tomato Sauce.

Cut and trim mutton chops as if for broiling; 10 or 12 may be enough for a dinner entree.

Break two eggs in a pan, add half as much water, beat together, dip the chops in it and then in cracker meal. Press on a good coating without rubbing bare spots for the grease to get in. Lay the chops in the wire basket and dip into lard that is hot enough to hiss. Cook about 6 minutes. Tomato sauce, No. 1120.

The best way to bread any article without using eggs is to mix together one-third flour and two-thirds cracker meal. Dip the piece of meat in it, then in a plate of milk, then in the mixture again, and let lie a few minutes before dropping it in the hot fat. Milk takes on a better brown color than a wetting with water would afford.

1236. Hot Spiced Pigs' Feet.

The same as *a la vinaigrette*. Boneless pigs' feet in a pearl-colored sauce.

Put on a pint of clear broth or stock, half a pod of red pepper minced in it and half a cupful of vinegar. When it boils thicken it with flour to the consistency of thin cream.

Throw in a tablespoonful of green pickle and the same of capers, and a little salt.

Have ready some shapes stamped out of slices of beets in vinegar, and a saucer with minced yolks of eggs, or minced parsley, and ornament the dishes with them as they go in.

1237. Hulled Corn or Home Made Hominy.

Steep a quart of white corn in weak lye for two days, wash in two waters and boil about 4 hours or until tender. The lye from the leach of wood ashes is the kind generally used, but a weak solution of concentrated lye will answer and if that is not available mix a handful of baking soda in water enough to cover the corn twice over and let steep in that. Wash well before cooking, eat with salt and milk.

In most large towns there are persons who make a business of supplying eating houses and hotels with the lunch and breakfast dish of hulled corn ready prepared.

Leland Hotel.

LUNCH.

Oatmeal and Milk   Buttermilk
Mush and Milk   Cracked Wheat and Milk
Graham Bread   Plain Bread   French Bread
Dry, Buttered and Cream Toast
Hulled Corn and Milk

SOUP
Consomme

OYSTERS
Raw   Stewed

HOT DISHES
Beef a la Mode
Mutton Chops Breaded, Tomato Sauce

COLD MEATS.
Roast Beef   Turkey   Boneless Pigs' Feet   Tongue
Potato Salad   Corned Beef   Chicken Salad
Ham   Chipped Beef   Sardines
Pickled Lambs' Tongue
Boston Baked Beans.

Mashed Potatoes   Boiled Potatoes
Boiled Rice   Stewed Tomatoes

Olives   Chow Chow
Pickled Cabbage   Pickled Beets

Cake   Ice Cream   Fruit

Ooiong, Black and Green Tea
Chocolate   Coffee with Cream
CHICAGO, November 18, 1883.

Among all the published bills of fare has anyone ever seen one of a hotel midday lunch? Here are two specimen cards. The regular Leland Hotel bill of fare is not in French like that of their banquet, but is as easy to read as this. There is an evident provision made for those who take their breakfast at the hour when others take lunch, and a good many people take dinner.

These luncheon cards are changed and printed anew every day, the same as the dinner bills. A number of such dishes as are used for these informal meals, and equally good for breakfast and supper, are found described in this and the adjoining pages. Specimens of breakfast and supper cards will follow further on.

COMMENTS.

These meals, it is seen, bring into requisition a number of those dishes that have delighted the hearts of all gourmands from Rabelais down (and the monks of St. Menehould might now be forgotten if it were not for the reputation they gained for their fried pigs' feet) but which for some cause do not seem fine enough for the dinner bill of fare. They are none the less necessary for the cook to know and practice. In many hotels the same list of secondary dishes is used to serve at supper, the regular dinner being in the middle of the day. The writer had business at a northern summer resort house a short time ago where three entrees of some kind were served at every supper, besides the usual supper dishes. In the South a similar variety of stews and minor dishes prevails at breakfast instead of supper.

Consomme paysanne is soup or broth in country style; a clear vegetable soup the same as No. 1233. But the distinctions are so nearly without a difference that the addition or omission of lettuce or cabbage is sufficient to change the name.

This bill of fare has choice dishes enough for an elegant Sunday dinner.

LUNCHEON.
1 to 2:30 p.m.
SUNDAY, October 21, 1883.

SOUP.
Consomme Paysanne

ENTREES.
Fried Chicken, Cream Sauce
Fillet of Beef Larded, Mushroom Dressing
(ORANGE WATER ICE.)

SALADS.
Potato   Mayonnaise of Shrimp   Celery

COLD DISHES.
Roast Beef   Spiced Pigs' Feet   Ham   Tongue

VEGETABLES.
Fried Corn   Baked Potatoes   Boiled Rice

Fruits in season.
Tea   Coffee   Milk
Dinner from 6 to 8 p.m.
GALT HOUSE, Louisville, Ky.

1237 a. Devils—What They Are.

It seems probable there would be no devils now if it were not for the packers of canned meats; the latter day tendency to pick and cut out and banish glycerinate, mollify or smooth over all the strong words would prevent these dishes ever being mentioned to ears polite if it were not for the rows of cans of devilled ham, devilled turkey, chicken, crabs, and the like, seen on the shelves at the provision stores. We don't know where these packers find the authority for calling such meats devilled; in this case they are simply finely minced and seasoned, all ready for spreading in sandwiches; devilled crab and lobster as sold in these closed tin cans are only the selected meat cut small, and ready to be seasoned, and variously prepared for the table. Proper devils, however, are broils or grills. Sir Walter Scott in *Guy Mannering* takes the reader into a hotel kitchen in Edinburgh, "where a number of cooks were employed in roasting devils on a gridiron." In Lever's *Tom Burke*, one officer asks another to come and take a devilled bone and a kidney with him, and in numberless instances we find mentioned Indian devils, wet devils and dry devils, devilled chickens, pigeons, rabbits, spareribs and everything that can be broiled, for they are always broils or grills (*grill* is the French for gridiron), the Indian devil being seasoned with hot East India sauces, the dry devil being simply broiled chicken on toast without a sauce. Singular that the true devils of half a century ago should be so completely banished and get so completely replaced by such new loves as crabs dressed *au gratin* and termed devils without reason. Should a customer come along, however, one of the old school, or one used to the London club house dishes, and call for a devilled kidney, or even a devilled woodcock, he will simply want it broiled, with butter, salt and pepper for sauce.

Eleventh Day.

Chicken gumbo soup.

Devilled ham—old style.
Young rabbit with Soubise sauce.
Macaroni and cheese—American.
Fricasseed oysters in border.
French toast, wine sauce.

1238. Chicken Gumbo Soup.

One of the first things required of a cook who goes south is to make the different sorts of okra soups. Okra is the seed pod of a tall garden plant. It is cooked as a vegetable, also, just the same as string beans. When the pods are young they will dissolve in boiling into a kind of gum and make the soup smooth and thick; the slices cut thin need not be strained out. But when the older pods are brought to the kitchen they can still be used for soup if no better can be had, and the soup must be strained afterwards, because they will not boil quite tender. The same with sliced and dried okra. It can also be bought in cans, and better yet in bottles in the form of a green powder called *filé* gumbo, (pronounced *filay* and meaning dried). It will be understood from this that the exact amount to use cannot be stated, but the cook will put in according to the kind. There should be boiled rice as a vegetable the same day.

8 quarts of soup stock.
1 large fowl.
4 slices of ham or salt pork.
2-quart panful of sliced okra.
½ cupful of minced onion.
1 bayleaf. 1 pod of red pepper.
1 cupful of flour.

Boil the fowl in the soup stock or stock boiler until tender, then let it get cold and after that cut it into neat small pieces. Fry (saute) the slices of ham and pieces of chicken in the same pan together until they are brown, then put them into the soup pot (there is always a second pot that your soups are finally brought together and finished in) to wait till the stock is seasoned and thickened in the other. Put the flour into the frying pan and brown it in the ham fat, setting it in the oven if necessary, then empty the contents into the soup and add the onion, bayleaf and pepper. Boil half an hour. Strain into the soup pot where the pieces of chicken are, add the sliced okra and boil slowly about an hour longer, skimming off the fat as it rises at the side.

It is a dark green soup. Put a tablespoonful of boiled rice in each plate as it is served. Take out the slices of ham, but serve the pieces of chicken in the soup.

1239. Devilled Ham—Old Style.

Old style is *à l'ancienne* in French, and new style is *à la moderne*.

This is a good dish for a stop-gap for days when there is nothing in market, or extra arrivals after an insufficient dinner has been prepared.

10 slices of ham or shoulder.
½ cupful of butter.
1 tablespoonful of dry mustard.
1 teaspoonful of black pepper.
1 cucumber pickle minced.
½ cupful of vinegar and water.

Broil the ham nicely over the coals. Mix all the other articles in a bright tin pan together and drop the hot slices of ham on top. When all are mingled and at boiling heat there will be a thick, yellow, pungent sauce in the pan and more slices of ham can be added as wanted.

1240. Stewed Rabbit, Soubise Sauce.

Cut rabbits in joints over night and steep in cold water to whiten them. Stew tender, time according to age, and have the liquor they stew in highly seasoned with salt and pepper, and if a piece of bacon in it all the better.

Meantime make the white onion sauce by chopping onions small and stewing in water until tender enough to mash, then put them through a coarse strainer or seive, add salt and milk to the puree, boil and thicken so that a spoonful poured over the piece of rabbit in the dish will remain and coat it over.

Sauce Soubise, or cream of onions, is named for its reputed inventor, the Prince de Soubise, elsewhere already referred to in this book. From this onion sauce, as a starting point, we find several other dishes labelled *a la Soubise* because they contain onions in excess, such as onion soups both white and brown, and fowls stuffed with onions. The Prince thus made famous, rescued from the oblivion into which all his friends and companions are faded and gone, is mentioned in a note to the *Scottish Chiefs* as having been, on the French side, present at the battle in which "Prince Charlie," of Scotland, met his final defeat, and his tent was found as full of perfumes and toi'et articles and all sorts of foppish appliances as an ordinary lady's boudoir.

1241. Macaroni and Cheese—Plain.

1 pound of macaroni.
1 cupful of minced cheese.
½ cupful of butter.
1 quart of water or milk.
2 tablespoonfuls of flour.
2 eggs. Salt. Cracker-meal.

Break the macaroni into finger lengths and throw it into a saucepan of boiling water. When it has cooked 20 minutes pour a'l into a co'ander to drain.

Put it in a 2-quart pan, mix the cheese and butter with it. Mix the flour smooth and add it to the water or milk, then the eggs and some salt, and pour it to the macaroni. Sift cracker-meal on top. Bake brown on top. Dish out with a spoon.

The use of a little flour saves eggs and is an advantage; but the dish of macaroni should never be dry and solid enough to cut in blocks. The quality of the cheese used also makes a great difference.

1241 a. Fricasseed Oysters in Border.

Scald the oysters in their own liquor. Strain the liquor from them into another saucepan, add an equal quantity of milk and a little salt and cayenne. When it boils add a little thickening, then two yolks of eggs and juice of half a lemon. Soon as it shows signs of boiling again put in the oysters.

Cut oval rings of puff paste and bake them, same as tartlets, in a pan. Place one such ring or border in the dish and fill with the yellow fricassee.

1241 b. French Toast, Wine Sauce.

20 slices of bread.
1 cupful of milk.
1 tablespoonful of flour.
2 or 3 yolks of eggs.
3 tablespoonfuls of sugar.

Mix the flour gradually with the milk in a pan, (or use a large spoonful of thickening instead) add the yolks well beaten. This is not a batter, but only thick as cream.

Dip one side of slices of bread in the mixture, place them with the dipped side up in a buttered baking pan, dredge granulated sugar over and bake them on the shelf in the range to get a good brown glaze on top. Serve in dish with wine pudding sauce.

Several different things are understood by the term French toast. We shall not attempt to determine which is the right article, as anything whatever may be termed French and there is nothing definite about it. The common, almost universal h tel French toast is the bread fried in batter at No. 256, which is a bread fri'ter, and the sauce makes it good. However, the best cooks make it other ways, either as above described or the same way prepared but browned on a griddle instead of in the oven, or else the bread spread with butter and sugar only, baked brown, then dipped in batter and fried.

The way we have given (No. 1241 a) is probably the best, and as a restaurant dish is most satisfactory if served in a soup plate of hot milk.

There is a great misuse of the words *aux* and *au* in bills of fare which have come this year from hotels of every section, from the most prominent as well as the obscure. Instead of *a la*, a considerable number have written *aux*, which is not the same thing, neither is it quite the same as our "with," and to use such in wrong connections so far from showing high-tone and learning, is just as bad as to write *a* eggs, or *them* molasses or any other sample of bad grammar. As near as can be explained as they are used in bills of fare, *au* means to-it, and *aux* means to-them. The first is right when that which follows is one thing, as *truffles au macaroni*; but *aux* must be used when it is several, as *macaroni aux truffles*.

We notice all the menus call it "St. Julien" soup if they have it at all; it should be known, however, that it is named for a New York restaurant keeper who was not a saint. It is the old French "saute soup" which Brillat-Savarin showed Julien how to make, in New York, and it took his name.

"We had hot spiced pigs' feet put in the entrees to-day and they were well received"—writes one of our pupils, referring to No. 1236, which appeared last week, and goes on—"I followed the reading of the letter, only after boning rolled each foot in a piece of twine to reboil in the spiced sauce; they unrolled in good shape on the small platters and with the sauce poured over and *garnished* with hard boiled yolks had an appetizing appearance—have had fine success in the plain, easy way these entree dishes are written."

That is right, and one thing well learned leads to others; now try calves' brains the same way, and we make this remark save the space of repeating the receipt for it.

[Having thus far digressed from the regular line let us add what the steward of a prominent club writes, for these are among the many evidences at hand that this is all considered very live matter indeed by a large and important class of readers of the NATIONAL HOTEL REPORTER. This correspondent says:

"Your books are all full of good sense for the benefit of both the cook and the steward; but this, I think, will be more valuable than either of the others, for it helps the cook out where he most needs help. The average cook does not make good soups, and his list of entrees is very limited. Having one of your books, however, it will be his own fault if he fail in either quality or variety."]

Pattern of the Hotel Menus of the Future.

MENU.

Stewed Oysters Consomme Royal

Kennebec Salmon, Hollandaise Sauce
Parisian Potatoes

Vol-au-Vent of Sweetbreads Chicken Croquettes

Roast Beef Roast Turkey
Sweet Potatoes Cauliflower

Saddle of Venison, Currant Jelly Lettuce Salad

Roquefort Cheese Crackers
Mince Pie Plum Pudding

Neapolitan Ice Cream

Cakes Fruit

Coffee

Thanksgiving, 1883,
St. Clair Hotel,
Cincinnati.

Twelfth Day.

Bouillon.

Antelope steak saute, French potatoes
Chipped beef in butter.
Minced kidneys on toast.
Fried sugar corn.

1242. Bouillon.

Bouillon is the liquor in which beef has been boiled; it is beef broth. *Bouilli* is boiled beef; it is the soup meat that has made the *bouillon*. *Bouillon et bouilli*, the soup first, and then the soup meat, is the common inartistic dinner of the common people, that French epicures have bandied jests about, while still respecting the simple excellence of the first part.

If through any accident your intended soup or soup stock is spoiled, you will find the very best remedy for the trouble by putting on some fresh cut beef and fresh trimmed beef bones in cold water with a turnip, carrot and onion, and letting it boil an hour. Then strain it through a coarse strainer that will let the beef tea particles go through; add a very little thickening, and some salt and pepper, and, if the quantity consumed is to be taken as an indication, you find the simple *bouillon* is as much thought of as any soup you make—that is, for once in a while. It is fine for a second soup when the other kind is rich and high flavored, and fine for lunch.

There seems to be a perversion of terms when the so-called *bouillon* served in cups at fashionable parties, is clarified into *consomme*.

It is true these names do not signify much, but if *bouillon* means anything it means beef broth with the beef essence left in it.

Consomme and bouillon, when served at parties' should have a slight seasoning of cayenne added, and a quarter slice of lemon dropped in the cup before filling.

1243. Antelope Steak Saute, French Potatoes.

Sauteeing is the way that is commonly known as frying, in a little fat in a frying pan.

Season the antelope steaks with salt and pepper and fry (saute) them as wanted, a few at a time in several small pans with a little fresh roast meat drippings. Add a little water to one or two of the pans when the slices are taken out and make a deep colored gravy to pour around in the dishes.

Cut potatoes with a scollop knife and cook them before the meal begins by stewing in fat and lightly browning in the oven and sprinkling with parsley, as directed at No. 953. Serve them as a border with the steaks.

1244. Chipped Beef in Butter.

For lunch, breakfast or supper, shave dried beef very thinly, either with a knife or inverted plane. Put into a pan enough butter to cover the bottom when melted, and then a cupful of the shaved beef. Dredge with pepper. Stir about. When fairly hot through it is done. May be served heaped up on thin toast or in individual deep dishes.

1245. Minced Kidneys with Ham.

2 beef kidneys.
½ pound of broiled ham—4 slices.
2 hard-boiled eggs.
12 slices of fried bread or toast.
Pepper and salt.

Mince the ham fine in a chopping bowl and set it aside to be ready. Cut the kidneys small, put them in a frying pan with a spoonful of drippings, or ham or sausage fat and shake them over the fire in the gravy that forms until the pieces are partly cooked. Too much cooking makes them hard. Drain them out with a spoon and chop fine. Put back in the gravy and the minced ham with it; add pepper and a little salt. Make hot without frying the moisture out. Dish on slices of toast and sprinkle with chopped eggs.

Regular dinner bill of the Brunswick, Boston:

MENU.

OYSTERS ON SHELL.
SOUP.
PUREE OF ASPARAGUS—aux croutons
CONSOMME OF CHICKEN
FISH.
BOILED PENOBSCOT SALMON—butter sauce
Hollandaise Potatoes   Cucumbers
REMOVES.
PHILADELPHIA CAPON, with pork—parsley sauce
LOIN OF SPRING LAMB—mint sauce
STUFFED CHICKEN—giblet sauce
SIRLOIN OF BEEF—mushroom sauce
ENTREES.
CROQUETTE OF SWEET-BREAD—perigord
BROILED ANTELOPE STEAK—au champagne
SMALL CHICKEN PATTIES—a la reine
PEACH FRITTERS, glace—en sabayon
VEGETABLES.

MASHED POTATOES	RICE	BOILED POTATOES
NEW PEAS	POTATOES	SPINACH
BERMUDA ONIONS		MACARONI

MAYONNAISE.

LOBSTER	CHICKEN	SHRIMPS

DESSERT.
BAKED INDIAN PUDDING

APPLE PIE		MINCE PIE
ASSORTED CAKE	MACAROONS	CHARLOTTE RUSSE
CONFECTIONERY		FROZEN PUDDING

ROMAN PUNCH

APPLES	ORANGES	BANANAS

COFFEE

Sunday, April 29, 1883.

COMMENTS.

The foregoing bill is of no particular occasion, but an estray of last April, used here to show one style of construction.

"Puree of asparagus with crusts"—the soup is made by using the thin, green stalks and heads of young asparagus because that can be cooked *green* instead of purple, and mashing it through a strainer in sufficient quantity to give a cream-like consistency to the stock. The common liking for bacon and cabbage is remembered in making this soup and a piece of bacon is boiled in it. There should also be some asparagus heads left whole to put in at last —*croutons* are dice-shaped pieces of bread toasted brown in a pan in the oven if to be *Conde* crusts, but if *duchesse* they are fried in clear butter—but the great Conde, who probably being the Bismarck of his day and being fond of these crusts in his soup, had none of our superfine American steam manufactured crackers, (oyster, soda, pic-nic, butter and Boston) if he had he would have liked them better than his crusts—at least that is the way with all of our generals and colonels. It is only about forty years since the first American machine-made crackers were sent over the water, and then the English thought them almost too good to eat. So when it is found in the old directions that all puree soups should have *croutons* served with them, it ought to be remembered that those poor unenlightened people had nothing else that was better, and while there is no harm in serving a *few* crusts, your people at table should not be annoyed by finding no room left in their plate of soup for the favorite oyster crackers.

"Perigord"—standing for sweetbreads a la Perigord, is simply an allusion to truffles in the dressing; because the best truffles come from Perigord— just as with us the best asparagus comes from New Jersey.

1246. Fried Sugar Corn, or Corn Fritters.

1 can solid packed corn.
Butter size of an egg—2 ounces.
½ cupful of flour—2 ounces.
1 teaspoonful salt.
½ as much pepper.
3 eggs.

Mash the corn to make it pasty, mix all the ingredients in, make flattened cakes with flour on the hands and fry (saute) them in a frying pan, brown on both sides.

To make corn fritters roll in shape of eggs with plenty of flour on the outside, and fry in the potato fryer immersed in hot lard or drippings.

This makes 25 or 30.

1247. Sautes—What They Are.

"I ask you not to meet Mr So-and-so and Lord What d'ye-call-him; I ask you to meet a *saute de foie gras*, and a haunch of venison." "Confound the man!" was my mental anathema— "Long life to the Solomon of *sautes*," was my audible exclamation— "I will most certainly pay them my respects. Never did I know before how far things were better company than *persons*. Your lordship has taught me that great truth."

The commonplace of those studied sentences of the novelist is that his lordship was going home to have some "fried" liver and bacon—sauteed, really, but very few of us have learned the difference of meaning of frying and sauteing as yet—and the other one said he would be on hand and did not care if there was not any company if the *saute* was good and hot and had a nicely seasoned gravy.

A *saute*, then, is good enough for anybody. There is not a cook in any hotel but what can prepare one and does, very frequently. There is no French knowledge required for it, all that is wanted is to know how to get rid of the superfluous grease, if there be in any, and to thicken and season the pan gravy so that it tastes good. We have mentioned incidentally many times over that the common frying of slices of meat in a common frying pan is *sauteeing*, and we have as much right to adopt that word and use it as to construct and adopt a new word for the telephone, when the language did not contain one ready.

When a party of travelers alight at a wayside inn and must have a meal prepared in the shortest time, the cook cuts up it may be a chicken into the frying pan, or perhaps a rabbit, or pork chops, or beef steak, or liver and bacon, cooks it over the fire, takes out the meat when done, stirs a spoonful of flour around in the pan, then pours in a little water and lets it boil up—that is a *saute* of chicken, rabbit or whatever it may be, and *it is fine enough to put in any bill of fare*, provided always that it be fresh cooked and hot just as it would be for a traveling party.

Napoleon's *chicken a la Marengo*, the dish said to have been praised by him when served on the battlefield, is a *saute* of chicken with mushrooms and wine added to the sauce. Somewhere we have seen an anecdote of Prince Talleyand and his cook, the Prince angry at having been kept waiting, "But the *saute*? your excellency." "It is perfection," replied the Prince. Every cook who reads this can prepare a saute of any kind of meat; but remember to pronounce it *sautay*.

Study of Notable Menus.

Annual Game Dinner and Thanksgiving: Windsor Hotel, Saint Paul, Minn.; Summers and Monfort Proprietors.

MENU.
Thursday, Nov. 29, 1883.

SOUP.
Marie Stuart

FISH.
Red Snapper
Boiled Potatoes

REMOVES.
Saddle of Antelope, Cranberry Jam
Roast Brant, Apple Sauce
Roast Turkey, Stuffed with Chestnuts
Young Black Bear, Marechale
Prairie Chicken, Stuffed
Haunch of Buffalo, Cumberland Sauce
Mallard Duck Canvas Back Duck Teal Duck

LUCULLUS' PUNCH.

ENTREES.
Red Squirrel Pot Pie
Wild Goose, a la Fermiere
Pheasant Saute, Hunters' Style.
Opossum, Braised, with Sweet Potatoes
Salmis of Grouse, with Mushrooms
Venison Steak, Sauce Dufour

Broiled Quail on Toast
LETTUCE SALAD

COLD.
Pate of Game Liver   Chaufroix of Woodcock
Snipe, en Bellevue

VEGETABLES.
Boiled and Mashed Potatoes
String Beans   Stewed Tomatoes
Green Peas   Green Corn

PASTRY.
English Plum Pudding, Brandy Sauce
Lemon Meringue Pie   Sliced Apple Pie
Macaroons Eclairs au Confiture Vienna Cake

DESSERT.
Nesselrode Ice Cream Orange Jellies Fancy Creams
Biscuits a la Vanilla

SWEET CIDER.

Oranges Apples Figs Nuts Raisins Malaga Grapes
Coffee   Cheese

Of the Windsor the 1st Steward is C. J. Monfort; Chief Cook, Louis Du Verdier; Pastry Cook and Confectioner, Louis Hanson.

COMMENTS.

The special feature of the bill is that all the meats are various kinds of game, from the soup which contains quenelles of partridge through the removes and entrées, the quail on toast—written there to observe the French form of a *roti* with salad,—to the three cold ornamental dishes; and it has been so managed that none of the kinds are named twice over, nor can it be fairly said that the same thing appears cooked in several ways at once. There is nothing that needs explanation. Lucullus is a good and favorite affix to anything that is fine and costly, that being the name of one of the most famous Roman high-livers.

The "à la Fermière" to the wild goose means, in Farmer's style—the reason why it is *fermière*, instead of *fermier*—farmer *ess* instead of farmer-feminine instead of masculine, is because all these qualifications are supposed to include the word *mode*, but to have dropped it for the sake of brevity, and *mode* being feminine, makes the style the same.

The above menu was beautifully printed on a large double gilt-edge card very finely engraved specially for this occasion.

Study of Notable Menus.

Christmas dinner at the Brunswick, Boston. Barnes and Dunklee, Proprietors, 1883.

MENU.

BLUE POINTS.

Puree of Tomatoes—croutons
  Consomme of Chicken—celery
Fillet of Flounder, breaded—colbert
  Parisian Potatoes.
  Leg of Mutton—caper sauce
  Bremen Goose—chestnut dressing
  Stuffed Chicken—giblet sauce
  Sirloin of Beef—mushroom sauce
  Small Chicken Patties—salpicon
  Potted Quails, truffled—sauce madere
  Terrine de Foie-Gras—de Strasbourg
Game Pie—chasseur Boned Turkey—jelly
Canvas-back Duck
  Prairie Chicken, larded—bread sauce
  Dressed Lettuce Dressed Celery
  Mashed Potatoes Boiled Potatoes
Rice Tomatoes Peas Turnips Corn
   Onions Squash
Lobster Salad Chicken Mayonnaise Shrimp Salad
  English Plum Pudding
Mince Pie Pumpkin Pie Apple Pie
Fruit Cake Chocolate Cake Swiss Meringues
  Champagne Jelly Confectionery
  Neapolitan Ices Roman Punch
   Roquefort Neufchatel
Apples Oranges Bananas Grapes
   Coffee

The Seward of the Brunswick is Charles A. Gleason; Chief Cook, Arnold Dedinger; Pastry Cook and Confectioner, Henry Mayer.

1248. Potting—What it Means.

Potted meats are both hot and cold dishes. It seems probable that the very ancient practice of packing down cooked meats in the form of a paste highly seasoned in small pots or jars made air tight at the top by a covering of melted butter, was the first thing intended to be expressed by potting, but as these meats are cooked in a covered jar in the oven, liked Boston baked beans, for example, and as described at No. 1189 for potted pigeons, there could be nothing more natural than to serve them hot, also, and call them potted meats even before they were potted.

However that may be, it is a term that is sufficiently easy to be understood where intelligible culinary terms are so few, and the way of cooking is of the highest degree of excellence. Almost every cooking range has one very hot oven, and another that never heats up above the medium. The cool side is the one to set the jar in, with its covering of paste, to bake for three or four hours.

Christmas dinner at the Burnet House, Cincinnati. Dunklee, Barnes and Zimmerman, Proprietors, 1883.

MENU.

Oysters on Half Shell
   SOUP.
Green Turtle   Consomme
   FISH.
Boiled Sheephead, Mashed Potatoes
   REMOVES.
Saddle of Mutton, with Jelly Roast Beef
 Roast Goose, Stuffed with Apples
 Roast Turkey, Cranberry Sauce
   GAME.
 Red Head Duck, Stuffed with Oysters
Broiled Quail on Toast
  Saddle of Venison with Jelly
   ENTREES.
Croquettes of Sweetbreads, with French Peas
 Hashed Turkey, with Poached Eggs
  Queen Fritters, with Jelly
   VEGETABLES.
Mashed Potatoes Boiled Potatoes Stewed Tomatoes
Rice Lima Beans Mashed Turnips
Sweet Potatoes Spinach Sugar Corn
Stewed Oyster Plant Onions
   COLD DISHES.
Cold Ham Celery Chicken Salad Cold Tongue
  PASTRY AND DESSERT.
Rice Pudding Plum Pudding Mince Pie Cream Pie
Roman Punch Charlotte Russe Vanilla Ice Cream
Assorted Cake   Oranges
Grapes   Bananas
  Coffee

1249. Salmis—What they Are.

This is one of the few necessary terms to use, because there is no other name. There is a thin distinction between *salmi* and *salmis*, but it is not observed and need not be. A salmi is a hash; a sa'mis is a dish of game recooked. It is as much as can be expected if bill of fare writers can adopt salmi as meaning one dish and salmis for more than one. It is made by first roasting the game (and we do not know why it should not apply to poultry as well), then cutting it up into a sauce prepared for it by boiling down the bones and fragments in broth well seasoned, then thickening and straining it. The various styles or "a la modes" attached half the time have reference to the kind of seasoning in the sauce, as a salmis sauce strong with onions has one name, but if with wine it has another—which would be all very pretty if it could be learnt—the other terms refer to the style of building up and trimming in the dish. But salmi or salmis can be used in the bill of fare without troubling about the after terms. A *salmi* of any small game is a more elaborate dish than a *saute* of the same thing, because it has a sauce carefully prepared instead of a quick-made gravy stirred up in the pan.

1250. Fricassees—What they Are.

This, the last of the terms which occur to us as having become partially known and are used because they are needed, is the least likely of all to be correctly used, for at least ten or twelve differently cooked dishes are called fricassees by the French masters, while domestic cookery calls any common white stew a white fricassee, and a brown stew a brown fricassee, but domestic cookery is wrong and stew is the better name. French fricassees are all alike in one thing, and that is in being served in the creamy, yellow sauce, thickened with eggs instead of flour, and containing either wine or lemon juice, called *sauce a la poulette*. Anything that is cooked, almost, from chicken breaded and fried to cucumbers sliced and stewed, is a fricassee if it has that kind of sauce to it, much the same as any kind of fowl or game is a *supreme* when it is in the sauce of that name.

Sometimes, instead of such a stew being called a fricassee it is mentioned as something—scollops of veal for example—"*en fricassee de poulette*," or it may be "*a la poulette*."

The difference between this and a supreme, is that the fricassee sauce has eggs in it, thickening it like a custard, and supreme sauce has not, and the same egg thickening makes the distinction between a fricassee and any common sort of stew.

MENU.

Blue points on shell
Celery

Green Turtle, a l'Anglaise   Scotch broth
Olives   Radishes
Cannellons Francaise

Baked Black Grouper, port wine sauce
Potato beignets

Sweetbreads glace, aux petits pois
Patties of parsnips

Roast sirloin of beef
Roast Turkey, stuffed with oysters
Baked sweet potatoes   Marrow asparagus
Sugar corn

JAMAICA RUM PUNCH

Roast quail, larded, with guava jelly
Lettuce, a la mayonaise

Boned capon   Shrimp salad

Boiled plum pudding, hard sauce
Pumpkin pie   Charlotte russe   Mince pie
Assorted cake Claret wine jelly Pineapple ice cream
Fruit   Cider   Biscuit   Coffee

THE WINDSOR, Denver, Colo., Christmas, 1883.

It would not do for all hotels to be alike, nor should a procrustean rule be applied when advice is asked as to which form of bill of fare should be adopted. The writer's own preference among all the specimens in these leaves is the Burnet House form, on the preceding page; but that is for the regular every day dinner, and its adoption does not prevent the use of a bill of the pattern of the two succeeding for a party dinner or supper. They are dinners to be served in courses. But the same dishes and the same number for each division, with the same simple expression of them in plain language, might be slightly changed in arrangement, and there would be the same table d'hote pattern to which we adverted above as near perfection as the exigencies of hotel business will ever allow us to go.

Cannellons,—mentioned as a hot side dish in the above bill, will be found explained at No. 241— these have a morsel of minced meat rolled up in them—potato beignets are potato fritters, No. 280, and they are fine and not common—patties of parsnips may be another form of parsnip fritters or croquettes.

Rissole—in the menu following, is the same thing as croquette, it being applied to the rolled form instead of the pear or other rounded shape; rissole and croquette both mean something crisp outside. The mince of fowl of this bill and the hashed turkey of the Burnet House bill are the same thing. It is a favorite dish at the fine restaurants and we cannot see but it is just as well presented in such words as if it had been covered with some such term as chaufroix or calmis, or anything else that would not have been understood and would have caused it to be left uncalled for.

MENU.

Blue points
Celery

Green turtle
Rissole of chicken

Boiled trout
Parisienne potatoes   Sliced cucumbers

Boiled turkey, oyster sauce
Sugar cured ham
Spinach   Asparagus

Sirloin of beef
Chicken, sage dressing
Mashed potatoes   Sweet potatoes
French Peas   Sugar corn

Supreme of sweetbreads, with truffles
Mince of fowl, with poached eggs

ROMAN PUNCH

Roast quail   Mallard duck
Lettuce, a la mayonaise

Chicken salad   Boned turkey

Mince pie   Plum pudding, brandy sauce   Apple pie
Claret wine jelly   Lemon jelly
Charlotte russe

Vanilla ice cream
Fancy cake

Fruit   Roquefort Cheese   Coffee
THE ANTLERS, Colorado Springs, Colo.

Study of Notable Menus.

Perhaps we cannot do better for an ending of the line of specimen dinner menus than to study the following for the benefit of such of our readers as still imagine some unapproachable heights of excellence existing in whatever is printed in French.

It was an ideal affair that was never realized, for as a meal the dinner was a bad failure; a fact that has nothing to do with the dinner as planned in the mind of one or two or more of the best informed and most experienced cooks in America. It is the menu of the dinner given to Mr. Henry Villard's party of German tourists, who came to participate in the Northern Pacific Railroad opening. It took place at a fine summer resort house, the Hotel Lafayette, Lake Minnetonka, September, 1883. The preparations for it were, however, made in New York. Without knowing for a certainty why the dinner was a failure we think—and every hotel man who has had to do with these too elaborate banquets will be ready to agree with us—that it was because the menu was in a language which the guests either did not understand at all, or did not understand the culinary terms; that the dinner was too tedious'y attempted to be served in courses, an intention which the party just from the wild west did not understand either, and began to leave the table before the second act of the formalities had commenced, thereby upsetting all plans and losing the best of everything which was reserved for the last. However that may have been, this is a genuine French menu in arrangemen, language, spelling and choice of dishes. It was neatly printed in b'ue on heavy bristol board, edged with blue silk fringe, and on the last page was the monogram in old script "N. P. R. R."

Blue Points sur coquille
POTAGES.
Bisque de crevettes   Consomme d'Orsay
HORS D'ŒUVRES.
Varies   Varies
Petites bouchees au salpicon
POISSONS.
Bass rayee a la Hollandaise   Filet de sole a la Joinville
Concombres   Pommes croquettes
RELEVES.
Selle de chevreuil a la Cumberland
Jambon d'ourson au chasseur
Tomates farcies
ENTREES.
Cotelettes de pigeonneaux, chevaliere
Petits pois Francais
Poitrine de cailles a l'Andalouse
Quenelles de perdreaux a la St. Hubert
Flageolets a l'Anglaise
Ballottines d'ortolans a la Perigueux
Fonds d'artichauts, Lyonnaise
SORBET.
Lucullus
ROTI.
Poule de prairie   Sarcelles
Salade escarole
PIECES MONTEES.
Paniers garnis aux fruits   Pyramide en nougat
Chalet Suisse   Chapelle Turque
Vues du Lac Minnetonka
Corne d'abondance
Chemin de fer du Northern Pacific entrent dans le tunnel Mullen
SUCRES.
Pudding a la Tyrolienne, sauce sabayon
Glace Napolitaine   Bavarois au chocolat
Petits fours assortis
Fruits   Fromage   Cafe
VINS.
Chateau Yquem   Amontillado
Johannisberger Cabinet
Chateau Cos d'Estournel, '74
Roederer   Pommery   Chateau Lafite, '65
Clos de Vougeot
Liqueurs

The above was the production, probably, of Eugene Mehl, for a long time chief cook of the Windsor and Brevoort Hotels, New York. It was reported early in the season that a French cook who had lately gained some reputation in the service of the President of the United States was engaged for this hotel, and he may have been concerned in it likewise.

TRANSLATION.

The names of the styles and the sauces are from an expensive French work but little known in this country, a book that is principally devoted to what has been called the "fuss and feathers of ornamental cookery."

OYSTERS—On shell.

SOUP—Bisque of prawns, and an amber clear soup.

SIDE DISHES—Various—such as olives, lettuce, caviar; and a hot patty with a little highly seasoned mince inclosed.

FISHES—Striped bass with Hollandaise sauce, and fillet of sole with a ragout of truffles and crayfish—cucumbers and potato croquettes.

RELEVES—Saddle of venison with Cumberland sauce—ham of young bear, hunters' style, or with game sauce—stuffed tomatoes (*farcies* is filled with *farce*, which is French for and the original of our forcemeat—there is no beef or other ordinary kind of meat in this menu.

ENTREES—Pigeonneaux is the French for "squabs" —cutlets as described at No. 1217—chevaliere style is breaded and fried—French peas with them—breast of quails, sauce Andalouse (No. 938)—quenelles of partridges, a paste made by pounding the meat fine, seasoning, making in shapes and poaching them in seasoned broth—St. Hubert is the patron saint of hunters—flageolets, French beans dressed with butter, salt and pepper—*ballottines* are rendered fillets in English, they are the breasts with wing joints attached, but we suppose that in this case the ballottines were the little butter ball birds boned and not divided, thus bringing the gradation of dishes down to the finest point because ortolans are the most rare and expensive of European birds, like our reed birds, but larger and fatter. Perigueux (the style of the people of Perigord) indicates truffles—bottoms of artichokes in a brown sauce.

PUNCH—Lucullus—an expensive punch like imperial, composed of several kinds of liqueurs and fruits and frozen a la Romaine.

ROTI—Prairie hen and teal duck—endive salad.

ORNAMENTAL PIECES on stands—baskets of fruits —almond candy pyramids—a Swiss chalet—Turkish chapel—views of Lake Minnetonka, done, probably, in sugar work—*corn d'abondance* is the horn of plenty, the figure that always appears whenever an old-style banquet is set out—the grand piece evidently was a representation of the railroad and train of cars entering a tunnel.

SWEETS—Tyrolean or Swiss pudding with wine custard sauce. Neapolitan ice cream (No. 126)—chocolate Bavarian cream (No. 187)—small fancy cakes and tarts of various sorts—fruits—cheese—coffee.

WINES—Choice brands.

The chief excellence of the menu consists in the selection of parts only of small birds—of the young pigeons only the principal joint of the wing with the entire breast, the quail the same but differently shaped and cooked, the partridges similarly selected meat, and the dish of ortolans was of a higher order still—all this because it makes common food expensive and capable of being shaped, flavored and ornamented until it becomes virtually a new product. But the people who dine cannot know of these things intuitively and without the necessary information they would better enjoy a plainer dinner.

Thirteenth Day.

Clam chowder—Boston style.

Roll of veal stuffed and braised.
Stewed lamb with tomatoes.
Salmon patties.
Charlotte of peaches.

1251. Clam Chowder—Boston Style.

2 quarts of clams and their liquor.
6 quarts of soup stock.
2 quart panful of raw potatoes cut small.
2 cupfuls of sliced onions.
2 or three slices of streaky salt pork.
2 teaspoonfuls of powdered thyme and savory.
1 tablespoonful each of white pepper and salt.
A little minced parsley for ornament.

The different articles should be made ready separately and placed convenient for use.

The belly pieces of pork which are cut off the roasts and dropped in the pickle keg from day to day, are the best for this purpose. Cut up a pound into small bits and fry them light brown in the pot the soup is to be made in; then pour off the fat. Put in the potatoes, onions, stock, clam liquor and seasonings, let boil until the potatoes are done, then add the clams cut small, and boil up once more.

The clam soup made with milk, at No. 823, and the Coney Island chowder, No. 1208, with the other kind above, make the three varieties most desired both for hotel and restaurant custom. They are all unequivocally good.

1252. Roll of Veal Stuffed and Braised.

There is always a surplus on hand of the cut of veal marked 9 and 0 on the diagram at No 996, and

The clam soup made with milk, at No. 823, and the Coney Island chowder, No. 1208, with the o her kind above, make the three varieties most desired both for hotel and restaurant custom. They are all unequivocally good.

1252. Roll of Veal Stuffed and Braised.

There is always a surplus on hand of the cut of veal marked 9 and 0 on the diagram at No. 996, and extending back to the leg. It is useless for roast or cutlets, but most excellent meat for entrees. Take the whole piece, full length, and make it all alike by cutting the bones out of the brisket and the firmest part of the gristle along the ridge, if large veal.

Make the veal dressing, No. 956. It is not best to use much, but rather a thin coating highly seasoned. Lay the veal suet and trimmings of the brisket in a saucepan, add an onion and small soup bunch, a sage leaf, and a little salt. Roll up the breast of veal, tie with twine, put it on top of the scraps and set it to cook with only a cupful of stock at first, and the lid on. When it has become set with cooking add a dipperful of stock and keep it simmering with the steam shut in for 2 hours, managing so that it will be boiled down dry at last. Then take up the roll of veal and brown it in one of the roast meat pans very quickly, not to dry the outside into strings. Pour the grease out of the saucepan, make gravy of the glaze that adheres to the bottom. See that when carved the roll is neatly sliced across and served with its own seasoned gravy.

1253. Stewed Lamb with Tomatoes.

4 pounds of breast of lamb.
1 pint cupful mixed vegetables.
1 pint of tomatoes.
2 tablespoonfuls of chopped parsley.
Salt and pepper.

Take two of the brisket and flank pieces marked 7 in the cut at No. 997. Saw across the bones making them less than two-inch lengths, divide them, two pieces of the ribs to each cut. Wash, stew in water enough just to cover, long enough to make the meat tender.

Cut carrots, turnips and onions in squares, and boil them in water separately; pour off the water when they are half done and put them in the stew, and also the tomatoes. Boil half an hour longer, thicken slightly if necessary, season, and at last throw in the parsley.

The above makes a very pretty dish. In dishing up take up two pieces of the meat for each dish and place them square in the middle of an individual flat platter, and dish the sauce and vegetables in order at each end.

1254. Salmon Patties.

Take cooked fresh salmon—canned salmon as good as any if in large pieces, or boiled salmon from a previous day—and some puff paste from the pie-making.

Roll out and cut about 10 flats like large biscuits but thin. Press a shapely piece of salmon down in each one, in the middle, and bake the patties of a nice color.

If good paste that will rise with high edges around the fish these are sufficiently ornamented without any additions when dished up. A Friday dish. Not many wanted.

1255. Charlotte of Peaches.

See Nos. 352 and 355. A sweet entree comes in good place for a Friday dinner, if ever.

Fourteenth Day.

Amber clear soup or consomme.

Stuffed shoulder of mutton.
Fricassee of veal and mushrooms.
Parsnip fritters
Croquettes of sweetbreads.

1256. Amber Clear Soup or Consomme.

2½ gallons of clear stock.
1 shank bone of veal.
1 fowl, or the drumsticks and trimmings.
1 onion and bunch of soup vegetables.
2 pounds coarse beef.
4 whites of eggs.

Roast the veal and fowl carefully in the oven the same as roasting dinner meat, but in a pan by themselves, and have a little butter in the pan as well as the veal fat. The object is to get a nice deep brown color, as well as flavor, to impart to the soup, and veal and butter are the best materials for the purpose. When brown put the meat into the soup pot with the stock and let boil. Pour off the grease from the baking pan, dissolve the brown glaze with water and put that in the soup, also the onion and soup bunch. Boil an hour. Next comes the clarifying process.

Chop a lump of lean beef like sausage meat and add the whites of eggs to it, and a pint of cold water. Stir to mix.

Strain off the soup that you have ready and mix the chopped beef and egg with it, then boil it again. It is like clearing jelly. The egg comes up on top, and when it is all cooked strain the clear soup first through a gravy strainer to remove the beef, then through a jelly bag or a napkin spread in a colander. Run it through twice.

The foregoing is the full detailed process of making consomme as fine as can be made, and once it is thoroughly understood all the different varieties follow as a matter of course. There are some advantages can be taken and substitutions made both to make the work easier and to suit the public fancy. You find a good many people objecting to the soup, which they declare is only like seasoned hot water, and you have to add four ounces of starch to give an appearance of strength. If boiled slowly after the starch is added it becomes just as clear as it was before. Then where there is poultry roasted every day the cook will reserve a dish of the drumsticks and backbones and necks at the carving stand to put in his brown stock, but if there is no such coloring a little burnt sugar must be used.

The chopped beef if not absolutely necessary nor even the white of eggs—it all depends on whether the consomme is wanted to be of the best or only ordinary. Season with salt and cayenne before sending in.

In connection with the above read the article referring to the many variations of clear soups at No. 1175 and the whole subject is covered.

1257. Stuffed Shoulder of Mutton.

Take the bones out of two shoulders of mutton at the time the meats are cut up for breakfast, that they may be ready early. It is done by beginning at the shank end and cutting close to the blade bone. Lay some pieces from the thick parts ove the thin places.

Make the bread dressing either at No. 942 or No. 1060—one has sweet herbs, the other sage, and both are good—and spread it over the meat. Roll up the long way of the shoulder; that is, with the shank end inside, because it slices much better so than if rolled the other way. Tie with twine. Put the rolled shoulders in to bake in a deep pan the same as if roasting turkey; cover with an oiled sheet of paper and keep cooking with always a little water in the pan, not less than two hours. Take off the twine and slice neatly and serve with a little gravy made in the pan poured around. See No. 1062 for this sort of bread sauce. There is no trouble whatever in disposing of all the shoulders of mutton in this way. They are nearly as good as fowls if cooked moist and tender with the stuffing seasoned as directed.

1258. Fricassee of Veal and Mushrooms.

A fricassee, having a smooth yellow sauce, cannot be made right by proceeding as for a common stew, because the gravy particles and scum from the meat would fill it full of specks and spoil the appearance.

Take the brisket of veal marked 9 at No. 996. 1 slice of salt pork.
One small onion, or three green ones.
4 yolks of eggs.
1 small blade of mace.
1 pod of red pepper.
1 lemon.
1 can of mushrooms.
Butter and flour and salt.

Wash the veal and drop it in the stock boiler to remain about half an hour, then take it up and when cool divide it across the ribs into pieces suitable for two to a dish. Draw some clear stock through a strainer and put the pieces of veal on in just enough to cover, to simmer for an hour. Put in also the slice of pork, whole onion and mace, and red pepper finely minced and a little salt. When the meat is done add a cup of flour thickening (to save eggs and be more satisfactory) and when that has boiled up best the yolks with a little milk, pour some of the stew to them, then pour all back into the saucepan, stir around once and take off before it boils. Finish with a little lemon juice.

Make the mushrooms into a brown saute in a frying pan. Dish up a piece of veal at each end of the dish and the sauce poured over them, and a tablespoonful of brown mushrooms in the middle. Leaf shapes of pastry may be used to lay in the dish for ornament.

1259. Parsnip Fritters.

1 pint of dry mashed parsnips—2 cupfuls.
Butter size of an egg.
2 tablespoonfuls of flour.
2 eggs.
1 teaspoonful of pepper.
Same of salt.

Stir all together. Have a saucepan of lard hot enough to hiss when a drop of water touches it. Dip a spoon in and then shape a fritter with it, drop in and fry light brown.

Serve either with gravy or as an accompaniment with some kind of meat.

1260. Croquettes of Sweetbreads — Toulousaine.

2 pounds of sweetbreads.
½ can of mushrooms.
1 cupful of butter.
Same of flour.
1 cupful of cream.
Same of broth or water.
Grating of nutmeg.
Juice of half a lemon.
Eggs and cracker-meal for breading.

Boil the sweetbreads first in salted water for a

time, according to kind—beef sweetbreads may need an hour. Cool them, cut in very small dice and the mushrooms with them.

Season with pepper, salt, nutmeg and lemon juice. Then make some thick cream sauce of the butter, flour and cream and broth and mix it with the minced sweetbreads. Spread the mixture in a pan and make it very cold. After that cut out pieces, roll them in flour, then dip in beaten egg and cracker-meal and fry in the wire basket in hot lard. Serve with a sauce in the dish or garnish of green peas.

A cheaper sort can be made by stirring up the minced sweetbreads with a cupful of panada and a couple of eggs, instead of making a cream sauce to set and bind the mixture.

Fifteenth Day.

Cream of celery soup.

Saute of young turkey.
Veal and oyster pie.
Calves' brains in brown butter.
French pancakes with jelly.

1261. Cream of Celery Soup.

6 quarts of soup stock.
2 quarts of milk.
1 cupful of minced onion.
Lean boiled ham—a small piece or knuckle bone.
2 or 3 heads of celery.
1 cupful of flour and same of butter.

Cut the outside stalks of celery into very small dice and boil them five minutes in water, then drain the water away.

Boil the stock with onions and ham in it; stir the butter and flour together in a saucepan and add them to the stock. When it has boiled up and thickened strain it into another saucepan, add the celery and let cook at the side until the celery is done—over half an hour. Have the milk hot ready and add it at last, along with salt and pepper and a tablespoonful of minced green celery leaf or parsley. Serve so that the squares of celery will be evenly distributed in the plates.

When the soup is rich it is as well to omit the butter and mix the flour with milk, for thickening.

1262. Saute of Young Turkey.

Very small and tender turkeys are more serviceable cooked this way than roasted, and it is a pleasant variation from the regular routine. Cut them up in joints and dust them with flour, salt and pepper. Put some fresh roast meat fat in the largest frying pan, and when it is melted lay in the pieces and cook them brown without burning. To insure the drumsticks and sections of the breast being well done keep the pan covered with a lid part of the time, but the goodness of anything cooked this way depends upon its being cooked quickly and without drying the meat. Then take up the pieces, stir a spoonful of flour around in the pan, add a pint of water, pepper and salt, boil up, and strain the gravy thus made over the pieces of turkey.

1263. Veal and Oyster Pie.

4 pounds of small pieces of veal.
1 quart of oysters.
1 quart of milk.
1 small onion.
1 pint of Parisienne potatoes.
2 tablespoonfuls of minced parsley.
4 pounds of pie paste.
Pepper, salt and thickening.

All the pieces of raw veal that will not make either roasts or cutlets are suitable for this—the neck, flank or brisket. Cut all to one size and steep in cold water some time before wanted.

Two hours before dinner set the veal on to boil with water enough nearly to cover, draw the oyster liquor by pouring hot water over through a colander, add that to the veal and carefully skim when it comes to a boil. Let cook an hour, add the milk, thicken and season it. Turn the stew into a baking pan, drop in the potato balls, the oysters spread over the top, and sprinkle with parsley. Cover with a pie crust and bake half an hour.

1264. Calves' Brains in Brown Butter.

Take six sets of brains, or about twelve lobes, which, being split, may be expected to make 20 orders; drop them into a saucepan of water in which there is salt and a little vinegar, and let slowly boil about 20 minutes. Pour all into a colander, letting the liquor run away. When the brains are cold remove all the dark streaks and skin. It is best to have them in a pan of cold water for this purpose. Slice each lobe in two, lay them out on a board, dredge with salt and pepper, roll both sides in flour and keep them ready until dishing up time. Then set a baking pan on top of the range with two-thirds fat from the roast meat pans and one-third butter, lay the brains in and brown them on both sides. Have some olives ready in a saucer and quarters of lemons in another. Serve the brains hot out of the pan with the froth of butter upon them, with olives and lemon in the same dish.

1265. French Pancakes with Jelly.

See directions at No. 259.

Pattern menu for a sociable affair where the losing party in a contest pays for the supper.

COMPLIMENTS OF THE LOSING SIDE,
WITH A BELIEF IN A HEREAFTER.

SCHNITGER, - Referee.
54   60

"To the Victors belong the Spoils."

MENU.

OYSTERS.
Raw   Fried   Stewed

Boiled Fresh California Salmon } Saratoga
Mountain Brook Trout   } Potatoes

Roast Turkey, Cranberry Sauce
Quail on Toast
Tenderloin Steak, with Mushrooms
Veal Cutlets, Breaded, with French Peas
Broiled Young Sage Chicken, with Jelly

Mashed Potatoes
Fresh California Cauliflower
Hubbard Squash

Shrimp Salad   Celery

Assorted Cake   Pineapple Ice

Fruit   Cheese   Nuts   Raisins   Coffee
THORNDCROH HOUSE, M. M. Towne, Prop'r.
Laramie City, Wyo., Dec. 18, 1883.

Sixteenth Day.

Tomato gumbo soup.

Breaded brisket of lamb.
Stewed pig's head, Russian sauce.
Spaghetti in cream.
Spanish puff fritters.

1266. Tomato Gumbo Soup.

6 quarts of soup stock.
1 quart or can of tomatoes.
2 cupfuls of minced vegetables.
12 cloves.
2 quart pan of sliced okra.
1 or 2 pods of red pepper minced.
6 spoonfuls flour and water thickening.

Set the stock on the fire an hour before dinner. Chop the tomatoes with the edge of a spoon into small pieces; let half the minced vegetables he onions; put everything in and let boil gently. Add thickening and salt at last.

1267. Breaded Brisket of Lamb.

Saw the briskets of lamb or mutton across so that the bones will be about two inches long. Drop the pieces in the stock boiler early and let them cook until very tender. Take out and press flat between two pans. When cold cut in convenient pieces, without removing the bones. Pepper and salt plentifully and then double bread them and fry in hot fat.

This is a good dish if properly managed, but does not look well unless breaded twice. The first coating may be done without using eggs, as at No.1235. May be served with any vegetable border or tomato or cream sauce.

1268. Stewed Pig's Head, Russian Sauce.

There is no satisfaction in trying to use very fat meat this way. Take the head of a small porker, saw it in two, steep in cold water an hour or two, wash it, cut out the ear, trim off all discolored portions carefully, put it in the salt meat boiler to cook about two hours. Then take it up and remove the bones.
Put into a saucepan
1 pint of strained soup stock.
1 onion cut across into small bits.
1 green pickle same way.
1 pod of red pepper. Butter size of an egg.
2 tablespoonfuls of dry mustard.
But not all at once,for the onion should stew awhile, then the butter and dry mustard be mixed together in a pan and stirred up with the onion sauce. Add salt. It makes a light yellow sauce, rather thick, with onions, pickles and red pepper in it. Put in the pig's head and slice it out as wanted.

1269. Spaghetti in Cream.

Spaghetti and macaroni can both he cooked the same ways;they are alike except in shape. Break up into finger lengths,boil in salted water about 20 minutes,drain away the water and put the spaghetti into a saucepan of rich cream sauce. It comes handy to prepare it so at times when there is no cheese within reach. At other times add chopped cheese and a sprinkling of parsley to it.

1269 a. Spanish Puff Fritters.

For all varieties of puff fritters see No. 275 AM. PASTRY COOK

PATTERN MENU FOR PRIVATE PARTY.

MENU.

Huitres en coquilles

      Chateau Yquem

Consomme en tasse

      Old Amontillado

Cassolettes au salpicon

Saumon au gratin, sauce Genoise

      La Rose

Filet de boeuf, roti au Madere

Petits Pois   Epinards

      Mumm's Ex Dry

Supreme de perdreaux aux truffes

  Asperges

Sorbet au kirsch

  Cailles roties

    Salade   Chambertin

Pouding Nesselrode Meringues panachee

Gelee au Marasquin Gateau assortie

  Fruits Roquefort

    Dessert

    Cafe noir

Matteson House, Chicago, Munger Bros., Proprietors; E. A. Smith, Steward.
JAN. 4, 1884.

Seventeenth Day.

Potato cream soup.

Baked spareribs, Robert sauce.
Corned lambs' tongues with brocoli.
Patties of calves' brains.

1270. Potato Cream Soup.

The French call potato soup *Potage Parmentier* after the man who first brought potatoes into France. Some of the Saratoga bills of fare have it "Jackson soup," but why we know not.
 6 quarts of soup stock.
 2 quarts of milk.
 8 large potatoes.
 8 spoonfuls flour thickening.
 1 cupful minced onion.
 1 knuckle bone of boiled ham.
 Salt and white or red pepper.
 2 tablespoonfuls minced parsley.
Strain the stock into the soup pot and boil it, and set the milk to gradually come to a boil at the side of the range, with the ham bone and onions in it, and minced red pepper.

Take a dipperful of good mealy potatoes out of the steamer and mash them, and mix the milk with them. Then strain the puree into the soup and when it boils up add sufficient thickening to make it like cream and to prevent the potato from settling to the bottom. Sprinkle parsley on top in the tureen.

1271. Baked Spareribs, Robert Sauce.

Divide spareribs into cuts of convenient size for one to each dish. Sawing is much neater than hacking, and leaves no splinters. Place in a baking pan, sprinkle with salt, pepper and powdered sage and bake in a very hot oven to imitate broiling in getting a quick brown without drying out. Serve with the sauce No. 908, in the dish.

1272. Corned Lambs' Tongues with Brocoli.

Take the tongues out of the pickle keg on the preceding day and boil with the salt meats. They take two or three hours to cook tender. When cold pare off all the white outside skin and split lengthwise in two.

Having the halves ready in a dish when the roast meat is done, after taking it out fry the tongues in the fat and glaze in the baking pan for about five minutes, then take them out slightly browned and glazed, and keep hot.

Brocoli is a kind of cabbage, entirely green, has the cauliflower flavor. Cook it the same as cabbage, an hour or more. Drain, add salt, pepper and a little roast meat fat and chop fine in the pan. Serve a spoonful in the dish and the lamb's tongue pushed down in the centre.

1273. Patties of Calves' Brains.

Set on a large frying pan with butter in it size of an egg, put in a pint of brains, dredge in salt and pepper and a teaspoonful of powdered sage. Scramble the brains in the pan same way as eggs. They will be done in about 10 minutes.

Prepare 12 vol-au-vent patty cases of puff paste, fill with scrambled brains, put on the lids, ornament with chopped yolks and parsley or a slice of lemon.

Something Practical for a Cold Supper.

A hotel keeper wrote from a railroad hotel where, perhaps, they do not run a printed bill of fare regularly, asking suggestions as to what sort of a bill he should provide for an anniversary supper and suitable dishes for it. Said he, "We shall have no hot dishes but oysters. We have looked through your books and find nothing suitable; they all have too many hot dishes."

About a month previous another hotel keeper had written the very same thing.

In reply to the earlier inquiry I had given it as my experience that after the most elaborate preparations of strange dishes with strange names have been made, the things which the company are unanimous in choosing and which it is important to have plenty of and to have waiters to supply them fast enough are very few. First of these is fried oysters—well fried, and garnished with lemons—then oysters in the other forms, cold roast turkey and chicken, chicken salad, ice cream, cakes and pastry and coffee. These do not make much of a show on a bill of fare and it is provoking to those who want to show the resources of the kitchen to find at least 150 out of 200 persons calling for fried oysters and disappointed if they are not abundant and making still heavier drafts on the coffee and cream when there is so much else that we think they ought to like better. I went on and suggested other good dishes both for use and appearance' sake and named about the proportions likely to be wanted of each. The supper for about 200 came off and apparently was satisfactory for it was much praised But the fried oysters were not there. Probably the hotel keeper was afraid to undertake the task, as I had intimated that it would take 12 or 15 waiters to supply fried oysters and coffee within the short limit of patience of his guests. But there were oysters stewed, scalloped and raw, and other dishes such as those in the bill below, and because these made but a small show of words a considerable space was filled up enumerating relishes which were thus made the heaviest appearing part of the supper. There is some sort of a difficulty in these matters not to be obviated on a first attempt. In responding to the second inquiry, I enclosed the first bill of fare, repeating in part what had been said to the other party; crossed out some things and suggested others, and the hotel keeper produced the following menu, which, under the circumstances as stated, must be regarded as an excellent pattern for other affairs of the kind. The letter inclosing the copy from which this is printed, is as follows:

"I also enclose our menu for banquet given last evening, which we made up from suggestions made by you, from what all said it was a complete success. Had about 140. Please accept thanks for your kindness.

Yours truly,

——————''

Ball Supper.

MENU.

OYSTERS.

Raw   Fried   Scalloped

COLD.

Roast Turkey   Tongue
Boneless Turkey in Aspic Jelly
Ham Sandwiches   Tea Biscuit
Lobster Salad   Chicken Salad
                Celery
Strawberry Jelly   Lemon Jelly
    Pineapple Jelly with Whipped Cream
Charlotte Russe   Vanilla Ice Cream
Fancy Cakes   Lemon Tartlets
        Knight Templar's Food
Neapolitan Cake   Chocolate Cake
                Fruit Cake
Swiss Cream Cheese   Edam Cheese
    Oranges   Bananas   Grapes
        Almonds and Raisins

Tea   Coffee

Eighteenth Day.

Andalusian soup.

Corned pork tenderloins in border.
Veal pot pie, country style.
Onions stuffed and baked.
Queen fritters, custard sauce.

1274. Andalusian Soup.

It is a strong brown soup with tomatoes.
7 quarts of soup stock.
1 quart or a can of tomatoes.
4 cloves of garlic.
1 cupful of minced onion.
Same of mixed vegetables — carrot, turnip, celery.
4 cupfuls of browned flour.

Throw a spoonful of butter and same of sugar in the saucepan of tomatoes and let simmer down rich at the side of the range. Boil the stock with vegetables in it, add browned flour or butter and flour and then the tomatoes. Strain through a fine strainer; let boil again slowly and skim from the side until the soup looks bright and smooth. Add cayenne and salt.

1275. Corned Pork Tenderloins in Border.

One of the prettiest borders for small entrees is finely shred Julien vegetables of mixed colors boiled done in salted water, then drained into a little saucepan of cream sauce, or brown or yellow sauce for variety. They must be neatly cut in one-inch lengths. Dishes so bordered would be called *a la Nivernaise*, in French, for no reason but because a part of France called Nivernon used to raise the best carrots and turnips and such, as our Michigan yields the best potatoes. Such a garnish costs little besides the time. Having prepared the vegetables take pork tenderloins that have been in the pickle about three days, boil an hour, split, and brown them quickly in a roast meat pan and dish up with a spoonful of the vegetables placed first as a border.

1276. Veal Pot Pie, Country Style

3 pounds of neck of veal.
1 pint of milk.
1 small onion and slice of salt pork.
White pepper and salt, and flour thickening.
Baking powder paste.

Stew the meat an hour in water just enough to cover and with the seasoning articles in it, then add the milk and thicken it to the consistency of cream. Put the stew in a deep pan that will go in the oven. Then mix up

4 cupfuls of flour.
3 large teaspoonfuls of baking powder.
1 coffee cupful of water. Salt,

The dough should be a little too soft to handle. Stir it well together with a stout spoon and drop portions close enough to touch all over the top of the stew. Bake about 20 minutes.

1277. Onions Stuffed and Baked.

6 or 8 large onions.
½ cupful of sausage meat.
½ cupful of bread crumbs.
1 egg.
1 cupful of brown sauce.
Pepper and salt.

Peel the onions and boil them in water 10 minutes; both to extract some of the strong taste and to make the inside easy to remove. Then drain them and push out about half the insides; chop these and mix with them the sausage meat, and bread crumbs, and egg, and a good pinch of black pepper, and little salt. Stuff the onions with the mixture and heap it a little on top to use up the surplus. Place them in a deep pan that will go in your steamer and let steam about an hour and a half. Then brown them off in the oven with the cup of gravy poured in the pan.

When not convenient to steam they can be simmered in gravy in the oven if kept covered with a greased sheet of paper. Any kind of minced cold meat, or part raw and part cooked without an egg,

can be made into a savory side dish in the above manner.

1277 a. Queen Fritters, Custard Sauce.

For all varieties of puff fritters and all sorts of sweet entrees see No. 274 AM. PASTRY COOK.

Regular Breakfast Bill of Fare of a summer resort. Hotel rates, $4 and $5 a day.

HOTEL KAATERSKILL

BREAKFAST.

FRUIT.

Coffee Chocolate Oolong and English Breakfast Tea
Cocoa Shells

Irish Oat Meal   Hominy Grits   Cracked Wheat

FISH

Broiled Salt Mackerel   Codfish, with Cream
Broiled Burlington Herring   Fried Pan Fish
Fish Cakes   Broiled Fresh Mackerel
Broiled Smoked Salmon   Broiled Fresh Salmon

BROILED.

Sirloin Steak   Veal Cutlets   Calf's Liver and Bacon
Ham   Breakfast Bacon   Mutton Chops
Tripe   Lamb Chops

FRIED.

Ham and Eggs   Clam Fritters
Veal Chops—plain or breaded   Breakfast Bacon
Liver and Bacon   Beefsteak, with Onions
Fried Hominy or Mush

MISCELLANEOUS.

Corned Beef Hash   Frizzled Beef in Cream
Stewed Mutton Kidneys   Stewed Clams
Stewed Tripe

EGGS.

Omelettes—Plain or with Parsley, Onions, Tomatoes,
Ham, Kidneys or Spanish
Boiled   Fried   Scrambled   Poached

POTATOES

Saratoga Chips   Baked   Stewed
Fried   Lyonnaise   Saute

BREAD

French and Graham Bread   Plain Bread
Kaaterskill Flannel Rolls   Graham Muffins
Corn Muffins   Potato Bread
French Rolls   Saratoga Rolls   Toast
Kaaterskill Flannel Cakes, with Maple Syrup

Nineteenth Day.

Scotch mutton broth,

Breaded calf's head, tomato sauce.
Beef stew with potatoes.
Minced Turkey with poached eggs.

1278. Scotch Mutton Broth.

8 quarts of mutton broth or stock.
8 tablespoonfuls of pearl barley.
1 pint of lean boiled mutton cut in dice.
Same of mixed vegetables, mostly turnips.
A bunch of parsley. Pepper and salt.
Wash the barley and put it on in plenty of water, let boil about two hours, then wash the blue-looking liquor away from it and keep it ready.
It can easily be managed to have this kind o soup when there is a surplus of lamb and mutton to be boiled and used. Cut the carrot, turnip, onion and celery in small dice, cook them in the broth and add the barley, meat, and chopped parsley at last. It should be but very slightly thickened if at all.

1279. Breaded Calf's Head, Tomato Sauce.

Saw the head in two, beginning at the crown, and take out the brains and tongue. Steep in a pan of cold water an hour or two, then drop it in the stock boiler and cook until the skin is tender enough to be cut with the point of a spoon. Some take but an hour, others two hours. Take it up and set away to become quite cold. After that take out the bones and cut the meat in pieces of suitable size for one to each dish. Dredge with salt and pepper, roll in flour, dip in egg and then in cracker meal and fry in hot fat. It is necessary to be particular to flour and coat the pieces well. The gelatinous calf's head looks only like a lump of grease if not perfectly breaded and then well drained.
Serve with good tomato sauce well stewed down in the dish, but not poured over the meat. The brains scrambled with eggs may serve for patties. The tongue either to cut up in soup or used as boiled tongue, or in a stew.

1280. Beef Stew with Potatoes.

2 pounds of pieces of beef.
8 potatoes.
1 onion. Salt and pepper.
Let the meat be one-fourth fat. The flank pieces that come off the ends of porter house steaks make the best stew. Having the pieces cut all to one size put them on with water enough just to cover and let stew slowly for two hours. Put in the onion cut small and potatoes whole; cook till done, add seasoning and thickening of flour and keep simmering at the side of the range until wanted.

1281. Minced Turkey with Poached Eggs.

3 pounds of cooked turkey meat.
1 quart of cream sauce.
A poached egg for each dish—18 or 20.
Read about cutting and carving fowls at No. 1015.
Cut the meat neatly into small dice. Make the white sauce as rich as supreme sauce, if wished, and put the cut meat into it. Dish a spoonful in the in dividual dish, press a hollow in the top and place a soft poached egg well drained from water.

HOTEL KAATERSKILL.

SUPPER.

FRUIT OR PRESERVES.

Tea   Coffee   Chocolate

FISH.

Burlington Herring   Fried Fresh Fish

BROILED.   COLD MEATS
Beef Steak | Roast Beef
Mutton Chops | Chicken
Ham | Ham
Lamb Chops | Beef Tongue
Deviled Kidney | Boned Capon

Spiced Mackerel. Sardines, Pickled Lamb Tongue

EGGS.

Fried   Scrambled   Plain Omelottes

POTATOES.

Fried   Lyonaise   Saute   Saratoga
Hashed Potatoes, with cream or browned

BREAD.

Corn Mush and Milk   Oat Meal and Vanilla Wafers
Toast   Tea Biscuit   Cream and Soda Crackers
Kaaterskill Flannel Cakes, with Maple Syrup.

Twentieth Day.

Fish mulligatawny soup.

Larded calf's liver, crisped onions.
Blanquette of lamb, Parisian style.
Fish fondue.
Turkey patties.

1282. Fish Mulligatawney Soup.

6 quarts of fish stock.
1 quart panful of pieces of fish.
6 or 8 green onions.
Butter size of an egg.
4 tablespoonfuls of curry powder.
1 pod of red pepper.
2 cupfuls of browned flour.
1 large lemon. Salt.
Some dry boiled rice.
If for a Lenten soup boil a large fish in water

with herb seasonings in it, as mentioned at Nos. 920 and 930. This gives you a good fish soup already half made. Some kind of firm fish that the meat will part in flakes, like snapper, carp or salmon, should be chosen. Pick it apart free from skin, fat or bones. Put the butter in a saucepan, slice the onions into it, with a little of the green tops.

Simmer until they are nearly dry and beginning to fry, then fill up with fish stock. Mix the curry powder and brown flour together, stir up with stock and add them for thickening. Let boil up, then strain into the soup pot, put in the fish, simmer at the side of the range and skim frequently, as the fat and skum rises at the side. Add lemon juice in the tureen. Serve a spoonful of boiled rice in the plates as well as the flakes of fish that are in the soup.

1283. Larded Calf's Liver, Crisped Onions.

It should be borne in mind that, however it may seem to be disguised by the various names which the cooks have been proud to bestow upon its different forms, liver and bacon has always been a favorite dish. The decided flavor has been employed in numerous ways to give life to other dishes that, if perhaps more delicate, still seem decidedly tame to palates that are sated with good things. Such zests as the liver forcemeat for spreading on the inside of boned quails and around the walls of a truffled cold pie, and such is pate de foie gras, imported in jars. Bacon is the natural concomitant; liver and bacon always go together. The liver flavor being universally approved there is only a question of kind. Goose liver ranks best and calf liver next. This kind is therefore scarce and dear in the cities, being always in great demand at the restaurants. Beef liver is next best and most generally available. Sheep liver is hard and not fit to use at all. For this entree take

4 pounds of calf's liver.
1 pound of fat bacon.
Spiced salt and pepper.
2 quart panful of sliced onions for border.

Cut the bacon in strips size of a common pencil; roll them in mixed spices or aromatic salt, draw them into the liver with a larding needle in such a direction that they will be sliced across when the liver is served.

Put the remaining scraps of bacon in a saucepan, the liver on top, a cupful of stock (and half as much sherry if you use it) and set it on to cook with a lid on. When the liquid is all boiled away as the bacon fries and browns turn the liver over to get a light brown on both sides. Then take it out, pour the grease out of the saucepan and make a thick-ened gravy of the glaze that remains, adding a seasoning of pepper, and strain it off.

To crisp the onions for a border to the dishes needs great care; slice them all to one thickness and fry them light yellow without blackening any, in a saucepan of hot fat precisely like frying Saratoga chips. The onions, of course, separate in rings. Put in a few at a time. They take but three minutes to cook. Drain in a colander. Place them with a fork in the dish, some gravy underneath and slice of larded liver in the midst.

1284. Blanquette of Lamb, Parisian Style.

Cook the breast of lamb whole (or any other part that may be to spare for this dish) by boiling in seasoned stock, then press it between two pans until cold and after that cut it in pieces suitable for the individual dishes.

Boil down the liquor the meat was cooked in until it is very rich; strain it through a fine seive, boil it again and thicken it, then thin it down with cream, making a white sauce of it, like supreme.

Prepare potatoes as directed at No. 953, stewing them in butter (which may afterwards be used for other purposes) because in water they would be sure to break and be useless. Sprinkle them with chopped parsley, but they should not be browned for this dish.

Make the pieces of lamb hot again in some seasoned broth. Dish up one or two pieces in a dish, cover with a spoonful of the white sauce and place a border of the potato boulettes around.

1285. Fish Fondue.

A fine dish for Lent and for Fridays. Take a boiled fish of a firm-fleshed sort—haddock, cod, pike, salmon, halibut, buffalo or carp—and when cold pick the meat from the bones in flakes or strips. After that proceed precisely the same as for macaroni and cheese, using the fish in place of macaroni. See No. 1241.

1286. Turkey Patties.

Prepare minced turkey as at No. 1281 for turkey with poached eggs. Bake oval shaped flats of puff paste; split them; dish a spoonful of mince on the bottom crust, put the top crust upon it and garnish with a sprig of parsley.

Special Breakfast Bill of Fare at a 4-dollar-a-day hotel.

BREAKFAST.

CHRISTMAS, 1883.

FRUITS IN SEASON.

Stewed Oysters   Fried Oysters   Broiled Oysters
Cracked Wheat   Oatmeal
Chocolate   Black and Green Tea   Coffee

BROILED FISH

Mutton Chops Ham Bacon Liver Tripe Veal Cutlets

Broiled Beefsteak, Plain, with Mushrooms, Onions or Tomato Sauce

Broiled Pigs' Feet   Pork Chops   Sausage
Pork Spareribs

FRIED CHICKEN.

EGGS.

Boiled, Poached, Fried, Shirred, Scrambled, Omelettes

POTATOES.

Lyonnaise   Baked   Fried   Saratoga
             Stewed in Cream

Graham Bread   Hot Rolls   Plain White Bread
Buckwheat Cakes   Corn Muffins

Luncheon, 1 to 2:30 p.m.   Dinner, 6 to 8 p.m.

Twenty-first Day.

French cream soup.

Young pigeon pie.

Saute of lambs' hearts—Toulousaine.

Artichokes in gravy.

Curry of veal with rice.

Orange fritters, port wine sauce.

1287. French Cream Soup.

This soup can be made equally as good as *potage a la reine*, which it closely resembles. Make the stock rich with plenty of veal necks and shanks or calf's head and feet. Take

5 quarts of veal stock,
3 quarts of milk.
1 head of celery.
1 cupful of minced onion.
A bunch of parsley.
1 large slice of ham.
1 cupful of butter.
2 cupfuls of flour.
2 tablespoonfuls of tapioca.
Blade of mace, cayenne, salt.

Set the stock on to boil and put in the celery, onion, parsley and mace.

Melt the butter in a frying pan, put in the ham and let it cook in the butter at the side of the range until it stops simmering and begins to fry, then stir the flour into it and let cook together, set just inside the oven, until it begins to show light yellow. This gives a good flavor, but there must be no brown color. Then put it in the soup, taking care it does not go in a mass to the bottom and burn. When it has boiled a short time and become thick add the milk, which should be hot, and strain the soup into the regular soup pot. Crush some tapioca, take two heaping tablespoonfuls and put in the soup and continue the cooking about half an hour longer. Season to taste.

It is a rule of the kitchen that the cook who makes the soup cannot salt and pepper it by the taste, but he adds what he knows must be an insufficient quantity of those articles and allows some other person fresh from the open air to be the judge. Most cooks by the time they have prepared an elaborate dinner can hardly detect a salt taste in the brine from a salt beef barrel, and cayenne makes no more impression on their palate than sugar or starch. The effect of the heat and fumes of the cookery.

1288. Young Pigeon Pie.

As old pigeons are hardly fit to be eaten at all, and at any rate must be cooked three or four hours, it is necessary to designate these used either young pigeons or "squabs."

2 dozen young pigeons.
1 pound of butter.
3 quarts of broth or water.
Flour thickening, pepper, salt.
4 pounds of pie paste.

The squabs can be picked dry, but a little easier if scalded. Singe and draw, splitting them down the back first, like broiling chickens, and then cut in halves. Wash and dry them, flatten a little with the side of the cleaver, pepper and salt and flour on both sides, then fry them slightly in the butter melted in the same baking pan the pie is to be made in.

When the squabs have acquired a light brown on both sides pour into the pan about 3 quarts of broth or water and set in in the stove that they may stew tender while you make the crust. See whether the flour on the birds has thickened the liquor sufficiently, and add salt and pepper. Cover with a thin sheet of short pie paste the same as directed for chicken pie at No. 1193, or with common puff paste if preferred. The difference between this kind of pie and the chicken pie referred to is in the pigeons being in a brown butter gravy instead of a stew. Guinea fowls, young chickens, quail and similar kinds can be made into pies the same way, with no seasonings, but brown butter and flour, pepper and salt, and they are among the dishes which nearly everybody calls for.

When the crust of your meat pie of any kind

"gives out," as is often the case when it is good, roll out a sheet of paste thin, lay it on a baking pan and mark squares, if there is time, by running a paste jagger over and across it. Bake it in ten minutes. Lay the squares on top of the remainder of the pan of pie.

1289. Sauto of Lambs' Hearts—Toulousaine.

To slice and cut the lambs' hearts in a large frying pan like any other saute is only a short operation, to be performed shortly before dinner. But to give the dish the style named commence somewhat earlier and make a forcemeat the same as if for stuffed onions (No. 1277) and add a little garlic to it. Make it up in small balls, about as large as walnuts, roll them in flour and bake them in a pan containing a little roast meat fat until they have a light brown color.

Serve two slices or half a heart with the saute gravy upon it and two or three or four of the baked forcemeat balls placed around, and two or three olives that have been made hot in a little brown sauce.

1290. Artichokes in Gravy.

Let the artichokes lie in a pan of cold water, the same as is the rule for cauliflower, spinach, etc., an hour or two before they are to be cooked. Wash well, and if the tips of the leaves are discolored, clip them; cut the artichokes in two and remove the stringy core. Have the water ready boiling, put in a teaspoonful of salt and baking soda the size of a bean, boil the artichokes about ½ hour or until the soft end of the leaf when pulled out proves to be tender. Drain and serve like cauliflower, 2 pieces in a dish, set upright, and roast beef gravy or brown sauce poured around but not all over them.

1291. Curry of Veal with Rice.

1 pound of veal,
2 tablespoonfuls of minced onion.
Same of grated cocoanut.
1 tablespoonful of curry powder.
Same of flour.
1 pint of broth.
Salt, cayenne, juice of half a lemon.
A quart of boiled rice.

Put the meat, cut in pieces, in a saucepan with a little fat or butter and the onion and let fry together a few minutes to acquire a light color but not brown.

Dredge in the curry powder, cocoanut and flour and stir until all are well mingled, then add broth or water, and milk of a cocoanut if at hand, cover and let stew slowly for an hour. Salt and small pinch of cayenne to be added at last, and the fat carefully skimmed off.

Cook rice specially for it, in loose, dry, distinct grains, slightly seasoned with salt and butter dropped on top to mix while cooking without stirring. Dish a light heap of rice at one end of the dish, and the curry in the remaining space.

1292. Orange Fritters with Port Wine.

Divide the oranges in sections by the natural divisions, removing the white pith and seeds, and drop them in a pan of hot syrup; out of that with a fork into a pan of flour and coat them with it, then into fritter batter (No. 1202) and fry in lard or oil, same as apple or peach fritters. Sauce No. 478 or 490.

Regular Breakfast Bill of Fare of a good 2-dollar-a-day hotel in the interior.

BREAKFAST.

FRUIT.

| Mocha Coffee | | Tea | | Milk |
| Cream | | | Chocolate | |

BROILED.

| Chicken | Tenderloin Steak | Lamb Chops | Ham |
| Breakfast Bacon | | Mackerel | |

FRIED.

| Sausage | Oysters | Cod Fish Balls |

COLD MEATS.

| Ham | Corned Beef | Chicken |

EGGS.

| Fried | Poached | Omelet | Boiled |
| | Scrambled | Shirred | |

POTATOES.

| Baked Sweet Potatoes | | Baked Potatoes |
| | Stewed Potatoes | Corn Beef Hash |

BREAD.

White	Graham	French Rolls	Dry Toast
	Buckwheat Cakes		
Milk Toast	Steamed Brown Bread	Oat Meal

Cook's Scrap Book.

BLANK PAGES FOR WRITING RECIPES UPON.

SCRAPS ABOUT EDIBLES.

A Typical American Dish.

The American edible clam of the Atlantic seaboard is not much larger than our scallop or scollop. Raw, it does duty for the oyster 'au naturel;" and in this simple condition it was likewise devoured by the Romans, vinegar being sometimes replaced by oxymel. When clams were eaten cooked, the disciples of Apicius and Lucullus placed the molluscs in a new stewpan with a little oil, sweet wine, and pepper. The coction was completed over a slow fire, and before serving much more pepper was added to the stew. Mrs. Hales—the Miss Acton of the United States—gives minute directions for frying, stewing, and steaming both hard and soft shell-clams, and for making clam-fritters; but, oddly enough, she omits any mention of clam-chowder. The observant M. Urbain Dubois, however, in his "Cosmopolitan Cookery," gives a sufficiently lucid "apercu" of clam-chowder; only he treats it as a "potage." "Clam-chowder soup," the German Kaiser's chef tell us, is made from the chopped flesh of clams placed in a well-buttered stewpan, and "accommodated" with onions blanched and minced, and a bunch of aromatics, salt, pepper, nutmeg, cayenne, and mace, the whole moistened with a sufficiency of wine and fish-broth. Prior to serving the soup is to be thickened with a handful of bruised "crackers," and fortified—for a mess of five dozen clams - with a bottle of Rhine wine. This is nearly, but not quite, the genuine article. M. Dubois has omitted an integral component of chowder, the pork. To find the "norma," or original basis, of chowder, we must go back to the venerable Mrs. Hannah Glasse, in whose culinary "Novum Organum," and under the heading of "A Cheshire Pork Pye for Sea," to which she specially directs the attention of master-mariners, there will be found the real foundation of chowder. "Take," says Hannah, "some salt pork which has been boiled; cut it into thin slices; an equal quantity of potatoes, pared, and cut thin; lay a layer of pork seasoned with pepper, and a layer of potatoes; then another layer of pork, and so on till your pye is full. Then add more pepper, lay some butter on the top, and fill your dish about half-full of soft water. Cover up close, and bake it in a gentle oven.

This is veritable chowder, and in the British navy was, during many generations, extensively patronized by our gallant tars, by whom it was known as "sea-pie," and sometimes as "lobscouse." On the shores of New England, however, it was popularized as "chowder," and with the addition of the sand-clams, which were so amazingly popular, it became "clam-chowder."

The oyster beds of Puget Sound are just now attracting attention. When railroad facilities are completed there is no reason why the northwestern section of the United States should not receive their oysters from this source. The gathering of oysters has been so far carried on by Indians, but lately white men have engaged in the business, and transplanting has taken place to the advantage of the oyster. Of late some very wonderful beds of oysters are described as being of unusual size, and though more meaty than those of the Atlantic coast, quite as well flavored.

A publication announces that there are daily eaten in London some thousands of the hind-quarters of frogs, "and truly delicious they are when nicely cooked in butter till of a rich brown color." We have never "spotted" the dish on a restaurant menu, and believe the statement to be incapable of verification. Apropos of frog-eating, however, we note that the Societe Protectrice des Animaux has issued a strong protest against the present mode of providing frogs for the dinner-table in France. It appears that the poor creatures when caught have the upper part of their legs, or edible portion of their bodies, ruthlessly cut off with a pair of shears. The frogs in their mutilated state being helpless, they are thrown aside. Numbers of them are stated to have been found eight or ten days after their mutilation crawling about on their fore-legs in a pitable condition. The society, therefore, recommends that some plan of killing them in the first place should be adopted.

How to Cook a Canvasback Duck.

To roast a canvasback duck, pluck the duck except the wings and head. Cut off the wings. Draw the whole inside and windpipe. Put alcohol in a small flat pan; set fire to it, and hold the duck over it one minute. Clean the duck by rubbing with a dry cloth. Cut off the neck and head. Take the skin off the head and remove the eyes. Put the head inside the duck, with the end of the bill just sticking out; season inside with salt and pepper, and truss in the ordinary fashion. The web feet are not cut off. Roast on the spit for about fifteen minutes more or less, according to size.

To broil a canvas-back duck. Clean as for roasting. Split the duck on the back, season and anoint with sweet oil. Put the duck in a double gridiron with hinge. Cook over a very brisk fire for about twelve minutes. When placed on a dish pour over it melted butter, with lemon juice, salt, pepper and chopped parsley. Canvasbacks should be served on hot plates.

At some hotels the strawberries stand from the beginning of the meal in glass dishes on the tables, smothered in pulverized sugar.

The codfish, when at home rambling through the submarine forests, does not wear his vest unbuttoned, as he does while loafing around the grocery stores of the United States.

Turtle a la Chinoise.

The flesh of turtles forms almost the staple food of the natives of large districts in the tropics, and is cooked in several ways. No method of culinary preparation that we ever heard of, however, would be more likely to please both *gourmet* and *gourmand* than the one credited to the fastidious citizens of Pekin. If you follow it, you will take a live turtle that you have previously deprived of anything to drink long enough to render him exceedingly thirsty; you will place him in a caldron of cool water in such a position that his body will be immersed, but that he will be unable to get his mouth down to it; at the side of the kettle, within reach of his turtleship, you will then place a bowl of cool and spicy wine. This done, set the caldron on the fire, and observe with glee the enrichment of your noble repast. Urged by thirst, the turtle eagerly drinks the wine; and as the slowly heating water in which he floats grows hotter and hotter, his thirst increases, and he drinks deeper and deeper of the wine, until suddenly he is boiled, and dies, full of wine, and fragrant through the uttermost fibers of his unctuous flesh with the rich condiment he has so plentifully imbibed. Luxury and art have reached their acme!—*Harper's Bazar*.

In the course of a conversation with a dealer in game, a Philadelphia Press reporter learned that within a few weeks past, since the advent of cold weather, a few venturesome spirits residing in that city decided to thoroughly test the value of the meat of the rat as an article of diet. The rodents had been caught and caged while young, and fed carefully upon grain and green food. The rats thrived upon the diet and their silky coats gave evidence of a thoroughly healthful condition. At the meal in question they had been carefully prepared, and were served with other viands. The flesh, after cooking, was found to be quite light in color, much more so than either the rabbit or the squirrel, and possessing a delicacy of flavor entirely unknown to either of the last mentioned animals. The experiment proved entirely successful and a diet of rats prepared under proper conditions was voted to be practical and economical.

Middle aged travelers can remember when native oysters were sold in London at sixpence per dozen; now they are thought cheap at six times the money, and it is a singular fact that they are at this moment dearer in London than they were in Rome when the Emperor Vitellius devoured them all day long, and Cicero sustained his philosophy by swallowing scores of the Rutupine luxuries brought from the coast of Kent.

Arcachon, in France, is justly celebrated for its oysters, for in fact a great part of our so-called natives are brought from there, kept one season in our English beds, and then sold under the name they have but little right to bear. The bay is full of "oyster parks," to each of which a floating domicile belongs, tenanted by a guardian always on the watch.

In Norway, where fish is prepared with much ingenuity in many ways, they make flour of the flesh of the fish ground to powder. It is used instead of rice and potatoes, and the biscuits made from it are said to be extremely nutricious.

The Duke of Sutherland, when visiting America, last summer, was so much delighted with the flavor of the black bass as served up by one of the Clan Chattan, Mr. John Sutherland, of New York city, that he made great efforts to secure live specimens for stocking a lake in his County of Sutherlandshire. Mr. George Shepherd Page, President of the American Piscicultural Association, took out a number in the steamship Spain, at the end of April, which reached Sutherlandshire alive and well. Mr. Page was invited to visit the Duke at Dunrobin Castle, where he has reported most favorably on the chances of naturalizing this fine fish in Scotland.

Winter Scenes.

No more the wildwood cheers our eyes
  With eglantine and aster,
No more the kine do kick the flies
  That tease them in the pastur'.
No more are rural maids employed
  In mashes with the "utter,"
But well they fill the aching void
  With buckwheat cakes and butter.

It is about now that the comic oyster winks with his pearly shell and laughs inside of himself in anticipation at the fun he will have at some coming church or Sunday school festival. Swimming around all alone in ten gallons of soup, boss of the whole thing, and not liable to get caught by hungry ladlers. But it's tew bad.

According to a Baltimore epicure, a highly satisfactory stuffing for a duck, whether canvasback or redhead, is made by grating enough bread to fill the bird, moisten it with cream or with milk, in which put a tablespoonful of melted butter; season with salt, pepper, etc., the rind of a lemon, a tablespoonful of chopped celery and the yolk of an egg. If the flavor of an oyster is to you delectable, he says, add a few raw oysters whole. A strip of bacon placed over the breast of the roasting duck gives a delicate, almost imperceptible flavor, and prevents it becoming dry.

It is asserted that the nutritiousness of apples has never been properly appreciated and that they are far more nourishing than potatoes. Cornish workmen say that they can work better on baked apples than on potatoes. There is a dish in Cornwall called squab pie, made of mutton with slices of potato apple and onion, and, strange as it may seem to many, it is excellent. Cornwall is the county for meat pies, as the miners carry their dinners with them in that form.

London is eating dried bananas and declares they are delicious. They come from Jamaica, where the method has been patented. Fruit prepared twelve months ago retains its flavor to a remarkable degree. The banana is cut in half lengthwise and subjected to slow drying, which prevents fermentation and decay. It is thought these dried bananas are to open up a new and important industry. They can be made into wine, eaten as they are, or cooked.—*Ex.*

Dried bananas are common at the street venders' fruit stands in Chicago.

Soups, according to Sir Henry Thompson, whether clear or thick, are far too lightly esteemed by most classes. They are too often regarded as a mere prelude to a meal, to be swallowed hastily or discarded altogether.

Among the palatable soups of the period is a bisque of crabs, but seldom is it prepared by the card.

Egg plant is a vegetable susceptible of being sent to the table in a dozen different styles and ways.

A Boston paper gives this as the way to make Lancashire pie: "Take cold beef or veal, chop and season as for hash; have ready hot mashed potatoes, seasoned as if for the table, and put in a shallow baking dish first a layer of meat, then a layer of potatoes, and so on, till the dish is heaping full; smooth over top of potatoes, and make little holes in which place bits of butter, bake until a nice brown."

The exportation of frozen meat from New Zealand to England has become successful beyond the expectations of its projectors. Recent sales of mutton have been especially satisfactory; indeed it appears that the value of a sheep is nearly doubled by conveying its carcass from Dunedin to London.

What Tripe Is.

[Burlington Hawkeye.]

Occasionaly you see a man order tripe at a hotel, but he always looks hard, as though he hated himself and everybody else. He tries to look as though he enjoyed it, but he does not. Tripe is indigestible, and looks like an India rubber apron for a child to sit on. When it is pickled it looks like dirty clothes put to soak, and when it is cooking it looks as though the cook was boiling a dish cloth. On the table it looks like glue and tastes like a piece of old silk umbrella cover. A stomach that is not lined with corrugated iron would be turned wrong side out by the smell of tripe. A man eating tripe at a hotel table looks like an Arctic explorer dining on his boots or chewing pieces of frozen dog. You cannot look at a man eating tripe but he will blush and look as though he wanted to apologize and convince you he is taking it to tone up his system. A woman never eats tripe. There is not money enough in the world to hire a woman to take a corner of a sheet of tripe in her teeth and try to pull off a piece. Those who eat tripe are men who have had their stomachs play mean tricks on them, and they eat tripe to get even with their stomachs, and then they go and take a Turkish bath to sweat it out of their system. Tripe is a superstition handed down from a former generation of butchers, who sold all the meat and kept the tripe for themselves and the dogs, but the dogs of the present day will not eat tripe. You throw a piece of tripe down in front of a dog and see if he does not put his tail between his legs and go off and hate you. Tripe may have a value, but it is not as food. It may be good to fill in a burglar-proof safe, with the cement and chilled steel, or it might answer to use as a breast plate in the time of war, or it would be good to use for bumpers between cars, or it would make a good face for the weight of a pile driver, but when you come to smuggle it into the stomach you do wrong. Tripe! Bah! A piece of Turkish towel soaked in axle grease would be pie compared with tripe.

Redsnapper loses its fine flavor by being sent North on ice, and is best eaten where it is caught, say epicures.

Roast grouse are often ruined by being allowed to stand after being taken from the fire, and thus become dry and parched. All game tastes best that is sent immediately from the fire to the dinner table.

Terrapin croquettes are something made by certain Philadelphia caterers to perfection, and as made by them constitute a dish fit to set before the king.

Mushrooms Not Poisonous.

People must talk and write paragraphs, but one that is now going the rounds should not be allowed to raise a new prejudice against the delicious and and wholesome edible mushroom, that is but just beginning to be appreciated in this country. The statement is made and backed up with some foreign name of a doctor that mushrooms are poisonous always; that the water they are boiled in is more poisonous; that mushrooms in the raw state are most poisonous, and their poisonous properties do not depart from them until they are dried and kept a certain number of days. It does not say whether they are to be dried in the dark of the moon or not. But the statement goes on that a dog fed on mushrooms died in a certain number of days from their effects. We do not know about the dog, there being no witnesses named, but think we could have killed him with peaches and cream, or peach and honey, or rock and rye, or almost any other thing besides mushrooms, if we had had a motive for it. It is not long since we read that a dog died because it was fed so many days on bread. Still, we have not given up eating bread. It has also been stated that the bread we eat is more or less poisonous, so is the meat, so is the air, the water, the paper on the walls, the paste it is put on with, the soap we use, the coffee, tea, flavoring extracts, tobacco, but they seem to be amazingly slow in operation. Some poisons are really quite wholesome and pleasant. Arsenic, as is well known, is quite extensively eaten for its fattening properties, and mushrooms cannot certainly be any worse than arsenic. That they are not is shown in their consumption in large quantities daily in the hotels and restaurants; and the sauces are made with the liquor they are boiled in. The customers make meals of them, the cooks make meals of them—these are the canned. Fresh mushrooms are cooked and eaten all through the season when they are obtainable, and some kinds that are not true mushrooms are sold and bought and cooked and served with equal harmlessness. The writer has gathered mushrooms and eaten them raw, as children do, in the fields where they grew in abundance, and stole the ketchup before it was finished making and absorbed mushroom poison in over way, along with bread poison, coffee poison, and all the rest. There is no need of proving that all these things are not poisonous as long as they continue to prove wholesome and beneficial, and no need to prove that even those foreign named doctors are quite harmless as long as matters turn out so serious with the unhappy canines.

In England 200 years ago pies and pastries were made of all sorts of good things—artichokes, marrow, dates, raisins, figs and ginger—and it is related that Page invited Falstaff and his friends to a dinner of "hot venison pastry," wound up by "pippins and cheese."

The Various Frying Mixtures, from Olive Oil to Butter and Lard.

From The Caterer.

There are several oily and fatty substances used for frying, which we name in the order of their cost. Olive oil is almost exclusively used in olive-bearing countries as the cheapest frying material. Here it is quite costly and but little used, save by the wealthy or the epicure who prizes it for the olive flavor it communicates to food cooked in it. Others, again, dislike and reject it for the same reason. Clarified butter comes next in cost and is prepared as follows: Put the butter into an enameled saucepan and melt it gently over a clear fire; when it begins to simmer take it off the fire, skim well, let stand in a warm corner till the buttermilk or cheesy matter has settled, then pour it off steadily from the sediment, through fine muslin, into a stone or glass jar, cover and keep in a cool place. It is the best of all frying material and greatly superior to lard, in that the slight flavor it communicates is quite pleasant and appetizing.

A third preparation, a favorite with many of the best European cooks, and a genuine mixture, is composed of equal measure of olive oil, butter, veal suet and leaf lard. The butter is first melted and stirred into the other three, already mixed and melted; then it is strained into a stone pot and kept always in cold place, well covered. The combined flavor of the four ingredients is acceptable to almost all tastes.

Fresh butter comes next and is much to be preferred to lard, but it has one objectionable quality. On account of the buttermilk and salt it contains it scorches and burns when subjected to a high or long-continued heat. This renders it unfit for the cooking of many delicate dishes. This tendency can, however, be much lessened by rubbing the frying-pan with a small muslin bag filled with prepared beef suet.

Lard is the common, well-nigh universal frying material in America, because it is cheap and to be had in every nook and corner of the land. Its free use has caused many a dyspeptic stomach. If used at all only the best leaf lard should be employed and rendered out by steam or boiling water, so as to avoid the burnt taste it gets if rendered on the open fire.

There are times, no doubt, when a civilized man may eat liver and enjoy it; but these times occur but seldom, and to most persons never. To the shipwrecked mariner, tossed in his frail boat upon the pitiless sea, the stock of old boots exhausted and all his companions eaten, then a small piece of of liver is not altogether unacceptable. (Said by one who doesn't know.)

An alleged new salad called Brussels is made of lobsters, oysters, chicken and tongue mixed with celery.

Salads and Salad-Making.

From London Society.

The obvious accompaniment to cold meats is salad, which may be truly said to fill the bowl which cheers but not inebriates. No wonder that, tradition tells us it takes three people to make a good salad; a sage, to contribute the salt; a miser, to add the vinegar, and a prodigal, to pour in the oil. To which may be added an untiring steam arm or electric motor, to stir up the mixture for an indefinite time. For, if "when taken, to be well shaken" is applicable to anything that enters the human stomach, it assuredly is to the assemblage of ingredients which go to make a finished salad. In default of an automatic mechanical salad-mixer, it is the host's duty to perform that task; and it is polite on his part to help himself first, because the best lies at the bottom of the bowel. *Fatiguer*, to fatigue the salad, is the French expressive description of how it ought to be turned over and over; so much so, that "Je vais le faire la salade" is a popular threat that a good drubbing instead of a good time, is coming. Another saying, "Bataillons de salade," battalions drawn promiscuously from divers and sundry corps of soldiers, is founded on the multiplicity of herbs eligible for the composition of a salad. The hemp plant was known as "Salade de Gascogne," Gascony salad, because it furnished ropes wherewith malefactors in the South of France were hanged. By such salad many a one has been choked, who previously had cultitivated the cause of his death— thoereby suffering a much worse malady than that implied by the proverb.

"Qui viu ne boit apres salade,
Est en danger d'estre malade."

"After salad take some wine,
And health with pleasure thus combine."

"Salad eaten, claret take,
And avoid a stomach-ache."

A glass of good Bordeau or Burgundy wine, or even of pale ale, with or after salad, is a better, and to many people, a more agreeable digestive than pepper—white, black or red—mixed with the vegetables as seasoning.

Seagulls' eggs were served at a recent dinner in Halifax, given to some Government officials, and were pronounced excellent. They were boiled hard and eaten with pepper.

Snails are not adequate in supply to the demand and are rapidly increasing in favor among our native epicures.

The Evolution of Bread.

Persons of extreme views are apt to maintain that all mankind, being normally savages, were as normally cannibals; but, leaving that moot question altogether on one side, it seems probable that humanity ate acorns long before they ate cereals or learned the art of making bread, and that the veneration entertained by the Druids of Gaul and Britain for the oak was due to the circumstance that its glands were the staple food of the people. Bread, properly so called, was transmitted by the Greeks to the Romans; and either the latter or the Phœnicians may have introduced the cultivation of corn into Gaul. While, however, the land was mainly covered with immense forests, a long time must have elapsed before the practice of eating acorns, chestnuts, and beech mast was abandoned, and even when corn was regularly grown, ripened and harvested, the grains were merely plucked from the ear and eaten raw or slightly parched. The next step was to infuse the grain in hot water for the making of a species of gruel or porridge, and a long time afterwards it may have occurred to some bright genius to pound the corn in a mortar or rub it to a powder between two stones. Subsequently came the handmill; but it was not until after the First Crusade that the windmill was introduced from the East, whither it had probably found its way from China. The first bread was evidently baked on the ashes and unleavened, and the intolerable pangs of indigestion brought on by a continual course of "galette" or "damper" may have suggested the use of a fermenting agent, which in the first instance was probably stale bread turned sour. Pliny has distinctly told us in his "Natural History" that the Gauls leavened their bread with yeast made from the lye of beer; yet, strangely enough, they abandoned the use of beer yeast, and did not resume it until the middle of the seventeenth century. Its revival in France made the fortune of many bakers; then the medical faculty sounded an alarm, declaring that yeast made from beer was poisonous. Its employment was prohibited by law in 1666, but the outcry raised by the bakers and the public was so vehement that in the following year the decree of prohibition was cancealed, with proviso that the yeast was to be procured only from beer freshly brewed in Paris or the immediate neighborhood. Some form of fermented bread, however, the French had been eating for 1,600 years in contradistinction to the gruel and pulse-eating Italians and Levantines and the purely vegetarian Hindus.

American Pie.

The foreign visitor to these shores has, with very few exceptions, denounced pie as a deadly invention of some culinary Satan. He has gazed with mingled pity and horror upon the native pie-eater, and has often been tempted to stretch out a hand to save him from a life of suffering and dyspepsia. Coming from a nation where pie is treated with no less contempt than is bestowed by Herr Bismarck upon the inoffensive and salutary American hog, he is unable to understand by what unlucky chance the American people have become a nation of pie-eaters. Every disagreeable peculiarity of American society he attributes to pie. Pie is responsible for every variety of evil in our politics. Ruffianism and crime are due to pie, and pie, indeed, is the source of almost as many ills as "that forbidden fruit whose mortal taste brought death into the world, and all our woe." Yet in spite of foreign scorn and prejudice the pie habit survives and each year adds thousands and thousands to the adorers of pie. The American love for pie can never be conquered. It is the strongest proof of American birth. The person who does not eat pie is regarded by Americans with distrust, and foreigners who do eat it are hailed as brothers. The United States will experience a thrill of satisfaction and good feeling to hear that the Czar has ordered 1,000,000 pies for his coronation ceremonies. It will rejoice to learn that there is at least one foreign nation that does not share the hostility felt by other great powers toward pie. Russia and America have always been on friendly terms, but this gratifying proof that the Czar is alive to the beauty and excellence of pie will unite them in the strongest bonds of sympathy and good-will.

Something About Salad Oil.

N. Y. Sun.

The gourmand who carefully makes up his own dish of cool looking salad is very apt to be deceived into believing that the rich gold colored oil he pours upon it is from the land of olives. It is an almost even chance that it is from the land of cotton, for the sale of cotton seed oil for olive oil has become so extensive that the Italian Government has begun to take strong measures toward keeping the former product out of Italy, where it is taken in Italian vessels from New Orleans, to be bottled and labeled, and returned to this country, so that merchants can say that it is imported. But, to those who dread the substitution of cotton seed oil for olive oil, there is comfort in the fact that the supply of the native product is limited, for planters whose lands are thin prefer to return the seed to them, and the cotton lands of the lower Mississippi, which do not need careful fertilizing, furnish the seed for the seventy cotton seed oil mills in the South. This enterprise is bound to remain confined to the South, for the seed is so bulky that transportation would not be profitable. That the manufacture of cotton seed oil, however, will increase is beyond doubt, as the raw seed goes through processes that nearly treble its value, and its oil is being used for paint and also for lubricating machinery.

An Incredible Story.

Pall Mall Gazette.

Not only has the intellect of the worm been sadly unappreciated for centuries till Mr. Darwin rehabilitated that sagacious reptile, but it appears now that his value as a viand has also been grossly misunderstood and underrated. A group of French gourmets, whose object it is to do for the cookery of the future what Wagner is doing for its music, are happily following up the labors of Darwin in this direction, and, having recently tried this tempting morsel, have communicated to a grateful public the result of their researches. Fifty guests were present at the experiment. The worms, apparently lob-worms, were first put into vinegar, by which process they were made to disgorge the famous vegetable mold about which we have heard so much. They were then rolled in batter and put into an oven, where they acquired a delightful golden tint, and, we are assured, a most appetizing smell. After the first p'ateful the fifty guests rose like one man and asked for more. Could anything be more convincing? Those who love snails, they add, will abandon them forever in favor of worms. And yet M. Monselet, the great authority in Paris, has told us sadly that no advances have been made in the art of cookery since Brillat-Savarin, and that all enthusiasm on the subject died out with Vatel when he committed suicide because the fish had not arrived for the royal dinner.

It was the Duke of Wellington, we believe, who referred to hash as "something left over from the fight of yesterday," but at some hotels they make it so nicely of lamb and potatoes that even epicures have expressed satisfaction with it.

There are three dishes, it is said, which if put upon the bill of fare of a London club, are devoured before all the rest; so that at 7 or 8 o'clock, when most members dine, there is nothing left of them. These dishes are Irish stew, tripe and onions, and liver and bacon.

SCRAPS ABOUT GREAT EATERS AND EPICURES.

Queer Customers of Cafes.

In M. Eugene Chavette's witty and curious little volume, published in 1867, "Restaurateurs et Restaures," some entertaining portraits are given of eccentric guests, celebrated at Parisian cafes. One of the most famous of these was Gourier, commonly called "The Fork of Death," a frequenter of the Restaurant Boovelet, who invited a victim to dine with him by the year, and slew him with high feeding. The first died of apoplexy after a six months' combat; the second held his own for two years, and then succumbed to a "liver complaint"—an indigestion brought on by over-indulgence in the liver of the Strasburg goose, "three days after," as Gourier sadly said, when gazing on the funeral from the window of the restaurant, "I had treated him to a new hat for his birthday." A third champion then descended into the arena, a long lean man named Ameline, who said as his invariable grace when sitting down to table with his host, "You rascal, I'm going to bury you;" while the host gently replied by way of "Amen," "Nonsense; the other two said the same thing." The crafty Ameline, however, took occasion to pick a quarrel monthly with his amphitryon, and, retiring sulkily to his tent, dieted himself on tea, toast, and senna, returning to the encounter mollified and refreshed after an absence of two or three days, during which Gourier lost still more ground by eating rapidly, and injuring his digestion by solitary and gloomy reflections. One day, after this duel had lasted three years, Gourier, who had just helped himself to a fourteenth slice of 4-year-old Welsh mutton, threw his head back. His companion, thinking he was about to sneeze, muttered the customery benediction; but Gourier fell forward into the currant jelly, dead as the mutton he so dearly loved. He who had taken the fork had perished by the fork. He should have imitated the prudent diner of the Cafe Riche, who always had two dozen saucers piled at his left when he sat down to table, and wore one between his collar and the nape of his neck throughout the repast, changing it as it became warm, as a preventive against apoplexy.

The heroes of gastronomy, including Mr. Walton himself, will gnash their teeth, which, excepting their stomachs, must be regarded as their most valuable possessions, when they hear of the exploit just accomplished by Thomas Clute, of Mount Morris, N.Y. On Feb. 6 that individual ate six quarts of sauer kraut within the space of thirty-seven minutes, and washed it down with a bottle of champagne. Having survived this feat in excellent condition he now offers to bet a reasonable amount that he can eat eight quarts of sauer kraut within an hour. This challenge is likely to result in an international contest, for Clute is not a German, and the children of the Fatherland will not tamely submit to his imputation on their capacity in the sauer kraut line.

Captain Morris, George the Fourth's boon companion, used to sing:
 Old Lucullus, they say,
 Forty cooks had each day,
And Vitellius's meals cost a million;
 But I like what is good
 When and where be my food,
 In a chop-house or royal pavilion.

 At all feasts (if enough)
 I most heartily stuff,
And a song at my heart alike rushes
 Though I've not fed my lungs
 Upon nightingales' tongues,
 Nor the brains of goldfinches and thrushes.

There was a good deal of monotony and variety about the monthly repast of the eccentric who used to dine at the Maison Phillippe, going conscientiously through the thirty-five or forty soups on the bill of fare, and topping off with a cream meringue. Another much pointed out diner frequented the Restaurant Vefour, distinguishing himself by his devotion to sweets—a plump and rosy little old gentleman, who had carried the Princess Lamballe's head round Paris on a pike in his salad days. Handel, who ordered the dinner for four, and, arriving alone, bade it be brought in "brestissimo—I am de gompany," was outdone by the man of an unbounded stomach who used to visit Vachette's every fortnight and call for the proprietor, Brebant, and give the following order: "My dear Brehant, I shall have six friends to dinner to-morrow" (mentioning their names); "all experienced diners, you see! Get us up a nice little dinner—70 francs a head, without wine. Have it served at 6 o'clock, post-office time; I have told them to be punctual." At 5:45 the host arrives, inspects the table, writes out the names of the diners and places their cards at their plates, arranges the relishes according to the taste of each, then takes out his watch. "Ah! 6 o'clock, and no one here." Brebant: "Perhaps you are fast?" "No, I always keep post-office time, and I told them 6 to the minute. I'll give them a lesson. Have dinner served." Brebant: "But they may have been unaccountably delayed." "Well, I'll give them five minutes' grace." After watching for them in vain, "Put on the dinner; they can overtake me." Then he fell to and devoured the dinner for seven, indulging in a monologue for the benefit of the waiter. "Why on earth did all those scoundrels fail to keep their appointment?" Coffee being served he sends for Brebant, and says, with triumphant smile, "You see, if I had taken your advice I'd be waiting for them still. I'll invite them again two weeks from now, and see if they will be more punctual " And two weeks later, the same comedy having been performed with due solemnity, the diner reiterates his determination with indignant vehemence. "D—n them! I'll ask them again; I want to see how far they will carry their brutal lack of politeness!"

What Bismarck Eats.

There seems to be something in the air and life of Germany extraordinarily favorable to the digestion. Bismarck has thriven on mixtures of champagne and porter washing down meals at the description of which the American trembles, but he does no more than the other most famous ruler of his country, Frederick the Great. Here is what Dr. Zimmerman saw him devour when a septuagenarian invalid: "A very large quantity of soup, of the strongest and most highly spiced ingredients, Yet spiced as it already was, he added to each plate of it a large spoonful of powdered ginger and mace; then a good piece of bœuf a la Russe—beef steeped in half a pint of brandy. Next he took a great quantity of an Italian dish, half Indian corn, half Parmesan cheese. To this the juice of garlic is added, and the whole is baked in butter until there arises a hard rind as thick as a finger. This, one of the King's most darling dishes, is called Polenta. At last, the King having expressed his satisfaction at the excellent appetite which the dandeloin gave him, closed the scene with a whole plateful of eel pie, so hot and fiery it seemed as if it had been baked in hell. At other times he would eat a large quantity of chilling and unwholesome fruits, especially melons, and then again a vast number of sweetmeats.

Byron's extravagant fondness for macaroni has been recorded in more than one sketch of his tastes and habits, but his biographers have omitted to mention the fact that he was wont to bestow his macaroni so thickly with slices of truffle that the result—his favorite dish—might have been more correctly described as "truffles au macaroni" than as "macaroni aux truffles."

There are many examples on record of a voracity almost incredible, and sometimes, indeed, including the most unlikely objects. Sparing my readers any such details, I prefer to relate two actual instances from my own experience, which do not require on their part any great effort of faith.

Some forty years ago I went to pay a flying visit to the vicar of Bregnier, a man of great stature, and known throughout the district for his power of eating. Though scarcely midday, I found him already at the table; the soup had been removed, as well as the meat boiled in it, and these two regular dishes had been followed by a leg of mutton, a fine fowl and a large bowl of salad. On seeing me he ordered another knife and fork, which I declined; and it was well I did so, for alone, and without any assistance, he quite easily got rid of everything, leaving of the mutton nothing but the bone, of the fowl nothing but the skeleton, and of the salad nothing but the bowl. Next they brought a cheese of considerable size and in it he made an angular breach of ninety degrees; the whole being washed down with a bottle of wine and a decanter of water, he then went to have his forty winks.

One thing which delighted me was, that during the whole of this performance, lasting nearly three quarters of an hour, the venerable pastor did not at all seem too much engrossed in his work. The huge pieces which he threw into his capacious mouth prevented him neither from talking nor laughing, and he despatched all that was put before him with as little effort as if he had only eaten a couple of larks.

In the same way General Bisson, who drank eight bottles of wine every day at breakfast, never seemed to be doing anything of the sort. His glass was larger than the others, and he emptied it oftener; but you would have said that he did it without any effort, and, whilst thus imbibing his sixteen pints he could as freely join in pleasant chat or give his orders as if he had only drunk a single bottle.

At the age of eighteen, General Sibuet had that happy appetite by which Nature announces her intention of completing a well developed man, when one evening he entered Genin's dining rooms, where the worthies of the place usually met to eat chestnuts over a bottle of white wine there called "cross grain."

A superb turkey had just been taken off the spit, a fine bird, golden, done to a turn, and scenting the room enough to tempt a saint.

The village worthies, not being hungry, took very little notice of it: but the digestive powers of young Sibuet were stirred within him, and with his mouth watering, he cried, "I have only just had dinner, yet I'll lay a bet to eat that big turkey all by myself."

"Done!" replied Bouvier du Bouchet, a stout farmer, who happened to be in the room; if you'll eat it, I'll pay for you; but if you come to a halt, then you'll pay, and I'll eat the rest."

Instantly setting to work, the young athlete detached a wing skillfully and swallowed it in two mouthfuls; then kept his teeth in play whilst taking a glass of wine as an interlude, by crunching the neck of the fowl.

Next he tackled the thigh, and after eating it with the same self-possession, took a second glass of wine to clear the way for the remainder. Very soon the second wing went the same road, and on its disappearance, the performer, as keen as ever, was taking hold of the only remaining limb, when the unfortunate farmer shouted in a doleful tone, "Ah! I see very well you'll win; but as I have to pay, leave me a small bit to myself."

Sibuet was as good natured as he afterwards showed himself courageous, and not only consented to his opponent's request, who thus had for his share the carcase of the fowl, but paid both for the turkey and the necessary accompaniments.

—*Brillat-Savarin.*

Some Noted Epicures.

From All The Year Round.

Among noted epicures of this era—Louis XIV—were the Marquis de Cussy, inventer of a cake which still bears his name; Camerani, a mediocre actor, but excellent stage manager of the Comedie Italienne, who employed his leisure hours in the composition of a soup, the materials of which were so costly as to be beyond the reach of the ordinary epicure; and Journiac de St. Meard, the same who during the Reign of Terror had miraculously escaped sharing the fate of his fellow-suspects in the prison of the Abbaye. According to contemporary accounts, it was his custom to take his place at the table early in the morning and never leave it before night; and it is recorded of him that, having invited a friend to dinner, he pressed him to partake of a particular dish, which the other declined doing, pleading as an excuse that he feared it might not agree with him. "Bah!" contemptuously exclaimed Journiac, "you don't mean to say that you are one of the idiots who trouble themselves about their digestion!"

Nor must a certain priest be forgotten, whose elasticity of conscience in culinary matters was proverbial. Being invited on a fast day to a repast befitting the occasion at the house of a noted lover of good cheer, he was on the point of helping himself to a dish, the odor of which singularly tickled his palate, when the lay brother who accompanied him enjoined him in a whisper not to touch it, adding that he had seen it prepared in the kitchen and that the gravy was simply the essence of meat. "Meddling fool!" angrily muttered his superior, pushing away the dish with a sigh of mortification; "what business had he in the kitchen? Couldn't he have kept it to himself until after dinner?"

We can remember many years ago conversing with an old gentleman who had been on intimate terms with Brillat-Savarin and Grimod de la Reyniere, and questioning him about them. "Brillat-Savarin," he said, "was the pleasantest and cheeriest of men, but he had one defect; he was inordinately fond of pork, and I recollect a dinner given by him at Villers-sur-Orge, on which occasion a delicately-prepared sucking-pig met with such general approbation that our host sent for the cook, and after complimenting him on his skill, declared his intention of bestowing on him a suitable recompense, and having ascertained on inquiry that M. Pierre's ambition was to marry a young girl whose face was her fortune, promised a handsome dowry to the bride, besides paying for the wedding dinner; so that the sucking-pig eventually cost him over 6,000 francs."

During the Consulate and the Empire the most fashionable "traiteur" was the Beauvilliers, whose splendid dining rooms in the Rue Richelieu were frequented by the best society in Paris. Unlike the generality of his colleagues, he was equally renowned for his polished and courteous manners, and for the orthodox propriety of his costumes; he invariably received his customers himself, and took infinite pains that everything set before them should be sufficiently tempting to induce them to repeat their visit. One day a gentleman, whom he recognized as a well known marquis, came in and ordered a "supreme de volaille" (a specialty of the establishment), which in due time was placed on the table. Beauvilliers, happening to pass by at the moment, glanced at the dish, and in spite of the remonstrances of the marquis pounced upon it, and delivered it to a waiter, directing him to have another prepared immediately. Then, turning to his indignant visitor, and deliberately savouring a pinch of snuff, "M. le Marquis," he said, "you will pardon the abruptness of my proceeding but the honor of my house is at stake. I regret that you should be exposed to a little temporary inconvenience, but I cannot allow my reputation to be compromised by a failure."

When the illustrious academicians, Villemain and Victor Cousin, were young students, they generally dined together for the sake of economy, their modest repast consisting of a single dish of meat, with now and then a couple of apples, one for each; by way of dessert. On these gala occasions Villemain, who had a weakness for this supplementary luxury, never omitted to start a subject of conversation on which his companion loved to air his theories; and while the latter declaimed and philosophised to his heart's content, quietly ate both the apples.

To the foregoing list of gastronomic celebrities may be added the names of three men of mark of our own time, Balzac, Alexandre Dumas and Rossini. The first of these, although sufficiently abstemious in other respects, had an inordinate predilection for pastry and fruit, devouring, as Leon Gozlan tells us, whole dishes of Montreuil peaches and juicy pears with Gargantuan facility. Dumas considered his culinary manual a masterpiece far superior to the Mousquetaires or Monte-Cristo, while the composer of Il Barbiere was never so happy as when superintending the preparation of a dish invented by himself. "I was born to be a cook," he exclaimed one evening, while presiding at the supper-table of his villa at Passy; "and have altogether missed my vocation!"

"But, maestro," objected one of his guests, "in that case we should have had no Guillaume Tell."

"Bah!" contemptuously retorted Rossini, "any one could have done that. Donizetti and Bellini can write operas, but if either of them were to try his hand at a timbale de macaroni aux truffes," helping himself largely as he spoke to the delicacy in question, "do you imagine for a moment that it would taste like this."

Epicurean Clergy

It is a remarkable fact that the epicures of the world should be so largely indebted to the French clergy for the luxuries they enjoy. It has been suggested that during the long season of Lent these holy men have been in the habit of relieving their privations by employing their ingenuity in the invention of pleasant foods and drinks in readiness for the return of the days of feasting. Whether there is any foundation for this or not is not positively known, but the fact remains that the clergy, from whatever cause, are capital inventors of all comestibles. One of the largest oyster parks in the country was started by the Abbe Bonnetard, the cure of La Teste, whose system of artificial cultivation was so successful that last year, of 151,000,000 oysters distributed through France, 97,000,000 were produced by the abbe. Canon Agen was the discoverer of the terrines of the Nerac. The rilettes of Tours are the work of a monk of Marmoutiers. The renowned liqueurs Chartreuse, Trappestine, Benedictine, and others betray their monastic origin in their names, and the strangest part of their production is that they should be the work of the most severe and ascetic of religious bodies. The Elixir of Garus is the invention of the Abbe Garus. The Beziers sausages were first prepared under the direction of the Prior Lamouroux. The popular Bergougnous sauce was first mingled by the Abbe Bergougnous. The delicate Floguard cakes are the invention of the Abbe Floguard. Even the immortal glory of the discovery of champagne is attributed to a monk. To these may be added the innumerable delicacies in bon-bons, confectionery, and the like, which owe their origin entirely to the nuns in the French convents scattered throughout the land.

Lovers of Truffles.

London Telegraph.

Herr Julius Olden, a contemporary eulogist of the truffle, boldly asserts that ever since the discovery of this toothsome tuber it has been beloved of poets and musicians above all other comestibles. Among its most renowned votaries he assigns front-rank places to Georges Sand—who bestowed upon it the fanciful title of "Fair Potato," and immortalized its merits in a metrical legend—Lord Byron and Rossini. Byron's extravagant fondness for macaroni has been recorded in more than one sketch of his tastes and habits; but his biographers, according to Herr Olden, have omitted to mention the fact that he was wont to bestrew his macaroni so thickly with slices of truffle that the result—his favorite dish—might have been more correctly described as "truffles au macaroni" than as "macaroni aux truffles." The Swan Pesaro was no less enthusiastic a truffle-worshiper than the author of "Don Juan." It was Rossini whose fertile brain, stimulated to superhuman activity by dread of an impending gastronomical calamity, invented truffle salad. He was dining one day with several celebrated epicures, at the table of Baron James Rothschild. The moment had arrived for serving the roti, when it was discovered to the horror of all present, that the Baron's chef had forgotten to provide any salad! Rossini was the only person who preserved his presence of mind. He called for truffles and the castors, cut up the former into delicate slices, mixed a sublime dressing with the contents of the latter, and in a few minutes produced a salad of so seductively delicate a flavor that his admiring fellow-gourmets unanimously christened it "the poetry of truffles set to music by Maestro Rossini."

The following anecdote of the Count Vittalio Borromeo and his famous chef is related: "The Count was a great epicure, and would sooner part with his best friend than with his cook. This culinary artist knew how to please his master with a variety of dishes, known only to himself, in fact his own production, among which was one, that for the delicacy of its meat, the aroma of its condiment, and the general care taken in its preparation, made it the favorite above all the rest, and for many years it held the monopoly of the Count's table. The cook died, and many filled his place, but to no satisfaction. Money was freely lavished but to no purpose. The Count was languishing for want of an appetite, until one day, after a careful investigation an old scullion, for many years an inmate of the palace, conducted the new cook to a remote sub-cellar of the palace, in a corner of which a large cage was built, and continually supplied with enormous rats, fed on meal and milk, fattened and purified, until ready to kill. These, and the ingenuity of the cook, kept for a long time the old Count in ecstasy over his table."

A Tableau.

Paris Paper.

M. Gaulthier de Rumilly, dean of the senate, received a visit a few days ago from his landlord. It was a question of repairs to to be made, and the senator explained what he wanted to have done. The proprietor listened attentively and promising to have everything done. Six o'clock struck.

"Six o'clock already," said the landlord.

"Exactly," replied M. de Rumilly; "but that doesn't matter, for I hope you will do me the honor of dining with me."

"You are very kind," replied the landlord, "but—"

"I insist; I shall not let you leave at this hour; your plate is already laid."

"It is impossible."

"I shall be angry."

"It is impossible, notwithstanding the desire I have to remain. My affairs call me elsewhere at precisely this hour."

"You do not wish to share my dinner?" said the senator, slightly vexed.

"You will understand why. They dine at M. de Rothschild's at 7 o'clock."

"Ah, you are his guest!"

"No, I am his cook."

Tableau.

Roman Cooks and Gourmands

Quarterly Review.

In Juvenal's time the salary of a good cook was ten times higher than that of a tutor, a man of learning and ability, who, according to Lucian, was deemed well paid with 200 sesterces a year. The salary of Dionysia, a danseuse, was 200,000. The houses and establishments of the two players in pantomime, Bathyllus and Pylades, rivaled those of the richest patricians. There were three Romans named Apicius, each celebrated for devotion to gastronomy. The second, who flourished under Tiberius, was the most famous, and enjoys the credit of having shown both discrimination and industry in the gratification of his appetite; so much so that his name has passed into a synonym for an accomplished epicure. After spending about £800,000 on his palate he balanced his books, and finding that he had not much more than £80,000 left, hanged himself to avoid living upon such a pittance Lempriere's version is that he made a mistake in casting up his books, and hanged himself under a false impression of insolvency. A noted betting man named Smith made a similar mistake in casting up his book for the Derby, and flung himself into the sea. He was fished out, discovered the mistake and ever since went by the name of Neptune Smith. Apicius unluckily had no kind friend to cut him down. The outrageous absurdities of Elagabalus equaled or surpassed those of Caligula and Nero. He fed the officers of his palace with the brains of pheasants and thrushes, the eggs of partridges, and the heads of parrots. Among the dishes served at his own table were peas mashed with grains of gold, beans fricasseed with morsels of amber, and rice mixed with pearls. His meals were frequently composed of twenty-two services. Turning roofs threw flowers with such profusion on the guests that they were nearly smothered. At the sea-side he never ate fish, but when far inland he caused the roe of the rarest to be distributed among his suite. He was the first Roman who ever wore a complete dress of silk. His shoes glittered with rubies and emeralds, and his chariots were of gold, inlaid with precious stones. With a view to becoming suicide, he had cords of purple silk, poisons inclosed in emeralds, and richly set daggers; but either his courage failed when the moment arrived for choosing between these elegant instruments of death, or no time was left him for the choice. He was killed in an insurrection of the soldiery in the eighteenth year of his age, after a reign of nearly four years, during which the Roman people had endured the insane and degrading tyranny of a boy.

The first rose of spring—the shad's.

The guests have dined, and the host hands round a case of cigars. "I don't smoke myself," he says, "but you will find them good; my man steals more of them than any other brand I ever had."

Ben. Butler is one of the biggest eaters that visit the Fifth Avenue Hotel. He devours an enormous quantity of meat, vegetables, milk, coffee, salads and sweets. A chicken disappears before him as though he was a Methodist preacher and it was a partridge. He doesn't affect wines. At his home he has several varieties upon his table, but he drinks only about a tumblerful of sherry. If he wants a drink he takes a glass of Jamaica rum, or the statesman's drink, brandy. He eats four meals a day, and is never troubled with indigestion. He smokes cigars that are strong enough to knock a marine over. Yet he prides himself upon his temperate life, to which he traces his prosperity.

TABLE ETIQUETTE

Use of the Napkin and Finger-Bowl.

(Laramine Boomerang.)

It has been stated, and very truly too, that the law of the napkin is but vaguely understood. It may be said however, on the start, that custom and good breeding have uttered the decree that it is in exceeding'y poor taste to put the napkin in the pocket and carry it away.

The rule of etiquette is becoming more and more thoroughly established, that the napkin should be left at the house of the host or hostess after dinner.

There has been a good deal of discussion, also upon the matter of folding the napkin after dinner, and whether it should be so disposed of or negligently tossed into the gravy boat. If however, it can be folded easily, and without attracting too much attention and prolonging the session for several hours, it should be so arranged, and placed beside the plate, where it may easily be found by the hostess, and returned to her neighbor from whom she borrowed it for the occasion. If however the lady of the house is not doing her own work, the napkin may be carefully jammed into a globular wad and fired under the table to convey the idea of utter recklessness and pampered abandon.

The use of the finger bowl is also a subject of much importance to the *bon ton* guest who gorges himself at the expense of his friends.

The custom of drinking out of the finger bowl though not entirely obsolete, has been limited to the extent that good breeding does not permit the guest to quaff the water from the finger-bowl unless he does so prior to using it as a finger-bowl.

Thus, it will be seen that social customs are slowly but surely cutting down and circumscribing the rights and privileges of the masses.

At the court of Eugenie the customs of the table were very rigid, and the most prominent guest of H. R. H. was liable to get the G. B. if he spread his napkin on his lap and cut his eggs in two with a carving knife. The custom was that the napkin should be hung on one knee, and the egg busted at the big end and scooped out with a spoon.

A prominent American at his table one day, in an unguarded moment shattered the shell of a soft boiled egg with his knife, and while prying it apart both thumbs were erroneously jammed into the true inwardness of the fruit with so much momentum that juice took him in the eye, thus blinding him and maddening him to such a degree that he got up and threw the remains into the bosom of the hired man plenipotentiary, who stood near the table scratching his ear with the tray. As may readily be supposed, there was a painful interim, during which it was hard to tell for five or six minutes whether the prominent American or the hired man would come out on top, but at last the prominent American with the egg in his eye got the ear of the high-priced hired man in among his back teeth, and the honor of our beloved flag was vindicated.

A Revolution in Carving

(Bill Nye's Boomerang)

Speaking about carving there is a prospect now that in our best circles, within a short time, the old custom of making the host demolish the kiln dried poultry at dinner will become extent, and that a servant at a sideboard will take a hand saw and a can of nitro-glycerine and shatter the remains, thus giving a host a chance to chat with his guests instead of spattering them with dress ing, and casting gloom and gravy over the company.

This is a move for which I have long contended. It p'aces the manual labor of a dinner where it belongs, and relieves a man who should give his whole attention to the entertainment of his friends at table. You would not expect your host to take off his coat and kill the fowl in your presence, in order to show you that it was all on the square, and it is not customary to require the proprietor to peel the potatoes at the table of his guest, to prove that there is no put up job about it.

Therefore, I claim that the lamented hen may be thoroughly shattered at a side table by an athlete at $4 per week, and still good faith toward the guests be maintained. If any one be doubtful or suspicious, etiquette will permit him to stand by the side of the hireling carver and witness the inquest. Still it would be better fun for him to sit at the table, and if the parts given him are not sattisfactory, he can put them in his overshoes protem and casually throw them out the back door while the other guests are listening to the "Maiden's Prayer" in the parlor.

Under the new deal the host will enjoy the dinner much more than he used to with his thumb cut off and a quart of dressing on his lap. No man feels perfectly at home if he has to wrap up his cut finger in a rag and then scoop a handful of dressing out of his vest pocket. Few men are cool enough to do this, laughing heartily all the time and telling some mirth provoking anecdote meanwhile.

It is also annoying to have twenty guests ask for the "dark meat, please," when there are only three animals cooked, and neither one of them had a particle of dark meat about her person. Lately

I have adopted the plan of segregating the fowl by main strength, using the fingers when necessary, and then wiping them in an off hand manner on the table-cloth. Then I ask the servant to bring in that dark hen we ordered, so that we might have an abundance of dark meat. If the servant says there is none, I smile and tell the guests that the brunette chicken, by some oversight, has been eaten in the kitchen, and I shall have to give them such relics as may be at hand. This simplifies the matter, and places me in a far more agreeable place relative to the company. My great success however in carving, is mainly confined to the watermelon. The watermelon does not confuse me. I always know how to find the joints, and those who do not like the inside of the melon can have the outside. Now, my great trouble with fowls is, that one day I have Nebraska chicken, and the next trip I have to assainate a Mormon Shanghai pullet, with high, expressive hip bones and amalgam paletot. This makes me nervous, because they are so dissimilar and their joints are in different places. The Mormon hen is round shouldered, and her collar bone is more on the bias than the Nebraska fowl. This gives a totally different expression to her features in death, and, as I have said, destroys the symmetry of the carve.

I began my education in this line by carving butter in hot weather, and gradually led up to quail on toast. In carving the quail, first mortgage your home and get the quail. The quail should be cooked before carving, but not until the chronometer balance and other organs have been removed. Place your quail on the toast in a sitting position, then, passing the dissecting knife down between the shoulder blades, bisect the polonaise.

Another method is to take the quail by the hind-leg and eat it asking the guests to do the same. This breaks up the feeling of stiffness that is apt to prevail at a formal dinner party, and, while each one has his or her nose immersed in quail, good feeling cannot fail to show itself.

An Essay on Roller Skates

[Laramie Boomerang.]

The roller skate is a wayward little quadruped. It is as frolicsome and more innocent looking than a lamb, but for interfering with one's upright attitude in the community, it is, perhaps, the best machine that has appeared in Salt Lake city.

One's first feeling upon standing on a pair of roller skates is an uncontrollable tendency to come from together. One foot may start out toward Idaho, while the other as promptly starts for Arizona. The legs do not stand by each other as legs related by blood should do, but each shows a disposition to set up in business alone, and have you take care of yourself as best you may. The awkwardness of this arrangement is apparent, while they are setting up independently, there is nothing for you to do but sit down and await future developments. And you have to sit down, too, without having made any previous preparation for it, and without having devoted as much thought to it as you might have done had you been consulted in the matter.

One of the most noticeable things at a skating rink is the strong attachment between the human body and floor of the rink. If the human body had been coming through space for days and days, at the rate of a million miles a second, without stopping at eating stations, and not excepting Sundays, when it strikes the floor, we could understand why it struck the floor with so much violence. As it is however, the thing is inexplicable.

There are different kinds of falls in vogue at the rink. There are the rear falls, and the front falls, and the Cardinal Wolsey fall, the fall one across the other, three in a pile and so on. There are some of the falls I would like to be excused from describing. The rear fall is the favorite. It is more frequently utilized than any other. There are two positions in skating, the perpendicular and the horizontal. Advanced skaters prefer the perpendicular, while others affect the horizontal.

Skates are no respecters of persons. They will lay out a minister of the Gospel, or the mayor of the city, as readily as they will a short coated, one suspender boy or a giddy girl.

When one of a man's feet start for Nevada, and the other for Colorado, that does not separate him from the floor or break up his fun. Other portions of his body take the place his feet have just vacated with a promptness that is surprising. And he will find that the fun has just begun—for the people looking on.

The equipment for the rink, are a pair of skates, a cushion, and a bottle of liniment.

"How do you like my waffles?" asked a society belle of her guest. "Could not be nicer," was the reply. "Did you really make these yourself." "Oh, yes, indeed, I read off the recipe to the cook and turned the patent flour sifter all by my self."

Mistress to new cook—"On Wednesdays and Saturdays I shall go to market with you." New cook—"Very well mum; but who's a going to curry the basket the other days?"

A New York plumber is said to have died from overwork. It is terribly hard on a man to hug the cook and solder a sink spout at the same time.

SCRAPS ABOUT COOKS.

An Opening for Young Men.

Daily National Hotel Reporter.

So many of the avenues opening to young men are so completely filled and even overcrowded that it behooves thinking people to find new paths by which those approaching manhood, in the country and city, may finally reach a competency and perhaps something more. The "National Hotel Reporter" believes it can point out such a path, and one, too, that is comparatively untrodden. The path to which we refer leads to the hotel kitchen, and the position which is sure to yield a comfortable and satisfactory income is that of chef or head cook. It is a position which rarely pays less than $50 per month and often double and treble that sum. In addition to this amount of cash received, the cook also has his "living" which, at a low estimate, gives him an income ranging from $70 to $200 per month, according to the skill and ability of the man employed. The "Reporter is sorry to make such a statement, but it is a fact that the majority of hotel cooks are worthless, unreliable, ignorant and given to dissipation. And yet those of them who are at all skillful can always find permanent employment at remunerative wages. Does not the hotel kitchen, then, offer rare inducements for young men, to educate themselves (beginning, of course, like all true students, at the lower rounds of the ladder) to fill the honorable position of master of the range? The subject is one which we earnestly commend to young men about to select a means of livelihood, and also to those practical hotel keepers who see that, sooner or later, something must be done to improve the character and standing of their kitchen forces.

They have at one of the leading restaurants in Paris a Chinese cook whose sole and exclusive duty it is to cook rice. It is claimed that he can prepare and serve it in two or three dozen different styles, and when Lord Lyons gives dinner parties he hires this culinary Chinaman for the special purpose of cooking a dish of curry and rice that is described as delicious.

The Union Universelle pour le Progres de l'Art Culinaire has just given a curious fete at the Palace theatre. After dancing had been vigorously carried on for some time a plentiful supper was spread on a number of large tables; no less than nineteen plats appeared in succession, each bearing the name of some distinguished cook, their inventor. M. Monselet presided, and among the numerous witticisms delivered by him perhaps the chef d'œuvre was an eulogium on a lobster, ingeniously prepared a la Belleville by "M. Mention." The prize, a gold medal, was subsequently decreed to M. Emile Vassant, chef to Baron Erlanger, for a poularde a la Anglaise, and the second to M. Berte, for his Monde des Oiseaux a la Toussenel. The third prize fell to M. Escoffier, the talented chef of the restaurant Castiglione, for a chaufroid d'alouettes, and M. Kaugenciser received a prize for a pain de foie gras.

Genius in the Kitchen.

Hartford Times.

Another branch of the subject which comes up yearly at the cooks' ball for discussion by the gourmands is the degree of ingenuity displayed by different famous cooks in devising new dishes and menus wherewith to tickle jaded palates. It is considered that for originality the palm should go to the chef of the French Rothschilds, whose patron in Christmas week, 1870, invited a select party of friends to the following dinner:

Hors D' œuvres

Butter   Radishes   Sardines   Ass's head, stuffed
Potages.
Puree of beans aux croutons   Elephant consomme
Entrees.
Fried gudgeons   Roast camel a la Anglaise
Civet of kangaroo   Roast ribs of bear
Rotis
Haunch of wolf, venison sauce   Cat with rats
Water-cress-salad
Antelope pie, truffled   Petits pois au beurre
Rice-cakes with preserves
Gruyere cheese
Wines
Xeres   Chateau Mouton Rothschild
Latour blanche, 1861   Rornancee Contil, 1853
Chateau Palmer, 1860   Bollinger frappe orto, 1827
Cafe et liqueurs

This dinner cost the Rothschild's chef three months' preparation, besides writing and telegraphing to the different parts of the world, and in money $400 a cover.

New York has 430 cooks who are members of the "Societe Culinaire." M. Fere, chef of the Astor House, is the manager of the American branch of the association, and the others are: Droln, chef to the King of Spain; Bobers, chef of the St. James Club, London, and Favre, of the Central Hotel, Berlin. The official paper is published at Geneva, Switzerland.

The chef of the Chinese Embassy in Paris has introduced baked ice as a gastronomic novelty and gives for it the following receipe: "Make your ice very fine; roll out some light paste thin and cut into small squares; place a spoonful of ice in the centre of each piece of paste and fold it up closely, so that no air may get in, and bake in a quick oven The paste will be cooked before the ice can melt.

Queen Victoria has recently received from the London Cooks' Company a beautiful plaque of hammered silver, which the Lord Steward of Buckingham has acknowledged for her in a gracefully expressed communication.

It was at the *petits soupers de Choisy* of Louis XV. that the *tables volantes* were first introduced. Those "admirable pieces of mechanism," as they are called by a distinguished gastronome, the poet Rogers, consisted of a table and sideboard, which, at a signal, descended through the floor, to be immediately replaced by others which rose covered with a fresh course.

His singular proficiency in the art of cookery, one of the few redeeming features in this worthless monarch's character, was derived, like his taste for working tapestry, from his youthful companions, the Dukes of Epernon and La Tremouille and De Gesvres.

But for the reign of Louis XVIII. being so recent our author would probably have referred to his qualities as a gastronome. In these he as certainly equalled Louis the Magnificent and his worthless successor, as he surpassed them intellectually and morally. His most famous *maitre d'hotel* was the Duc d'Escars, of whom a Quarterly Reviewer says that, when he and his royal master were closeted together to meditate a dish, the Ministers of State were kept waiting in the antechamber, and the next day the official announcement regularly appeared—"*M. le Duc d'Escars a travaille dans le cabinet.*"

The king had invented the *truffes a la puree d'ortolans*, and invariably prepared it himself, assisted by the duke. On one occasion they had jointly composed a dish of more than ordinary dimensions, and duly consumed the whole of it. In the middle of the night the duke was seized with a fit of indigestion, and his case was declared hopeless; loyal to the last, he ordered an attendant to wake and inform the king, who might be exposed to a similar attack. His majesty was roused accordingly, and told that d'Escars was dying of his invention. "Dying!" exclaimed Louis le Desire; "dying of my *truffes a la puree?* I was right then; I always said that I had the better stomach of the two."

Money is a good thing, even to a cook, but it is not the chief thing in life—to a cook. The famous Careme, the friend of princes, who boasted that the fate of Europe often depended upon the kind of sauces he served up at political banquets, died in 1833, before he had attained his fiftieth year—killed by his passion for work "The charcoal kills us," he said, "but what does that matter? The fewer years, the greater glory." Careme was not a man to care for money, and the world is fortunate in having some disciples worthy of him.

Parlor Cookery.

Harper's Bazar.

Another set, less lofty, have descended to the kitchen, and call themselves the "Pancake Club." This club aims at the mastery of the culinary art, and its *batterie de cuisine* is indeed formidable. There are silver chafing-dishes, faultless trivets, and alcohol lamps enough to sin a Monitor at least. These amateur Brillat-Savarins aim at breakfast-table and supper cookery, the oysters, kidneys and deviled turkey being all cooked on the table. The idea is that a theatre party shall, after enjoying the play, come home and cook their own supper. Also the breakfast for the early bird who must be down-town to catch the Wall Street worm—this hasty meal shall be cooked for him by a loving wife or daughter on a silver chafing-dish or heater before his eyes. This is an admirable idea. These noble girls mean to learn how to make the most delicious Persian coffe, to attack even the kitchen range, and to make all the pancakes possible, to realize that title "dainty dishes" to its fullest extent. Of course one evening a week they appear in costume—white apron and cap—and treat their admirers to a supper all cooked by themselves.

The Lady Amateur Cook.

Cook's Letter to a Friend.

Our Lady Amabel she've took lessons, so as to help us in the cooking. One day down she comes to make a apple pie. I'd made the paste ready for 'er to roll and buttered the dish, and Jane had peeled the apples, and John and Robert stood over 'er with the things, and 'Liza had hot water for 'er to wash 'er hands in when she'd done. So it was a nice "help," you may be sure! Hows'ever, she did it, and I baked it; and upstairs they all said as there'd never bin known sich a pie—tho' it were as sour as warjuice, for, lor', if she hadn't forgot to put in the shuggar!

A great cook is a great man. For instance Fere, of the Astor House, is an aristocrat in his dominions, and when away from his fires lives in excellent style upon a salary of $4,000 a year. One of his sons is a promising young artist engaged upon the "Graphic" in this city. Fere's position requires a knowledge of accounts as well as of cookery. He has to study economy, the prices in the markets, study out new dishes, and keep an eye upon his twelve cooks, eighteen assistants and ten carvers. His work begins at 6 o'clock in the morning and ends at 7 in the evening, and during that time he oversees the preparation of food for 3,000 persons. M. Fere's secretary is a real count, de Moisenu by name, who has been naturalized and has no other ambition than to make the Astor House table the best in the country.—*Cor. Hartford Times.*

Cooks of the Olden Days.

The cook of the middle ages was a lordly autocrat, and his scepter, a long wooden spoon, was also used as a means of punishment. Brillat-Savarin tells this story:

An Italian prince, who had a Sicilian cook of great excellence—the cooks of Sicily were famous even in the days of ancient Rome—was once traveling to his provincial estates, taking with him his entire batterie de cuisine and his Sicilian cook. At a point where the narrow path along the precipice turned the angle of a projecting rock, the prince, at the head of his long cavalcade, heard a shriek and the splash of a body falling into the torrent far below. With a face white with terror, he pulled up, and, looking back, exclaimed:

"The cook! the cook! Holy Virgin, the cook!"

"No, your Excellency," cried a voice from the rear; "it is Don Prosdocimo!"

The Prince heaved a sigh of profound relief. "Ah! only the chaplain!" said he. "Heaven be thanked!"

French Cooking.

At the beginning of the sixteenth century, Englishmen and Frenchmen were on a parity of capacity as cooks. Perhaps, as having finer meats, England slightly surpassed its neighbor, but the character of the cuisine of the two countries may be accurately appreciated from the description of the banquet of Gargantua in Rabelais. Nothing could be more abundant or more barbarously coarse than that monstrous feast. It was Gouthier of Andernach, the German physician of Francis I., who came to put an end to the reign of culinary barbarism in France. The great reformer of the French kitchen was a Huguenot, and died in 1574 at Strasburg, an exile from the land for whose digestion he had done so much; but the seed which he had sown bore good fruit, and its cultivation was continued by that admirable cook, Catherine de Medicis, who had brought with her from Italy the best traditions of the Florentine cuisine, next to the Roman the grandest in Europe. There were then formed in Paris two companies of cooks—the cooks proper and the patissiers, but in 1770 the two guilds were united by a decree of Parliament as the jurande and maitrisse of the Queen, an old Gallic word signifying cooks. It was from this fact that France dates her supremacy in the restorative art.

An Ingenious Cook.

Near, in the opinion of the Greek poet Euphron, are the poet and the cook. Both, he says, attain by an ingenious audacity the apex of their art. And to show the intellectual daring of the cook, he tells the following story: Nicomedes, the great King of Bithynia, being once on a time some twelve days' journey from the sea, had a sudden longing for a loach. Some lexicographers explain the word used by Euphron as "smelt," but the general consensus is in favor of the former interpretation. His cook served him in twenty minutes this very fish. Everybody wondered, for the season, to add to the difficulty of the exploit, chanced to be midwinter. It is said that once while Selden sat in the assembly of divines at Westminster, a warm debate arose about the distance from Jericho to Jerusalem. Those who contended for the longer distance were about to yield to the argument of their adversaries that fishes were carrried from one city to the other, when the celebrated lawyer cried out, "Perhaps the fishes were salted," upon which the dispute was renewed with increased vigor. But the loach in the present case was quite fresh. How then was it procured? French cooks can, it is well known, make a delicious soup out of an old shoe, but the curious device of the cook of Nicomedes will be found equally clever. He took a turnip and cut it into the figure of a loach. He then boiled it gently over a slow fire, added a certain quantity of oil and salt—not that indefinite amount familiar to us in modern cookery books as a "pinch," but measured with exact and learned discrimination—and completed the dish by the sprinkling of a dozen grains of black pepper. Nicomedes, devouring the disguised turnip with a good appetite, told his friend that it was the finest loach he ever ate in his life.

Concerning a subject upon which the "National Hotel Reporter" has had considerable to say of late, the New York "Graphic" of recent date prints the following well chosen words: The best hotel cooks in New York are French, generally from Alsace. They get from $150 to $200 per month, and in a few cases more. This includes board and wine. They learn their business in Paris, and are often men of more than ordinary intelligence and education. They have at command an array of French culinary authorities to which, in cases requiring reference, they turn, as does the lawyer to his "old masters." No young American enters regularly on the "profession" of a cook. He is "above it," and generally such profession is above him. He had rather try to be a lawyer and end he becoming a lawyer's assistant at some nameless price per week, *not* inclusive of board and wine.

SCRAPS ABOUT LANDLORDS AND HOTELS.

Carving the Goose.

Oliver Wendell Holmes

Were this a pulpit, I should doubtless preach,
Were this a platform, I should gravely teach,
But to no solemn duties I pretend
In my vocation at the table's end,
So, as my answer, let me tell instead
What Landlord Porter—rest his soul—once said.
A feast it was that none might scorn to share;
Cambridge and Concord's demigods were there—
"And who were they?" You know as will as I
The stars long glittering in our Eastern sky—
The names that blazon our provincial scroll
Ring round the world with Britain's drumbeat roll.
Good was the dinner, better was the talk ;
Some whispered, devious was the homeward wa'k;
The story came from some reporting spy,
They lie, those fellows—O, how they do lie!
Not ours those foot-tracks in the new fallen snow—
Poets and sages never zig zagged so.

Now Landlord Porter, grave concise, severe,
Master, nay monarch in his proper sphere,
Though to belles-lettres he pretended not,
Lived close to Harvard, so knew what was what,
And having bards, philosophers, and such
To eat his dinner, put the finest touch
His art could teach, those learned mouths to fill
With the best proofs of gustatory skill,
And finding wisdom plenty at his board,
Wit, science, learning, all his guests had stored
By way of contrast, ventured to produce
To please their palates, an inviting goose

Better it were the compa y should starve
Than hands unskilled that goose attempt to carve;
None but the master artist shall assail
The bird that turns the mightiest surgeon pale,

One voice arises from the banquet hall—
The landlord answers to the pleading call;
Of stature tall, sublime of port, he stands,
His blade and trident gleaming in his hands ;
Beneath his glance the strong-knit joints relax
As the weak knees before the headsman's ax.

And Landlord Porter lifts his glittering knife
As some stout warrior armed for bloody strife ;
All eyes are on him , some in whispers ask
What man is that who dares this dangerous task?
When, lo! the triumph of consummate art,
With scarce a touch the creature drops apart,
As when the baby in his nurse's lap
Spills on the carpet a dessected map.

Then the calm sage, the monarch of the lyre,
Critics and men ot science, all admire
And one whose wisdom I will not impeach,
Lively, not churlish, somewhat free of speech,
Speaks thus : "Say, master, what of worth is left
In birds like this, of breast and legs bereft?"

And Land'ord Porter, with uplifted eyes,
Smiles on the simple querist, and replies
"When from a goose you've taken legs and breast,
Wipe lips, thank God, and leave the poor the rest."

When the world was younger, says the New York *Graphic*, and this city was younger and smaller than now, hotel landlords were more primitive in their ways, and used to sit at the heads of their own tab'es and carve the breakfast beefsteaks. When Warren Leland so carved at the old Clinton Hotel there used to put up at his house a rich, old and penurious oountry merchant, whose stinginess at home had earned him the reputation of "counting the potatoes that went into the pot for dinner." And this worthy would always manage to obtain a seat at Warren's elbow. "Mr. Leland," he would observe on seating himself at the brea fast table, "I slept very well last night—very well, indeed. I am not at all particular where I sleep. I can put up with most any sort of a room--but, Mr. Leland, will you oblige me with a bit of steak cut there - just there?" and with this he would delicately touch with the end of his table knife the central and most juicy and tenderest portion of the tenderloin brought hot to the table. And this he would eat with well-timed deliberation, so as to finish just as the next relay of tenderloin was brought on, when he would again remark : "Mr. Leland, your beds are very fine, indeed. I'm not a all particular where I sleep, but would you oblige me with another steak, just there?" and again the tip of his knife would hover over the steak where it cut the easiest and was most tempting. And so on until the end of the breakfast and chapter. Warren Leland, Sr. now tells the story with artistic gusto and humor.

The Delaware river method, of planking shad is as follows : Scale the fish, split it open down the back, carefully remove the roe and entrails and wash and dry it with a cloth. Then spread it on its back and fasten it with two or three nails upon a hic'ory plank thoroughly hot. Of course but one side of the fish is exposed to the fire, the heat of the plan' cooking the other. Set the plank and fish at an angle of forty-five degrees before a clear hot fire of live coals and bake it to a rich brown color, basting it every litt'e while by means of a soft brush with a thin mixture of melted butter an flour. When done serve it upon the plank on which it was cooked : send plank and all to the table In the meantime the roe should be parboiled, then egged, rolled in cracker dust or bread crumbs and fried and sent to table with the fish. Housekeepers can obtain the planks ready made and fitted with wire fastenings for planking shad at the house-furnishing warehouses. This is the way to broil a shad: Clean, wash and split the shad, wipe it dry, and sprinkle it with salt and pepper. Rub a double wire broiler with suet or other fat, place the fish upon it, and put it over a clear fire and broil it to a golden brown color. Then place it on a hot dish and pour plain melted butter over it, seasoned with salt and pepper. This is a delightfully appetizing dish for breakfast.

If broiling be for any reason impossible, a shad may be fried, thus: Clean, wash and split the shad in two, then cut each half crosswise into three parts, season well with pepper and salt and dredge them with flour. Have your frying material smoking hot, lay in your pieces of fish and fry them to a nice golden brown, drain and lay them on a hot dish, pour plain melted butter over them and serve piping hot.

The news that "The Cock," in Fleet Street, London, is to be demolished announces the disappearance of the resorts which are intimately associated with the characteristic life of London for centuries, and with the most famous names in English literature and history. Many a pilgrim to London would hasten first of all to the site of the old Tabard Inn in Southwark, and search curiously for some trace of Dame Quickly's tavern in Eastcheap, or Beaumont and Jonson's "Mermaid," or Dryden's "Buttons," or Dr. Johnson's "Mitre." London indeed, swarms with taverns and clubs and resorts so intimately identified with the most interesting traditions that old London itself vanishes as they disappear.

"The Cock," of which there is a characteristic picture upon another page, is not only rich in old reminiscence—for it was unaltered since the days of James I, and Pepys made merry there in 1668 —but it has acquired fresh charm in recent times from Tennyson's "Will Waterproof's Monologue," in which that thoughtful roisterer apostrophizes the "plump head waiter of the Cock." In Dicken's *Life and Letters* there is the same friendly feeling for the tavern as a seat of good fellowship. Thackeray is never more charming than when he is playfully gossiping or moralizing about the good places for good dinners, and when he was in this country, he was never more at home than when, at the "Century," he was seated with his cigar and his "modest glass," ruling with gentle sway, like Addison with his pipe, in his familiar realm.

Such associations as those of the famous London resorts of wits and poets and statesmen and scholars are of great value to any city. As they disappear the city is robbed of an influence which, although a mere sentiment, is most elevating and persuasive. The universal instinct of men which builds monuments and other memorials of the famous dead, the heroes and patriots, the poets and story-tellers and orators, is akin to that which fondly cherishes the material objects with which they were associated, and preserves their autographs and every personal relic. New York has retained very few buildings which have any striking or interesting connection with the past. The most interesting of them is probably Fraunces' Tavern, at the corner of Broad and Pearl streets, where Washington parted with his officers. But although London still teems with them, even London will have lost a charm which no splendor of architecture or convenience of building can restore, when the most famous "Cock" in the world is gone forever.—*Harpers Weekly.*

Mr. Abner C. McIlrath, who kept a famous hotel for thirty-six years, six miles from Cleveland on Euclid avenue, has been gathered to his stalwart fathers. He was a mighty fox hunter and a remarkable athlete. Six feet six inches and a half tall, his average weight was about 264 pounds, but yet he is said to have frequently on foot run down foxes. He once lifted with his hands from the ground an iron shaft weighing 1,700 pounds, which would be equal to lifting double that weight were be harnessed with straps to weights and allowed to lift under the best advantage. Two men would hold a string two inches above his head, and he would step back two or three steps and jump over it without touching it, making the leap about six feet nine inches in height. He has been known, rather than to lead his horses around to the other side of the barn, to put his long arms under a horse and lift it up to the floor of the barn, which happened to be three or four feet above the ground. In Buffalo he once wrestled with and threw with ease Charlie Freeman, the "American giant," who afterward in England defeated "Tipton Slasher" in a prize fight. Another feat of the hotel keeper was his chase on horseback of a fox one December over frozen Lake Erie far from sight of land. He lived to the age of seventy years, having been a paralytic for four years of life as a result of exposure during a fox hunt. He was borne to the grave Saturday by six of his tall sons, four of whom are six feet four and a half inches high and the other two just six feet, and whose combined weight is 1,305 pounds.

At most Italian restaurants on the authority of the London *Caterer*, cotellettes milanese, consisting only of a veal chop or cutlet encrusted with bread crumbs and egg, with the traditional quarter of lemon to stimulate the palate, is a standing dish-

SCRAPS ABOUT DINNERS.

A President's Dinner

To return to Washington's dinner, the writer of the description continues: "First was soup, fish, roasted and boiled meats, gammon, fowls, etc. This was the middle. The middle of the table was garnished in the usual tasty way with small images, flowers (artificial), etc. The dessert was first apple pies, puddings, etc.; then iced creams, jellies, etc.; then watermelons, muskmelons, apples, peaches, nuts. It was the most solemn dinner I ever sat at," continues Maclay. "Not a health drank, scarce a word said, until the cloth was taken away. Then the President, taking a glass of wine, with great formality drank the health of every individual by name 'round the table. Everybody imitated him—charged glasses, and such a buzz of 'health, sir,' and 'health, madam,' and 'thank you, sir,' and 'thank you, madam,' never had I heard before.

"The ladies sat a good while and the bottle passed about, but there was a dead silence almost. Mrs. Washington at last withdrew with the ladies. I expected the men would begin, but the same stillness remained. The President told of a New England clergyman who had lost a hat and wig in passing a river called the Brunks. He smiled and everybody else laughed. He now and then said a sentence or two on some common subject, and what he said was not amiss. The President kept a fork in his hand when the cloth was taken away, I thought for the purpose of picking nuts. He ate no nuts, but played the fork, striking on the edge of the table with it. We did not sit long after the ladies retired. The President rose, went up stairs to drink coffee—the company followed." This precedent was followed at President Arthur's dinners last year.

Prince Napoleon, while a prisoner at Conciergerie, had his meals from one of the most illustrious restaurateurs in Paris, and they were excellently chosen. One day when a correspondent called on him he had for breakfast "œufs brouilles aux pointes d'asperge," mutton cutlets a la Napolitaine, cold capon, cheese and grapes. His dinner consisted of potage Voisin, fillets of sole, Tournedos (an admirable fillet of beef) and salad. Upon this fare one might worry along, even in captivity.

The New York "Thirteen" Club has lately partaken of its seventh annual dinner. The menu was printed on cards cut in the shape of a coffin lid and the repast consisted of thirteen dishes. The organization has thirteen times thirteen members, the initiation fee is $13, the monthly dues are 13 cents, and, still, despite the awful significance of this showing, there are applicants for fellowship awaiting the death of present members.

A Mediæval Dinner.

A mediæval dinner was recently given in Basle in honor of the mediæval collection in that city, and to augment its funds. The guests, 120 in number, were summoned by the blare of trumpets to the table which was splendid with old plate and drinking vessels loaned by the venerable guilds of the city. The first course was beer soup of the middle ages, and the last was "gofreu" and "aenisbred," baked after the models exhibited in early German pictures. Wine of the middle ages was not to be had, but a loving cup of Markgrafter of the vintage of 1715 was sent round the table. Two pianofortes made in the years 1720 and 1750, furnished the accompaniments to the songs in a tone "remarkably thin, but at the same time exceedingly tender and refined." The guests wore modern garments, but the servants were appropriately dressed, and the furniture of the hall and the decorations of the table, to the smallest detail, were conscientious reproductions of the middle ages.

A birthday cake with sixty-five tiny candles was a table ornament at the dinner to Mr. Evarts on Saturday.

At a dinner party in New York the other evening the menu, printed on white satin, came from beneath the wings of a tiny swan placed beside the plate of each guest. The swans were retained as souvenirs, and when their heads were pulled off were found to be intended for match boxes.

Ice cream was served at a hunt dinner the other night in the form of whips, spurs, saddles, caps, and other freezing reminders of the Long Island hunting field.

At a recent private dinner served at Kinsley's, in Chicago, the ice cream came to the table in the form of asparagus stalks and bananas. Cakes filled with cream were made to take the form and appearance of baked potatoes, and the deception was so perfect as to excite the wonder and admiration of all present.

For a dinner for eighteen gentlemen on Thursday, a florist made a centre-basket remarkable for its size and display of selected flowers. It was six feet in diameter. There were one thousand rich roses and a garden of lilacs, violets and other spring blossoms. The centre of this piece was a circle of lillies—amaryllis, vitata and callas. The cost knots were of hyacinth sprays and roses. The same night a dinner for 125 at Delmonico's was decorated with rose baskets fringed with ferns.

At a dinner party recently given in New York the menus placed at the plate of each guest cost sixty dollars apiece. They were in the form of a picture, a beautiful work of art, which could afterwards be used as a drawing room ornament. An English gentleman, in whose honor the entertainment was given, spil'ed some wine over his, which ruined it. Not wishing to lose so costly and beautiful a souvenir, he went to Tiffany's and had a duplicate made.

A Memphis paper says: "The Fontaine german" in this city was the biggest affair of the season. The supper was very elaborate. The most unique and striking feature of the repast was produced on the cutting of six grand centre cakes. In each of the cakes had been placed six live birds—doves in some, in others quail—and on opening them these feathered guests fluttered their wings, and, rising in the air, perched on the doors and heavy window sills, from which elevated and lofty positions they gazed down on the brilliant assemblage.

It is related of the famous Spanish banker, Don Jose de Salamanca, who died recently, that in 1858 he gave a single dinner that cost $90,000.

The gallant Colonel Tom Ochiltree of Texas, gave a supper to a party of friends in Washington a few nights ago that is said to have cost $500.

The dinner of the Standard Collar Club at the Hotel Brunswick on Wednesday night was attended by thirty gentlemen. The menus were hand painted, and cost ten dollars each. The dishes were ornamented with sugar collars, and the bird musical dinner favors held collars in their bills.

Nearly all the large office buildings and banks down-town have their own restaurants, which are presided over by a steward, a chef and a corps of waiters and attendants—but few people have an idea how systematically such a department of a great institution is managed. Take the Western Union Telegraph building as an example. There are more than eleven hundred employes on the pay roll, and of these fully eight hundred regularly eat in the building. To feed these the meats are put on the fire every morning at four o'clock, and when cooked are carried to the steam tables. Beef, ham, tongue, vegetables, tea, chocolate and milk are the ordinary dishes served for dinner, which is charged at cost price, ten cents. This meal is served to all—no distinction is made from the lowest to the highest official of the company. No wine, liquors or ale is allowed. The men are waited on by men and the females by women. If any one desires a steak an extra charge of ten cents is added. A ticket entitling the owner to as many meals as there are numbers on it, is sold, the ticket being punched every time a meal is eaten. Breakfast is served at seven, dinner from twelve to one, and after that hour for head officials; tea at five and supper at midnight. If any of the lady employes is taken sick or feels unwell a hot cup of tea is sent down from the kitchen, which is on the top floor, and no charge whatever is made. The dining room is large, thirty by eighty feet, thorough'y clean and located on one of the upper floors.—*N. Y. Gastronomer.*

"Ain't this a little high?" asked a timid tenderfoot of a Deadwood tavern-keeper who had charged him $1.50 for his dinner. "It may be a little high," replied the host, fumbling with the handle of a revolver in the cash drawer; "but I need the money." He got it

Shovel and pick brigade—a party of Americans at dinner.

"George, dear, don't you think it rather extravagant of you to eat butter, with that delicious jam?" "No, love, economical. Same piece of bread does for both."

Cheyenne society is harrowed up over a question of etiquet. People are divided in opinion as to which coat sleeve a man should wipe his mouth with after eating soup.

The London *Caterer* tells of a novelty the golden pudding, which comes on the table as a bag of gold, such as is delivered by banks, and upon being opened, imitations of money, fruits and confectionery are disclosed

One of Benjamin Franklin's Dinners

A century ago one of the notable ladies in Philadelphia society was Mrs Mary Ruston, and if proof were wanting that the people of those days appreciated the joys of the table it could be found in her receipt book, now owned by Charles M. Pennypac er, one of her descendants. Mrs. Ruston was in the habit of recording in this book particulars of the elaborate dinners at which she was present. Thus it appears that on one occasion Dr. Franklin regaled his guests with clam soup, breast of veal ragouted, forequarter of roast lamb, four small chickens, pigs' feet, a pair of roast ducks, and a roast leg of mutton, with numerous vegetables served from the sideboard, and filled up the services with a dessert of green currant tarts, jellies, truffles, blanc mange, cranberry tarts, English and Swiss cheeses and cheese cakes.

INDEX.

The Numbers Refer to the Article, and Not to the Page.

A half-shell roast, 811
Andalusian, fish sauce, 938
Antelope, 1004
Apple sauce for meats, 1031

Bacon and spinach, 1093
   liver, 1125
   breakfast, broiled, 1126
   hog, cutting up a, 1011
Bass, sea, 984
   black, fried, 876
   striped, broiled, 883
   with green peas, 927
Bear meat, 1007
Beef, cutting up the loin, 989
   fore quarter, 994
   round, 995
   roast, rare, 1090
   natural gravy, 1020
   roast, well done, 1021
   rib ends, 1022.
   flank, 1023
   boiled horseradish, 1076
   salt vegetables, 1077
   corned cabbage, 1078
   heart, 1087
Beefsteak, broiling, 1099
   devilled, 1111
   English mushrooms, 1107
   French, 1103
   Hamburg, 1115
   maître d'hotel, 1104
   Milanaise, 1113
   natural gravy, 1100
   old fashion, 1101
   porterhouse broiled, 1102
   sauce piquant, 1105
   Spanish, 1109
   with champignons, 1106
   onions, 1112
   oysters, 1114
   tomatoes, 1110
Black bass, 876
Bloaters, Yarmouth, 973
Bluefish, baked, 954
Boiled dinner, New England, 1080
Boning and rolling meats, 1025
Bordelaise sauce, 910
Boston fancy stew, 827
Box stew, 815
   fry, 816
Breading and frying, 872
Bread stuffing for fish, 942
   for poultry 1060
   sauce brown, 1062
Broiled chicken, 1132
   oysters stuffed, 813
   crumbed, 831
   on toast, 832
   in bacon, 851
   quail on toast, 1133

snipe and plover, 1134
Brook trout, 865
   boned, with bacon, 866
   fried plain, 869
   breaded, 871
Brown oyster sauce, 854
Buffalo, 1009
Buttered eggs, 1142
Butter sauce, 916
   common, 917

Cabbage and corned beef, 1078
   to boil, 1079
Canned salmon, 975
Canvasbacks, 1072
Capersauce, 928
Capon roast 1056
Carp, baked plain, 944
   Espagnole, 941
   German, 939
Cases, oysters in, 817
Catfish steak, 966
Celery sauce, brown, 1059
   white, 1092
Champagne sauce, 1040,
Cheese omelet, 1148
Chestnut sauce, 1053
   puree, for turkey, 1054
Chicken boiled, salt pork, 1089
   egg sauce, 1090
   broiled, 1132
   Maryland, 1063
   spring roast, 1057
   stuffed, 1061
   liver omelet, 1150
Chutney, home-made, 909
Chowder, clam, 862
   fish, 863
Chops, pork, 1122
   lamb, green peas, 1121
   mutton, 1117
Cisco, 895
   potted, 896
Clam chowder, 862
   soup, 823
   fritters, 859
   without eggs, 810
   soups, 822
Clams, fricasseed on toast, 861
   soft shell, 816
   roast, 811
   scalloped in shell, 838
Corned Beef and cabbage, 1078
   tongue, boiled, 1085
Codfish boiled, 914
   balls, 980
   stuffed, oysters, 958
   salt, stewed, 982
   in cream, 981
Cooking terrapin, 803
Crabs, soft shell, boiled, 806

fried, 807
Cream sauce, 931
   bechamel, 932
Cranberry sauce, 1047
   jelly for game, 1048
Creole beefsteak, 1109
Croquettes of potatoes, 946
   small balls, 951
Crimping fish, 911
Croustades or bread shapes, 849
   of oysters, 850
Cure hams, to, 1013
Cutting up a porker, 1010
   bacon hog, 1011
   fore quarter, beef, 994
   fowls, 1015
   ham, 1014
   turtle, 1017

Dauphine potatoes, 918
Devilled beefsteak, 1111
Dry stew, oysters, 826
Duchesse potatoes, 957
Duck, canvasback, 1072
   domestic, 1064
   mallard, 1073
   redhead, 1072
   teal and butterball, 1074
   wild, common, 1071
   young domestic, 1066
Dutch sauce, 891

Easy, broiling of fish, 1131
Economy of broiled meats, 1130
Eels, 970
Elk, 1005
English steak with mush'ms, 1107
Egg sauce, 936
Eggs boiled, 1138
   buttered, 1142
   fried, 1140
   omelets, 1144
   poached, 1139
   scrambled, 1141
   shirred, 1143

Fancy roast oysters, 840
   stew, 827
Fillets of fish, 889
   white fish, 947
   with quenelle dressing, 960
Finnan haddies, 976
Fish, crimped, 911
   forcemeat, for, 950
   quenelle, 961
   a Southern way, 963
   a plain bake, 964
   chowder, 863
   sauce royal, 887
Fowls, to cut up, 1015
   truss, 1016

roast, celery sauce, 1058
Fresh mushrooms, 1108
   water perch 891
   mackerel, 924
French beefsteak, 1103
fried potatoes, 943
Fricasseed clams, 861
Fried oysters, without eggs, 809
   single breaded, 829
   double, 830
   parsley, 867
   peas for garnish 940
Fritters, oyster, 858
   clam, 859
   without eggs, 810

Game
   antelope, 1001
   bear, 1007
   buffalo, 1009
   canvasback, 1072
   ducks, common wild, 1071
   elk, 1005
   mallard duck, 1073
   'possum, 1008
   quail, 1133
   Rocky mountain sheep, 1003
   rabbit, 1135
   read-head duck, 1072
   snipe and plover, 1134
   teal and butterball, 1074
   squirrel, 1136
   venison, 1006
   wild goose, 1067
   wild turkey, 1055
Giblet sauce, 1069
Goose, domestic, 1064
   wild, roast 1068
Grayling, 894

Haddock, boiled, 914
   smoked, 976
Halibut steak, 904
Hamburgh steak, 1115
Ham and eggs, 1124
   boiled, 1086
   to cure, 1013
   to cut up, 1014
   about roasting, 1038
   roast with spinach, 1035
   breaded, 1041
   with wine sauce, 1039
   omelet, 1147
Herring, lake, 890
Hollandaise sauce, French, 899
   English, 890
   original, 891
   potatoes, 923
Honeycomb tripe, broiled, 1128
Hotel beef and beefsteaks, 987
   broiling, 1098
   turkey and chicken, 1044

Jelly, cranberry, for game, 1048
   omelet with, 1155
Jowl and spinach, 1093

Keep'g meat to make ten'r, 1096
Kidneys broiled, 1129
   omelet with, 1149
Kippered salmon, 975
Kromeskies, oyster, 857

Lamb, roast, 1026
   chops with peas, 1121
   cutlets, 1002
   side of, 1001

Lake herring, 890
Loaf, oysters in, 848
Lobster sauce, 934
Liver and bacon. 1125
   broiled, 1127
Lyonaise potatoes, 1116

Macaroni and oysters, 814
Mackerel, Spanish, broiled, 886
   baked, 949
   fresh, broiled, 888
   boiled, 924
   salt, 971
Mackinaw trout, 874
   fried in eggs, 875
Maitre d' hotel sauce, cold, 880
   hot, 925
Mallard duck, roast, 1073
Meats, boning and rolling, 1025
Milk stew, oyster, 824
Minced potatoes, 868
Mint sauce, 1027
Muscallonge, boiled, 927
Mushrooms, fresh, 1108
Mustard sauce, 973
Mutton, cutting up, 999
   chops, broiled, 1117
   dish of, 1118
   English, 1000
   tomato sauce, 1119
   roast, 1024
   boiled, caper sauce, 1081
   side of, 998

New England boiled dinner, 1080

Omelet,
   with cheese, 1148
   chicken livers, 1150
   ham, 1147
   jelly, 1155
   kidneys, 1149
   onions, 1146
   oysters, 833
Omelet, with parsley, 1145
   rum, 1154
   tomatoes, 1153
   plain, 1144
   souffles, 1156
   Spanish, 1152
Onion and parsley omelet, 1146
Oppossum, roast, 1008
Ox-heart with gravy, 1087
Oysters,
   box stew, 815
   fry, 816
   broiled in bacon, 851
   crumbed, 831
   plain, 832
   stuffed, 813
   croustades of, 850
   fried single breaded, 829
   double breaded, 830
   without eggs, 809
   fritters, 858
   fancy roast, 840
   stew, 827
   in cases, 847
   in a loaf, 848
   kromeskies, 857
   macaroni, with, 814
   omelet, 833
   patties, 846
   pie individual, 843
   hotel entree, 845
   pot pie, cheap, 844
   raw, 864

   on half-shell, 837
   roast fancy, 840
   pan, 841
   shell, 839
   sauce, brown, 854
   good, 853
   white, 852
   sauteed in butter, 828
   · scalloped silver shells, 855
   large pan, 834
   restaurant party, 835
   individual, 836
   soup, 819
   brown, 821
   French way, 820
   stew for fifty, 808
   milk, 824
   plain, 825
   dry, 826
   fancy, 827
   steamed shells, 842
   stuffed, 813
   stuffing for turkeys, etc., 855
   truffled, 812

Pan-roast oysters, 841
Panada, 962
Parsley sauce, 919
   fried, 867
   omelet, 1145
Patties, oyster, 846
Perch, fresh water, 891
Pie, oyster, 843
Pickerel, 115
Pickle sauce, 1082
Pickled salmon, 974
Pike, boiled, 918
Pig, roast, apple sauce, 1034
   sucking, 1032
Piquant sauce, 1084 ad 1105
Plaice and flounders, 966
Plover, broiled, 1134
Poached eggs, 1139
Porker, cutting up a, 1010
Pork roast, 1030
   sausage, 1012
   chops, milk gravy, 1122
   salt slices of, 1123
   sauer kraut and, 1094
Porterhouse cut, the, 988
Possum and coon, 1008
Potatoes,
   boulettes, 953
   cake for fish, 959
   croquettes, 946
   in small balls, 951
   dauphine, 948
   Dutch fried, 878
   Duchesse, 957
   Francaise, 943
   fried plain, 873
   frizzed, 862
   Hollandaise, 923
   Lyonaise, 1116
   maitre d'hotel, 921
   minced, 868
   pancakes, 893
   parisienne, 953
   Saratoga chips, 870
   sauteed, 878
   shoestring, 882

Quenelle forcemeat, fish, 961
Quail on toast, 1133

Rabbit young, broiled, 1135
Radish greens, 1037

III

Raw oysters and clams, 864
Red snapper, 912
  grouper, 9-7
Remarks on frying fish, 872
Restaurant tenderloin, 990
Roe shad, fried, 885
Roast clams, 811
Robert sauce, 907
Rocky mountain sheep, 1003
Round of beef, 995
Rum omelet, 1154

Sage and onion stuffing, 1033
Salmon, boiled, 922
  steak, 902
    maitre d' hotel, 897
  canned, 975
  salt, 974
Sauce,
  apple for meats, 1031
  Andalusian, 938
  bechamel, 932
  Bordelaise, 910
  bread, brown, 1062
    English, white, 1062
  brown oyster, 854
  butter, 916 and 917
  caper, 928
  celery, brown, 1059
    white, 1092
  champ'ne for roast ham 1040
  chestnut, 1053
    puree, 1054
  chutney, 909
  cranberry, 1047
  cream, plain, 931
  egg, 936
  fennel, 924
  giblet, 1069
  Hollandaise, 899
  lobster, 934
  maitre d' hotel, 880
  hot, 925
  mint for lamb, 1027
  mustard, 973
  oyster, 852
  parsley, 919
  pickle, 1082
  piquant, 1084 and 1105
  Robert, 908
  royal, 887
  shrimp, 913
  tartar, 1049
  tomato, 120

    wine for fish, etc., 955
Sauer kraut, 1095
  with pork, 1094
Sausage, good pork, 1012
Sauteed oysters without eggs, 828
  potatoes, 878
Scallops, to cook, 861
  in batter, 860
Scalloped oysters, 834
  clams, 838
Scrambled eggs, 1141
Sea bass, baked, 984
  Shad, broiled, 884
  roe, fried, 885
    boiled, 926
Sheephead, fish, 933
Shirred eggs, 1143
Smelts, breaded, 983
  au beurre noir, 892
Smoked haddock, 976
  herring, 977
  white fish, 979
Snipe and plover, 1134
Soft-shell crabs, boiled, 806
  fried, 807
Soup, oyster, 819
  clam, 822
  chowder, 823
Soles, 967
Spanish beefsteak, 1109
  omelet, 1152
  mackerel, 886
Speckled trout, 952
Spinach, to cook, 1036
Spring chickens, 1057
  Maryland style, 1063
Squirrel broiled, 1136
Steak, catfish, 906
  halibut, 904
  salmon, 897 and 902
  fish, stewed, 935
  trout, 898 and 903
  restaurant tenderloin, 990
  porterhouse, 988
Steamed oysters, 821
Stewed terrapin, 805
Striped bass, 883
Stuffed oysters, 813
Stuffing for fish, 942 and 956
  oyster, 855
  common for chickens, 1060
  sage and onion, 1033
  chestnut, 1052
Sturgeon, 968
Sucking pig, roast, 1032

Sweet omelet, 1155

Teal duck, 1137 and 1074
Terrapin, to dress, 803
  baked in shell, 804
  stewed, 805
Tenderloin steak, 990
Tomato omelet, 1153
  sauce, 1120
Tongue, boiled, 1083
  corned, 1085
Trout, a la Genevoise, 969
  brook, boned, 866
    or speckled, fried, 869
    breaded, 871
    with bacon, 865
  a la Colbert, 879
  Mackinaw, 874
  fried in eggs, 875
  boiled, 920
  speckled, fine herbs, 952
  broiled, 877
  potted, 896
Tripe, broiled, 1128
Truffled oysters, 812
Turbot, 965
Turkeys, 1015
  boiled oyster sauce, 1088
  roast, cranberry, 1046
  stuffed, 1049
  brown oyster, 1050
  stuffed with oysters, 1051
    chestnuts, 1052
  wild, roast, 1055
Turtle, 1017

Veal roast, 1028
  with dressing, 1029
  side of to cut, 996
  tenderloins, 997
Venison, 1006
  roast, 1043
  baked in paste, 1042

White fish, boiled, 930
  broiled, 881
  fillets, 947
  salt, 972
Wild goose and brant, 1067
  roast, 1068
  ducks, 1071 and 1075
  turkey, 1055
Wine sauce for fish, 955

Young ducks with peas, 1066

BOOK OF SOUPS AND ENTREES.

Amber clear soup, 1256
Andalusian soup, 1274
Antelope steak saute, 1243
Apple fritters with sauce, 1202
Artichokes in gravy, 1290
Asparagus soup, 1222.
Backbone stew, egg dumplings, 1230
Baked celery and cheese, 1206
  corn custard, 1231
  fish and cheese, 1285
Barley soup, 1278
Beef, a la mode, 1234
  chipped, in butter, 1244.
  ribs with Yorkshire pudding, 1264
  small fillets in glaze, 1199
  stew with potatoes, 1280
Blanquette of lamb, 1284
  of sweetbreads and oysters, 1185
Boston clam chowder, 1251
Bouillon or beef broth, 1242
Brains in brown butter, 1264
  in patties, 1273
Braised fillet of beef, 1216
  roll of veal, 1252
Braising, what it means, 1214.
Breaded calf's head, tomato sauce, 1279
  cutlets, 1188
  ribs of lamb, 1267
Calf's head fried, 1279
  head in omelet, 1223
  liver, larded, crisped onions, 1283
Calves' brains sauteed, with olives, 1264
Celery and cheese baked, 1206
  cream soup, 1261
  stewed in cream, 1211
Chicken, breast of, in form, 1183
  broth, 1215
  cutlets with vegetables, 1217
  gumbo soup, 1238
  pie, American style, 1193
  pies, small, French, 1224
Chipped beef in butter, 1244
Clear soups, 1175
  amber, or consomme, 1256
  turtle soup, 1187
Coney Island chowder, 1208
Corn custard, baked, 1231
  fried, or mock oysters, 1246
  hulled, or home-made hominy, 1237
Corned pork tenderloins, 1275
  tongues with brocoli, 1272
Cream fritters, 1186
  of asparagus, 1222
  of celery, 1261
  of potatoes, 1270
Croquettes of sweetbreads, 1260
Curried tripe, Italian, 1201
  veal with rice, 1291
Devilled beefsteak, 1111
  ham, old style, 1239
Devils, what they are, 1237
Egg dumplings for stews, 1230
Egg plant fried, plain, 1200
Eggs poached, in sauce, 1212
Entrees, common sense about, 1162
  rule of, 1170
  sweet, use of, 1168
  vegetable, or garnishes, 1169
Espagnole or brown sauce, 1172

Farina cake with jelly, 1213
Fillet of beef, braised, 1216
  larded, with mushrooms, 1182
Fish dinner bill of fare, 985
  fondue or baked with cheese, 1285
  soup, mulligatawney, 1282
French cream soup, 1287
  pancakes with jelly, 1265
  toast, wine sauce, 1241b
Fricandeau of minced veal, 1209
Fricasseed oysters in border, 1241a
Fricassee of veal and mushrooms, 1258
Fricassees, what they are, 1250
Fritters, apple, 1202
  bell, 278
  corn mock oysters, 1246
  cream, 1186
  fruit, 253
  orange wine sauce, 1292
  parsnip, 1259
  peach, sabayon sauce, 1207
  pineapple, with curacoa, 1227
  plain, 255
  potato, French, 280
  queen or Boston puff, 274
  Spanish puff, 275
Game dinner bill of fare, page 361
Geese livers in cases, 1195
Gumbo soup, 1238
Hulled corn and milk, 1237
Irish stew, 1280
Kidneys and ham, minced, 1245
Lamb, blanquette of, 1284
  cutlets with vegetables, 1188
  fries sauteed in butter, 1194
  hearts, Taulausaine, 1289
  stew with potatoes, 1253
  tongues with brocoli, 1272
Larded fillet of beef, with mushrooms, 1182
  liver, crisped onions, 1283
  sweetbreads with peas, 1205
Macaroni and cheese, American, 1241
  French, 1225
  and tomatoes, Italian, 1218
  in cream, 1269
Minced kidneys and ham, 1245
  turkey with poached eggs, 1281
Mushrooms stewed, in croustades, 1184
Mutton chops, breaded, tomatoes, 1235
  loin of, stuffed, 1198
  shoulder rolled, braised, 1257
Onions crisped, garnish, 1283
  stuffed, baked, 1277
Orange fritters, 1292
Ox-tail soup, 1192
Parsnip, fritters, 1259
Patties, calves' brains, 1273
  chicken, 1224
  salmon, 1254
  turkey, 1286
Poaches with rice, 1196
Peach fritters, 1207
Pie, chicken, American, 1193
  pigeon or squab, 1288

  veal and oyster, 1263
  veal pot-pie, 1276
Pigeons potted, with jelly, 1189
Pigeon pie, 1288
Pigs feet, vinaigrette, 1236
  head stewed, Russian sauce, 1268
Poached eggs, Andalusian, 1212
Pork backbones or chine, stewed, 1230
  tenderloins corned, glazed, with cabbage, 1210 1275
Potato cream soup, 1270
Potting, what it means, 1248
Pumpkin bread, for lunch, 1232
Quail, minced, or chaudpaid, 1191
Rabbits, smothered, country style, 1229
  stewed, soubise sauce, 1240
Rice croquettes, sabayon, 1220
  peaches, with, 1196
Roll of veal, braised, 1252
Salmis, what they are, 1249
Salmon patties, 1254
Saute of young turkey, 1262
Sautes, what they are, 1247
Scotch broth, 1278
Soups, clear, or consommes, 1175
  full, 1176
Soup, amber clear, 1256
  Andalusian, 1274
  bouillon or beef broth, 1242
  chicken, 1215
  clam chowder, Boston, 1251
  clam chowder, Coney Island,
  clam, cream, 822 1208
  cream of asparagus, 1222
  cream, French, 1287
  cream of chicken, 1203
  cream of potatoes, 1270
  fish mulligatawney, 1282
  gumbo, 1238
  making, in general, 1174
  ox-tail, 1192
  oyster, 819
  potato cream, 1270
  Scotch mutton broth, 1278
  Spring or Printaniere, 1197
  stock, making, 1179
  tomato gumbo, 1266
  turtle, 1181
  vegetable, 1228
Spaghetti and tomatoes, 1218
  in cream, 1269
Spareribs baked or broiled, Robert, 1271
Squab or pigeon pie, 1288
Stuffed onions, 1277
  tomatoes, 1190
Supreme of sweetbreads, 1226
Supremes, what they are, 1221
Sweetbreads, croquettes of, 1260
  larded, with peas, 1205
Terrapin in cases, Maryland, in shell, 804 1219
  stewed, 805
Tripe curried, Italian, 1201
Turkey minced, poached eggs, patties, 1286 1281
Turkey poult, saute, 1262
Veal and oyster pie, 1263
  curry with rice, 1291
  pot-pie, country style, 1276
Veloute or white sauce, 1173

INDEX OF FRENCH TERMS.

Antelope, Saute of, aux Pommes, Française, 1243
Artichokes (fonds de artichauts) a l'Espagnole, 1290

Beef is Boeuf, 989
  a la mode, 1234
  dried, au beurre, 1244
  petits filets de, en demi-glace, 1199
  stew a l'Irlandaise, 1280
  filet de, piqué, aux champignons, 1182
  filet de, braisé, 1216
  entrecote a l'Anglaise, 1019
  a l'écarlate, 1078
  a la jardinière, 1077
  grenadins of, a la diable, 1111
  emince de, a la Hamburg, 1115
Beefsteak is Bifteck, 1099
  aux mousserous, a l'Anglaise, 1107
  aux pommes Française, 1103
  a la maitre d'hotel, 1104
  a la Milanaise, 1113
  au naturel, 1100
  a la menagere, 1101
  a la sauce piquante, 1105
  a la Creole, 1109
  aux champignons, 1106
  aux ognons, 1112
  aux huitres, 1114
  a la sauce tomate, 1110
Brains (cervelle de veau) a la Milanaise, 1264
  en petits pates, 1273

Calf's head is Tete de veau, 1279
  a la Venitienne, 1279
  a la Chartreuse, 1223
Celery is Celeri, sauce, 1059
  and cheese a la Piemontaise, 1206
  a la Bechamel, 1211
Clams, a la paulette, 861

Duck is Canard, young duck is caneton, 1066
Caneton a l'Anglaise, 1066
  au cresson, a la Française, 1072

Fish is Poisson, page 335
  rechauffe of, a la Chartreuse, 1285
  bisque of, a l'Indienne, 1282
  Truites, petites, bardes, 865 and 866
  Trout fried, aux pommes Saratoga
  Trout, a la chevaliere, 871
  Truite du lac, a l'Italienne, 875
  Trout broiled, a la Colbert, 879
  Smelts sautes, au buerre, 892
  Salmon steak broiled, a l'Anglaise 897
  Salmon or trout, a la Hollandaise, 898
  Pompano grillée, a la tartare, 902
  Bass ragée, fillets of, a la maitre d'hotel, 883
  Red snapper boiled, sauce aux cressettes, 912
  Rock Bass, a la Printamere, 929
  Whitefish, a la Bechamel, 930
  Mackerel boiled, a l'Anglaise
  Sheephead boiled, sauce homard, 933
  Red Grouper, a l'Andalouse, 937
  Carp baked, a l'Americaine, 939
  Carp baked, a l'Espagnole, 941
  Salmon trout baked au gratin, 945
  Whitefish, fillets of, a la Mackinac, 947
  Spanish mackerel, farcis aux pommes croquettes, 949
  Trout baked, aux fines herbes, 952
  Bluefish baked, a la Bordelaise, 954
  Codfish baked, a l'Ostende, 958
  Muskallongo or pike, a la Chambord, 960
  Red drum, a la Creole, 963
  Whitefish a la Point Shirley, 964
  Soles, fillets of, a l'Anglaise, 967
  Salmon trout, a la Genevoise, 969
  Sea Bass, a la Port Royal, 984

Fowls is Volaille, chickens are poulets and poulardes.
  Chicken, boudins of, a la Richelieu, 1183
  cutlets of, a la Julienne, 1217
  pie a l'Americaine, 1193
  a la Marengo, 1247
  a la Maryland, 1063
  a la crapaudine, 1132
  Bouchees de volaille, 1224
Fritters are Beignets, 255
  Beignets de bouillie, 1186
  de mais, 1216
  de pommes, 1202
  a l'ananas, 1227
  aux fruits, 253
  a l'orange, au vin, 1292
  de peches, au sabayon, 1207
  soufflés, 247
  soufflés a la vanille, 275
  de pommes de terre, 280
  de pavais, 1259
  aux huitres, 858

Game is Gibier; game dinner, page 361
  Bear is Ours; young bear is ourson, 1007
  gigot (leg) de ourson, 1007
  Deer is Daim; cotelettes do, same as 1243
  Prairie hen is Poule de prairie.
  Quail is Caille; sur canape, 1133
  chaudfroid of, 1191
  galantine en bellevue, 802
  Rabbit is Laporeau; gritté, 1135
  a la fermiere, 1229
  a la Soubise, 1240
  Teal duck is Sarcelle; roti, 1074
  Venison is Venaison and Chevreuil.
  Selle (saddle) de, 1043
Goose is Oie; young goose is oison, 1064

Ham is Jambon, grillé, 1124
  roast aux epinards, 1035
  a la diable, 1239
  a la Westphalienne, 1039

Lamb is Agneau, 1026
  blanquette of, a la Nantaise, 1284
  cutlets a la Printaniere, 1188
  fries, sautes au buerre noir, 1191
  hearts, a la Toulouse, 1289
  haricot of, a la jardinière, 1253
  tongues, a l'Allemande, 1272
  cutlets, aux petits pois, 1121
  cutlets, a la marechale, 1235
  epigramme of, a la chevaliere, 1767
Liver and bacon saute of, 1247

larded, a la Lyonnaise, 1283
Foies-gras en caisses, a la Bordelaise, 1195
Pain de foies de paulardes, 802
Lobster is Homard, 746
  Homard, buisson de, 746
  Homard, mayonnaise de, 746
Mutton is Mouton, 999
  gigot (leg) de sauce capres, 1081
  cutlets en canapes, 1118
  rouleau of braisé, a la Bretonne 1257
Oysters are Huitres, page 350
  Croustades of, a la Montglas, 850
  a la brochette, 851
  Kromeskies of, a la Russe, 857
  a la creme, 815
  farcies aux truffes, 812
  en caisses, 847
  a la Milanaise, 814
  Omelette aux huitres, 833
  Vols-av-vent garnie aux huitres, 846
  Bouchees aux huitres, 846
  Petits pates aux huitres, 845
  Huitres sur coquille, 837
  Huitres au graten, 834
  Salade de huitres.
  Huitres en aspic.
Petoncles (Scallops) a la Marseillaise, 860
Pork is Porc, 1010
  chine of, a la fermiere, 1230
  cochon de lait (sucking pig), 1032
  cutlets, a la bourgeois, 1122
  scallops of, a la Flamande
  fillets of, a l'ecarlate, 1275
  Pigs head, a la Russe, 1268
    feet, a la vinaigrette, 1236
Salad is Salade; dressing, 707
  Salade de chou-fleur, 699
    celeri, 706
    concombres, 772
    escarole 768
    laitue, 767
    pommes, 723, 730
    harengs, 726
    legumes, 701
    crevettes, 733
    macedoine, 724
    a la Russe, 745
    a la Hollandaise, 725
    a l'Italienne, 744
    a la jardiniere, 710
  Mayonnaise, sauce a la, 693
  Mayonnaise de homard, 746
    de volaille, 759
    de poisson, 750
    de crevettes, 733
Soups thick or full are Potages, 1176

Potage a l'Andalouse, 1274
  creme d'asperges, 1222
  a la creme, 1287
  creme de volaille, 1203
  a la reine, 1203
  Parmentier, 1270
  a l'Indienne, 1282
  gumbo a la Creole, 1238
  a la fermiere, 1228
  aux queus de boeuf, 1192
  huitres a la creme, 819
  huitres a la Marseillaise, 820
  huitres a l'Ostende, 821
  a l'Ecossaise, 1278
  d'orge, (barley soup) 1278
  gumbo aux tomates, 1266
  tortue verte, 1181
  tortue claire, 1187
  bouillon or beef broth, 1242
Soups, clear broths are Consommes, 1256
  Consomm clair, 1256
    de volaille, or of chicken, 1215
    Printaniere, 1197
    paysanne, 1233
    au riz (with rice), 1175
    Imperial (with custard shapes) 1175
    royal (same as imperial) 1175
    aux pates d'Italie (alphabet macoroni) 1175
    aux petits pois, (with green peas) 1175
    au chou-fleur, (with cauliflower) 1175
    au vermicelli, 1175
Spaghetti, a la Palermetane, 1218
  a la Bechamel, 1269
Sweetbreads are Ris de veau, 1205
  supreme of, aux truffes, 1226
  croquettes of, a la Perigneux, 1260
  piqué, aux petits pois, 1205
  and oysters, a la Cherbourg, 1185
Turkey is Dinde, young turkey is dindonneau.
  aux marrons, 1052
  eminco of, aux œufs poches, 1281
  aux huitres, 1051
  a l'Anglaise, 1049
  a l'Americaine, 1046
  Dindon sauvage roti, 1055
  Petits pates de valaille, 1286
  Dindonneaux sautés, 1262
Veal is Veau, 1028
  and oyster pie a l'Anglaise, 1263
  curry with rice, a l'Indienne, 1291
  pie a la paysanne, 1276
  rouleau of, braisé sauce au vin, 1252
  fricassee of, a la Toulouse, 1258
  fricandeau of, a la Bourgeoise, 1209

C. F. GUNTHER,
CONFECTIONER
78 MADISON STREET, CHICAGO.

DEALER IN

**ALL KINDS OF PAPER CASES FOR COOKS,
ORNAMENTS,
FANCY MOTTOES, FINE CONFECTIONERY FOR THE TABLE, ETC.**

SEND FOR CATALOGUE.

Jameson · and · Morse :

❀ Job · Printers · and · Publishers ❀

164 Clark: Chicago.

MENUS, BALL PROGRAMMES AND HOTEL WORK GENERALLY.

HENRY A. SLOAN,
WHOLESALE DEALER IN
Poultry, Game, Oysters and Fish

GAME A SPECIALTY.

NO. 86 ADAMS STREET,
CHICAGO.

✢ Purchasing Agency ✢

If you need any articles that are not advertised; anything that the merchants do not keep on hand or do not understand by the names that caterers, stewards, cooks and bakers know them by, write, and I will try to procure what is wanted.

JESSUP WHITEHEAD,
Publisher of Hotel Cook Books,
Care NATIONAL HOTEL REPORTER, CHICAGO.

www.ingramcontent.com/pod-product-compliance
Lightning Source LLC
Chambersburg PA
CBHW031444160426
43195CB00010BB/835